ROLLING COFFINS

Experiences of a M

in the Bloodiest Year

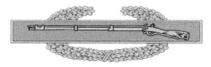

Brian Richard Esher

Photo courtesy of the 25th Infantry Division Association.

25th Infantry Division

4th Battalion 23rd Infantry Mechanized

First Edition

PAGE PUBLISHING, INC.
New York, NY

First originally published by Page Publishing, Inc. 2014

ISBN 978-1-63417-110-6 (pbk)
ISBN 978-1-63417-111-3 (digital)

Printed in the United States of America

DEDICATION

To the guardian angel who watched over me in Vietnam, helping me to survive while so many others did not.

Further dedicated to my wife, Cristina, my son Justin, my brother Robert, and my partners at STORM, who encouraged me to write about my experiences, and to Tom Foster, who served with me briefly in Vietnam; Cain Bridgman, who helped save my life and recommended me for the DSC; and to Major Norman E. Orr, who let things slide while I was serving under him in Vietnam.

ROLLING COFFINS

Brian Esher SP4
Vietnam April 11, 1968-April 11, 1969
25th Infantry Division, 4th Battalion, 23rd Infantry, Company A,
3RD Platoon, Track 3-2

Edited by Joan Porter

CONTENTS

Chapter II
Vietnam

Chapter III
Combat Infantryman

Chapter IV
Back in the Field

Chapter V
House Cat

Chapter VI
Back to the World

Chapter VII
Fort Monmouth New Jersey

CHAPTER VIII
After the Army

ACKNOWLEDGMENTS

I want to thank the 25th Infantry Association for posting numerous pictures, *Tropic Lighting News* issues, and other valuable information I used to research this book. I specifically want to recognize LTC Clifford Nielson for posting his diary while he was the commander of the 4/23 of the 25th Infantry to the Web site. This was most helpful to me in doing research and for placing the many incidents in my memory in a time sequence and in perspective of the bigger picture. I also want to thank retired LTC Cain Bridgman for spending time with Tom Foster and me, explaining some of the big picture battles and incidents we were engaged in while serving under him in Vietnam. Without Cain Bridgman, I might not be here to tell this story! Additionally, I wish to thank Tom Foster, who was involved in several battles with me and helped me to remember specific incidents and details.

I also want to thank my friends Nick Pierce and Jeff Ruege, who after reading the book helped to identify errors in the initial release, my wife Cristina for her support and to Joan Porter who did the final editing of the book.

PROLOGUE

As I am writing this book some forty-five years after I served in Vietnam, I am sure that many of my recollections are clouded by time. Some of the incidents are as clear as if they happened yesterday, and others are somewhat vague. As an infantryman I did not keep a diary, nor did I write many letters back home. We were fighting for our lives and the elements, and unlike senior officers who had writing materials and the time to reflect, we did not. Likewise, we rarely knew where we were at any point in time, why we were there, and what others were doing around us. To the infantryman, his world is a very small place, knowing only what is going on a few hundred yards around him at any one time. Being scared, dog tired, hungry, dirty, wet (or dusty, depending on the season), hot, cold, infected with ringworm and jungle rot, constantly attacked by insects and reptiles, and generally miserable most time did not help for us to record our experiences. Yet I have a vivid recollection of many of the battles and incidents which impacted me during my five months in the mechanized infantry.

I have read well over a thousand books on war and history and more than a hundred books specifically on the Vietnam War. I have a much better appreciation and understanding of what happened to me while in Vietnam than I did at the time. Likewise, I have done research and have many of my documents, records, and awards from Vietnam for reference. I have also met at least two of the soldiers I served with who helped fill in the blanks for me. I am especially grateful to retired LTC Cain A. Bridgman, who was our battalion operations officer (S-3 Major) during my service and who helped get me out of our dangerous ambush on Friday, September 13, 1968. Later, then Major Cain A. Bridgman recommended me for the Distinguished Service Cross, our country's second-highest medal for valor, which I ultimately was awarded. I linked up with Cain some forty-five years later to thank him and to talk about our service. He was most helpful in giving Tom Foster, another survivor from our platoon, and me an overview of some of our operations and filling in recollections of specific incidents. Cain was wounded by a mine explosion under his APC on the same road where I was wounded just a month previously. Cain also received a Silver Star, the country's third-highest medal for valor, during his service in Vietnam. Likewise, my new friend, Tom Foster, who I met some forty-three years later by chance in Roswell, Georgia, also served in my unit. Without knowing each other at the time, we served in adjoining squads and tracks for two weeks in constant combat before we were both wounded on the same day in May of 1968. On this day, Tom was shot twice by an AK-47 and evacuated to Japan whereas I was sent to the hospital and then back to the field. Tom served the five months prior to my joining Alpha Company and was wounded twice and received a Silver Star Award for bravery in action.

I was also fortunate to locate in my research the daily diary of LTC Clifford C. Neilson (Colonel retired), who was our battalion commander from May 12 through November 13, 1968. His diary was most helpful in determining where our company was each day, and it mentioned many of the operations and battles in which I took part as an infantryman. Obviously, with a thousand men and five companies under his command, his view was on a high level. He would have had little or no knowledge of what happened to our platoon or squad and certainly not to me as an individual line soldier. Some of his recollections conflict with mine as we had very different experiences and viewpoints. I saw things in my immediate area while he had an overview of the situation. I was also in the direct line of fire, so every moment to me was life or death whereas he had the advantage of viewing the situation from afar and not under fire.

One of the most difficult aspects of writing this book was to place the many incidents I recall in some semblance of order and to attempt to tie them to dates. In this, Lieutenant Colonel Neilson's diary was most helpful. I tried as much as possible to tie my experiences to the colonel's diary where he mentioned our company's operations. I tried to match up my experiences and the specific "incidents" I recall with his diary as it was much more accurate than my memory, especially when it comes to dates and places. Sometimes incidents mentioned by Lieutenant Colonel Neilson and my experiences happened about the same time, but the dates do not align exactly. For example, I recall when one of our soldiers was run over by a tank. I was perhaps one hundred yards away when it happened and saw the bloody aftermath. The lieutenant colonel's diary notes a similar incident but several days earlier when I was in our base camp recovering from wounds. In fact, being run over by an armored vehicle almost happened to me on several occasions. I heard of it happening to others a couple of times but did not witness these other events myself. In his notes, Lieutenant Colonel Neilson notes that a major on his staff was run over by a track. Of course, many times we operated independently — as platoons, squads, and even as individuals (such as listening posts or LPs with two men or ambushes with three to four soldiers), so what I was doing on a specific date could differ significantly from what our company was doing. For example, my platoon or squad could have been guarding a bridge, outpost, or section of a road, while the colonel's notes would have mentioned our company operating in a different place with different experiences. In some situations, such as the ambush on September 13, 1968, my recollection on the ground is far different than what the colonel recorded in his diary. My awards, notes from the original debriefings, and historic documentation match my recollections and conflict with the colonel's. In this instance, I have pointed out where there are differences between the two versions of the event since we both participated in the action, me through the entire action and the colonel after the major ambush was affected.

One might ask why I did not use more names of soldiers with whom I served. The answer is that I rarely knew anyone's name. We used nicknames, last names, or ranks to communicate with other soldiers. Likewise, since I joined Alpha Company as an individual replacement I did not know anyone prior to joining my unit. Then I was either in battles where there was no time to get to know anyone or I was wounded and evacuated. When I returned, there were always many new replacements, and many of the soldiers who I served with before were killed or wounded. Our squad, platoon, and a good deal of our company were essentially wiped out several times in the five or so months in which I served in the field. So each time I returned from being wounded, there were new people manning our platoon and squad. Even the lieutenants and platoon sergeants did not last very long. In a five-month period, we had three or four different lieutenants and as many platoon sergeants. A couple of these lasted only a few days, as was the case with one of our new lieutenants and a platoon sergeant who both were wounded at the same time. In another situation, where a tank was stuck in the mud and we were attacked that evening, a new platoon sergeant joined us in the morning and was killed by an RPG that very evening. On several other occasions, both the platoon lieutenant and sergeant were either killed or wounded in the same firefight so that we had no continuity of command at the platoon level or below. As an SP4, I was often in command of our squad (which called for a sergeant) and once of our platoon (which called for an officer position) as I was the ranking soldier left fighting. At the same time, we lost some five or six of our tracks (armored personnel carriers, or APCs) to RPGs so that we never had an APC much longer than a month or so. On one occasion, we conducted operations and went into battle with an APC which had the back ramp (entire back side of the APC) pulled off while trying to pull a tank out of the mud. Thus, the enemy could shoot through the back of the track and kill the driver and track commander who had no protection at all from even small-arms fire. Such was the desperate situation under which we fought and conducted everyday operations.

One of the major errors in command decisions for the US Army was how they sent in replacements for the infantry (military occupational status, or MOS, of 11B or light weapons infantryman). The fact is that so few men were actually engaged in infantry combat, I estimate less than one in twenty army soldiers based on what I have read. Of course, they took the bulk of the combat-related casualties. It was well known from experience in WWII that by keeping the infantry units in the field as long as possible, they were forced to send in replacements while the combat units were engaged in active combat. This caused far more casualties than was necessary because the replacements never had a chance to learn the critical real-world skills necessary to survive as an infantryman in combat. Furthermore, it resulted in a very difficult challenge for new replacements as they did not know anyone in their new units, and most experienced soldiers ignored them since they were the most likely to get killed or get someone else killed. Since we were constantly short of experienced NCOs (noncommissioned officers) and officers, no one had the time to even help new replacement soldiers learn the ropes. You simply learned by doing or did not survive. In some cases, new replacements were given the most dangerous assignments, such as walking point, so that others in the squads would survive at the expense of the new replacements. This faulty approach resulted in a significant loss of unit cohesion and was detrimental to the combat effectiveness of the line infantry units. My own personal experience bore out all of these drawbacks. For all the time I was in the infantry, my unit was out in the field on operations against the enemy except for occasional two- or three-day visits to our base camp. We never really had time for training, retrofitting, or integrating new replacements and equipment into our unit. Everything, including new soldiers, was replaced out in the field so that we could continue operations against the enemy. No one took the time to teach me much of anything, and I learned everything the hard way, by doing it and making mistakes along the way. Frankly, I was very lucky that I survived.

Another point worth making is about the many untrue rumors about the Vietnam War and those who served. Unfortunately, many people have believed these rumors, which were spread by the media and others who avoided the draft and were never in Vietnam. Without going into the merits of many of the more common rumors, the truth is that we soldiers did not lose the war. In fact, the USA had pulled out of Vietnam two years before the South Vietnamese government fell to the North Vietnamese Army (a larger army than General Patton controlled during WWII). The politicians, especially the Congress of the United States, let South Vietnam fall because they cut off military aid to the South and would not let our Air Force come to the South's assistance in 1975.

Another rumor about the soldiers is that they were baby killers, drug addicts, and they did not measure up to their fathers, the brave soldiers who won WWII. This is nonsense. While serving in Vietnam, I do not recall any of our soldiers being evacuated with battle fatigue or cowardice. The only exception to this was, as I found out from Tom Foster some forty-three years later, that I was not the only survivor of the friendly fire 105 artillery short round. I had mistakenly thought that the 105 artillery round had killed everyone on our track except myself. But Tom told me that there was another soldier who survived physically, but not mentally. This soldier had served with Tom for many months, going through some of the worst battles of the war. After he, too, was blown off our track and likely received a concussion, he simply had hit the end of his endurance after seeing all of his buddies killed by our own artillery! The only situation where I can recall drugs in our unit was with one soldier whom everyone called Pothead. Once when we were going into a battle, he was so stoned that he fell off the track as it was going over a rice paddy dike. He had so little respect in the squad that no one told the driver to stop and pick him up. He was later killed or wounded because of his own stupidity. On a battlefield, you needed all your wits and senses to survive, along with a great deal of luck!

While I was in the field infantry, we were in almost constant contact with the enemy or booby traps and mines. For a comparison, let's contrast our situation to one of the largest battles in WWII, that of Okinawa. During the Battle for Okinawa, which lasted for about three months, there were some 541,000 USA soldiers who participated, of which there were 183,000 combat troops. There were about the same number of troops in Vietnam during 1968, but with about a quarter as many combat troops. On the *best day* in Vietnam, there were only 43,500 USA combat troops in the field out of a total of 545,000 USA soldiers. Since most of the time I was in the field, we operated with half strength in our combat unit. It was likely that we rarely had this many combat troops in the field at any one time. Of course, there were some 1,500,000 South Vietnamese troops, but for the most part they stayed near their bases and were certainly not actively pursuing the enemy in our area of operations (AO). There were other free-world troops in Vietnam, but none that I saw who fought as infantry in our AO. In the Battle of Okinawa, the US soldiers were attacking an island about sixty miles long and two to eighteen miles wide. They attacked with supporting ships and aircraft and faced an enemy of around 110,000. This is an advantage in combat soldiers of 1.8 to 1. In Vietnam, we faced an enemy of around four to five times (around 500,000, over 300,000 in Tet alone) as many men as they did in Okinawa, in a country the size of the USA state of Washington in square miles. Most of the time while I was in the infantry, we were vastly outnumbered by the enemy in the larger battles.

During the three-month battle, of Okinawa USA losses totaled 12,274 USA soldiers killed and 36,707 wounded. An additional 26,000 American servicemen were evacuated with so-called non-battle injuries. Most of these non-battle injuries were neuropsychiatric disorders, or battle fatigue. In the Vietnam War, only 5 of 1,000 troops were evacuated due to battle fatigue. During 1968 in Vietnam, the USA suffered some 14,589 battle deaths and over 100,000 wounded or almost a third of all casualties during the entire Vietnam War. While the casualties of the enemy during the war ranged widely, a conservative estimate of the enemy killed during the first nine months of 1968 is 150,000 to 160,000 with twice that many wounded or captured. Remember also that while these battles and timing were very different, the Vietnam War was a small unit war fought in very close quarters, mostly by companies and platoons, whereas the WWII Battle for Okinawa involved many more USA combat soldiers and larger combat formations. In my unit, the 25th Infantry Division, we took 34,484 casualties during the Vietnam War. This is almost twice as many the division suffered in WWII (5,532) and Korea (13,685) combined. Thus, you can determine for yourself if the war in Vietnam and soldiers fighting measured up against the brave fighting men of WWII.

INTRODUCTION

I decided to write about some of the incidents which happened to me while serving with the Army as an infantryman in Vietnam in 1968. My sons and a couple of Vietnam veterans I have recently met encouraged me to do so. It is forty-five-plus years after the events described in this book, so I am sure I have some things incorrect and others confused. What I found most difficult was trying to place the sequence of events in the proper order and time frames and remembering people's names. The specific incidents I recalled are very clear, and indeed I recall some details as if they happened yesterday. Most memories are vague, and the fear I felt experiencing the horrors of a firefight—with its killing, blood, guts, smells, dirt, death, and dying—now appear more like a bad dream than the vivid picture they once were in reality.

Anyone who has experienced combat would understand the depths of feeling that has been stamped on your memory. Here it is, some more than 45 years after I returned home from Vietnam, and there is rarely a day that goes by that I don't think about something that happened to me during the very long year I spent in there. The good news is that it has never impacted me in a negative way, as it has with others. Since coming home to "the world," I have been grateful for everything that God has given me. The opportunities that this great country has afforded me and the success I have earned is beyond my wildest dreams. Since Vietnam, I have had a very positive outlook on life in general and never really looked back. Rather, I have always looked to the future and planned ahead to make myself, my family and businesses I have run a success. To me, every day above ground is a good day. Every time I have a difficult situation, I think just how good I have it compared to when I was nineteen years old in the jungles of

Vietnam, and then the problem fades in significance. It certainly puts our everyday lives into perspective. I guess that is why I have never really been depressed or overwhelmed by adversity.

One of my hobbies is travel and history. I am especially interested in how soldiers experienced combat throughout history. It is interesting how I can relate to the experiences of soldiers of centuries ago and can imagine their fear and trials as they were forced into fighting for various causes. Our war in Vietnam was different in many ways from prior wars, but also more similar in other ways to wars that preceded it. In fact, we even used some of the same equipment in Vietnam as they did in WWII. My experiences in Vietnam were more closely tied to those of the soldiers fighting the island-hopping campaigns in the Pacific against Japan in WWII than the current wars in Afghanistan and Iraq, in which my son Justin participated as a Captain in the US Air Force.

What is interesting is that two men in combat can have very different experiences even if they are only yards apart. In discussion with another veteran of A Company of the 4/23, Tom Foster, he and I were only one squad/track apart (3-2 and 3-3). Yet even though we were only yards apart, we had very different experiences. I did not even know Tom, yet he was right next to me on several occasions. He was on the track in front of mine on my first day in joining A Company and another time when we were wounded on the same day and likely dusted off together! (A "dust off" is an evacuation of wounded soldiers by helicopter)

In many of the war movies you see, the men are always talking, even during the fighting. In real combat, it is so loud, with dust and smoke from explosions everywhere. Basically, you can't hear much of anything after the first few minutes in a firefight and can only see what is going on in the immediate area around you. There are times in battle you cannot see anything but smoke and dust or, as in the case of jungle fighting, a few feet in front of you. In the jungle and fighting in the forest, it is easy to get separated from the rest of your unit, which is very dangerous as your own men or weapons can kill you just as easily as the enemy. My own experience was that about one in five or 20% of the casualties we experienced in our unit was from friendly fire.

In a battle, most everyone is scared and trigger-happy and will react instantly by shooting at the slightest movement or anything that looks like a target. In a firefight, the noise of rifles, automatic weapons, grenades, mortars, rockets, artillery, and armored vehicles is overwhelming. If there are aircraft overhead dropping bombs or shooting cannons, this too adds to the noise, confusion, and reduced visibility. You can barely hear what someone next to you is saying, much less commands from yards away. Besides, we were never closer than about twenty feet from our other soldiers, and often in attacking, we had APCs to either side, firing their .50-caliber machine guns. If you stayed closer than fifteen to twenty-five feet, you presented too tempting a target for enemy machine guns or mortars. Thus, we always were spread out far apart to present smaller individual targets for the enemy. To communicate, we used simple hand signals. Basically, in battle you were so scared and hyped up on adrenaline that you needed to focus all of your senses on what was going around you, not trying to yell something clever to the soldier next to you. Especially since they would not have a clue what you were saying even if they looked your way rather than at the enemy, which was not a good thing to do. During the Vietnam War, we did not wear any ear protection, so for days after a battle your ears were still ringing. To this day I still have ringing in my ears. This made going out on ambushes or LP (listening post) more difficult as your hearing was impaired from the noises of battle during the day. When you are too near an explosion or get a concussion from rockets or mines, you often damage you eardrums and bleed from your ears, as happened to me twice during my tour. A battlefield is not a healthy place to be, even if you are not wounded or killed.

CHAPTER I

Drafted into the Army

October 26, 1967

My story of a short road to the jungles of Vietnam began around October 12, 1967, when I received my draft notice to report for induction on October 26, 1967. I had recently been kicked out of the University of South Florida, where I attended one semester. One of the students was a brown belt in karate and always went around threatening people with his karate stands. While he never bothered me, when I was drunk, I finally had had it and went after him. He ran into the bathroom and locked himself into a stall. I proceeded to pull the door off the hinges and broke up a few things in the dorm, including the karate kid. Unfortunately, that plus a prior stint in the Tampa City Jail for fighting and a few other such incidences, helped to encourage the dean to ask me to leave his school. Standing in his office on my final day in college, the Dean told me I was "crazy," and I guess he was right!

Anyone who lived through the 1960s as a young man, with the country engaged in a war and a much divided population, can understand our outlook on life. Frankly, we made the small number of people who protest today look tame in comparison. This was a wild time, and we all felt like we had to make every day count, since something out of our control was going to happen to us (which in fact did—the draft). Thus, we were wild and lived life to the fullest every day.

In the summer of 1967, I was working at ITT Rayonier, and while there, I was having a ball dating and raising hell in general. I was fortunate to have the lab director, Mr. Tabkee, or Tabkee man as we called him, understanding and forgiving of our antics. He was an older chemical engineer and a very nice and caring man. Today I would have been fired many times over for the things we did as lab technicians, and the disruptions to his experiments they were trying to conduct while we played games. Everything to us was a game. An example is that one of the technicians (a real Latin lover boy) enjoyed urinating in the test pulp. This created a problem in that the engineers were trying to make the paper as white as possible and could not understand why it kept turning yellow during the test. As I was kind of wild and spent most nights chasing women and staying out all night, I made a rather comfortable bed for myself out of filter material under one of the lab benches, complete with a filter blanket. Unfortunately, Mr. Tabkee would visit our lab during my sleep time, but he let it pass as I worked hard when I was awake. Like I said, thank God I was working in the sixties and not in the twenty-first century.

At this time, ARAMCO, the Saudi Arabia oil company, was hiring mercenaries to patrol its desert pipelines. They were paying the unbelievable sum of $50,000 (a fortune in the sixties) for one year's work with all room and board paid. They would have the $50,000 waiting for you when you returned, or give it to your relatives if you failed to come back. To a wild young man of nineteen making a couple of dollars an hour, this seemed like a good idea. In fact, one night in a bar, a friend and I agreed we would go down and sign up. The next morning, instead of going to sign up to be mercenaries, we went to the draft board in Morristown, New Jersey, and signed up for the early draft. I felt like I was going nowhere with my life and was getting tired of the unknown of when the draft would call us up. At that time it was a certainty that if you were not in college, you would be drafted. So we decided we were tired of waiting and would go for the adventure of Vietnam and the army. If you were drafted, odds were you would go to Vietnam as cannon fodder (infantry). Of course, I did not tell my parents but kept it to myself.

Much to my surprise, the draft board accommodated us, and shortly thereafter, I received my draft notice. In fact, it was only fourteen days later, which was a real shock! At this time I did not know that the United States was building up troops to their wartime high, and that they were desperate for replacement infantry. On October

12, 1967 I received my draft notice with "Greetings" from Uncle Sam, instructing me to report for duty just 14 days later.

One fact to keep in mind for today's youth is that at eighteen, when we were eligible for the draft, we could not vote and, in most states, not drink. Both required you to be twenty-one years old. Only in the state of New York could we drink, so we spent many nights traveling to NYC or Staten Island to raise hell in bars. So we were required to put our lives on the line at eighteen (although most were drafted after their nineteenth birthday) by being drafted, yet we could not vote. If you refused to go into service when drafted, you could go to jail. Talk about being unfair. So we changed this when we were able to vote after we got out of service.

Drafted into the Army

October 26, 1967

On a cool morning in October 26, 1968, my mother dropped me off at the Square in Morristown, New Jersey, in front of the selective service office. When I arrived, I recognized only one person whom I had known from a drinking bar called the Library. I don't recall his name, but he was a union construction heavy-equipment operator. We hung around until most of the draftees showed up, and then we were told to board buses. I sat next to him for the ride to Newark, New Jersey.

Upon arrival at the induction center, we were met by a lifer (professional career soldier) master sergeant (six stripes—three on top and three on the bottom). He hustled us off the bus barking orders. Most of the men had brought some luggage or at least an overnight bag as we were given no instruction: other than to report at such and such an hour, on a specific day and location. We were sent upstairs into an induction center. Here we were told to strip to our shorts and line up for medical inspections. One by one in line, we went through a series of medical evaluation stations where we met with medical doctors and army medics. They checked our eyesight, teeth, reflexes, private parts, hernia, and conducted other such evaluations. They also asked each of us a series of questions concerning our health, and as I recall, we had to take some sort of written test. Basically, the army was so desperate for men that if you had two of everything you were supposed to have, you were inducted.

In our group, there was one huge individual who was grossly overweight. He kept bragging that "they can't draft me, I'm too fat." Later I saw him in basic training running around the exercise field with his uniform hanging off him while we were eating. He was in the Fat Man's Platoon, where they ran, exercised, and generally starved the fat men until they dropped to an acceptable weight.

After our perfunctory medical exam (if one could call it such), we were shuffled into another room and told to get dressed. While there, one of the lifer sergeants, a few inches shorter than I was, ordered me to empty the garbage pail and get a broom. I told him to "fuck off" as I wasn't in his fucking army yet! He went into a tirade, and said he would handle me soon enough. I told him again to "fuck off and go pick on someone else who gives a shit!" I was not happy being treated like a dog and figured he couldn't do anything anyway, as I was still a civilian.

Later we were told we all passed and were going to be inducted into the army. I do not believe anyone failed no matter what their condition or aptitude. We were then walked into a room where an officer told us to repeat after him a pledge, after which we were inducted. No one refused, and all of us were then in the army as buck privates, or E-1 (enlisted grade 1), the lowest of the low! After that, we were taken back outside to waiting army green, or OD (olive drab), buses. The sergeant who went into a tirade over me did not bother me again. I would have ignored him anyway. No one informed me that I needed to follow the orders of a sergeant! Even though I knew enough that this was true, I would simply play dumb, which would work for me many times in the future.

We then boarded the buses, and they told us that we would be transported to Fort Dix, New Jersey, for training. While we were getting ready to leave, a smart-looking marine sergeant boarded the bus and asked for volunteers to join the finest branch of the service—the marines. No one volunteered, and so he looked around and then said for everyone in the first two rows to get up. They got up, and he marched them off to "volunteer" for the marines! I was in the middle of the bus so I learned a valuable lesson—never be the first ten or the last ten in line. Stay hidden in the middle and never volunteer for anything.

We took a long ride to Fort Dix on the buses, and no one said much of anything. I got the feeling that no one really knew anyone else on the bus. Everyone kept to his own thoughts, including me. When we arrived at Fort Dix, it was dark. We had eaten lunch at a diner around the corner from the Newark processing center using coupons the army provided. I, for one, was getting hungry, but no one seemed to give a damn about feeding us. The bus driver was a soldier who said little or nothing other than we were going to Fort Dix and "you will see." Upon arrival, we were rushed off the buses at double time (quickly without running) and told by a couple of sergeants to line up in several rows facing forward.

Fort Dix, New Jersey, Processing and Basic Training

October 26, 1967–January 11, 1968

After lining up at Fort Dix, we were marched off to our barracks. These barracks were brick and looked fairly modern, so I did not think they would be too bad. However, as it was late fall in New Jersey; it was getting pretty cold at night. We found out that the army did not believe in heating the barracks, or at least if they were heated, it was only just above freezing. I remember that the entire time I spent at Fort Dix I was cold, always cold, even under the covers, or rather the single woolen cover on the bunks. We were assigned bunks and then marched off to the mess hall. They did not give us enough to eat as everyone, no matter what size, got the same allocation on metal trays. Since I ate a lot, I was always hungry throughout my army days, until after Vietnam when I was assigned to Fort Monmouth, where you could have all you wanted to eat. After dinner, we were marched off to the supply center, a wooden building with stacks of army supplies. Here we were fitted (that is a joke) for black army boots and army fatigues, caps, jackets, gloves, underwear, socks, etc., and given two of everything. We were also given a woolen blanket and duffel bag (a large military bag for storing our clothing and personal items) to hold everything. I did not think it would all fit, but by pounding the duffel bag on the floor, you finally managed to fit it all in. This would be my only luggage during my twenty-two months in the army.

Then we were marched back to our barracks and shown how to make up our bunks. The NCOs in charge yelled every command and explanation to us like we were deaf. I guess they did it to impress us, but mostly it was annoying. Each of us had a bed with a wooden OD (olive drab) green locker at the foot of the bunk beds, which were stacked one on top of the other. We were then told about how all of us would have turns pulling fire duty for each hour during the night. By this time it was late evening, and we finally got to go to sleep. At 0500 we were awakened, and a new day started. More formations, they cut off all our hair, gave us a variety of tests and shots, and issued us weapons. Anyone who called the rifle a gun got punishment in the form of push-ups. In fact, the drill instructors, or DIs (who wore Smokey the Bear hats), looked for people to step out of line so they could make an example of them.

We were required to take a battery of tests called the AFCT. This stands for Armed Forces Classification Tests. These tests helped determine where you would go for assignment to different military occupation specialty (or MOS) within the army. Getting into the infantry required only a score of 70, which is pretty low. Of course, as draftees, the army wasn't interested in training us for a job other than the infantry. Most of the draftees during this period were destined as replacements for the infantry. After taking the tests, one of the administrators asked me several questions. One of the questions was, "What would you like to do?" I told him, "I want to go home!" In reality, unless you enlisted for three years, you really didn't have a choice of where you served or what you would be doing.

Training went on every day, and we learned about the uniform code of military justice, ranks in the army, how to salute, the Geneva Convention (North Vietnam was not a signatory), how to march, how to shoot weapons, how to exercise, how to use bayonets, how to go over obstacle courses, first aid, and everything else you needed to know about the army. We had many lectures and even films on such interesting subjects as frostbite, where they showed soldiers with their frostbitten black toes being peeled off, and all sorts of venereal diseases (VD) you could contract and what they would do to the male genitals. They even showed us prophylactics and how to use them, which most of us chucked at during the demonstration. The first aid training came in very handy in Vietnam and even several times after I was out of the military. After the army, I saved one man's life when he would have bled to death, and another time pulled a pilot from a small aircraft after he crashed. We also learned how to make our bunks (so a coin could bounce off them) and take care of our gear, weapons, and personal items. We used Brasso for polishing belt buckles and shoe polish to spit-shine boots. We had to pay for those items ourselves. For these essentials, we were given an advance on our pay of $25. A big deal since we only made about $78 a month (less deductions such as income and Social Security taxes) as buck privates. Polishing our boots and brass was an exercise in futility, as we would polish them at night only to get them full of mud and snow the next day. We learned the old army saying "Hurry up and wait," as we double-timed everywhere and then waited in lines for everything. We were required to repeat our service number before every meal and whenever asked. Mine started with a "US" since I was drafted. Serial numbers beginning with an "RA" were for those who signed up for a three-year hitch in the regular army. We also needed to remember the serial number of our M-14 weapons. Additionally we learned never to volunteer, or to look idle, as you would be volunteered for extra duty.

One time, a couple of us had some free time after exercises. We were standing around our barracks, talking. A sergeant came along and, typical of those days, volunteered us for duty at the supply stores building. Then he marched us off and turned us over to the supply sergeant. The supply sergeant pointed to a stack of woolen blankets and said, "You can go back to your barracks when all of these are folded and stacked up on the shelves." There were literally tens of thousands of them. We started folding them and soon realized that we would never be able to fold all of the blankets in a few hours or even a full day. So we hatched a scheme. We would fold enough blankets to make a stack of blankets in the front, and then throw the unfolded blankets in the back of these folded blankets. As the shelves were huge and deep, this worked very well. So when we had piled up all of the unfolded blankets behind the folded row, we asked one of the other sergeants in the supply building if we could leave. Not knowing how many blankets there were, he agreed and dismissed us. We were always looking for shortcuts and ways to play the army game against them.

My worst experience was getting inoculations. We were marched down to the medical building where we were lined up and told to take off our shirts leaving on only undershirts. Then we went through what I can only describe as a line of torture where we received two shots at the same time in each upper arm with a gun which injected us with the inoculation. They hurt like hell, but if you moved, the gun would lacerate your arm, and you had to get the shot all over again. The soldier in front of me collapsed and passed out. Two medics simply picked him up by each arm and dragged him through the line. He received every shot like everyone else, and at the end they put him down in a cot along with several others. It was like a human assembly line. Then we received a shot in the Gluteus Maximus with what one can only describe as a horse needle. At the end a medic with a cruel streak stabbed you in your finger with a small scalpel and took a sample of your blood. Later these blood types would be placed on your dog tags along with your name, serial number, and religion. At the end we were given a shot record, which listed all the inoculations we received. We were told never to lose this card because if we did, we would have to get all of these shots again! Apparently, the army did not keep medical records on its soldiers! I carried my shot record through the entire war and still have it today. One time when I was going for R&R from Vietnam, I was told by one of the friendly medics that I was missing a shot and would not be allowed to leave Vietnam without it. So I borrowed his pen and forged a line that I had received this shot. Unfortunately, to this day, I don't recall which shot I forged. Apparently, it was not important as I didn't get any permanent diseases in Nam outside of the normal field aliments. One of the shots, I believe it was for yellow fever, hurt so badly, and it semi-paralyzed the left side of my body to where I could not button up my shirt. All I wanted was to get away from that torture building, so one of the guys helped me on with my field jacket, and I left. After the shots you were given the afternoon off to recover. I felt sick for a few days afterward, but the feeling came back in my left side after a few hours.

We ran everywhere, which I learned to hate. Running in combat boots with a rifle and pack was no pleasure, especially when the rifle hit you in the helmet every time your foot hit the ground. The army did not give us sneakers at that time. You wore only boots for training and different shoes when in your dress uniforms. But the physical part of the training was relatively easy for me. I was five feet eleven inches and 185 pounds and had been lifting weights and playing sports most of my young life, so none of the exercises or obstacle courses were very difficult for me. Men who grew up in the fifties and sixties were much slimmer than today. We typically had only one fat guy in our classes and groups where we hung out versus a third of youths today. Other recruits had more difficulty with the exercises and obstacle courses. It was very difficult especially for fat people, who were placed into the Fat Man's Platoon. Here overweight recruits were placed in a special platoon where they ate only what everyone else ate, and they did much more physical exercise than normal recruits.

I enjoyed the firing range where we fired the M-14 rifle, which was most accurate. In Vietnam we would use this as a sniper rifle with a mounted infrared scope. I had fired a .22 rifle in my youth but never anything as powerful as the M-14. One demonstration which stuck in my mind was how powerful an M-14 was when it hit an object. We were in stands having a lecture on the M-14 rifle. The DI placed a .50-caliber metal ammo can full of water on the ground and placed a GI helmet on top of it. Then he fired a single round from the M-14 into the can. The can exploded, and it threw the helmet ten feet into the air! Then the DI said, "That is an example of what would happen to your head if you were shot by an M-14 rifle!" It sure made you think about keeping your head down in combat.

Real Basic Training

October 1967

One of the more memorable "basic training" episodes was when we first joined our basic training units. Our entire company was herded (we were treated like cattle) into a large hall with a stage up front. Our head drill instructor was standing on the stage and announced in his Southern drawl, "Today you nasty-ass recruits are going to be taught how to keep your dirty asses clean the army way. This is your first and last instruction on basic army hygiene!" Then he proceeded to explain while showing us how to wash our asses, under our arms, our crotch, feet (between the toes), hair (with army soap bars), and other parts of our anatomy. He explained how to shave with army razors, brush our teeth with army OD toothbrushes (which can also be used to clean you weapon), and brush our hair, which got a chuckle out from everyone since our hair had all been shaved off. I couldn't believe that the army had to show people how to clean themselves. Most of us thought it was ridiculous. I found out later that some of the draftees actually did not know basic hygiene. Some of the men were really filthy, especially the American Indians, who were the dirtiest people I have ever come across in my life. They never took a shower nor cleaned themselves. Later they would find out what a GI shower was when their bunkmates got tired of the smell and dragged them off to the shower and scrubbed them down with stiff army cleaning brushes and brown soap.

At the end of the lecture and demonstration, the head DI told us he was going to demonstrate how we were to wipe our asses with one sheet of toilet paper per day. He explained that the army only allotted one sheet of toilet paper per day per soldier. Given the very basic and graphic demonstration we had just witnessed, we all fell for the joke but did not realize it until much later. I remember thinking to myself, "The army is nuts if they think you can only use one sheet of toilet paper a day!" The head DI took out of his pocket a single sheet of toilet paper and held it up for all to see. Then he folded it in half and folded it twice more until it was in a wedge shape. He held it up for all to see again. Then he tore off a very small piece from the end of the folded toilet paper. He then explained, "Tear off a very small piece and put this in your pocket!" which he proceeded to execute. Then he unfolded the single piece of toilet paper, which now had a hole in the middle where he had torn off the end of the folded piece. I kept thinking to myself, "This guy is nuts!" No one said a word; they just watched in fascination. The head DI stuck the index finger of his right hand through the hole he had created in the single sheet of toilet paper. He then proceeded to demonstrate wiping his rear end with the toilet paper! Then he held up the single piece of toilet paper in his right hand and used his left hand to close the paper around his index finger and demonstrate how to clean your finger off after wiping. I recall thinking, "You have got to be kidding!" Then he said, "Now remember the piece I told you to put in your pocket," as he retrieved the small torn-out center of the toilet paper sheet with his left hand. Then he said, "This is to use to clean under your fingernail," and proceeded to use the small piece of paper to demonstrate cleaning the fingernail of his index finger. No one said a word, and he did not laugh or show any emotion! But then he announced, "Attention! This lecture is over!" and walked off the stage. I, for one, and most everyone else thought that this demonstration was for real just like the rest of the lecture. No one ever told us it was a sick joke, but we figured it out later when there was still a roll of toilet paper in our latrine (dormitory-like bathrooms). An interesting side note to this lecture was how the barracks latrines were laid out and our one roll of toilet paper was handled. In addition to the urinals, all of the toilets were lined up side by side with around twelve inches between each toilet. As everyone had to get ready to go at once, all the toilets were occupied whenever our platoon used the latrines. So you had some forty men using the latrines at one time with around ten or twelve toilets lined up in a row. There was one roll of toilet paper for the entire latrine. So when you were finished and you needed toilet paper, you asked that it be passed down to you from the other side of the row of men doing their business.

Pugil Stick Training

Another memorable incident took place when we were being instructed on Pugil stick training. I had been getting in trouble quite a bit in training and had been assigned KP (kitchen patrol) most every weekend. Two of the DI assistant buck sergeants (E-5 rank) were always ragging on me. Both were Vietnam vets, and one, the shorter of the two, had been shot through the mouth where the bullet had gone through his open mouth and out one of his cheeks. He had a round scar on his cheek to prove it. They thought they would teach me a lesson by beating my head in while demonstrating how to use the Pugil sticks. They volunteered me to fight with the sergeant. The Pugil sticks were four-foot-long rounded poles about three inches in diameter with large vinyl pads at each end. The idea was to hold the Pugil sticks with both hands and hit the other opponent with the pads, knocking him down or at least senseless. It was designed to instill aggression and learn how to fight using a rifle as a weapon. It was also physically challenging, similar to a boxing match. As protection, you wore a football helmet, gloves and a pad outside your uniform to protect your crotch. After suiting up in the helmet and crotch pad, the DIs announced they would show us the proper way of using the Pugil sticks to disable the enemy. The smaller sergeant then quickly attacked me with the Pugil stick, hitting me with several hard blows to my head. I had never used these weapons before, so he used his skill to his advantage. It was hard to hit him, but he seemed to be able to hit me at will and continued doing so before I had a chance. I was really getting pissed off and became aggressive and out for blood. I thought he was going to kill me if I didn't do something different. So when he came at me again, instead of holding the Pugil stick with two hands, I let go with the left hand and used the end of the Pugil stick like a sword. This was totally unexpected by the sergeant as the Pugil stick was not meant to be used in this manner. My Pugil stick caught him under his chin while he was moving rapidly toward me! The blow knocked his head back, and he stumbled backward. Quickly I grabbed the Pugil stick with both hands and swung it like a baseball bat, which was another unorthodox move. By this time my blood was up, and I wanted to kill this son of a bitch who had been hounding me for weeks. This was my chance to do it legally. After all, I was just a trainee who was being made an example. My baseball bat blow spun the sergeant around so that his back was toward me and his head bowed down. I was out to kill him, so I raised the Pugil stick up and hit him as hard as I could on the helmet with the wooden shaft of the Pugil stick. The blow hit him with a loud crack, and it knocked him down on his knees. I was about to hit him again when several of the DIs and assistant sergeants grabbed the Pugil stick and pulled me off from killing him! They were really pissed that I had knocked down the sergeant and was obviously trying to kill or at least hurt him badly. This was exactly my intention, after he beat the shit out of me with the Pugil stick. This was not how the demonstration was supposed to go, and I was the one who was to be taught a lesson, not the sergeant. That ended my Pugil stick career, as I was not allowed to use them again. Of course, I had to do more push-ups and got assigned more KP. Afterward the sergeant, who was older than me but smaller, told me he would love to take me out back and beat the shit out of me. I told him I would look forward to it anytime he had the balls. He never did follow up on his threat, and after that, he left me alone. I think we both ended up with more respect for each other. The bigger sergeant, who likely could have put me in the hospital if we got in a fight, told me later, "You're lucky I don't take off my stripes and teach you a lesson." Then he added, "Anytime you want to try that shit with me, just meet me behind the barracks and I'll take off my stripes." Being a wise guy but not stupid, I replied, "If I meet you out back, I'll bring an entrenching tool!" With that he just gave me a look that could kill and walked away shaking his head. I never asked him to go out back, and he backed off on harassing me after that. He turned out to be a decent guy who also had been drafted.

Kitchen Patrol

Kitchen patrol, or KP for short, was used as punishment for recruits who got out of line. I got KP more than my share of the time. KP meant that you had to get up around 3 a.m. and be marched off to the mess hall where you worked all day cleaning pots (large kettles), ovens, peeling potatoes, mopping floors, cleaning out garbage cans, and generally doing whatever the cooks didn't want to do. You worked hard from early in the morning until everything was cleaned after dinner. Sometimes you worked until eight or nine at night. If the pots had any grease on them at all, the mess sergeant would throw everything on the floor and you had to clean it all over again. One thing I remember was peeling potatoes. You peeled potatoes with a potato peeling machine which looked like a small washing machine. Inside the "washing machine," instead of a smooth surface where you would place clothes, it had a black sandpaper type of surface. As water was run into the potato peeling machine, the potatoes were peeled very quickly. This was necessary since there were mounds of potatoes to peel and feed an army. When I first used the potato peeling machine, I left the potatoes in too long, and they came out more like marbles. This did not endear me to the mess sergeant.

I quickly discovered that there was no communications between the platoon sergeants and the mess sergeant. All the mess sergeant knew was he was to be assigned five men from such and such a company but did not know their names. So after a while, when we had time off, I simply bugged out on the way to the mess hall since it was dark and no one had my name. I would then get extra sleep and hang out around the base if it were on a Sunday when we had off. Other times they identified who was on mess duty with a towel tied around your bunk. So after everyone went to sleep, I would get up and tie the towel on my bunk around someone else's bunk. At 3 a.m. there would be a lot of objecting that they did not have KP, but their protests were ignored. Anyway I got out of a lot of KP using these techniques. Another way I got out of extra duty was to have my then girlfriend, Barbara, come down to Fort Dix and go to the commanding officer's building. She told him that we were engaged and that she had not heard from me since I was drafted. This worked like a charm. The CO felt sorry for the girl, and I was called off KP and given a ten-hour pass to spend with my girlfriend. We quickly left the base in her VW car and spent the afternoon in a local hotel. We did this twice, once with the base CO and once with our battalion CO. Both times worked great!

Hand Grenade Practice Range

BASIC COMBAT TRAINING SUBJECTS

SUBJECT	HOURS
1. ADMINISTRATIVE PROCESSING	24
2. COMMANDER'S TIME	25
3. PROFICIENCY TESTING	4
4. ACHIEVEMENTS AND TRADITIONS	2
5. MILITARY COURTESY AND CUSTOMS	3
6. CHARACTER GUIDANCE	4
7. CODE OF CONDUCT	1
8. MILITARY JUSTICE	3
9. COMMAND INFORMATION	1
10. DRILL AND CEREMONIES	40
11. PERSONAL HYGIENE	1
12. FIRST AID	8
13. CHEMICAL, BIOLOGICAL, AND RADIOLOGICAL WARFARE	4
14. GUARD DUTY	4
15. INSPECTIONS	28
16. PHYSICAL TRAINING	26
17. ORIENTATION IN COUNTER-INSURGENCY OPERATIONS	1
18. PHYSICAL CONTACT CONFIDENCE TRAINING	26
19. GRENADES	4
20. INDIVIDUAL WEAPONS QUALIFICATION: BASIC RIFLE MARKSMANSHIP COURSE	83
21. CLOSE COMBAT COURSE	4
22. INFILTRATION COURSE	3
23. INDIVIDUAL TACTICAL TRAINING	14
24. MARCHES AND BIVOUACS	30
25. COMBAT FIRING	4
26. DRIVER EDUCATION	2
TOTAL	352

Another incident in basic training was at the hand grenade practice range. Here we used inert grenades (without explosives or detonators) as opposed to the live ranges, where we used live hand grenades and bullets. We would practice throwing grenades from various positions and from foxholes, behind obstacles, and out in the open. The target was a series of rings around an artillery shell stuck in the ground in the middle of the circles. The distance was about fifteen to twenty yards near the maximum range a normal soldier could throw a hand grenade. The idea was to hit the artillery shell with the grenade, which was very difficult.

One day our top sergeant (an E-8 rank or first sergeant) was walking with another DI behind the rows of artillery shell targets for the grenade range. As he walked behind my target, I tossed a grenade as far as I could behind the target shell and damn near hit him in the head. Getting hit in the head with a steel hand grenade would ruin your day. Immediately the top sergeant came over to where I was standing and started yelling at me that I could have killed him. I said something like "Gee, First Sergeant, I didn't know I could throw it that far. I was just aiming at the target, and it must have gone too far!" I don't think he bought it, but what else could he say? I was just a dumb recruit! I never saw him walk behind the grenade targets ever again. But I was not one of his favorite recruits after that. I just didn't like being pulled out of civilian life to be basically a slave to the army, being constantly harassed and taking orders from everyone above me, which was basically everyone in the military. Some of them dumb as dirt!

Guarding an Empty Warehouse with Live Ammo

One of our final exercises near the end of our basic training was to pull guard duty all night with live ammo. By now it was in the dead of winter in Fort Dix with snow on the ground, and it was cold as hell. I was assigned to guard an empty warehouse. All night long I was required to walk around this warehouse, being relieved only when a sergeant relieved me. It was a very cold night, and I was not looking forward to walking around all night guarding a vacant warehouse. We were issued three live rounds for our M-14 and told to load them into our magazines, but we were not to shoot them ever! The top sergeant took me aside and said, "Now, Esher, this warehouse you are guarding is empty. I don't give a damn what happens, you are not to shoot anyone or anything around this warehouse. There is nothing in there of value, and I don't want to have to write up a bunch of reports because some stupid recruit shot someone. Understand!" I said, "Well, First Sergeant, if there is nothing to guard, then why is the army having me guard it?" He got red in the face and said, "Just guard the warehouse like you're told, but don't you shoot anything." Those are real bullets!"

So I replied, "Well, First Sergeant, if the army wants me to guard it, I will surely guard it because it must be important!" He got very angry and simply said, "Don't you shoot off one of those goddamn rounds, Esher," and stormed away.

So I was dropped off in the middle of a bunch of empty warehouses and told to walk around the building until relieved. Just to be a wise guy, I told the assistant DI sergeant who dropped me off, "Well, Sergeant, I will guard this building with my life and challenge anyone who comes close. After all, the army thinks it is so important that they want me to guard it, so I will!" The assistant DI sergeant got angry and said, "Esher, don't you shoot anyone when they come to relieve you or anyone else for that matter. This is an empty warehouse. This is serious business with live rounds!" I replied, "Yes, Sergeant, I will do my duty." He walked off pissed, but I'll bet he didn't want to be the one to drop off another recruit to relieve me with live ammo. I knew I had several hours of guard duty before someone came to relieve me. I would be damned if I was going to walk around in the snow all night freezing my ass off. I figured they were cautious enough not to try to surprise me as I had live ammo and they didn't know what I would do. So I walked around the warehouse a couple of times to have my footprints show in the snow. Then I found an unlocked door, and I snuck into one of the empty warehouses and fell asleep. At least I was out of the wind. After a couple of hours of guard duty, I heard someone calling my name and beeping a jeep horn. I got up and walked outside and came around the side of the building like I had been guarding it all along. As I suspected, the sergeant did not want to come near the warehouse I was guarding. The procedure was for me to approach the sergeant with my rifle at the ready position (across my chest, barrel facing upward), release the magazine, and open the chamber, proving there was no round in the chamber, then hand the magazine to the sergeant and report on my watch. I followed the procedure, and the sergeant took the magazine, inspected my rifle, and appeared relieved. On the way back, he said, "It's a damn good thing you didn't fire off a round, Esher. The first sergeant was afraid to give you live rounds in the first place." I didn't say anything but chuckled to myself.

Live Fire Course

One of the final exercises we went through in basic training was the live-fire obstacle course. Here we went out at night and had to crawl through barbed wire and around obstacles while .50-caliber machine guns fired live rounds over our heads. Throughout the course, there were sandbagged emplacements where explosives went off right next to you. It was scary, and we had been warned never to stand up or we would be killed. In actual fact, the machine guns were on elevated platforms, and if you stood up, they would have still fired over your head. It was a scary exercise, but at least you knew what it was like to have live round fired over your head and explosions next to you as you crawled through barbed wire.

Basic Training Graduation

January 11, 1968

I went through most of basic training without any issues. None of the physical and mental tests were that difficult for me. The one test I hated the most was running a mile with full pack and gear within eight minutes. Some of the men whom I went through the training with were not very bright. They had trouble with even the most basic tasks and commands. Most of the wrath of the DIs and assistant DI sergeants were directed at these men. The DIs and sergeants were trying to get them through as best they could. Some didn't make it and had to go back through basic training all over again. We found out later about the McNamara Project 100, where they drafted people with marginal IQs, and some of these were obviously in our basic training company. After a while I got along with most of the DIs and sergeants, and they didn't seem to hold a grudge. After graduation, I found out that the two assistant DIs were also draftees finishing their tour of duty. Neither one had any love for the army. They went through the motions like I did but mostly in front of the lifer DIs. Even the sergeant I hit with the

Pugil sticks didn't hold a grudge. He told us some good points about being careful in Vietnam.

The day before we were to graduate, we were told there would be postings at the company HQ for our next assignment. Everyone was anxious to see not only where they would go next but what kind of MOS they would be assigned. Most of the draftees thought we would all be chosen as infantry and sent to Vietnam, which turned out to be true. However, in the back of everyone's mind, we were hoping for some other, any other, assignment besides the infantry. Before we were sent to Vietnam, there was one more step along the way—AIT, or advanced individual training. We were called by name into groups and then taken to the company HQ building. There we were told by the first sergeant of our designated MOS and next duty assignment where we would go for additional specialized training. We all knew that the infantry was the worst MOS, and the very worst place you could be sent for AIT training was to Tigerland in Fort Polk, Louisiana. When it came time for my group to report, the first sergeant looked up at us and smiled, saying, "Well, boys, you're all going to be real infantry combat soldiers and are going to Fort Polk for AIT." Then he added, "Ah, yes, the famous Tigerland, good preparation to get you ready for Vietnam!" With that, he handed us our orders in a manila envelope to take with us. My thought at that point was I wished I had hit him in the head with the grenade. Then the realization of where I was going and what I was destined to do hit home. We all walked away in shock since everyone was hoping for some other assignment. Not only were we going into the infantry and a sure trip to Vietnam, but we were going to the dreaded Tigerland, the worst place in the army for AIT training—a double strike against us!

We had a graduation ceremony in a huge empty building (it was January in New Jersey and very cold) where guests were invited. We marched in company formations before a viewing stand, awards were given out, and the band played. The chaplain said invocations, and we heard several speeches by our officers. Upon graduation, I was promoted to private first class (or PFC) as were most of the men. My mom came down with my girlfriend to the graduation. After graduation we had the rest of the day off and our first weekend passes. I drove home and spent the rest of the weekend at my girlfriend's apartment. Too soon the weekend was over, and I had to report back to base to be transported to Fort Polk.

What I recall most about basic training in Fort Dix, New Jersey, was just how cold it was to be outside all day long in the winter. We froze our rears off most of the time and were glad to get indoors even if it was for a boring training session.

Tigerland, Fort Polk, Louisiana

January 15–March 15, 1968

Tigerland was located in a remote area of Fort Polk, Louisiana. It was known that this was a staging area for those infantry troops going to Vietnam. In fact, it was guarded by MPs (military police) such that we needed a pass to go to the regular (non-infantry) locations within Fort Polk. For some reason I was selected as the acting corporal (you were given corporal stripes on an armband) in charge of taking the soldiers in our company on the plane and to the airport. We were driven in a bus to Newark Airport and boarded a commercial flight to what I believe was New Orleans Airport. I had never flown before, and neither had anyone else. Everyone roamed around the airport, so it was like herding cats to get them on the plane. I held all the tickets for everyone, so I had to make a roll call and hand out the tickets just before boarding.

When we arrived at the airport, we were met by a military bus which took us to Fort Polk. None of us had ever been to the south, so everything was new to us. Louisiana had a lot of swamps, lakes, and rivers and was a lot hotter than New Jersey. We thought that at least we would not be freezing on maneuvers like we were at Fort Dix.

When we arrived at Fort Polk, we were taken to the North Fort known as the famous Tigerland. Tigerland was located a few miles from the main fort. We processed into Tigerland and were assigned to training companies and barracks. The barracks were old WWII wooden barracks elevated off the ground with a latrine (community bathroom) at the back. As usual, we were harassed by the DIs who liked to yell, and we had to run everywhere. The big difference in this training and basic training was this training was much more focused on the use and care of weapons. We also learned the use and care of the new M-16 rifle, which is the one we would use in Vietnam. We no longer used the M-14 rifle in day-to-day exercises, but we did fire it as it was still being used in Vietnam as a sniper rifle. We trained on the M-16 rifle, the M-79 grenade launcher, the M-60 machine gun, the 1911 .45 pistol, the .50-caliber machine gun, the LAW 3.5-inch antitank rocket, hand grenades, Claymore mines, and other types of land mines. We also spent a lot of time on patrol and on land navigation. As everyone knew we were going to Vietnam in the infantry, everyone was on a razor's edge, and it didn't take much to set people off. Thus, there were many fights, and tempers flared easily. The training was difficult and concentrated, and they tried to make it as real as possible. There was even a full Vietnamese fortified village in Tigerland with enemy, tunnels, and booby traps where we practiced. As we marched around, the army tried to indoctrinate us to hate the enemy and prepare us to kill the enemy by singing marching songs such as "*I want to go to Vietnam, I want to kill a Vietcong.*"

McNamara Project 100,000

When I was in AIT (advanced individual training) in Tigerland, we had a several soldiers who were mentally unable to perform as infantry soldiers. Two of them were American Indians (we called both Chief) who apparently did not speak English, and at least one other soldier had a very low IQ. These individuals were unable to understand even the simplest requirements of a soldier. They had difficulty marching and going through the arms training, were unable to assemble and dissemble a rifle, and did not understand the basics of the equipment and armaments we had to handle as infantry. However, the DIs or drill sergeants were under orders to graduate everyone. Thus, they faced a dilemma. In order to graduate an infantryman, all soldiers had to be able to assemble and disassemble his weapon and become proficient in the use of other infantry armaments, such as hand grenades, machine guns, LAWs, etc. So the way they handled this was really unconscionable. They would simply leave the room and tell everyone that no one could eat or go on leave or other such motivation until everyone had assembled his weapon. They knew we would help these individuals to assemble their weapons so we could go to eat or on leave. In the other qualifications, a sergeant would simply assist the low-IQ troopers in throwing the grenade or firing a LAW, etc. The result was that these low-IQ soldiers were graduated and likely sent to their death in Vietnam if they wound up in the infantry.

McNamara's Project 100,000 was a program conceived by McNamara in 1966 to fill the replacement needs of the army in Vietnam. Because LBJ (President Lyndon Baines Johnson) refused to call up either the military reserves or the National Guard to provide replacements for troops in Vietnam, McNamara had to find troops someplace. Basically, McNamara's solution was to "lower the standards" for draftees. Project 100,000 lowered draft standards in both physical and mental abilities so that draftees who previously failed minimum military qualifications could be drafted. For example, those unable to speak English, those of low aptitude, those with physical impairments, those too short or too tall, and other categories. According to information I researched, there were some 320,000 to 354,000 volunteers and draftees who entered the military under this program. The majority were volunteers, accounting for 54% of the total. The individuals who were drafted were apparently given different draft numbers (beginning with the digits US67 for those who failed the minimum IQ tests) and were called the "Moron Corps" by the army. Apparently, the Moron Corps were sent into combat in disproportionate numbers. Some 40% were trained for combat versus 25% of general draftees. Likewise, blacks made up some 41% of the Moron Corps. According to some research, some of those drafted had IQs as low as 62! After WWII, the lowest draft IQ legally allowed was 80.

Pueblo Incident and North Korea

January 23, 1968

A few days after we arrived at Tigerland, the North Koreans attacked and captured the USA spy ship USS Pueblo operating off the shore of North Korea on January 23, 1968. While we knew little about the incident, the rumor around the camp was that we may be going to war with North Korea. We had only been in infantry training a few days, and we knew that in any war, we would be the first to go upon graduation. We were all nervous about being sent to Vietnam, much less North Korea, to fight. Some of us knew how bad the fighting was in North Korea, and we didn't want to go and face the Chinese and North Koreans. You will recall that the Korean War had ended in a temporary armistice on July 27, 1953. That was only fifteen years earlier, so the Korean War was still fresh in everyone's mind.

A couple of days after the spy ship Pueblo was captured; we were scheduled to receive a briefing on jungle diseases and survival in the tropics. So after exercises and marching, we were led into a briefing hall. We were seated and the training drill instructor began the briefing. About a minute into the briefing, another sergeant walked onto the stage, looking very nervous, and handed the DI giving the briefing a piece of paper. Then he exited the stage. The DI stopped the briefing and looked at the paper. Then he said, "The United States has just declared war on the Democratic People's Republic of North Korea!" There was dead silence in the room. To this day I still get chills down my spine thinking of that moment. I was shocked along with everyone else in the room. Here we thought we were all going to Vietnam and fight an enemy who was running around in black pajamas and the most we had to watch out for was booby traps. At least that was what we had been told by the army. Now we were going to face the North Koreans and Chinese, who had millions of men, tanks, and artillery! We were all scared shitless and in shock. Then after an eternity, the DI on the stage said, "We now will switch this lecture on jungle diseases and survival to cold weather survival." You could have heard a pin drop even though the hall was filled with several hundred men.

Finally after another minute or so, the DI on the stage said, "This is not true, but you have to be adaptable and be ready for anything in the infantry. But we may yet be going to war with North Korea, so take your training very seriously." Everyone in the room let out a gasp of air. We were all still in a state of shock over the declaration of War with North Korea. I thought to myself, "These people are nuts. All they ever do is fuck with us." But I, along with several hundred others, was relieved that it was all a farce.

This was typical of how we knew nothing except what the army wanted us to know and how they screwed with us all the time, both mentally and physically. Remember, back in those days on base we had no TVs, radios, Internet, newspapers, telephones, or any other communications with the outside world. The only exception was when we were let off base, which was only a couple of times toward the end of our training. Then we would only be allowed a twelve-hour pass to go to Leesville, which was a local town near the base. Then we would be transported back and forth to Tigerland via a military bus. Leesville was not much of a town, and it was nicknamed Disease Ville by the troops for obvious reasons.

It is interesting to note that the USS Pueblo (AGER-2), officially called a naval intelligence ship, is the only USA ship still being held captive at this time. It is held by the North Koreans in the Taedong River in Pyongyang, North Korea. They use it as a floating museum.

Getting Extra Sleep

After a week or so, I figured out that the DIs did not take role call until after the company went on a several-mile run before breakfast each morning. So I would line up with everyone else, and then when the platoon moved out for the morning run, I would bug out and crawl under the barracks to get some extra sleep. When the company returned, I would simply crawl out from under the barracks and join the formation for roll call. This worked fine for a week or so, and I was enjoying my extra sleep and avoiding the run, which I hated anyway. One morning while I was sleeping under the barracks, I felt something wasn't right. It was dark, so I couldn't see anything, but as I stirred awake, I felt like something was pressed up against me. Turned out it was a very large snake! Now I don't like snakes anyway, but a large snake sleeping with me really freaked me out. I knew he would bite me if I tried to move or push him away. I slowly inched away from the snake, which was quite happy using my body heat to stay warm. Thankfully, he stayed where he was while I moved away. Then I quickly crawled out from under the barracks. I did not see what kind of snake it was, nor did I try to find out. I just wanted to get as far away from the snake as possible. After that, I decided that running wasn't so bad after all.

From Private to Captain

February 1968

Tigerland was a tough place. You need to understand that a good many of the men were drafted and not very happy to be in the army. Others were given a choice by judges to go in the army or go to jail. Everyone in Tigerland knew where we were going, and we were not happy about being a grunt in Vietnam. There were also gangs of soldiers who roamed Tigerland at night and would attack and rob smaller groups or individuals who happened to be walking around by themselves. There were blanket parties for soldiers who harmed the platoon or got on the bad side of some of the soldiers. Then there were GI brush parties. In the case of our platoon, we had two American Indians who barely spoke English and never took a shower. They were filthy dirty and no one wanted to be near them. Both were referred to as Chief. After a while, everyone was tired of having them hold up the platoon and being filthy dirty. The DIs used peer pressure to keep the platoon in line. For example, if someone forgot to wear their hat or gloves, then everyone had to take them off and be cold or wet all day. The DIs stressed, "Everyone must be the same all the time!" One night everyone in the platoon got together and dragged the two Chiefs into the showers and scrubbed them down with stiff hard-bristled cleaning brushes. It was very painful, and the Indians got the message and occasionally took a shower. Anyway, they were more responsive to not screwing up.

One of the guys we hung around with for mutual protection in our platoon was a graduate medical doctor (MD) who had been drafted. He refused to accept a commission as captain and work for the army as a doctor. He wanted to only serve two years, not the four- or

Subject	Hours
Administrative processing	10
Commander's time	27
Character guidance	2
Command information	4
Physical training	24
Drill and ceremonies	12
Inspections	14
Land navigation	18
First aid	4
Graduation	1
Bayonet	2
Field fortifications	3
M1911A1 pistol	8
M79 grenade launcher	4
3.5-inch rocket launcher	6
.50-caliber machine gun	8
Land mine warfare	8
Survival, evasion & escape	9
Individual combat actions	15
Introduction to armored personnel carrier	1
Technique of fire & tactics, rifle squad	56
Proficiency test	4
Weapons demonstration	2
Communications	10
M16A1 automatic rifle	28
M60 machine gun	40
Patrolling	32

AIT Training at Tigerland, Fort Polk

six-year commitment by accepting a commission. So the doctor did everything that we did. He was singled out by the DIs for special treatment whether he deserved it or not. I am sure they were directed by the army to lean on him so he would give up and accept a commission. After going through about five or six weeks of AIT training and harassment, he had had enough. He told us he was giving up and going to accept a commission. We all liked him and were sorry to see him go, but I am sure every one of us would have done the same. We thought we would never see him again. Well, we were wrong. About a week before we were to graduate from AIT, he returned to our company area and stopped by to see us after exercises. He "locked the heals" (made them stand at attention) of the DIs and NCO's on his way to our amusement. It was great to see him in a captain's uniform. Unfortunately, I never saw him again after we left Tigerland.

Fight with the Acting Corporal

February 1968

During AIT and basic training, the training instructors would appoint one or two of the trainees as acting corporals. I assume the purpose of this exercise was to identify those with leadership to determine if they should go to the NCO school or "shake and bake" school as we called it. However, most of the trainees selected wound up going to AIT and Vietnam along with me, so I am not sure of the purpose. As I mentioned earlier, I was selected to take a group of recruits to AIT from basic, and I was for sure not a model soldier. Anyway, they often selected men on a rotating basis, as was the case in Tigerland.

The DIs appointed one of the college boys (college graduates) who was older than most of us and was also an athlete in college to be our platoon corporal along with another trainee. The platoon corporal had corporal stripes, which you wore on your right arm over your fatigues. Most of the guys appointed took the job in stride and didn't pay much attention to the job, other than doing what they were required to do in marching and formations. But this college Joe let the temporary stripes go to his head. After a while, he started pushing other trainees around like he was a DI. On a couple of occasions, he pulled me out of formation and made me do push-ups in front of the DIs, who of course would back him up. Otherwise, no one would have paid any attention to him. After one such incident, I went up to him when we got back to the barracks and told him, "You pull that shit again with me and I'm going to kick you in the balls!" He stood over me at about six feet two inches and perhaps 200–210 pounds. I was five feet eleven and 185, but in the best shape of my life. He replied, "We'll see about that," and then walked away.

A couple of days later we were getting ready for formation, and I was picking up my gear off my bunk. We went everywhere with rifles, packs, and helmets. As we lived on the second story of the billets, we all had to go downstairs to exit onto the company formation area. I was walking toward the stairway, and the college boy corporal started pushing some of the recruits saying, "Move it, move it, let's go, move it." One of the guys he pushed bumped into me when I was at the top of the stairs. I turned around and said to the college boy corporal, "Hey, you asshole, you're gonna push someone down the stairs." With that, he pushed aside the soldiers in between us and lunged at me with his hands outstretched to push me. When I saw that, I dropped my rifle off my shoulder, grabbed his wrist with my left hand, and yanked him forward as my helmet fell off my head. The move caught him unexpectedly, and he was pulled off balance with his rifle over his shoulder and pack on his back. I was at the top of the stairs and was not going to give him the chance to take a swing at me, so I punched him in the face with a right hook, which knocked off his helmet, and he fell down the stairs. The stairs in the barracks were wooden and very steep. As he was falling, his gun was still slung over his shoulder, and it hit him in the head. I jumped on top of him, boots first, as he hit the bottom of the staircase. Then I started kicking him in the head and torso just to be sure he would not get up. I was mad as hell and going to kill the son of a bitch. I was taking my built-up aggression out on him. After a couple of kicks, some of my friends pulled me off, saying, "The DI is here!" They pulled me back and were holding my arms just at the DI entered our barracks. He bellowed to the entire barracks as he entered, "What the fuck is going on here?" Then he saw his acting corporal crumpled up at the bottom of the stairs, full of blood, and several guys holding me. He yelled at both of us, "What the hell is going on here, troops?" I was raging mad and didn't say anything, nor did anyone else. He looked at his acting corporal and asked, "Are you OK?" The acting corporal was still stunned and had a very bloody nose and cut lip. He nodded his head but said nothing. With that, the DI said to no one in particular of the assembly of soldiers standing at attention, "You men get him up NOW!" Then he said to the acting corporal, "Get cleaned up and report to me!" He looked over at me with a glaring look and said, "Did you do that?" I said, "Yes, Drill Sergeant." He just looked at me and then said, "Get the hell out of here and don't let me catch you doing that shit again, you hear me, soldier?" I replied, "Yes, Sergeant!" Someone handed me my helmet and rifle, and I double-timed it outside along with everyone else. We lined up in formation and went about our training as if nothing had happened. Nothing was ever mentioned to me again of the incident. I have no idea what our DI told his acting corporal, but he came back without his temporary corporal stripes. After that, the college boy never said anything to me again and generally stayed away from me, which was all I wanted in the first place.

An Unpleasant Surprise for a Drill Instructor

February 1968

We spent a great deal of time out in the boondocks of Louisiana. It rained frequently, and we were wet both from the rain and the swamps of Tigerland. This day we had been out all day wearing large, very heavy rubber boots over our GI leather boots. When mud stuck on them, they were so heavy it was a chore just to walk on flat land. Anyway, we crossed creeks, walked up and down hills, and generally spent the day wearing ourselves out. At the end of the exercise, we were exhausted. We all were convinced that the drill instructors were sadists. The last part of the exercise was to charge up a steep hill and attack an enemy-fortified position. At the top of the hill were the DIs and assistant DI sergeants yelling at us to attack. Our platoon DI was especially hated universally by the soldiers in our platoon. He was a tall thin black DI who was not very well educated but was all army. He was full of the army chicken shit and used his position of authority to demean his men and make our lives miserable for no apparent reason. Everyone hoped he would break his neck or fall off a cliff. This day while we were struggling to charge up this muddy, steep hill, he was standing at the top yelling profanities at us, telling us how worthless we were and his normal repertoire of raw insults. I was about halfway up the hill, struggling to make it to the top, when I saw the hated DI sergeant hit the dirt and crawl way from the crest of the hill. I had no clue why he did that, especially since it was very muddy and he didn't like to get dirty. He was above getting dirty; he was the boss, and he let everyone know it. I believe the assistant sergeants even hated him. Anyway, as we found out later, one of the recruits in our platoon had smuggled a live round from the firing range. As this recruit was charging up the hill shooting blanks (bullets with power but no projectile), he slipped in the live round and tried to kill the platoon DI. Apparently, he came very close as the DI sergeant hit the dirt and crawled away quickly. He was a Vietnam vet and knew what live fire going over his head sounded and felt like. Immediately we were ordered, "Cease fire, cease fire, the exercise has been called off. Stay where you are and advance no further!" I had no clue what was going on, but something certainly upset the instructors. It finally dawned on me that someone had fired a live round at our platoon sergeant. I looked around, and several of the exhausted men in our platoon were smiling. They too figured out what was going on and their only regret was that the soldier missed.

At this point it is worth mentioning that live rifle rounds (bullets) were strictly controlled in training. We were never allowed to carry live rounds unless it was on the live firing ranges. An exception was only one time when I carried three live rounds on guard duty in basic training. When we left the firing ranges, we had to yell out to our sergeants and DIs, "No brass, no ammo, Sergeant!" To obtain a live round, you had to take one of the rounds you were given for firing practice and hide it on your person. If you were discovered with live ammo, it would be a court-martial offense where you could go to the brig (jail).

Shortly, we were told to remove the magazines from our rifles and clear our weapons, then sling them over our shoulders and proceed to the top of the hill. At the top of the hill, the platoon sergeant was red-faced mad, stomping around and yelling and cursing at everyone. We were told to line up in formation and to keep our arms slung. After we lined up, we were told that we would have a rifle inspection and to order arms. Here you kept the rifle in two hands diagonally held across your chest. Then the DI grabbed every soldier's rifle and sniffed the barrel, looking intently into the eyes of each troop. Then he asked, "Did you shoot a live round at me?" Everyone answered, "No, Drill Instructor." It seemed to me that it would be impossible to determine who shot the live round at the drill instructor since everyone had fired blanks through their rifles. Then we received a dressing down, which ended with the platoon drill instructor saying, "All of you are going to pay for this until someone comes forward with a name!" Then we were marched back to our barracks.

Later that night each of us was taken to the company office and questioned by an officer who was conducting an investigation. You went into the company office, and the door was shut behind you so that you were alone with the officer. I stood at attention and told the officer my name, rank, and serial number. Then the officer, a captain as I recall, asked, "Did you shoot a live round at Drill Instructor So-and-So?" I replied, "No, sir!" Then he asked, "Do you know who shot the live round?" Again I replied, "No, sir!" He asked me a few other questions, which I answered. Then he asked what I thought of the drill instructor. I replied, "Not much, sir!" "Why?" he asked. I said, "Because he is a real son of a bitch, sir." He did not act surprised, so obviously I was not the only person who felt that way. He asked a few more questions, and then asked, "What would you think if he was killed?" The question surprised me, and I thought for a moment, and then figured, what the heck, I would tell him the truth, so I replied, "That wouldn't break my heart, sir!" He looked up a bit surprised and then said, "That's all, Private!" So I saluted, did an about-face, and left the office.

Afterward, several of the guys I hung around with compared questions and responses. Most of the questions were about the same as were many answers. The funniest response to a question was from a Southern boy who spoke slowly with a thick accent. He was asked by the captain, "Did you shoot at the drill instructor?" He said, "Yes, sir!" With that, the captain looked up, excited, and said, "So you shot the live round at Drill Instructor So-and-So?" He replied, "No, sir, not a live round, but I aimed my rifle at him sure enough!" So the captain then asked, "Well, how do you know you didn't have a live round in the chamber?" The Southern recruit answered, "Because, sir, if I did, I wouldn't have missed!" We all had a great laugh at that response. We never did find out who shot at the DI, but I had a few candidates in mind. All three had been given the choice of going to jail or going into the army by a judge. All three were from NYC. So my guess is one of them did it. Anyway, too bad he missed. Nothing ever came of the investigation, and the only result was that the drill instructor backed off our platoon a bit. I guess he got the message.

Staying Awake All Night to Guard our Position

February 1968

One of the exercises we had during training was to spend a couple of days and nights outdoors in bunkers. We trained all day in the rain and mud and then had to spend the nights in bunkers with nothing more than our field jackets for warmth. The exercise was to familiarize you with what standing guard would be like in Vietnam in the field. Of course, it was not really close to what we did in Vietnam, but I guess it was a good try at simulation. The idea was that during the night the DIs and sergeants would try to sneak up on our perimeter. We were to fire at them with blanks if we identified anyone outside the wire. Inside our perimeter the sergeants prowled around trying to catch someone on guard asleep. We were to receive some sort of punishment if anyone in our bunker was caught sleeping. We had three men to a bunker, so you shared the guard duties one hour out of three. We were all very tried from doing field exercises for two days and nights. We had an M-60 machine gun in our bunker along with two M-16 rifles. During the night, someone fell asleep during guard duty in our bunker. Of course, in Vietnam this could get your throat slit or get everyone in the company killed. It was raining hard, and you could not see very well at all. When one of us woke up, we found that our machine gun and one of the M-16s had been taken. We knew right away that we had been had by the sergeants, and we were going to be in trouble for losing our machine gun. The DIs and assistant DIs stayed in the field with us, but they had a heated, lighted tent with cots. The tent they were in had a large central area and a smaller area to enter and exit, which sheltered them from the outside. For their protection from recruits who might want to get even, they had guards around the tent all night long. We went over to the bunker next to us and found that they too had their machine gun stolen. Then in checking with several others in our platoon, they too had weapons stolen. In all, there were perhaps ten to fifteen weapons and machine guns taken during the night. So we hatched a plan. We would sneak into the sergeants' tent and steal them back. But first we had to get rid of the guards. Someone came up with the plan to just relieve them. What a simple but great idea. On guard duty, you stayed at your post until you were relieved by the next person in the schedule. Guard changeovers were normally done after an hour. The next problem was that too few of us still had weapons, and it would be suspicious to relieve a guard without a weapon. We solved this problem with a finger. As it was raining hard and we all had on ponchos, all we had to do was hold our fingers up inside the poncho to make it look like it was the barrel of a weapon sticking up. The guards had their own tent separate from the DIs' tent, where they went to bed down when they were off duty. These soldiers were not from our unit but likely holdovers from a prior training group. So four of us went near the end of a shift up to each of the guards and said we were relieving them. As they were all too eager to get out of the rain and into a warm tent, no one put up any fuss. So after all of the guards left, we snuck into the outer tent, where all of our weapons had been placed. We could hear the DIs and sergeants laughing about how they stole this gun and that one and how they couldn't wait to see the faces of the men in the morning when they woke up to find their weapons gone! So we quickly gathered up the weapons and handed them to the men who lost them, queuing up outside the DIs' tent. After this, we quietly went back to our bunkers. I assume other guards came and found that there was no one guarding the tent, but they simply assumed someone had relieved the others and went about doing their hour of guard duty.

No one dared fall asleep on guard duty after that. But it was unnecessary since the sergeants had done their worst and went to bed thinking how they had gotten us and looking forward to the morning. Next morning we were called out to formation. Everyone had their weapons. The DIs and sergeants didn't say a word to anyone and pretended that nothing had happened. I guess they had the surprise of their lives when they awoke to find that all the rifles and machine guns they had stolen had disappeared. Since they had been had, they said nothing at all. So we all had a good laugh at the DIs that day.

Lock Down and Investigation

February 1968

Training at Tigerland was very intense, and the DIs tried to make it as stressful as possible. They also did all they could to instill in us full aggression by harassing us and pitting one against the other. Fights in Tigerland were commonplace, and it was one tough place. We even had roving gangs (mostly of black soldiers) at night that would go around in groups of ten to twenty and assault and rob anyone they could catch. On more than one occasion I was chased by them coming back from the Enlisted Man's Club or Post Exchange (PX for short) on the weekend. We almost never saw any MPs, and at night the gangs waited in the dark areas of the fort, which was most of the fort, and even near the barracks.

One day we had just fallen out for our morning formation and run. We would fall out with full gear for roll call and then go on a three- to five-mile quick-step run in formation before breakfast. If we were spending the day in the field or the live-fire range, we would quick-step run all the way, which was about five miles. Then we would eat in the field with hot chow served by the cooks using oblong camouflaged insulated cans to store and serve the food. Too often we had shit on a shingle, or chipped beef which to me looked like puke and tasted about the same. This day we heard a commotion coming from the training company next to ours. All of a sudden our DIs and assistant DIs took off and left us standing at attention. Only one sergeant stayed behind, keeping us at attention. We heard yelling and shouting, and from where we stood, it looked like the entire company next door had gone wild and was rioting. After a couple of minutes, the sergeant who had been watching the commotion next to us told us, "You are to fall out and go back in the barracks and stay there until you are ordered out! Get moving now!" We did as we were told and quickly began moving back to the barracks. Our formation was in the rear of the barracks in an open area surrounded by several barracks. The company which was rioting was just off to our left in an adjacent open area between their barracks. All of the barracks faced outward from the formation area so that to get to our barracks we had to go around the side to enter in the front. As we moved around front, the riot next door spilled over into our area. None of us wanted to get involved, and we tried to get into our barracks, but fighting was happening all around us. To me it looked like everyone was going crazy, throwing punches, kicking, and ripping at each other and the DIs and sergeants. Someone yelled they had entrenching tools, just as the four of us who hung around together pushed through our door. I never did see anyone swinging entrenching tools, but several others did. We rushed up to our top floor while fighting was going on right outside our door. Some of our platoon was drawn into the fight as they tried to get back into our barracks.

We quickly got our entrenching tools, which were stored with our gear in the bunks. It was the one part of our gear that we often did not have to carry unless we were out in the field. We unsheathed the entrenching tools and extended them just in case. Then we stayed where we were on the top floor and guarded the stairs so only our platoon could come up. Several of our guys came up the stairs with bloody noses and cut lips, but most made it back without getting hurt too badly. We still had no idea what was going on and why so many men were fighting. Soon we heard the MPs coming in Jeeps, and we watched as they waded into the fray with batons swinging. They were trying to drag the DIs and NCOs out of the crowd. Others were pushing the rioting men backward. There were not enough MPs to handle the crowd of angry men, and soon they took off with the DIs and sergeants they retrieved from the rioters. After that, the fighting began to die down just as quickly as it had started. Groups of soldiers were yelling at each other, but most began to drift away. There were a lot of soldiers down on the ground, and many were really bloody. Some of their buddies were helping them up, and others were carrying some of the more badly injured away. After about fifteen minutes, the crowd had thinned, and the MPs returned with reinforcements. They began manhandling the soldiers who remained back toward barracks and yelling at them to get inside. A couple of MPs came into the bottom level of our barracks and said, "You are all to stay where you are. No one is to move outside. You are under lockdown until further notice!"

We all stayed inside since most of us had not been involved in the riot. The few of our platoon who had been injured trying to get into our barracks were being cleaned up and helped by their buddies. Most of the guys on our floor had made it back to the barracks without incident. There were only a couple of bloody noses and swollen eyes and lips. Shortly thereafter, we heard the post ambulances come, and they took away several of the injured. A couple of men from our barracks on the first floor were taken to the hospital. One trainee in our platoon never came back as we were told he had a broken arm. We still did not know what had started the riot. Afterward there were MPs stationed outside all the barracks, and no one was allowed to enter or leave. Even our DIs and sergeants were not allowed to enter. As usual, no one told us anything.

After a few hours, several MPs entered our barracks with an officer. We were told that there was going to be an investigation. Everyone was told to stay inside by his bunk until called. Then the MPs started calling groups of five men at a time and escorting them to the company administrative office. When it was my turn, five of us who bunked together were called to follow the two MPs. All of them were armed with .45 pistols and batons. Some outside had M-16 rifles. They all looked stern and like they meant business. One of the MPs escorting us had a black eye from the skirmishes. We marched over to the CO's office as we were told. Inside we were questioned one by one by a captain with two MPs standing in the room. I was asked what happened and how the rioting started. I told the captain I had no idea and explained that I was just standing in formation like everyone else when it began. He asked what I did after the rioting started, and I told him we went back to the barracks like we were told. He wrote down the names of the men I returned to the barracks with, and then I was dismissed. As we played no part in the riot, our platoon was questioned and returned to our barracks.

The questioning went on all day, and we lay around the barracks and did nothing. I went to sleep. They did not even let us out of our barracks for lunch, and I was getting hungry. Late afternoon, our DI and sergeants came into the barracks and told us to fall out without our gear. We fell out, and we were marched to the mess hall to get something to eat. We were given no explanations, but the mess hall was not as crowed as usual. We saw other platoons marching around but without any gear, which was unusual. Later we returned to our barracks and were told that the rest of the day would be spent on cleaning our weapons and gear for an inspection at 6 p.m. We had the inspection and training continued the next day as usual. We were told nothing at all about what happened by our DIs. They simply continued as if nothing had happened.

The scuttlebutt over the next few days finally gave us some insight into what had caused the riot. Apparently, there was a lot of bad blood between the officers and NCOs and the recruits of the company next to us. That was not surprising as we too hated our NCOs along with one of the young lieutenants who also harassed us with chicken-shit push-ups. At formation time the company lieutenant called out one of the recruits for some minor infraction. He was told to do twenty-five or fifty push-ups. The way you did push-ups was to say, "One Drill Sergeant, two Drill Sergeant, three, Drill Sergeant," and so on. If an officer told you to give him fifty, you would say, "One sir, two sir, three sir," and so on. Apparently, this soldier had been pushed to the breaking point. So when he went to do push-ups for the lieutenant he said, "One, fuck you sir, two fuck you, sir, three fuck you, sir," and continued shouting as loud as he could. With that, the entire company began to laugh, and the DIs and sergeants tried to get control and started yelling. The soldier on the ground continued saying "fuck you" to the officer, and he too was yelling for the troop to shut up! Finally, the platoon DI grabbed the man and pulled him to his feet. When he did, the man took a swing at the DI and hit him in the face. With that, the riot started, and everyone started going crazy and swinging at the DIs and themselves. It was a highly charged environment, and everyone took advantage of the situation to settle old scores not only with the DIs and NCOs but with fellow recruits as well. Then things got out of hand, and some of the recruits got knives and entrenching tools and even empty rifles and were using them as weapons against each other. We only caught the overflow of the riot, which spilled over into our barracks.

After the investigation, the company who rioted was broken up into other companies, and some of the men went to the brig. There were also a lot of casualties who went to the hospital and never returned to the training. The DIs and NCOs were also reassigned. Our training went on as usual, less one of the men who had been hospitalized.

Escape and Evasion

February 1968

One of the exercises we went through in Tigerland was escape and evasion. We were told that we would be taken out to a remote area of the fort, dropped off, have to prepare our own food and use a compass to navigate through the swamps to get back to camp. We were also told that there would be enemy soldiers trying to capture us. If we were captured, we would be tortured just like if we were in Vietnam. The DIs emphasized, "You don't want to get captured." It could take us several days to get back to camp barracks.

Late that afternoon we were shipped out to a remote area of Tigerland in cattle cars. These were army cabs with trailers which had no sides or top. They held a whole platoon or about forty soldiers. We sat on benches located on each side of the trailers open to the weather. If it rained, we were told, "It doesn't rain *in* the army, it rains *on* the army!" We were given a briefing on where we were generally located and how we would need to get back to the company area using our compasses. Then we were given instructions on how to break a chicken's neck, pluck its feathers, clean it with our bayonets, and cook it in our steel pots (helmets). All the guys I hung around with were from the NYC area, so we had never killed or cleaned a chicken. Most of us thought chickens came wrapped from the frozen food counter. We watched as some sergeant from the Deep South took a chicken by his neck, held it against his body with his left arm, and quickly snapped its neck! Then he showed us it was dead, but it was still kicking its feet. This was not very appetizing to me, although by this time we were starving, since we hadn't eaten all day after breakfast, which of course was the point of the exercise. Then groups of five of us were given live chickens and told to kill, clean and eat them. I feel sorry for the poor chicken they gave us. None of us had a clue as to how the sergeant efficiently killed the chicken, although several of us tried, but it didn't work. We finally wound up bludgeoning the chicken to death with the handles of our bayonets. Then we tried to gut it with dull bayonets, which are made for stabbing, not cutting. Unlike in the movies, bayonets are not sharpened, as they are designed only for stabbing, not cutting. A knife is made for cutting, but of course, the army did not provide us with knives. Then we tried to pull off the chicken's feathers. Good luck with that. The feathers didn't want to come out, and when they did, the carcass of the chicken looked like it had a bad hair transplant. Then we gathered sticks and did our best to light a fire. The wood was wet, and it didn't want to cooperate with us. Finally, we got a small fire going, or rather a smoking bunch of wood. We couldn't get the water to boil no matter what we did. I can still visualize the five of us hunched over the steel pot with smoke all over the place and the chicken's head hanging over the side of the pot. After a while we gave up on trying to cook the chicken. By this time the DIs were telling us we had to get ready to run for it. So we retrieved the steel pot, and the volunteer who used his helmet put it back on his head. For those who are wondering, a helmet at that time was made up of two parts. A steel pot (where we cooked or tried to cook the chicken) and a fiberglass helmet liner, which fit on your head underneath the steel pot and contained the webbing which fitted the helmet to your head.

We were then marched off to a firebreak approximately fifteen yards wide with telephone poles running down the middle. This cleared area was between where we were bivouacked with the chicken incident and the woods or, rather, swamps. We were told to head into the woods/swamps and then navigate via our compasses. We were told to go in groups of two men each, which would give us the best chance of not getting caught by the enemy, who were all over the woods and swamps waiting to catch us. The five of us who hung around together and tried to cook the chicken had decided we would meet together as soon as we got into the woods so we could travel together with more men. This way we had a better chance of fighting off any enemy, as we had no intention of being captured. As soon as we formed in groups of two and were waiting to be told what to do next, a starlight flare was fired, and the enemy came out from behind bushes on the edge of the woods and tried to capture anyone they could get their hands on. Seeing the flare, my partner and I sensed that this was a setup and jumped for the woods. We took off, but waited just off the firebreak for the rest of the guys to meet up with us. Two of the other guys caught up with us as they were just to our right when the flare went off.

We heard the other guys coming toward us, but to our surprise it was four of the enemy! They grabbed one of the guys from NY, who was a tough ironworker (he later lost both legs in Vietnam to a Bouncing Betty mine). The enemy said, "You're captured," and he punched him in the face and said, "Like hell." Then the other enemy tried to grab us, and we punched and kicked anyone who tried and told them to get the fuck away from us! They didn't want to get in a fight, so they gave up and went looking for easier pickings. Then we walked into the woods and waited for the rest of the guys. The flare was still lighting up the area, and we saw one of our mates come running up to us. He told us that they were attacked by the enemy and his partner was captured, but he wrenched himself free and escaped. We had heard about getting captured and decided that we would try to see if we could break him out of the enemy stockade. We waited until the flares ran out and all was quiet. We did not see any more enemy soldiers lurking near the firebreak, so we figured they were busy with the men they captured. We also thought that, before they got organized and were trying to handle the men they captured, we could use this confusion to get our man out of the stockade. The stockade contained several buildings with a fence with barbed wire at the top. As we approached the stockade, the enemy soldiers were putting the recruits they captured into the pens and moving around others. Some of the men's hands were tied. So we moved up near the fence where we could see what was going on and see if we could find our friend. The enemy guards were looking inward to guard the prisoners, not outward, because they didn't expect any recruits to try to break in. They thought we would all be long gone. We had no problem approaching the wire, and soon enough we saw our missing partner with his hands tied behind his back, standing in an open area of the stockade. The stockade was not very well constructed, so we simply grabbed the bottom of the fence, pulled it up in a remote area, and motioned for our friend to come over. Then we pulled him through the fence with his hands still tied and took off! No one saw us, nor did they come looking for us. If they did, we were prepared to fight it out with them as we were not getting captured. We untied our missing soldier's hands and were on our way.

As we moved through the woods and swamps, we heard many others moving along in front of us. We figured that it was unlikely that more enemy would be hiding in the woods and swamps, so we pushed ahead making as much noise as we pleased. Everyone else hid from us, thinking we were the enemy trying to capture them, which was fine with us. The woods and swamps in Tigerland were a mix of steams, wetlands, thick woods, and thickets. It was pitch-dark, so you couldn't see much of anything. We tried to navigate using our compass, which was difficult as we didn't have any flashlights and the woods were so thick you could not make out landmarks to aim for as we had been taught. The other problem was that when we came to a stream, we could not jump across; we thought we could walk through them. Unfortunately, they were perhaps only five feet wide but also almost three to four feet deep. So we got quite wet, and we were all cold. After we were walking for perhaps an hour, we were thinking we just wanted to get out of the woods and swamps, and that we didn't really want to spend the night cold, wet, and hungry. It was very quiet in the woods, and I thought I had heard what sounded like a truck shifting gears off to our left. We were told that we were on a remote area of the fort where there was only woods, but I was sure I heard a vehicle of some type far in the distance. We talked about it for a minute and decided we would head off in the direction of the vehicle and see if we could find a road. After we trudged through the swamp for another twenty minutes in the direction of the possible vehicle, we heard another vehicle. This time everyone heard it, so we continued moving in that direction. It took us another hour or so to make it to the road, much longer than we thought it would take, since sound travels very far at night. The road was paved and elevated with telephone poles running alongside, so we knew it would eventually led us to civilization. It was getting late at night by this time, and there was no traffic. The road appeared to be heading in the direction we were told to go, so we simply followed it. We were still cold and hungry, but at least walking was easy, and we were out of the swamps with fewer insects and no snakes.

We walked down the road for an hour or so when we saw the headlights of a vehicle approaching. So we stood off to the side of the road and put our thumbs out for a ride. We could see the lights were too high for a car, so we figured it was a truck. As it got near, we recognized it as a 2 ½-ton army truck. The driver slowed as we appeared in his headlights and came to a stop next to us. We were saved from a long, cold walk and a miserable night in the woods. The driver called out, "Who are you guys?" We said, "We are lost and are trying to get back to Fort Polk." He looked at the state of our clothes and said, "Hop on, I'm going that way." So we jumped on back of the truck, and he took off. It turned out that we were not in as a remote of an area of the fort as we thought because we arrived at Tigerland after about a half an hour. The driver stopped by the Post Exchange in Tigerland and said, "You guys will have to get off the truck now!" We thanked him for the ride and jumped off the truck. We were in good shape now as all we had to do was to get back to our barracks and sneak in. Since it was well into the early morning hours, there was no place to get something to eat, so we walked back to our barracks. There was no one in the barracks, and all the lights were off. So we went to the showers, cleaned up, and jumped into bed. In the morning, we were still alone in the barracks, as apparently no one else had made it back to the main part of the fort. They all had a miserable night trying to evade the enemy and spending the night in the swamps. So we got dressed in clean fatigues and went off to one of the other chow halls, where we hoped no one would pay us much attention. We saw a company of men lining up in one of the chow halls, so we simply joined the back of the line. As we looked like every other recruit, we went through the chow line without a problem and sat down for a hot meal. We were not allowed to go back for more food, so we left after the first serving. We walked around until we found another mess hall and waited for some more recruits to form a line. Then we joined them and got another serving of food. After that we walked around the fort like we owned the place. We did not want to go back to our barracks in case one of the DIs was waiting for us. Around midday, we went to chow again before joining another group of soldiers in another mess hall. Then we wandered around a bit and figured that some of the men would be getting back by now. When we returned to our barracks, a handful of guys were just getting back all muddy and wet. So we went back into our bunks and went for a nap. All that day, stragglers of groups of men came back to the barracks and cleaned up and went down the mess hall to get something to eat. So we joined them for another meal. We didn't tell anyone how we had hitched a ride back to the camp; we just pretended like we had gone through the swamps like everyone else.

Later that afternoon one of the assistant DIs came into our barracks and began taking the names of the men who had made it back. By now about half the platoon was accounted for, and more stragglers were coming in all the time. We gave the sergeant our names and then continued to relax in our bunks. The rest of our platoon eventually straggled in after dinner. Most of our platoon looked like they had been through hell and back. It was a good exercise, but nothing like what we would experience in combat, where you were out for months and always tired and hungry. Not to mention real enemy trying to kill you.

Live-Fire Training

February 1968

We had numerous weapons training courses with live-fire exercises. We were trained on the M-16, M-60 machine gun, 1911 .45 pistol, M-79 grenade launcher, .50-caliber machine gun, hand grenades, and the LAW antitank weapon. I shot expert (highest score) on most weapons and marksman on the M-60 machine gun (second-highest score). I enjoyed firing all these weapons, especially the machine guns and the LAW. We only got one shot with the LAW as it was very expensive to fire. We were told that each .50-caliber bullet costs the equivalent of a beer. I would later shoot a lot of beers-worth of ammunition with the .50-caliber (called MA Duce) in Vietnam.

The M-16 was much lighter than the M-14 rifle that we trained on in basic training, and it had much smaller bullets. It was also not as accurate as an M-14, but I liked shooting it much better and had no trouble shooting expert. We were also trained to react to pop-up targets and to shoot without aiming instinctively. This was one of the more useful training methods which came in very handy in Vietnam. Weapons training and maintenance was one of the courses I took very seriously.

Obstacle Course

February 1968

In addition to running and calisthenics, we spent time running the obstacle course. This involved climbing over and under obstacles, using ropes to swing over water, using our hands to maneuver over monkey bars, climbing up a very high (thirty feet or so) tower and back down the other side, crawling under barbed wire, rappelling down walls, and, my favorite, crossing a pond on a large rope, using your hands to pull you along while crossing your feet to hold on. I liked this because a couple of the men fell into the pond where they were plucked out by soldiers in a boat. In the Tigerland days, all these exercises were done with boots (which were very slippery on the bottom as they were smooth leather) and in some cases backpacks, web gear, helmets, and sometimes rifles, which made things much more difficult. We did not wear anything other than combat boots in training. I never had much of a problem with any of these challenges. The only one I really did not like was climbing up the thirty-foot tower, which had thick boards mounted on telephone poles spaced four feet or so apart. After a company of men went over this obstacle, the boards got muddy and wet and were very slippery. When I got to the top, I didn't like how high I was and always got nervous climbing over the top and then down the other side. Of course, I also hated the running, especially with my rifle where it hit you in the helmet on each step when slung over your shoulder. To pass, you had to run the course in under 8 minutes with your full combat clothing, gear, pack and rifle. I made sure I made it just in time because if not you had to go thru the exercise again and again until you passed.

Orders for Vietnam

March 6, 1968

Just before we graduated from AIT at Tigerland, we were given our orders to Vietnam. My orders were dated March 6, 1968, and stated, "*FNE report to US Army personnel Center, Oakland Army Terminal, BLDG 640, Oakland, California not later than 1200 hours on 10 APR 68.*" We all knew we were headed for Vietnam during our training, but when we received the orders it really hit home. Deep down we were all hoping that somehow something would change and we would be sent someplace else, anywhere else but Vietnam, especially since we had been trained and classified as infantry—the worst job in the army. My MOS was an 11 Bravo, or light weapons infantryman. Basically, cannon fodder or a grunt (named for the sound you make when lifting a seventy-pound pack on your back).

Graduation from AIT

March 15, 1968

I graduated from AIT on March 15, 1968. After graduation, we were given our first leave since being drafted into the army. I left the base with a group of other soldiers and went to the airport to fly back to my parents' home in New Jersey. I had leave until I had to report to Oakland Army Base at noon on April 10, 1968.

While at home, I spent some crazy days drinking and running around after women. Strangely enough, in those days, we were not allowed to drink (in New Jersey, but New York was still eighteen years of age) until we were twenty-one years old, nor were we allowed to vote. We were considered too young to vote or drink, but not to be killed for our country. After we returned home, many of the vets helped to change the voting laws to allow people under twenty-one to vote, but then they did away with the draft. So the inverse of what happened to us—we had none of the privileges of being a citizen but had the responsibilities. Today the kids seem to have none of the responsibilities but all the privileges. That aside, my friends and I carried false IDs, which were in the form of draft cards. We simply photographed them and changed our birthdates. In the military, I did the same with my military ID. Unlike today, no one really cared that much about drinking. So about every night we went bar-hopping, looking for girls, when we were not on a date. One evening I was speeding down a highway in the vicinity of Morristown, New Jersey, and was pulled over by a policeman. He gave me a ticket even after I told him I was on my way to Vietnam, so I simply ripped it up in front of him and told him I didn't give a shit! Many months later while I was sitting in a rice paddy, I received a notice from the Morristown sheriff's department saying that there was a warrant out for my arrest. So I wrote back across the face of the notice, "*Come get me . . . please!*" Then I sent it off without a stamp (we did not have stamps of course, so we simply wrote "Free" in the area where a stamp was supposed to go) but never heard from them again. I guess they had a laugh in the sheriff's department when they received my response from Vietnam.

AWOL from Oakland Army Base

April 8–9, 1968

When I arrived at Oakland Army Base on my way to Vietnam, I was shuffled into a bus along with other soldiers and driven to a very large aircraft or a dirigible hangar in a fenced-off area of the base surrounded by MPs. There must have been thousands of soldiers in this hangar with bunks two rows high as far as the eye could see. Everyone in the hangar was on their way to Vietnam. We simply had to wait in the hangar until our names were called, and then we would be escorted by MPs to a waiting aircraft and flown to Vietnam. Obviously, they were not taking any chances with soldiers going AWOL as we were guarded or behind barbed wire fences everywhere we went.

After arriving and placing my duffel bag on the bunk, I got to talking to a couple of troops around me. None of us had been in California and we had always heard stories about the wild girls so we decided that we would have a good time before we left for Vietnam. As we were all in the infantry, we had nothing to lose. After all, what were they going to do to us, send us to Vietnam?

The only problem was the ten-foot-tall fence with barbed wire on top, plus the MPs. Climbing the fence was compounded in difficulty because the entire perimeter of the fence was lighted around the hangar. When it turned dark, we snuck out of a side door of the hangar which the MPs had left unguarded. Then we ran to the fence and climbed over, and we were on our way. We started walking to San Francisco, not knowing how far it was or exactly where we were going. Fortunately, a truck stopped and asked if we needed a ride. The driver had been in the military. We hopped into the truck and drove into San Francisco.

We spent the evening in San Francisco, bar hopping until it was very late at night. When we were going from one bar to another, an MP Jeep pulled up to us, and the MPs asked for our passes. Of course, we had none, so they told us to hop in, and they took us to the MP station. After getting our names and ranks, they drove us back to the hangar with all sorts of threats about being AWOL. Anyway, nothing happened to us; they just returned us back to the hangar.

The next day, my name was called, and I was told to get my gear and load up on a bus, which carried us to the airfield to go to Vietnam. We loaded up on a chartered Boeing 707 Jetliner with stewardesses and flew off to Vietnam. Everyone was quiet and most slept during the flight. The aircraft carried approximately 160 soldiers and the civilian crew. Everyone kept to his own thoughts, and there was not much talking at all. After a long journey of perhaps fifteen hours, we landed in Japan, where we were allowed to de-plane the aircraft and go into the lobby while the aircraft refueled. An hour later, we re-boarded and flew on to Vietnam.

CHAPTER II

Vietnam

Arrival in Vietnam and In-Country Training

April 11, 1968

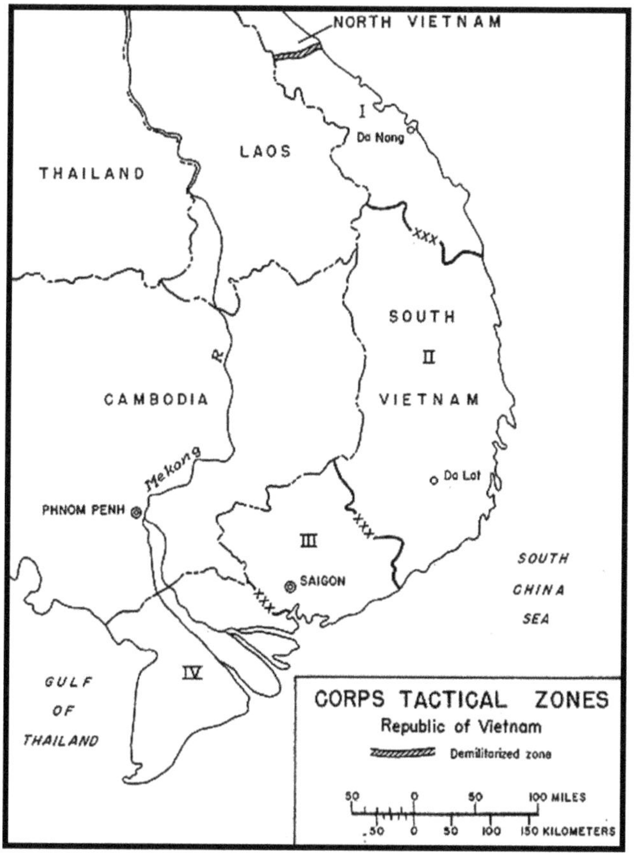

We landed in Ton Son Nhut Air Base just north of Saigon, Vietnam. The trip had taken about nineteen to twenty hours from when we left "the world" in California. When we de-planed the aircraft, the first thing that hit us was the stifling heat, humidity, and the smells. As we were leaving the plane, a line of soldiers was waiting to board the aircraft and fly home. Some of the soldiers called out, "Welcome to Vietnam," "You're in for the shit now," "Welcome to VN, you FNGs [Fucking New Guys]," and other such words of encouragement. Most of the ones talking tough turned out to be "house cats," or REMFs (Rear Echelon Mother Fuckers) as they were called by the men in the field doing the fighting. What I noticed was that a few of the men who looked the most rugged said nothing and just stared ahead. They were much skinnier than the rest, with sunken eyes. These were the infantrymen who were doing the fighting. I wondered if I would wind up looking like them after a year. What I didn't realize then was that these were the lucky ones who survived an entire year.

Ton Son Nhut Air Base was a massive military base with all sorts of aircraft taking off and landing. There were soldiers and civilians all over the place. The first thing you noticed about the Vietnamese was how small and wrinkled they were. The women especially looked very old with black teeth. We found out later that the women, who looked like they were eighty years old, were only half that age. Because of the hard life, poor diet, various parasites and disease, drying sun, which wrinkled their skin, and chewing Betel Nut, which turned their teeth red then after many years black, they all looked much older. Another shock to most of us was that when we went into the latrines or toilets there were women, cleaning the urinals and toilets right next to the men while they were doing their business. No one seemed to pay any attention to them, so we just took a leak with them cleaning next to us. Apparently, they were treated as ghosts in Vietnam. After relieving ourselves, we grabbed our duffel bags (our only baggage), and we loaded onto olive drab military buses similar to civilian buses, except for the wire mesh covering the windows. The driver explained that the wire was there to protect the bus from civilians who might throw hand grenades at the bus as it passed by. This made me feel very vulnerable without a rifle to fight back. As we were driving to the 22nd Replacement Depot (REPO DEPO) in Long Bien, we noticed all the sandbagged revetments and barbed wire surrounding all the military sites, plus the guards, both US and ARVN (Army of the Republic of Vietnam). Then there was the libretti's (small three wheeled motorized vehicles) full of people and the motorcycles with two or even three people hanging on riding en mass all around with no pattern of traffic. The young women wore pants with a long slit type of dress covering over the pants. The Vietnamese police wore white. Later we learned the Americans called them the White Mice. We would have some run-ins with them in the future. All of this was new and strange to us since few of us had ever been outside the USA. I had only been to one country outside of the USA, Canada, which was very similar to the United States.

When we arrived at the Repo Depo, we were ushered into wooden buildings with tin roofs. Halfway up the walls were screens which went to the ceilings for ventilation. Of course, there was no air conditioning in any of the buildings. There our names were compared against a roster, and we filled out a bunch of forms. One of the forms was called a Next of Kin form, in which you indicated whether you wanted your family notified in the event you were slightly wounded. As I didn't trust the army, I checked yes. As a result, my mother would have some hair-raising moments when soldiers came to her door telling her I was wounded and in the hospital. Other times she simply received a telegram indicating I was slightly wounded. We also filled out wills where we noted to whom our $10,000 life

insurance policy would be given upon our deaths. Life was cheap for the army in those days. The army also gave us a copy of a booklet called *A Pocket Guide to Vietnam*, which were we told to read to familiarize ourselves with the Vietnamese people and culture. Additionally, our US dollars were converted to MPC (military pay certificates), which looked like a foreign currency. MPC could only be used to purchase goods from the military PX. US dollars were illegal to have in your possession as they were worth more than the official exchange rate of around 100-plus *Piasters* (South Vietnamese currency) to the US dollar. You could also elect to have your pay deposited directly into a military savings account where you would receive 10% interest on any monies you deposited while in Vietnam. I had the majority of my pay deposited in this account, except around $50 a month left for spending money. This turned out to be an excellent decision on my part as I left Vietnam with $1,100 in savings. Back in those days, this was a lot of money. When I landed in Vietnam as a private first class, or E-3, my base pay was $137.70, plus overseas pay of $16 and combat pay of $65, so I was making $218.70 a month. After the initial processing of paperwork, we were then assigned to one of the military hooches and told to relax for a few hours. I fell immediately to sleep. A few hours later, which felt like minutes to me, an NCO woke us and told us to fall out in formation. We were taken (not marched, which was a positive change) to another building where we received other briefings. One I recall was about taking malaria pills daily and weekly. We were required to take a small white pill daily and a large orange pill weekly. What they didn't tell us was that the large orange pill gave you diarrhea, which was quite a problem if you were humping the bush in the infantry. We also were given a debriefing on venereal disease and warned about all the many forms of VD you could catch in Vietnam. One was supposed to be incurable (the black syphilis), which if you caught, you would never be allowed to go back to the USA. This was a typical army myth told to the soldiers, and most of us believed only half of what we were told by the army anyway. Then we received our new unit assignments in Vietnam. I was to be assigned to the 25th Infantry Division located in Cu Chi, with subsequent assignment to the first brigade 4th/23rd Mechanized Infantry. When I heard "mechanized infantry," I thought

I had hit pay dirt. Better to ride around in armor than to hoof it as a grunt in the jungle. Of course, I knew nothing at all about the mechanized infantry, and I would find out later just how wrong I was!

After receiving our assignments, we were given orders in triplicate to take with us in a manila envelope to our new division. We were told that we had the rest of the afternoon off but to be ready at 6 a.m. outside our hooch to be transported to Cu Chi. That evening, I went over to the Enlisted Man's Club where they served beer. In the club was a mix of house cats and men going through the Repo Depo either in or out of country processing. Of course, the FNGs who just arrived in the country were anxious to talk to the men who had served a year and were going home, especially men who were in the infantry. They were easy to identify because they had the worst-looking uniforms and had a CIB (combat infantryman's badge) stitched on top of their left-hand uniform pockets. After a while a few of us FNGs gathered around a couple of infantry men who were leaving the country. They didn't want to talk much, but after we bought them a few beers, one of them opened up. He was from a leg infantry unit in the 25th Division, but I don't recall which one. Several of the guys were asking him questions about his unit and what it was like in the field and firefights. I listened intently, hoping to gain some knowledge which might help me stay alive. I remember one of his key gems of advice was to always dig in whenever you had the chance, and "don't fuck with booby traps!" I put this advice in the back of my head and followed it to the letter throughout my tour in the infantry. When he asked where I was going, I replied optimistically, "I'm going to the 25th Division, 4/23rd [pronounced "the fourth of the twenty-third"] Mechanized Infantry." I thought for sure as a leg infantryman he would congratulate me on getting into the mechanized infantry. To my surprise he looked worried. Then he said, shaking his head, "That's a real bad unit, they are always in the shit! They call those tracks rolling coffins because they are moving targets for the enemy rockets and mines. They can hear you coming from a mile away and are always ambushing the mechanized units. They send them out whenever someone is in the shit, so they are always getting engaged. The 4th of the 23rd is one of the worst, taking all sorts of casualties!" My heart sank; instead of hitting the jackpot,

I landed in shit! Now I was really concerned. The rest of the night I spend worrying about what I had gotten myself into and what tomorrow would bring.

I fell asleep that night thinking about what would happen next. Fortunately, I was dead tired since we hardly had gotten any sleep from the plane ride and then immediately went into processing. I always manage to sleep well regardless of what is on my mind. In the army I could fall asleep during the ten-minute smoke breaks they gave us during training. I figured I should try to sleep as much as possible through the miserable two years so it would go faster. Next morning at 5am, we were awakened and told to report to the mess hall. We had no showers or running water, so we all had to pile outside in the dark and brush our teeth and shave with a Lister Bag full of water. A Lister Bag is a large military canvas bag which carries water and is hung from a pole such that you can drain water from a valve at the bottom. The water tasted foul and full of chemicals. It was also a brownish color. We relieved ourselves by urinating in piss tubes, which were nothing more than metal shell casings driven into the ground surrounded by gravel and sprinkled with DDT to keep away the flies. For taking a dump, we had a small shed with toilet seats on top of a long bench with fifty-five-gallon drums cut in half to catch the feces. These half drums of feces were later taken out from under the toilet bench and filled with diesel fuel and lit on fire to burn the waste. This burning shit was in large part the dominating smell which hung over the entire Repo Depo. We would find out later in the infantry that the men who received three Purple Hearts were given this "house cat" job, which was coveted by all of the men in the field. Burning shit all day was far better than humping the bush for Charlie and getting shot or killed. At the time, none of us FNGs hoped we would ever get this job. Again how wrong we were!

We were loaded up on the buses and taken to the airstrip where about thirty or so of us were loaded on C-130 or C-47 transport aircraft, sitting on nylon web seats along the sides of the plane, with large cubes of cargo in the center, on rollers. The plane took off and rose very quickly. From the air, the land looked very lush, but we saw a lot of bomb craters in the forest and jungle. We also saw some rows of trees which looked like nurseries, but were in fact rubber plantations. In less than twenty minutes, we landed in Cu Chi, which was apparently very close to the airport. The plane kept its engines running while it dropped its huge back ramp, and we all filed out with our duffel bags. Then it continued down the runway and took off again for some remote air base to the north. We were greeted by a soldier who was driving a deuce and a half (2 ½-ton truck). The deuce and a half was one of the key workhorses of the military transport system. It was open in the back (in cold weather, they had a canvas cover), and we climbed in two at a time using the steps on the underside of the back ramp which opened downward. After we all squeezed in, the driver took off driving to the 25th Division reception and training area for new soldiers.

Cu Chi was a dusty, barren base camp with vehicles moving all around and artillery going off all the time. There was a complete absence of trees of any sort, just a lot of red dirt. It was noisy and dusty and had columns of smoke all over the base camp from the burning shit. It smelled like cordite, burning shit, and diesel fuel all at once. The dust was everywhere and covered everything with a red dusting. We were dropped off by the truck in front of a building which by this time was becoming familiar to us a one-story wooden building with screens halfway up the sides and a tin roof. This was the reception center for new soldiers. We entered the building and gave the clerks our orders. I was among some twenty or so 11B infantrymen. We were sent to the infantry training section of the base camp for five days of in-country training by the division. Here we went through the normal routine of being assigned to barracks and then we were issued new tropical uniforms, jungle boots, web gear, helmets, flak jackets, bayonets, other gear, M-16 rifles, and magazines. We were also issued live ammunition for the first time and told to keep our weapons loaded and with us at all times. The magazine was to be kept in the rifle, but no rounds were to be chambered in base camp, and of course, the safety switch was to be kept on at all times.

We spent the next several days going through what I would term "refresher courses" on infantry tactics and weapons practices with various weapons in live-firing exercises. We fired M-60s, M-79 grenade launchers, and of course, M-16s. During these live-fire exercises, we zeroed in our M-16s to get them ready for combat. We also cleaned them several times and were constantly told to keep the weapon clean and had to learn the serial number of our assigned weapon, a standard procedure in the army. We were also given a comic book type of instruction book on cleaning the M-16 rifle.

We were given instruction on the various booby traps and mines that we would encounter in our area of operations, or AO for short. Then we did some physical sweeps around the base camp to get us acclimated to the heat and terrain. During these sweeps, we did not encounter any enemy or booby traps. It is likely that the sweeps were conducted in known safe areas near the base camp. I got to know a couple of the guys going through training, but only about ten of us were destined for the 4/23rd. After being in the country for seven days and training for five days, I was sent via convoy to Tay Ninh to join the 4/23rd Mechanized Infantry.

I was assigned to a large convoy transporting supplies and some replacements to Tay Nin Base Camp. The convoy had perhaps fifty or so trucks and was escorted by APCs which rode at the front, middle, and rear of the column. Later this would be my job. I rode shotgun in a deuce and a half which had a compressor in the back. The truck was driven by a Korean civilian who was a contractor for the US Military. He and several other Koreans were responsible for maintaining electric generators which powered Tay Ninh Base Camp. He was a bit crazy and, while driving fired a small .38-caliber pistol at a farmer's water buffalo which was in the middle of a rice paddy. Fortunately, he missed. Driving in the convoy down dirt roads caused a lot of dust, and it was hard to see the road. The road was so narrow that only one large military vehicle could pass at one time. The civilians had to move to the side of the road when a military convoy passed. I would find out later that this dirt road was a major highway for Vietnam called Route 1. It ran from Saigon to the village of Go Dau Ha and then onto the Cambodian border. At Go Dau Ha, we continued onto Route 22, to the city of Tay Ninh, where the 25th Division had a base camp for the 1st Brigade and my unit, the 4th of the 23rd. We passed several small villages and temples on the way along with heavily wooded areas and many rice fields. Many of the buildings were damaged, and we viewed several destroyed vehicles along the way. The country smelled like a combination of rotten vegetation, spoiled fish, and shit. The convoy moved fairly rapidly at perhaps twenty-five miles an hour, which was fast considering the poor state of the roads and the civilians crowding the sides of the road. The convoy kept rolling and never stopped until we arrived at the gates to Tay Ninh Base Camp. We saw parts of the city of Tay Ninh, which was larger than any of the other villages we passed.

My first impression of Tay Ninh Base Camp was it was a smaller version of Cu Chi. It was dusty and dirty like Cu Chi, without any trees or vegetation. The roads in the base camp were oil-covered dirt to keep the dust down. But everything picked up the oily dirt as it drove over the roads. There was a front gate with sandbagged emplacement all around and barbed wire everywhere. Before we got to the base, we went through a small shanty town in which the buildings appeared to be made of beer cans or boards and straw for roofs. As we pulled into Tay Ninh, the various vehicles went separate ways, delivering men and goods around the base camp. My Korean driver said goodbye and dropped me off by the airfield.

The airfield was a long runway with steel and earth revetments on one side which housed many helicopters. These were to protect against mortars and artillery. There were bunkers everywhere, and many of the buildings had sandbags halfway up the sides. I gathered with several other men who had been dropped off at the airport. Shortly, trucks and jeeps began to arrive to transport the men back to their units. Trucks would pull up, and the driver would ask if anyone was in unit so-and-so. Then a bunch of guys would pile on. A couple of junior officers were picked up in jeeps. Before long, a driver came by in a truck and asked, "Anyone for Alpha Company 4/23rd?" A group of five or six soldiers who had been in training with me at Cu Chi jumped on the truck. There were two sergeants and the rest PFC's. Very soon most of these men would be killed by a short round (ordnance which lands short of its intended target) without ever firing a round at the enemy.

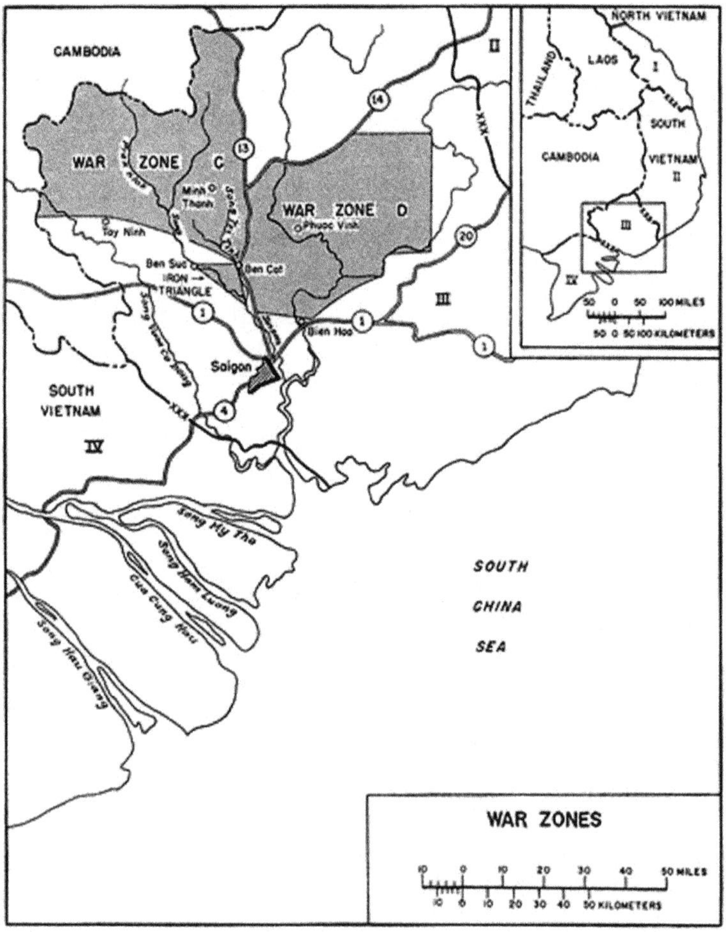

We were dropped off in the company area and reported into the company operations office. There we met the first sergeant, or top, and the company clerk. We gave him our orders, and each of us was assigned to a hooch. Then we were shown the company mess hall where we got something to eat. The cooks were called cookie, a derogatory term used by the infantrymen who did not respect the cooks. They did not fight and did not come to the field to feed us very often. The cooks stayed away from the fighting men when they came in from the field, which was rare. They also stayed away from the wounded and recovering soldiers in the company area. They would get a much worse reputation later on when they made the company sick with rotten chicken!

We were told we would be assigned to a specific squad in the field and we would leave tomorrow to join the company with the supply convoy. The company area was similar to the buildings we had stayed in during orientation training in Cu Chi—slightly elevated off the ground, wooden buildings with wooden floors, tin roofs, and screens halfway up the sides. There were sandbagged bunkers next to each hooch and a mess hall which looked like every other building except that it had a cement floor. There was a shower made up of fifty-five-gallon drums elevated in the air with valves at the bottom for releasing the water. The "shit house" was typical of those we experienced in Cu Chi with fifty-five-gallon drums cut in half to catch the feces ultimately to be burned with diesel oil. The shit burner, or Sierra Bravo (call letters for *S* and *B*), was a large Hispanic soldier who we found out had been wounded three times, thus earning the honor of becoming our company's Sierra Bravo. After that, we looked upon the job of burning shit very differently!

After processing into our company area, we had time to load up with ammo and grenades from the armory and square away our gear for the field. Everything else we carried with us from the States was left in a duffel bag hung on nails above our assigned bunks. The wounded men who were recovering were most helpful in instructing us on what to take to the field and what not to take with us. We learned to use empty .50-caliber ammo cans, which were waterproof, to store our personal effects, such as writing instruments and soap, shaving supplies, combs, and toothpaste. We also learned that we needed to carry two canteens of water and lots of hand grenades. The men also told us what we could expect in the field, and I listened very carefully as this advice could keep me alive.

A Company Clerk Kills Himself

April 20 or 21, 1968

We processed into Alpha Company and were getting our gear together for the trip to the field the next day. Our company was in the field, and we had heard that they were "engaged," meaning that they were in combat or contact with the enemy. The only troops in the base camp area were wounded troops plus a small administrative and support staff comprised of the first sergeant, executive officer (called the XO), company clerk, supply sergeant, cooks, and armory soldier. I arrived in Tay Ninh with perhaps six or so replacement soldiers for Alpha company, two of which were "shake and bake" sergeants (instant NCOs) newly arrived in Vietnam. We were being outfitted with gear and weapons in preparation for us to join our company the next day. I was walking to the armory to draw some additional ammo and gear when I noticed the company clerk walking down the stairs from the HQ hooch. He had a .45-caliber pistol in his right hand and then placed the gun to his head and fired! The blast shot off the top of his head, and he fell down the stairs in a pool of blood. I was shocked and ran over to him along with one or two others who were in the company area. Someone, I believe it was the first sergeant, wrapped a towel around his head where his brains were oozing out and told me to hold the towel while he ran for the jeep. A couple of men helped load the company clerk in the back of the jeep while I sat next to him holding the towel around his head. He was barely alive and growling in a low guttural tone. We raced to the 24th Evacuation Hospital, which was on the base. He was taken into the hospital on a stretcher where he died or was dead on arrival. There was nothing anyone in the world could have done to save his life!

I couldn't believe that with the safest job in our company the clerk shot himself with a .45 pistol. No one knows if he did it on purpose or by mistake. Either way, it was quite a shock as I had just met the man who processed me into the company. Quite a welcome to my new unit! If people were killed so easily in base camp, what could I expect when I was in the field with the enemy? My uniform was full of blood, and I took a shower and changed into my second set of jungle fatigues. Little did I know that my second set of fatigues (we were issued two sets) would be full of blood the next day!

Battalion S-3 Major Gored by Water Buffalo

April 1968

In early April, when A and C Companies of the 4/23rd Battalion were sweeping an area for NVA, the battalion operations officer, or S-3, Major was overseeing the operation. Captain Bridgman was the CO in charge of C Company while Captain Glory (fictitious name) was in charge of A Company. The progress to sweep the area was held up due to heavy vegetation and later by a wounded water buffalo that was hiding in a thicket of bamboo with her calf. The infantry was hesitant to move forward until they could locate and exit around the water buffalo. Both companies had experience with water buffalos and were most cautious to go near these massive animals, especially if one was wounded or with a calf.

The major was annoyed that progress was being held up by a water buffalo. He told then Captain Bridgman that he was going forward to see if he could move things along. Captain Bridgman warned him to be careful. The major proceeded to the front and, with a couple of soldiers, entered the bamboo thicket searching for the water buffalo. Unfortunately for the major, he found the water buffalo, or rather it found him. Apparently, the wounded water buffalo was threatened and was protecting its calf. With the water buffalo at around two thousand pounds with fierce horns, being in a confined area with such an animal is not a good thing. Anyway, the buffalo charged and caught the major behind the knee and threw him up with one of his horns, gashing the major with a wound from his knee to his rear end. The men with him reacted by killing the water buffalo with M-60 rounds. Medics from both C and A Company rushed to his aid, as this was a life-threatening wound. Later he was dusted off in the lieutenant colonel's helicopter and later evacuated out of Vietnam. I personally did not see any of this as I was either in another area or had yet to join A Company.

The way we heard the story later, it was somewhat colored, like many rumors in the army. We heard that the "stupid major" tried to ride the water buffalo and it gorged him and he was never seen again by our unit. As with many second hand accounts, there was some truth and some fiction in the story.

What happened later on was to have a significant impact on me personally. After the evacuation of the major, Lieutenant Colonel Fullerton needed a new battalion operations officer, or S-3. Thus he promoted Captain Bridgeman to become the new battalion operations officer in charge of operations. Some forty-five years later, then retired Lieutenant Colonel Bridgeman told Tom Foster and me this story, clarifying both the incident with the water buffalo and how he became our operations major. Major Bridgeman would later play a critical role in my future in A Company.

CHAPTER III

Combat Infantryman

Basic Organization of the US Army in Vietnam

Before going into the details of my experiences in the field in Vietnam with A, or Alpha, Company, it is worth explaining the basic units within the army and how a mechanized infantry company is organized and staffed.

The basic organization of the army of Vietnam is as follows:

- US ARMY VIETNAM—commanded by a full or four-star general. In my situation it was General Westmoreland, later superseded by General Abrams.
- CORPS—made up of several divisions, typically commanded by a three-star or lieutenant general. Lieutenant General Walter T. Kerwin Jr. was in command of II Corps Field Force some of the time while I was in the field.
- DIVISIONS—commanded by a major general or two-star general. My division, the 25th Infantry Division, full staff or TO (table of organization) in Vietnam was comprised approximately of 17,000 soldiers. More often than not, it was understrength, averaging around 15,000 troops. It was a large division comprised of HQ, medical (one battalion), support (eight battalions, plus four companies, plus four detachments), artillery (five battalions), aviation (one battalion), armor and reconnaissance (two battalions, plus one company), and four or more infantry brigades. In the 25th Division there were a total of nine infantry battalions.

From time to time there were others assigned to the 25th, including Air Force contingents. While I was in the 25th Division, it was commanded first by Major General Fillmore K. Mearns and later, in August of 1968, by Major General Ellis W. Williamson.

- BRIGADE—this is comprised of some 3,000–4,000 men organized into HQ, support, and four or more infantry battalions. The brigade was commanded by a full colonel (called a full bird due to his collar insignia of an eagle). Our brigade CO was initially a Lieutenant Colonel Wolf, who was relieved on August 26. Then Colonel Robert L. Flair assumed command of the brigade. He was full of stupid "spit and polish" ideas and was all about getting promoted and building a name for himself. As far as I could tell, he was universally disliked by both officers and men. We all thought he was out for the glory and promotions at the cost of our lives. He was shot at in his helicopter by our own troops during a battle! He later became a three-star general (Lieutenant General). Each CO of the brigade had a staff of officers reporting to his in addition to the battalion commanders. Typically, these staff positions were majors and lieutenant colonels.
- BATTALIONS—in my case this was a mechanized infantry battalion. It was commanded by a lieutenant colonel (LTC or, as we called them, light colonels). Our battalion was commanded by LTC Avery S. Fullerton when I first arrived in the 4/23. After May 15 the battalion was commanded by LTC Clifford C. Neilson. There were four infantry battalions in our brigade. A battalion was made up of four companies, including an HQ company with a recon platoon, flame track platoon, and a heavy mortar (four duces, or 4.2-inch heavy mortars) platoon. Our battalion had approximately 907 men authorized. My unit was called the 4th of the 23rd. This means the 4th Battalion, 23rd Infantry. We were known as the Tomahawks. The breakdown of the "authorized" fully

manned manpower (in the field we were never close to this staffing):

- A, B, and C Companies—each company had an "authorized TOE (Table of Organization and Equipment)" total of 188: 6 officers and 182 enlisted.
- HQ Company—total of 194: 17 officers and 177 enlisted men.
- Service (Delta)—total of 149: 7 officers and 142 enlisted men.
- Total 907 men: 42 officers (2 of them warrant officers) and 865 enlisted men.

Each battalion CO had a staff which included an executive officer (called an XO), who was second in command, and S-3 or operations officer, and S-2 or intelligence officer plus various other officers. In our battalion our S-3 or operations officer was Major Cain A. Bridgman, who will be mentioned several times in this book. The S-3 or operations officer commanded two or more companies in the field and generally pushed the company commanders to complete their missions (often the "bad guy" so the lieutenant colonel could be the "good guy" with the company commanders). S-4 was the logistics officer.

- COMPANIES—there were four mechanized companies in our battalion. Companies A or Alpha (my company), B or Bravo, C or Charlie, and the HQ Company. The TOE for our company was 188 men, 6 officers and 182 enlisted men. While I was in the field, our average strength, including everyone back in base camp (support), those on leave and recovering, was more often than not under 100. More importantly, the majority of the shortages were in the front line infantry where we typically had less than half of our authorized strength! The HQ Company also included the weapons platoon, which had four tracks with mounted 81 mm mortars in them for close-in support. It also included a recon platoon for scouting and protection of the HQ officers. When I first arrived, the company commander, or CO, of Alpha Company was Captain Glory (fictitious name). He volunteered Alpha Company for many dangerous missions and did not seem to give a damn how many of us got killed! The grunts (infantry) that I knew all were rooting for him to get shot. As far as I know, he was universally disliked by the infantry men because he tried to get us killed so he could get promoted and earn a name for himself. Eventually, he was promoted to a full colonel and retired from the army. I heard he was wounded on his second tour. That doesn't break my heart since he was heartless as far as I am concerned. The rumor was that Captain Glory went off the deep end when his RTO was killed next to him in a battle, and that is why he left Alpha Company, but this was only a rumor. Either way, most of us infantrymen were glad he went away regardless of the reason.

In the second half of May of 1968, a new CO of Alpha Company took over, Captain Henry Montgomery. He was welcomed warmly as he cared about his men and tried to limit the casualties. He was quite an improvement over Captain Glory. One of his RTOs was a short soldier named Luther Williams.

- PLATOONS—our infantry platoons were made up of 48 authorized manpower (1 officer, plus 47 enlisted men), and we resided on four APCs or tracks (M113 Armored Personnel Carriers armed with .50-caliber machine guns plus other weapons we could procure) in each infantry platoon. Sometimes the forward observer (FO) would accompany us on maneuvers. A forward observer was an artillery officer (usually a lieutenant) who called in artillery strikes for our company. One FO I especially remember who accompanied us many times was 2LT John Russell of Corpus Christi, Texas. I stayed close to him many times as he always knew where we were on the map and was good at calling in supporting artillery. Unfortunately Lieutenant Russell was later killed. I do not recall most of our platoon lieutenants' names as we seemed to go through them every month. According to Lieutenant Colonel Neilson's diary, Lieutenant Elbert was in command the day we were ambushed near French Fort on September 13. He was killed in that ambush.

- SQUADS—a squad in our unit had 11 enlisted men authorized. There was one squad for each of the four authorized tracks. This included a track commander (authorized as a sergeant) who sometimes sat in the .50-caliber cupolas, a driver for the track who was also responsible for field maintenance, and nine infantry, called the dismounted team. For most of the time I was in the field, we were lucky if we had all four tracks and perhaps four to six men per track, including the T/C (Track Commander) gunner and driver. This meant that we only had two or four men on the ground as infantry!

  We were always short of officers and sergeants. Thus after I was in the field for several months, I frequently was the highest-ranking man in our squad as a SP4 and thus was the squad leader. A few times there we no officers or sergeants left alive in our platoon as was the case after the battle of Tay Ninh in August 1968. Since I was a draftee as opposed to regular army, we never were promoted because the army wanted to save the promotions for regular army (RA serial number designation) soldiers even though we did the job!

Armored Personnel Carrier M113-Rolling Coffins

I was assigned to a mechanized infantry company, which operated as a mobile striking force with armored personnel carriers, or APCs for short. In Vietnam, we interchangeably used several terms to describe APCs, including tracks, vipers, and rolling coffins. The term "viper" was used in our unit for a period of time to confuse the enemy. However, along with call signs, I am sure this did not fool the enemy for long as they constantly listened into our communications.

The APC I was assigned to was officially known in the military as the armored personnel carrier M113. It came in a variety of different models. It is the most widely used armored personnel carrier in history with some 80,000-plus built. Basically, the four models we had in our battalion were the infantry carrying APCs which is the one I rode, the mortar APCs, which carried a 81 mm mortar, the Zippo track or flame-thrower track, and the command track, which carried the commanding officer (CO) and his support team. There were other variations of APCs, but these four types were the ones I used or worked with while in the mechanized infantry. My APC was armed with a Browning .50-caliber machine gun, plus a variety of other weapons we carried inside. The basic M113 weighted 12.3 tons and was 15 feet 11.5 inches in length, 8 feet 9.7 inches high, including the .50-caliber armor shield, and was 8 feet 2 inches wide. It rode on tank-like tracks and was steered by laterals or two levers controlling each track for turning. The engine was in the front compartment and was a six-cylinder 275 hp diesel engine (some of the earlier models were gas, but this proved to be too dangerous when hit by rockets or mines). It had an automatic transmission, so shifting gears was not necessary. It was designed to carry a squad of men consisting of a crew of two (driver and track commander who manned the machine gun and the radio) and eleven infantry inside. However, we never carried that many men in practice as we were always short of men. More likely was a crew of two and three to six infantry in the squad or about half our authorized strength. We also never rode inside the APC; we always rode on top so that our chances of survival were improved if the APC hit a mine or if it was hit by an RPG rocket.

APCs were essentially carriers of supplies, ammunition and explosives of all types including satchel charges full of C-4 explosives, boxes of hand grenades and rockets (LAWs). This is why we called them "rolling coffins"! When they were hit by mines and especially RPGs their contents exploded creating a firestorm and often blowing the track completely off the road. Of course anyone inside the track was killed and most times everyone on the top were killed or grievously wounded. It was a lucky individual who survived with minor injuries by being thrown off the track by the explosion and landing in a heap sometimes twenty to fifty yards from the track. Everyone involved had a concussion from such an explosion even if he survived.

The APC had very thin aluminum armor (0.47 to 1.5 inches) which could stop a light rifle round and some indirect shrapnel but no bullets of a larger caliber. It was very vulnerable to mines and rockets, which is how we lost most of our APCs. I believe we went through five or six different APCs in as many months while I was operating in the field, all of which were hit by RPG rockets. The operating range of the APCs was three hundred miles, and it could achieve speeds of forty-two miles per hour, although we rarely went this fast. The APC could also float and navigate through calm water at around 3.6 mph swimming speed. We often went through small rivers and streams, so this feature was very helpful.

We often used the APCs to mow down jungle to make a path as we pursued the enemy, who tended to set up their base camp in remote, heavily wooded, or jungle areas (we called the boondocks). The only problem was in crashing through the jungle, they would knock down vines, trees, and brush which was full of biting insects of all types. Especially painful were the hornets and red ants, both of which lived in trees. The tracks would knock down the trees, and these insects would come crashing down on top of the tracks, angry at being disturbed and biting anyone on the APC. The red ants were of a very large type with large jaws who made a nest of tree leaves and when disturbed swarmed out of their nest, biting anyone they encountered. The hornets and bees were of all types, and everyone had painful bites. We were constantly being bitten by insects (not to mention rather large mosquitoes and nits) in the jungles and woods. We would also encounter land leeches, which lived in trees, which would also fall down on us, looking for blood! Almost everything we encountered in Vietnam seemed to be out to get us. It was a very hostile place to walk around and live in day-to-day.

First Day in the Field Short Round

April 22, 1968

My first action in battle was a short round incident, on or about April 22, 1968.

Up to this point I had never received any training or familiarization with mechanized infantry, nor had I even ridden on an APC. As replacements we would be joining our unit while under fire, attacking the enemy. We were also told that the battalion had been fighting for a long time prior to our arrival and that they had taken heavy casualties, and thus they urgently needed replacements. After receiving our weapons, ammo, and other gear, we assisted in loading additional ammunition and supplies in the tracks and supply vehicles that would be accompanying us to join our company in the field. Obviously, we were all nervous about joining a new unit where we knew no one and very little about combat and would immediately come under enemy fire.

At around 3 p.m. we were loaded on several tracks (M113 Armored Personnel Carriers). We moved out of Tay Ninh Base Camp to join our company somewhere in the jungles and rice paddies of Tay Ninh near the Cambodian border. I was assigned to Track 3-2 along with eight other replacements. I met several of these replacements in the 25th Division in-country orientation just days before. Some I met only the same day. None of the replacements went through either basic training or AIT (Advanced Infantry Training) with me in the States. I recall we had one buck sergeant, who I believe was a "shake and bake" (an enlisted man who went through a quick military course to become a buck sergeant, E-5, who did not have the years of experience required to become a regular army NCO). This was necessary as the army was in dire need for NCOs for the infantry. There were several other PFCs (private first class), including myself, in the replacements. I believe the only experienced personnel on the track were the driver and the track commander, who was a sergeant and one SP4 grunt.

As we moved out, there were several APCs in front of us and some resupply vehicles following behind us. We were the last in the line, followed by a deuce and a half trailing a water tanker. Fortunately for me, I was riding on the left-hand side, leaning my back against the armored .50-caliber machine gun turret. This random selection of my position is what saved my life that day.

We had been traveling perhaps an hour and a half when we saw a firefight in the distance. We could hear the sounds of explosions and artillery in the distance and see smoke rising from the battlefield. We were all nervous and anxious for what would happen next as we approached our company who was engaged in a firefight with the enemy. We were traveling through a flat grass covered open area with no roads and a few large trees. We were traveling in line where the drivers were keeping inside of the tracks of the vehicle ahead. We were told that this was SOP (standard operating procedure) so that only the first track would hit a mine if we traveled through a minefield. This is why we also traveled through open fields rather than on roads in many cases. It seemed we were traveling in an uninhabited area where there were no roads, villages or farms. On the right and left of the field there appeared to be thick woods or semi-jungle areas. Daylight was fading as daylight goes quickly in the tropics. It was the dry season, so we were kicking up dust as the track ground forward through the fields. However, the dust was minimal and visibility clear as we were traversing through grass-covered fields, not on dirt roads.

I was looking ahead in the distance toward the sight of the battle and watching the tracks traveling in front of us to see where they were headed. Then without warning a huge explosion occurred next to our track and I was blown off the track. The next thing I remember I was laying on the ground with a terrible headache, and my body ached all over. I felt like I had been in the losing end of a fight and had the shit kicked out of me! I could not hear very well, and my head hurt like heck, and things were confused and moving all around me. I did not understand exactly what had happened, although I knew we had been blown up by something huge. As I sat up I felt wet and sticky and found that I was covered in blood and guts. My first thought was that we had hit a mine and that I had been wounded in the explosion. I instinctively felt around to see if I had any missing parts or limbs. Everything seemed confusing to me as there was smoke and soldiers moving around me. Someone came up to me and was asking if I was OK. I guess I responded that I seemed all right, and he helped me up. What I saw then was quite shocking. Strewn around me were several dismembered bodies of the replacements who were riding on the track just seconds before. Still on the track were the driver, track commander, and several others who were decapitated or dismembered. Blood and purplish-gray brain and body parts were all over the field and track on which I had been riding. It seemed as if the explosion took place on the right side of the track and blown most of us off the track on the left-hand side. I had a concussion from the blast and was disoriented seeing and hearing everything around me in kind of a dream like slow motion fog.

I was helped up and assisted in walking to another track where I sat down against the side of the track, facing away from the destruction and death of my former track and fellow replacements. Someone handed me my rifle and gear. Everything was still confusing to me at that point in time while I tried to shake the dizziness in my head and make some sense of what had happened. It seemed to me that everyone who had been riding on the track had been killed except me.

After a while (I have no idea how long we stayed cleaning up the mess and what happened to my track after that) I was helped onto another APC, and we continued going forward to meet up with our company. It seemed to me that we drove on for quite a while in the dark before we met up with our company. I recall someone telling me that we were not hit by a mine but rather a "short round." At that time I did not know what a short round meant. I later found out that it was our own artillery which had dropped a round on us rather than on the enemy several clicks away (a click is 1 kilometer or .62 of a mile). I believe that the caliber of the short round was either a 105 howitzer or perhaps a 155 round.

My uniform was covered in blood and guts from the other KIAs (killed in action), but I had no visible wounds other than I could not hear very well and had a severe headache and sore muscles that I never knew I had all over my body. When we arrived at the company, I was escorted to see the company commander, a "Captain Glory." He appeared to be an Asian American of short stature with glasses. His RTO escorted me into his command track (an oversized APC which was several feet higher than the normal profile APC and was roomier inside with numerous communications gear and antennas protruding from the top). I believe there were another officer and sergeant present along with other HQ company enlisted and NCOs present. I was not feeling very well after being blown off the track so things were still a bit foggy to me and I still could not hear very well. I believe there may have been some other replacements in attendance. I recall that Captain Glory was not very friendly and said very little. He sort of welcomed us to Alpha Company and then assigned us to fill in as replacements in various platoons. He seemed preoccupied with the conduct of the battle and did not spend much time with us and did not mention anything about the dead or what happened to our track. He looked strangely at my uniform (being covered in blood) but said nothing.

When we met up with the company, they were formed up in a circle with the APC facing out and surrounding the command track with several of the supply vehicles in the center of the circle. Infantry were around the perimeter in bunkers in between the tracks. I was escorted to my platoon where I met my platoon sergeant, a lifer E-6 staff sergeant. I don't recall his name but he was not very friendly and told me to get some sleep as we would be attacking in the morning and that I would be his replacement RTO. I instantly fell into a deep sleep with my headache, body ache and the strain of the events of the day. I was shaken awake by one of the soldiers after what seemed like an hour or so later, which was actually several hours later, in the early morning before light (around 5am). We had no breakfast or even a hot drink as no fires were allowed and we were to move out immediately. I reported to the Platoon E-6 as ordered not feeling very well from head to toe and still shaky from being blown off the track the evening before. I was told to carry the PRC 25 (we called it a PRICK 25 Radio) radio and stay next to the SSG and do as I was told. I was given a call sign and told to monitor the network for orders from the CO and transfer requests from the SSG over the radio. This was not too intelligent as I had difficulty hearing due to the concussion. With that introduction we moved out across a field into my first battle.

Until the summer of 2009, when I met another survivor of my old unit in Company A, 3rd platoon, Tom Foster, I thought that I was the only survivor of the short round incident. In fact Tom told me that he had been riding on the track directly in front of our track when the short round hit to the right of our track. Tom told me that he knew the track commander and driver of the track who had been in the country with him for several months. Tom had arrived in Vietnam in January 1968 just prior to the Tet Offensive. He had been in several firefights and had already been wounded once prior to this point in time. Tom told me he remembered the incident well and that one other soldier had survived the explosion. In fact he thought that this soldier was the only survivor and was surprised that I too had survived. Tom told me that he had to help remove the bodies from the APC after the short round hit. The other survivor had been a combat veteran with the third platoon. But after the shock of the short round killing everyone in the squad he got "combat fatigue" and could not function and was sent to the rear for medical treatment. He never returned to the company.

Tom Foster

The story of how I met Tom Foster is an interesting footnote. In the summer of 2009 I was living in Alpharetta, Georgia, with my wife Tina. We decided to attend the Memorial Day celebrations in Roswell, Georgia. After the speeches and celebrations were over, we walked through the displays of military vehicles, weapons and equipment, mostly from WWII and Vietnam. As we walked by a display with Vietnam weapons and equipment, I was explaining to Tina which items I used in Vietnam. As it happened, Tom Foster was manning the display as I explained the equipment to Tina. Tom overheard our conversations and asked if I was in Vietnam. I said yes and noticed he was wearing the emblem of the 25th Infantry Division. I explained I was also in the 25th as an 11B. Tom asked what year, and I responded 1968–69. He said he was in Vietnam in 1968 as a grunt, too. I asked what unit he was in, and he said Mechanized Infantry. I responded that I was also in the Mechanized Infantry. He asked what unit, and I said 4/23rd Infantry. He responded he, too, was in the 4/23rd Company A. I said I was in Company A also, Third Platoon. Tom looked closely at me and exclaimed he was in the Third Platoon also. Then he asked who the CO was? I said at that time Captain Glory (I used the actual name of the CO). Then I asked what track he was on and he said 3-3. I said I was on Track 3-2. Thus not only were we in the same unit at the same time, but we were in squads right next to each other! Yet we did not even know one another in Vietnam.

Tom and I met later for lunch and took along pictures of when we were in Vietnam, hoping to recognize something familiar to each of us. At lunch I discussed my first day in the field and the short round incident. Much to the surprise of both of us, Tom told me he remembered the incident well, since he was on the track in front of us, and that he knew some of the soldiers killed that day. In fact, he was surprised that I was on the track, since he thought everyone had been killed except one soldier he knew who was later dusted off (helicopter medevac) to the rear due to the trauma of the experience of all of his buddies killed by our own artillery.

RTO for a Day

April 23, 1968

My second day in combat was as the RTO (radio telephone operator) for our platoon staff sergeant. He was an E-6 staff sergeant but he was the highest sergeant in the platoon. He was one of the few "lifers" (regular army career soldiers) in our platoon. The platoon sergeant obviously wanted to keep the "new guy" close to him and he also needed a new RTO as the old RTO had been wounded and evacuated the day before. I had never even handled a PRC-25 radio. I guessed I was going to learn on the job under fire. I had less than no interest in carrying a radio as I had heard that it made you a target for the enemy—just what I needed in my second day of combat.

We moved out and immediately made contact with the enemy. They were dug in and we were attacking across open ground. I was trying to follow the platoon sergeant with the radio and not get shot at the same time. He would move ahead and get behind some cover and if I didn't immediately follow him he would motion for me by rapidly waving his arm. When I joined him he would sometimes grab the mike and speak with the platoon lieutenant. My job was to monitor the net and if the lieutenant called the sergeant I was to motion for him to grab up the headset. With all of the noise and bullets hitting next to me I could hardly hear and besides I was more interested in staying alive than listing to the radio.

About halfway through the day things were getting really hot as we closed on the enemy bunkers. The sergeant and I were taking shelter behind some felled trees while he was discussing the situation with the lieutenant. I recall that the lieutenant was yelling for him to move out and the sergeant was saying we were pinned down and could not move. The lieutenant did not care and told him to move out. The sergeant had had enough and got very angry, started cursing out the lieutenant and said, "Come on, we're moving out." With that he yelled for the platoon to move out and attack the enemy bunker complex. Then he started to run half crouched to a downed log ahead and to the right of our position. I began to run behind him to catch up. At that moment a machine gun opened up on the sergeant hitting just behind him as he ran to my front. If he moved any slower he would have been killed for sure. Seeing the machine gun zeroed in on the sergeant there was no way I was going to try to make it across that killing field. So I ran back to the protected position behind the log where we were previously. Some of the other troops who advanced likewise came under heavy automatic weapons fire. Some were hit and everyone else jumped back under cover.

Seeing that I was not moving, the sergeant motioned for me to join him. I thought it was suicide to try to run in front of a machine gun which had us zeroed in. In fact the enemy was firing at everyone, laying down a wall of fire. I shook my head and made a cutting motion with my hand across my neck indicating it was a bad idea. The sergeant then started frantically motioning for me to join him and making angry faces and apparently cursing at me. Either way I was not going to get killed, no matter how angry he got.

About that time the lieutenant called and asked what was going on. I told him we were pinned down by machine guns and could not move. He said, "Get me the sergeant!" I told him, "The sergeant is not here. He is pinned down on the other side of the field." The lieutenant said, "I don't care. Go get him." I told him I couldn't move as a machine gun had me pinned down. He started yelling that he didn't give a damn and that I should "go get the sergeant!" I just ignored both of them as there was no way I was going to try to run across an open field with a radio on my back, making a target for every enemy gunner. I simply held up the receiver to indicate the lieutenant wanted to talk to the sergeant. This only made him madder, and he waved his arms frantically. I would not move, as I knew what awaited me if I tried to run toward the sergeant. Of course he was smart enough not to try to run back to where I was hunkered down, having had too close a shave the first time. So we both stayed in position. I figured if the radio was that important to him, let him come to me and risk the machine gun. I was certainly not going to get shot simply to get him the radio.

Everyone stayed where they were for perhaps fifteen or twenty minutes. The lieutenant told me again to get the sergeant, and the sergeant kept motioning for me to come to him. I assume that the lieutenant called in either mortars or artillery, as it started hitting the enemy bunker line dug into a hedgerow. After the fire slackened, the troops began to raise their heads and return fire. The sergeant got up on one knee and started yelling, cursing and frantically motioning for me to join him. With that I ran over to him as fast as I could at a crouch, fully expecting that the enemy machine gun would open up on me. I kept on thinking that the radio on my back was a bull's eye for every enemy gunner. Fortunately the machine gun had either been knocked out or decided to move out, so I was able to run across the field and jump behind the cover where the sergeant had been hunkering down.

Needless to say the sergeant was cursing and calling me every name in the book for not joining him. I didn't say anything and just carried the radio, keeping my thoughts to myself.

We over-ran the enemy bunker line, collected our dead and wounded, and set up a night laager. After the battle the sergeant told me to take off the radio and return to my squad. He would get another RTO who was not a coward! Of course he didn't mention that he too would not tempt fate and run over to the radio across the open field. Frankly, I didn't give a damn what he called me. I was alive and would likely not have been if I ran across that field. Best of all I didn't have to carry the radio any longer, getting a bull's eye off my back. After that the platoon sergeant had it in for me, and would give me the shitty assignments when he could. Months later this situation would result in the incident at the Hoc Mon Bridge where I threw him in the river.

APCs carried Our Equipment, Gear, and Ammunition

Our tracks carried everything we needed while in the field. They carried us into battle along with all of our weapons, survival and personal gear. On top they had a .50-caliber machine gun in the turret. Inside they carried our other weapons: M-60s, an extra .50-caliber (we had an extra one on our track) machine gun for the bunker, extra barrels for the machine guns (they burned out), asbestos gloves for changing .50-caliber machine gun barrels under fire, LAWs, 90 mm recoilless rifle, C-4 explosives, mines, trip flares, smoke grenades, hand grenades, satchel charges, ammo for all of our weapons, sandbags, starlight scopes, sniper rifles (M-14 with an infrared scope), a flame thrower (one) and personal gear was carried inside the tracks. We also carried water, clothing, c-rations, medical kits, shovels and a pick for digging, maintenance equipment and supplies for the tracks and engines. On the outside we carried Marston mats on the sides to protect us from RPGs (not that they did much good) and for building bunkers, concertina wire for night laager positions, and sandbags to protect us when on top of the tracks. Sandbags added extra weight so we were told not to place them on the track but we did anyway. I also had an aluminum chair I took from a Vietnamese and mounted it on top of our track to sit in while moving so as to keep my butt off the hot metal in the sun. You could literally fry an egg on the metal surface of a track in the dry season!

First Kill "He Popped Up Right in Front of Me!"

April 24, 1968

We were in a firefight moving up behind the tracks since we were getting intense fire with automatic weapons from a tree line. The entire company was engaged in the fight. Each platoon was advancing slowly in line, firing as we moved forward. I was holding onto the back of the track with a stiff arm. You did this because if the track backed up it would run over you. With a stiff arm it would push you back and you would have a couple of seconds to get out of the way. There were three others with me moving up behind our track. The track commander was firing the .50-caliber machine gun and periodically we would fire from behind the track when we had a target.

As we moved closer to the wood line, everyone began moving out in front of the track firing in a line as we moved toward the enemy entrenchments. I was walking rapidly with the other three in our squad (as usual we were grossly understaffed) firing as we went. We were all running low on ammo, so I went back to the track to retrieve some M-16 ammo before we got to the enemy line. I opened the door to the track while it was moving forward and retrieved some M-60 belts and M-16 bandoliers. I draped these over my body so I had my hands free to fire my weapon.

As I was running forward to get in line with the rest of my squad, an NVA soldier popped up directly in front of me. He came out of the ground, perhaps ten feet in front of me, and opened up with his AK-47 on full automatic shooting at the back of my squad who had just passed over his spider hole. He likely got off four or six shots before I shot him in the back on full automatic with my M-16. All of this took just split seconds! Then I moved forward and fired into the hole to make sure anyone else in the hole was also dead. Then I threw in a hand grenade for good measure. Fortunately, all of his rounds were wide of the mark, and he did not hit any of the three men in our squad. After that, everyone was very careful to watch the ground for more spider holes.

I shared the ammo with my squad, and we advanced into the enemy trench line, killing all of the NVA who were in the trenches and bunkers.

Hit in the Back by a Spent Round

Between April 24 and April 31, 1968

After my first day of battle, being blown off my track by our own artillery, we were engaged in firefights every day. At night we set up night defensive positions. A couple of days later we were advancing across an open field. We advanced in a line firing as we went, usually with the APCs firing their .50-caliber machine guns along-side of us. The idea was that the massive firepower would keep the enemy's heads down so we could over-run their defensive positions. In theory this sounded good, but in practice the enemy was often dug into bunkers and kept firing as we advanced across the field. More often than not, they had automatic weapons and mortars, both of which were deadly in open fields. As we advanced, the enemy let loose with a massive amount of automatic weapons and RPGs to keep the tracks from advancing further. After a few RPG rounds the tracks backed up and the infantry hit the dirt. I jumped behind a berm which was perhaps two feet high and two to three feet thick. Rounds were hitting all around us and flying through the air. They sounded like angry hornets flying through the air. I moved up closer to the berm laterally because mortars were hitting around us. We were pinned down with no place to go. There were men on both sides of me perhaps ten yards apart hugging the berm. We could not move forward or backward without being hit by machine gun or mortar fire. While I was lying against the berm with the rest of our squad wondering what to do next, I was hit in the small of my back by a round. It knocked the wind out of me, and it felt like someone had run up behind me and hit me in the small of my back with the end of a broom handle. For a moment I was not sure how badly I had been injured. All I knew is that I had been hit in my lower back and it hurt like hell! I could not move without severe pain and could not speak since it knocked the wind out of me. As it turns out, the round that hit me must have compressed the nerves in my back and temporarily paralyzed my lower limbs, or at least made it unbearable to move. All I know is that I was in severe agony. I lay against the berm for I don't know how long until I got my breath and voice back. It hurt just to breathe. When I could, I yelled, "Medic!" Shortly thereafter, our doc came running through the fire and jumped down next to me. Medics were very brave men. While everyone else was hugging the dirt, they had to run through fire to come to the aid of wounded. He leaned over and yelled in my ear, asking, "Where are you hit?" All of us were half deaf by the noise of explosions and gunfire. At that time we wore no ear or eye protection as soldiers do today. I told the doc, "In my back." He pulled up my flak jacket and shirt and started cursing. "Goddamn it, you asshole, you were hit by a spent round." He put a .51-caliber Chicom (Chinese .51-caliber) heavy machine gun round in my hand and took off for someone else yelling for a medic. I had no idea of how badly I had been wounded except that moving any part of my body hurt like hell. I thought to myself that no one gives a shit about me. Here I am wounded and not even the doc gives a shit.

We stayed pinned down in this position for perhaps a half to three quarters of an hour before our artillery began to whistle over our heads and pound the enemy bunkers across the field. Gradually, I began to recover my sense of feelings in my lower body and I could move without it hurting. I felt around my lower back and could not feel any blood. I knew I had been hit, but did not understand how there was no blood. I was more concerned that I may have been paralyzed as it hurt just to move my legs or shift around. In the meanwhile the artillery kept pounding the bunker line of the enemy.

The artillery barrage went on for at least twenty minutes to a half an hour. Then I heard someone yell, "Move out!" and some of my platoon began to peak their heads over the top of the berm. No one was in a hurry to advance until they knew the enemy had been decimated. I still was hurting so I really did not want to move out, especially with someone shooting at me. Soldiers were passing the word along the berm that we were going to move out when the artillery stopped.

About this time the APCs began to move up to my position against the berm. Our tracks were slowly moving, firing their machine guns as they went. Gradually everyone began to get up firing their weapons and moving ahead in line with the tracks. I did not want to be left behind so I painfully rose and began firing my M-16 at the enemy positions. Every time I took a step my back hurt like hell! I was trying to keep up with everyone and not to lag behind; we needed to stay in line so as not to shoot each other. We moved across the field shooting at the enemy bunker line. When I reached the bunker line, I threw a grenade in the bunker next to the trenches where the enemy had been shooting at us. There were several dead lying in the ditch. I shot them just to be sure. The artillery had killed a lot of the enemy and thus had significantly reduced their firepower.

After we overran the enemy bunker line, resistance more or less ceased. The surviving enemy had retreated and we were only getting sporadic gun fire. I sat down beyond the enemy bunker line and took a drink. My back was killing me and I didn't want to walk any further. One of our squad who was to my left on the berm asked, "Where are you hit?" I took the .51-caliber bullet out of my pocket and pointed to my back. He looked at my back and said, "You are lucky that it was a spent round or it would have cut you in half." At the time, I was not feeling very lucky, just very sore!

Later the doc came over to me and said, "You sure are lucky it went through the berm before it hit you, or you would not be here." He told me to take it easy for a few days. Then he went over and spoke to our platoon staff sergeant. The platoon staff sergeant came over to me with the doc. The doc showed him my back and told me to show him the spent round. I showed them the spent round and the platoon staff sergeant simply said, "You're lucky," and walked away. Fortunately he listened to the doc and let me rest that evening.

Next day we continued fighting, making contact with the enemy every day.

First Ambush and the "Fuck You" Lizard

Between April 24 and April 31, 1968

Every third night we were sent out on an ambush. Usually a squad was supposed to go out on an ambush. However, we were so short of soldiers that we often went out with only three soldiers on ambush. The remainder of the squad manned the defensive perimeter of our night laager position or was on listening post. This time we went out with the staff sergeant and a handful of men.

"Fuck You" Lizard

The so-called "fuck you" lizard, as we GIs called it, is technically a Tokay gecko. It is a nocturnal arboreal gecko which inhabits tropical rainforest trees and cliffs in Southeast Asia. It is known as Tac Ke' in Vietnamese. It also frequently adapts to rural human habitats, roaming walls and ceilings in search of insect prey. When spending time in native Vietnamese houses, it was common to hear them scampering along walls during darkness, only to wake up face-to-face with a very large and menacing lizard just inches away. A most disconcerting situation for the uninitiated! I recall my alarm waking up next to such a lizard when sleeping at a Vietnamese house. My host had a good laugh at my alarm and said to leave them alone as they killed the bugs and mosquitoes in the house.

It is the second-largest gecko species, attaining lengths of up to twenty inches and weighing fourteen ounces. The Tokay Gecko is very aggressive and is capable of inflicting a painful bite, so it is better if you leave them alone, even if in your house.

Being the "fucking new guy" (FNG), I was assigned to be the "point man" or first man walking to our ambush sight. The squad staff sergeant was following behind me with a handful of our squad. We were to set up perhaps a quarter of a mile from our defensive position. We were walking across field in-between tree lines. This is a very vulnerable position as you cannot see anyone hidden in the tree line but they can see you moving across a field. The grass in the field was about four and a half feet high and we were walking slowly to make as little noise as possible. I was scared to death as I had never been on an ambush before and didn't really know what I was doing. It was probably a mistake to place a new man on point with zero experience. But that is how they did things in Vietnam. Give the FNG the most dangerous jobs so they would be killed first!

The night was dark and you could only see a few yards in front of you. As I walked along, all of a sudden I heard an NVA soldier say very clearly, "Fuck you!" I thought I had bought the farm and had walked into an enemy ambush. At the same instant, I noticed an NVA helmet just above the top of the grass. I froze as I didn't know if I should fire, hit the ground, or run! Then the NVA said "Fuck you" again! About this time (it felt like a minute but more likely it was seconds), the staff sergeant grabbed my arm and looked at me with a "what's up" expression. I pointed to the NVA helmet in the grass and looked back at him, knowing he heard the NVA say "Fuck you." He leaned over and said quietly in my ear, "Don't worry, it's a lizard." I was in disbelief, and I wasn't buying anything he said, as I didn't trust him. I still wouldn't move, believing we were in the middle of an enemy ambush—besides who would believe that a lizard could talk. He gave me a slight shove and motioned to move out. I wasn't moving. He then took the point himself. When the next soldier in line caught up with me, I figured the only thing to do was to follow the staff sergeant.

This was quite a fright for a new soldier on his first ambush. As it turns out, this was one of those Tokay geckos whose croak sounds exactly like "Fuck you." The NVA helmet turned out to be a bush.

Listening Post (LP)

Listening Post (LP) was where two men crawled outside of our defensive position and set up for the night perhaps fifty yards beyond the outer defensive wire (concertina wire). The idea was that if the defensive position was attacked, the LP men would give warning of the attack, providing those in the defensive position time to get ready for the attack. In fact in an attack the most likely outcome would be that those in the LP would be killed immediately as you would be caught between the attackers and your own men! Two nights out of three we were outside the wire on either LP or an ambush.

Abandoned by Our CO and Cut off at the Fortified Farm House

April 28, 1968

After being hit in the back by the spent round, the next memorable battle I recall was at the fortified farm house. Our platoon was ordered to attack this farm house across an open field. It was fortified with a fighting trench surrounding it and with machine guns and a platoon of enemy guarding the position. As we found out later this was the forward position of a much larger group who was concealed in a wood line beyond the farmhouse. Our squad was on the left side of the farm house with other squads to the left of our position. Tom Foster's squad was to our right. We were around four hundred to five hundred yards away taking sporadic small arms fire from the farm house and the wood line beyond.

The field beyond the farmhouse had been bombed by some large 250- or 500-pound bombs as there were craters behind the farmhouse. The farmhouse had been damaged indirectly by the bombs exploding to its rear, but the bunkers which were in the tree line had not been bombed. At the time we were not aware of the presence of the enemy fighting positions in the tree line, only that we were taking fire from the fortified farmhouse and fighting positions surrounding it.

While we were preparing to assault the farm house someone in our squad suggested that we blow it up with the 90 mm recoilless rifle. One of the "old-timers" (being in our unit three months or longer qualified you as an old-timer) asked if I wanted to try my hand at the 90 mm. I said sure, as I had never fired one before. I had fired the LAW recoilless weapon which was much smaller.

90 mm Recoilless Rifle

The M-67 90 mm recoilless rifle is a like a large LAW or a Bazooka on steroids. It is a large tube 3.5 inches in diameter, 53 inches long, and weighs 35 pounds unloaded. It is mounted on a bipod, and it has a handle underneath and an optical sight on the left hand side. It is breach loaded from the rear. The round it shoots is about 3 inches in diameter and weighs slightly more than 9 pounds. The back blast is a fan-shaped area 5 meters wide behind the weapon that extends some thirty yards (twenty-eight meters) to the rear when fired. To put the size of the weapon in perspective, the most commonly used USA tank in WWII, the Sherman Tank, has a cannon bore of 75 mm. Thus the M-67 90 mm recoilless rifle bore is 15 mm larger! Believe me, the 90 mm packs quite a wallop. Shooting it off of your shoulder is quite a thrill!

The old-timer told me it was just like firing a LAW but much bigger. He quickly instructed me on how to aim through the scope and fire the weapon. He pointed out similarities with the LAW of which I was familiar. The big difference is the size of the round and the back blast. He cautioned me that I must not even put my finger on the trigger until he taped me on the head indicating the round was loaded and armed. He also said that I had to aim and fire quickly because, as soon as I stuck my head up to fire, the enemy would try to take my head off. He also said, "Always keep the barrel pointed toward the house and aim for the middle of the house." He cautioned, "No matter what happens, even if rounds come close to you, do not lean back or point the barrel toward the sky as the back blast will blow us both up!"

I carried the 90 mm, the old-timer carried two rounds, and we ran forward toward a berm perhaps thirty yards to the right and fifty yards in front of the rest of the platoon and APCs. The APCs were firing their .50-caliber machine guns, and everyone else was firing weapons at the farmhouse and tree line to keep the enemy's head down. Once we made it to the berm, we ducked down and crawled off several yards to confuse the enemy as to where exactly we were setting up. I laid parallel to the berm and made sure as much of my body was away from the back end of the 90 mm rifle as possible. Then I placed the 90 mm at ninety degrees to my body with the front facing toward the farmhouse. My partner asked if I was ready and I nodded yes.

My partner loaded the round in the 90 mm rifle and closed the breach, then moved quickly out of the way to my front along the berm. Then he indicated the weapon was loaded and ready and gave me a thumbs-up. He put his hands over his ears and hugged the berm. I was anxious to fire the 90 mm so I quickly popped my head up and rested the 90 mm on my shoulder, in a one legged kneeling position, the same as how we were taught to fire the LAW. I placed my eye against the rubber eye scope and fortunately zeroed in on the farm house quickly, aiming at its center. Then I pulled the trigger! KABOOM! The rocket went off with a deafening roar and a flash of light. The back blast blew up the ground behind and in front of us into a pall of dust and smoke. The noise and smoke was like being directly under a tank's cannon when it fired!

An instant later the farmhouse exploded in a ball of flame and debris. A direct hit with my first try! I now understood why the old-timer was more anxious to cover his ears than to fire the 90 mm. I couldn't have been more pleased after seeing the farmhouse explode from the round. My partner tapped me on the back and gave me a "thumbs-up." I think he said, "Good shot," but I couldn't hear a damn thing he was saying. He indicated that we should shoot the second round, and I nodded my head in agreement. When the smoke cleared, we went through the same drill of loading the weapon. This time I fired the second shot and aimed once again at the center of the farmhouse so as not to miss. KABOOM! The rocket hit again and blew up more of the remaining farmhouse. Both of us thought that no one could have survived those two hits so our job would be much easier attacking the farmhouse.

After that we returned the 90 mm to the track, got our weapons and lined up with the rest of the squad, who was forming up to move out and attack the farmhouse. I grabbed my M-16, which was my normal weapon at that time. Several men in our platoon gave us the thumbs up for good shooting. We began to cross the field in line with the track, firing as we went forward at a fast walk. There were other platoons to our left and right moving out toward the farmhouse.

As we moved out toward the farmhouse, the sporadic fire we had been receiving intensified. It appeared there were still quite a few survivors from the 90 mm blasts and the .50 caliber firing. What we did not recognize at the time is that much of the shooting was from the wood line directly in back of the farmhouse rather than from the farmhouse and trenches around it. Our company walked rapidly in line charging the farmhouse with all weapons firing. When we got near the farmhouse, the 50s and M-60 machine guns plus the individual weapons of the company were chewing up everything that moved. By the time we got to the trenches surrounding the farmhouse, all of the enemy soldiers were dead. There were dead NVA bodies and body parts all along the ditch. I was near the left center of the ditch, and I plugged a couple of the dead bodies as I walked by to be sure they were really dead. I saw others in my squad do likewise, as this was SOP (Standard Operating Procedure) so that none of the NVA would come alive and shoot us in the back. The APCs of our platoon stayed in front of the farmhouse, providing protecting cover in the event of an enemy counter attack.

Our platoon proceeded to cover the ground in and around the farmhouse, making sure that all enemy were dead. We had had no casualties in our squad up to that point. Then we formed up at the end of the farmhouse where the back-end of the trench surrounded the farmhouse. By this time the firing in front of us had almost stopped, except that there was firing to our right and left against the attacking squads. The APCs did not catch up with us, which turned out to be a grave mistake. Our platoon leader yelled for us to move out and pointed toward the fortified wood line. It was here that we discovered the immense bomb craters from previous aerial bombings. We quickly formed up and proceeded to cross the open field between the farm house and the tree line. The squads in our platoon on either side of us were already proceeding toward the wood line, as was the rest of the company. What we did not realize is that we were walking into a well-planned trap of the enemy.

As we proceeded across the open field, we got about halfway to the tree line and all hell broke loose. The enemy had us zeroed in with two machine guns on both sides and automatic weapons directly in front. All of the machine guns were hidden from view in large camouflaged bunkers and covered fighting trenches. Additionally they had mortars concealed behind the tree line. While we were completely exposed, the mortars, machine guns and infantry automatic weapons hit us at once. Half the squad was mowed down immediately. Then the NVA dropped mortars on us for good measure. We needed to get out of the "killing zone" fast or join the dead. With bullets and mortars going off around me, I hit the dirt and quickly crawled back toward the bomb crater that I had just passed, perhaps twenty or so yards to my rear. Three others made it to the bomb crater. We peeped over the edge of the bomb crater to return fire and saw others in our platoon taking cover in other bomb craters. There were five or six of our platoon dead lying in the field we just crossed. From the bomb crater, we could see that we were in the middle of the killing zone the NVA had prepared for us. Due to the heavy machine gun and rocket fire, the tracks had pulled back, and it appeared we were the only ones left alive in the killing zone.

Abandoned by Captain Glory

We found out later that so many of the company had been killed or wounded in the attack that the CO, Captain Glory, had told everyone to pull back. Of course we had no way of knowing this, nor could we have pulled back if we wanted to, being stuck in the middle of an open field. We were abandoned by the company to our own devices. This was typical of Captain Glory, who seemed to care nothing for our lives.

From our positions at the top of the bomb crater, which was some twenty to thirty feet deep with very steep sides, we knew we were in big trouble. We were receiving heavy and accurate machine gun fire every time we popped up our heads, and the NVA were walking the mortars across the battlefield. Obviously they were trying to drop mortars on us in the bomb craters. It didn't take us long to agree to retreat to the ditch by the farmhouse where we had more cover. We maneuvered around to the rear of the bomb crater, which was not easy, given the steep grade, and got ready to crawl to the ditch, perhaps twenty-five yards away. That is a long way to crawl when someone is shooting and dropping mortars on you.

We crawled out of the bomb crater at the same time, crawling as fast and low as possible. The enemy gunners tried to hit us but all three of us made it back to the ditch. About the same time several other survivors of the platoon made it back to the ditch. Several were wounded, one seriously. We had no medics, so the wounded had to lie in the ditch and wait for help. There was little we could do for them, especially since any movement brought down a hail of bullets. The ditch was only about three feet deep and had blood-filled water in the bottom, along with many enemy dead and body parts. We kept our heads down once in the ditch. Some of the men were yelling to return fire. That made little sense to me as the enemy was in bunkers and we couldn't see a thing. Better to conserve our ammo in case they attacked us. Once in a while I would raise my gun up by one hand (keeping my head down) and fire off a couple of rounds just to let them know we were still alive and waiting for them should they attack. Over the course of the day, a couple of other wounded survivors made it to the ditch so that there were about six of us in the ditch.

One of the survivors of our platoon had the platoon radio with him. He was calling for someone in our company to bring up the tracks and medics for the wounded and to get us out of there. No one even tried to help us. As I was at the opposite end of the ditch, I don't know what was said over the radio, and the RTO didn't communicate with me or anyone near me. After we made it to the ditch, our mortar platoon was dropping mortars on the enemy bunker line. However, it did little good because we continued to receive machine gun and small arms fire, although the mortars and RPGs had stopped firing at us. We stayed in the ditch all day, waiting for someone to come help us or for an opportunity for us to retreat. While we were in the ditch, two of the men who were sticking up their heads to fire were shot in the head and killed instantly. One of these was the radio operator. I shared ammo with some of these men since they had used up all of their ammo. I was concerned that we were going to run out of ammo, so I was careful not to fire at the wood line in spite of the others yelling to return fire. They were afraid of a counter attack and wanted the NVA to know we were waiting for them if they did. I was not so sure this was a good idea as I wanted real ammo in the event of an attack.

The severely wounded man died sometime during the afternoon. We stayed in the ditch for the rest of the day, and no one came to help us. One time I rose up to fire in the direction of the enemy (we could not see a thing) to see if they were positioning for an attack, and a green bamboo viper slithered right in front of my rifle barrel just as I fired off a round. The muzzle blast knocked him away from me. This was not a good day. While lying in the ditch, I (and the others) ran out of water and it was boiling hot. I remember a duck of some sort with a bunch of chicks kept running back and forth through the ditch and over me trying to get away from all of the noise and firing. The ditch stank of human blood, dead bodies and waste, and we had to lie in it all day or risk getting shot in the head.

We had been cut off from the rest of the company all day. It was getting toward dusk (late afternoon in the tropics) and we were all almost out of ammo. By this time there were only three of us left alive and it was obvious to us that Captain Glory was going to let us die in place. I was alone at the far end of the ditch. I didn't like being there alone as I would be the first one killed if the NVA attacked. I also wanted to get away from the machine guns so I crawled along the ditch until I reached the other side which was closest to where the rest of our company had retreated. The other two surviving soldiers were further down the ditch keeping at the bottom of the ditch. I had only one magazine of ammo left (typically eighteen rounds). I had to crawl over the dead bodies of both the enemy and our own men. When I got to the end of the ditch, one of the enemy dead made a grunting noise. Thinking he was alive, I opened up on him making him grunt more and wasting valuable ammo. I laid next to him for what seemed like forever, and he continued to make grunting noises freaking me out! It was either stay next to him or crawl back to the front of the ditch. I decided to stay next to the grunting dead enemy.

I was perhaps ten yards away from the other two survivors who were not firing but like me waiting to see what we would do next. One of the guys had the radio but apparently it no longer worked. Thus no one even knew if we were alive. Occasionally, one of us would stick up our heads to see what the enemy was doing. Mostly we could see nothing and the artillery/mortars continued to drop round in their general area.

It continued to get dark. It gets dark very quickly in the tropics. One of the guys looked over the berm and began to frantically indicate that the enemy was advancing on our position. I had a few rounds left, and the others were either out or had only a few rounds left. I also had several grenades which I always carried. However, they would be useless against AKs and machine guns as I would be cut down as soon as I rose up to throw a grenade. We all looked at each other and crawled together. Everyone agreed that we should make a run for it as we didn't have a chance otherwise. For some reason, I grabbed the radio as we had always been told to save the radio. That was a bad mistake.

All of this took only seconds, and we jumped up and began running for the company perhaps a quarter of a mile away (it seemed like a very long way to us). They had settled into a night laager position where they circled the APCs, dug in and put out the typical three concertina barbed wire protections. We could see the NVA approaching our position in a line firing as they came on to us. We ran like hell moving side to side to make it more difficult to hit us. I was running as fast as I ever have run in my life. I could feel the bullets hit the ground near me and wiz by. I felt like the radio was drawing more fire at me so I threw it up in the air making sure that the enemy saw me get rid of the radio. I never missed a step while doing so. We covered about a third of the way to our lines when one of the soldiers running next to me went down. I kept running thinking he was killed and if I stopped I would quickly join him. I don't know where the other soldier was except he was not keeping up with me. Amazingly, I was getting close to our company night laager. It was still light enough for them to see we were GIs, but not wanting to take a chance I was yelling, "Don't shoot! Don't shoot! We're Fucking Americans!" No one but an American can curse like that. I did not want to get shot by one of our trigger happy soldiers as we were so full of mud and blood that no one could tell the difference between us and the enemy.

As I ran toward the barbed wire line (which was piled three high-two rolls on the bottom and one on top) at top speed and I didn't even slow down. I simply jumped head first over the wire and then got up and kept going until I reached the middle of the night laager. Both of the other two soldiers had also made it back to our line, including the soldier who was shot next to me. Apparently he had been shot through the shoulder. It had knocked him down, but his adrenaline was so high, he simply got up and began running back to the company, arriving shortly after the other soldier and I arrived.

Once safely behind our lines I collapsed trying to catch my breath. I was dehydrated and could hardly speak as my throat was so dry. Someone handed me a canteen for a much needed drink. I wasn't back in our lines two minutes and Captain Glory came strutting up to me with some of his HQ staff in tow. I was still sitting on the ground as he hovered over me and said something like "Where is my radio!" I was so angry I couldn't see straight and didn't give a damn about Captain Glory or the army at that point. Here was the SOB who left us to die, and all he cared about was the damn radio. I looked up at him and said, "You want the fucking radio, then you go get it!" Then I got up and walked away cursing at the SOB. He didn't say anything after that and I went looking for my track so I could collapse in peace! I had had it!

Some forty-plus years later when I met Tom Foster, it turns out that he too was in this battle and remembers the attack on the farmhouse. He recalled it being blown up with the 90 mm, and he was also caught in the ambush while advancing across the field. However, his squad came back to rescue him with his APC and thus he was able to retreat and join the rest of the company. An interesting fact is that Tom was the one who originally procured the 90 mm recoilless rifle for our company! His story of the battle follows:

Tom Foster Silver Star

Tom Foster remembers this battle well as he received a Silver Star (third highest medal in the military for Bravery) on this day. Tom was assaulting the tree line to the right of the farm house. He recalled when the farm house was blown up, but did not know that I had fired the 90 mm. Just as our squad was halted in our attack, Tom's squad was likewise devastated by the enemy automatic fire. We got about halfway across the field in our assault, and Tom and his squad got almost to the wood line where the enemy had dug in and had traversing machine gun fire on our platoon. In the assault, several of Tom's squad who were on the ground in front of the tracks were killed. During the assault, his platoon sergeant had frozen and was no longer able to direct the squad assault. Recognizing this, Tom took over command of the squad and continued the attack against the dug-in enemy fighting bunkers and trenches in the wood line. As Tom approached the wood line, his squad APC was halted, as both the track driver and track commander had been killed by the machine gun fire. The track sat idle in the field, yet remained unharmed. Tom realized that the attack had failed, and that the rest of the company had pulled back. He was not aware that our squad was likewise almost wiped out, and the few survivors had retreated back to the bomb craters and later to the farmhouse fighting ditches which the enemy had occupied. While Tom and his dysfunctional sergeant were pulling back from the wood line, a track charged the enemy bunkers, and the track commander told Tom to hop on! After loading his killed and wounded squad members into the track, Tom and the sergeant jumped on the track. Tom called in to the CO and gave him a status report about the failed attack and casualties. He was told to pull back with the rest of the company. He then made a fighting withdrawal from the open field. Later he was able to give the CO information on the disposition of the enemy troops in the wood line which he had approached closer than anyone else in the company. As a result the CO was able to adjust the company mortars to land on the enemy trench line and bunkers rather than behind them, where they were falling during the assault. The award of the Silver Star better describes the valiant actions Tom took that day. See adjacent award.

DEPARTMENT OF THE ARMY
HEADQUARTERS, 25TH INFANTRY DIVISION
APO San Francisco 96225

GENERAL ORDERS
NUMBER 4583

25 June 1968

AWARD OF THE SILVER STAR

1. TC 320. The following AWARD is announced.

FOSTER, THOMAS L. US54811460 (SSAN: 327-36-9676) SP4 E4
Co A, 4th Bn, 23d Inf, 25th Inf Div
Awarded: Silver Star
Date action: 28 April 1968
Theater: Republic of Vietnam
Reason: For gallantry in action: Specialist Four Foster distinguished himself by heroic actions on 28 April 1968, while serving with Company A, 4th Battalion, 23d Infantry on a combat operation in the Republic of Vietnam. When his unit came under intense enemy fire, Specialist Foster took command of his platoon after all of its leaders had been wounded. He fearlessly rallied his men and organized them to continue the attack against the enemy. Exposing himself many times to the intense enemy fire, Specialist Foster directed the fire of his men, then climbed on the platoon's command personnel carrier to give a situation report to the company commander. He supplied his men with ammunition, directed the evacuation of the wounded, and finally directed the platoon in a withdrawal at the order of the Company Commander. Specialist Foster's personal bravery, aggressiveness, and devotion to duty are in keeping with the highest traditions of the military service and reflect great credit upon himself, his unit, the 25th Infantry Division and the United States Army.
Authority: By direction of the President under the provisions of Executive Order 11046, dated 24 August 1962, and USARV message 16695, dated 1 July 1966.

FOR THE COMMANDER:

OFFICIAL:

Clarence A. Riser

CLARENCE A. RISER
LTC, AGC
Adjutant General

B. F. HOOD
Colonel, GS
Chief of Staff

DISTRIBUTION:
D (Modified) Plus
2-CO, 1st Bde, 25th Inf Div
3-CO, 4th Bn, 23d Inf
10-Act Br
1-Rec Br
4-Indiv cone
1-Div SGM
2-CG, USARV ATTN: AVHAG-PD

5-CG, II FFV ATTN: AXV-AGP APO 96225

SPECIAL DISTRIBUTION:
1-TAGO ATTN: AGPE-F

Award of the Silver Start to Tom Foster in the Fortified Farm House Battle

Strange Night Defensive Position Exit

Between May 1–5, 1968

One of the strangest incidents I experienced in Vietnam was in the first week of May 1968. Since joining A Company, I had been in constant combat. From the first day I joined the company and was blown off my track by a short round until I was wounded two weeks later. We had been in firefights all day when we broke off contact with the enemy and set up a night laager position. We stopped in an open field surrounded by heavy vegetation. When we set up a night defensive position we "circled the wagons" setting up a circle of APCs with bunkers built in between. Then we set up three rolls of concertina barbed wire in front of our position. It was exhausting work digging bunkers, filling sandbags and setting up barbed wire and trip flares after a day of fighting in 110- to 120-plus degrees temperature. Then we had to pull guard duty, man listening posts and go out on ambushes. We were always exhausted going around in kind of an infantry man's stupor twenty-four hours a day.

After setting up our position and digging in, I laid down next to the track in exhaustion. By this time it was late at night and pitch dark. In Vietnam there were no lights and the night came quickly and was very dark (especially in the jungle). I had fallen into a dead man's sleep when someone placed his hands over my mouth and looked into my eyes and put his finger over his lips. He motioned for me to get up and be quiet. I instantly was awake, thinking it was my turn for guard duty. He told me to mount up on the track as we were moving out. Moving out in the middle of the night was not good news! I asked what was up in a low voice, and he just put his finger to his lips, indicating to be silent. I gathered my gear and jumped on top of the track. Everyone else did likewise as the tracks were around us. It was very quiet. I asked one of the guys on top of our track who was looking through the starlight scope what was up. He handed me the starlight scope. When I looked through the starlight scope I was stunned! There, not twenty yards in front of our barbed wire, was what looked like a company-size attack force of NVA crawling up on our position!

The most amazing thing about this incident is that no one on either side opened fire on the other! The driver started up our APC and, along with the others, our company moved out. We left the wire and the bunkers behind as we drove away across the field. We did not open fire on the NVA and they did not fire one shot as we moved out. We had no idea what just happened. Later I heard that our platoon was told that there were gooks in the wire and not to fire, just load up quickly as we were moving out! No one on our track knew why or for what reason we did not open fire.

Later we drove for a while and caught up with a company of legs (regular infantry) who were hidden in a defensive position in a ravine. I believe the leg company was the Wolfhounds. We set up a night laager around them and stayed for the night. Nothing happened and we moved out at dawn. Later that day we got into another firefight, but without the leg infantry unit. None of us ever received an explanation of why we did not open fire on the NVA or why they did not fire on us. It made no sense to any of us as we had been heavily engaged in fighting the days before and after.

Years later when Tom Foster and I were discussing battles when he and I were in the 3rd platoon, he remembers the same incident. He also is at a loss as to what happened that night.

Never Too Much Ammo or Water

After being cut off at the farmhouse and running out of ammo, I decided that I would carry as much ammo as possible so I would never run out again. I would sacrifice carrying other things but never ammo or water. Without water in the tropics you would dehydrate very quickly and be ineffective. So we carried two canteens full of water plus decontamination pills in the event we were near a water source. Sometimes when it was very hot and we were on foot, I would go without my flak vest and even a helmet, but never without water, ammo and hand grenades. In working with tankers, I got one of them to give me a "tanker ammo magazine case" for their burb gun magazines (machine guns used by tankers). This ammo case was about 11 inches long by 5 1/2 inches wide and 3 inches thick and had both a shoulder strap and loop for connecting to a WEB belt. It was made of canvas material similar to that of a WEB belt, so it was very durable. It could hold twelve M-16 magazines of 18 rounds each or 216 rounds total. We only loaded 18 rounds in our magazines even thought they were designed to hold twenty rounds. With 18 rounds the magazines tended to feed better and keep the M-16 rifle from jamming. Magazines were loaded very quickly by using 10-round clips of 5.56 mm or M-16 ammunition and a loader device which hooked on top of the magazine. You simply placed the loader on top of the magazine, then connected the ammunition holder, and pressed down with your thumb thus loading 10 rounds in the magazine. I carried this ammo case through my entire five months in the field.

In addition to the tanker ammo case full of M-16 preloaded magazines, I carried a standard pouch or sometime two which carried four additional preloaded magazines each, plus the magazine in my rifle. Then I would carry at least one and most times two or three bandoliers of M-16 ammo. Each of these M-16 bandoliers had seven pockets which held twenty 5.56 mm rounds each or a total of 140 bullets. In addition every soldier carried two 100-round bandoliers of machine gun bullets for the M-60 machine gunner. The machine gunner carried 800 to 1,000 rounds himself. This is what I carried when humping the M-60.

In addition to carrying bullets and magazines, I carried at least four and most times six hand grenades which I hung from my flak vest. There were loops to place six hand grenades on the chest of the vest. If we were in fights where I thought there would be enemy bunkers I would carry a LAW used to blow up bunkers. Thus I carried seventeen to twenty-one preloaded magazines of ammo for the M-16 bullets containing 306 to 378 bullets, plus another 140 to 420 M-16 bullets in bandoliers. Then I carried another 200 rounds of M-60 machine gun bullets and sometimes a LAW. We also used the claymore mine bags to carry extra clips and hand grenades if we were going in to attack a base camp with many bunkers and tunnels. As I mentioned we were loaded down with ammo and water because you did not want to run out. I rarely if ever carried my bayonet and traded off this weight for more bullets.

Stuck Behind a Termite Mound

May 1–5, 1968

We were once again sweeping a heavily wooded area without our tracks. We came to a deep depression or stream which precluded APCs from crossing as we did not have bridging equipment and the sides of the depression were too steep for the tracks to climb. So our squad and another squad were ordered to proceed ahead without the tracks on a reconnaissance mission. The others stayed behind with the tracks to provide security. There were only about ten to twelve men in the reconnaissance force. We were to continue searching for the enemy base camp and then disengage if we found the enemy and call in mortars and artillery. As usual we felt like bait. Of course the lieutenant stayed behind to "coordinate" support if or more likely when we got into trouble.

We had just crossed the depression and climbed up the steep sides and re-entered the heavily wooded forest. It is likely we were in the Ho Bo or Bo Loi Woods. Both of these heavily wooded areas were havens for the NVA. I was walking right point along with one other person walking off to my left with the others following. Typically in a full platoon formation three of us would walk point out front of the main body of the platoon. This time there were not enough of us to have three men up front. We proceeded slowly forward when I came upon an open meadow surrounded on all sides by woods. I stopped as this was a perfect place for an ambush. Most of us thought we should go no further but the platoon sergeant wanted us to proceed across the field. Several of us told the platoon sergeant crossing the field was a bad idea. He insisted, and the rest of the recon team got in a linear formation to cross the meadow. Inside the meadow there was sparse vegetation, a few trees and perhaps fifty-plus large termite mounds. Some of these were taller than a man. We didn't get very far into the meadow before someone on our team opened up on the wood line in front. He had seen some movement and opened fire or perhaps just wanted to see if any enemy was in the wood line. Either way, this was the signal for the NVA to open up on us with a machine gun and automatic weapons.

Instantly, we all hit the dirt and I got behind a large termite mound and began firing at the wood line, keeping our fire low so as not to shoot over the enemy heads. A bullet kicking up dirt in front of you tends to make you want to keep your head down, whereas bullets going over head do not. Bullets going over your head sound like angry hornets flying next to your ear. When they cut through the foliage overhead or your side it is not a secure feeling.

The sergeant immediately made hand signals to pull back, and his RTO (Radio Telephone Operator) was calling in for support on his Prick 25 radio (nickname for a PRC-25 Portable Radio). Some of the men immediately pulled back to the wood line where we had just emerged. The other half of us, including the platoon sergeant and RTO were pinned down in the field by the heavy automatic fire. Fortunately for us, it appeared that there was perhaps a half of a squad (five to six men) firing on us, but they had a machine gun. Thus it was unlikely they would assault us until they had reinforcements and determined how many of us there were. This was most likely an enemy outpost guarding a larger enemy base camp.

As the machine guns and automatic weapons swept the field they chopped down part of the termite mound I was taking cover behind. The bullets went through the mound and broke off large chunks as they passed through. Fortunately they were shooting high and I kept as low as possible behind the largest mass of the termite mound at the base. Unfortunately, as the mound was destroyed all of the termites came out crawling all over me and they were not too happy. Mad termites bite! So I was in a quandary, either stay where I was and get bitten by termites, or run for it and chance getting shot when I moved. After a while I couldn't take it anymore as the damn termites were all over me. There were millions of them. So when the enemy was firing at others in the recon team, who were likewise trying to retreat, I began crawling away to the next termite mound about twenty yards to my rear. Fortunately the brush was high enough to mask my movements so I made it to the next mound. The enemy must have thought I was still behind the larger termite mound, so every once in a while he would traverse and shoot up the mound again.

I didn't want to return fire since they would see where I was firing from and I had zero cover except for the termite mounds. I still had termites crawling all over and biting me. I couldn't get them all off of me while crawling and I was afraid to make too many movements as it would draw the enemy's attention! About that time our mortars began falling near the enemy. This was good news as the fire slackened. So I used this opportunity to speed up my crawling going from mound to mound. The mortars began to hit on top of the enemy as their fire was adjusted by our RTO. So I was able to move quickly along the ground until I got into the woods. There I positioned myself behind a fallen tree in a slight depression. Only then did I return fire and swat at the termites still biting me. They were still everywhere on my body, gear and clothes. I wasn't the only one either. Several of the others in the recon team also had the same experience as I with the termites. Those caught behind the termite mounds had termite bites all over. As we did not wear any underwear (it would cause chaffing when wet so we did not wear any), the termites got in some very uncomfortable places.

Fortunately no one was killed, just a bunch of us were lunch for termites. I don't even think anyone was wounded and if they were they were able to walk out on their own since we did not carry anyone out. After we returned no one went back to the field. It was simply pounded with mortars and as it was getting late, we boarded our tracks and returned to our night laager position.

Almost Crushed Between Trees

May 1–5, 1968

We were sweeping a heavy wooded or jungle area. The undergrowth, trees and vines were very thick. Because you could not see very far in the jungle, we were walking ahead of our APCs which were knocking down small trees and brush pushing through the jungle. I was walking to the right of our APC with other soldiers on either side of me. We were perhaps fifteen feet apart, but I could not see anyone else. I could hear them using jungle axes (a very heavy machete) to cut through the jungle and move ahead. I was likewise using a jungle axe, chopping my way through the undergrowth. I was trying to stay ahead of the tracks, which were getting closer since they were moving faster than the infantry on the ground. This was dangerous situation, in my opinion, as we would walk right up to an enemy bunker and not see it if it was three feet in front of us.

To avoid a large tree, the APC on my left shifted toward me. It was perhaps twenty feet away. I was concerned because they had the engines revved up to high speed so they could "climb" trees and push them over. The trees they were pushing over were getting too close for comfort. I was caught between the brush and jungle around me and the trees and brush the track was pushing over me. I tried to move to the side by chopping the jungle faster to move further way from the path of the APC. Unfortunately I was losing the battle. Then the track pushed over a large tree which came crashing down on top of the jungle undergrowth, pinning me between the branches and jungle brush. I was stuck, and the APC kept climbing the tree that was beginning to crush me! I was yelling at the top of my lungs, but the driver kept revving up the engine so he could not hear me. I thought I was going to get crushed to death. I had to do something quick or I was going to get crushed by the track. I thought my only chance is to fire at the APC to stop it. Unfortunately I was pinned to the tree branches and brush and could barely reach the trigger of my weapon, much less aim it. So I slipped off the safety (we always kept our weapons on safety unless we were firing) and fired a burst. Fortunately the barrel of my M-16 was facing downward so I didn't shoot anyone, but by that time I just wanted to stop being crushed. When my weapon fired, the track stopped and immediately backed up a few feet. They did not know I was being crushed, only that someone had fired and there was likely enemy close. This was a big concern to the APCs since they could be easily blown up by an RPG at such close range. Finally someone recognized that I was being crushed and came over to help. They had to hack away the tree branches and jungle brush to get me out from under this mess.

After I was extracted from my trap, I moved to the back of the APC and climbed on top. I was still hurting from being crushed in my chest and was in no mood to go ahead of the track again. I jumped up on the track and for the rest of the day rode on top. Needless to say the jungle was very thick, and all we did was mow down a bunch of jungle and wear out our troops in a worthless exercise. Yet again another misadventure directed by our leaders.

Soldier Bucked into a Bomb Crater

May 1–5 1968

We were operating in the same thick jungle area as the previous day when I was almost crushed by the APC. The jungle was too thick for APCs so we were operating apart from them in a different area. We were sweeping the area for a suspected enemy base camp. I was in the back of a column that was hacking its way through the jungle. We moved single file, since the vegetation was too thick to move in more than one column. Everyone took turns hacking through the jungle to make a path for the others following. You could only wield a jungle axe for about fifteen minutes and then you could not hold your arm up any longer, so the next person in line would take over. Everyone else followed. I believe we were only making about one click, or one thousand meters, in a full day of going through the jungle.

The word was passed for the doc up front. We were told to hold up because someone had been hurt. We had no idea of what had happened so we simply spread out on the path we had made and settled down for a drink of water or perhaps some C-Rats (you ate and drank when you could). Several men went forward including the doc (medic). We were then told to move forward and set up a defensive perimeter. As we moved forward we came upon a huge bomb crater perhaps thirty or forty feet deep. It was surrounded by jungle and you didn't see it until you were on top of it. It turned out the point man was cutting through the jungle and came upon the bomb crater. As he emerged from the jungle a deer bucked into him, knocking him into the bomb crater. The sides of the crater were very steep, and he fell rather hard into the bottom of the crater. He apparently broke some of his ribs in the fall and could not get out of the bomb crater unassisted. We had no ropes, nor did we carry a stretcher for wounded. So we set up a defensive perimeter around the bomb crater while our platoon lieutenant tried to figure out how to get the wounded soldier out. I went off into the jungle to set up a defensive perimeter with the others.

It took most of the day to get the soldier out of the bomb crater. I was not involved in the extraction, but was later told several men climbed down and more or less dragged the soldier out of it without ropes. There was simply too much jungle, and we had no tools to cut down enough of the jungle to bring in a dust off helicopter. So the soldier had to walk out of the jungle on his own, helped by a couple of soldiers. This must have been very painful with broken ribs. As far as I recall, the wounded soldier never returned to our unit in the field.

Firefight at the Hoc Mon Bridge Factory

May 1–5, 1968

We were sweeping Route 1 from the area of Tay Ninh south toward Saigon and Tan Son Nhut Air Base. As we approached the Hoc Mon Bridge we noticed many of the civilians running away from the area. As we approached the Hoc Mon Bridge, there was a destroyed factory off to the right hand side. One of our units was guarding the bridge and told our lieutenant that there were enemy soldiers firing at them from the destroyed factory. So we proceeded over the bridge and dismounted. We immediately began taking small arms fire from the factory. From what we heard, this was a textile factory which was destroyed during the Tet attacks earlier in the year. Much of the factory was still standing, but it was in ruins. It was a very large concrete and brick structure by Vietnamese standards. We proceeded to assault the factory with our tracks providing cover with their .50-caliber machine guns. This was the first time I had ever fought in an urban environment. The ruins provided cover for the enemy and we did not know where he was hiding. Apparently there were not very many enemy soldiers in the ruins so the fight was not a large affair, but there were a lot of rooms and hiding places for the enemy to conceal himself and fire at us. After a short firefight we continued to carefully and methodically comb through the ruins where we discovered several enemy dead. The rest appeared to have retreated when we assaulted. We continued searching through the ruins but found no other enemy nor did we receive any further incoming enemy fire. The firefight and searching the factory had taken the better part of the day. By this time it was late afternoon so we policed up the enemy weapons and mounted our tracks. We then moved down Route 1 to our FSB north toward Tay Ninh.

Author riding on APC "running the roads"

Wounded the First Time

May 6, 1968

Since joining my unit I had been in constant combat for two weeks. Every day I thought it would be my last day! Apparently everyone else in the line felt the same way. Every day more and more of our company were killed or wounded. While I was there I don't recall any new replacements in our platoon. We were just being ground down day-after-day with no end in sight. It was just a matter of time before it was your turn. The odds would eventually catch up with you. Every day and every night we were sleep deprived, low on food (we ate only C-Rations or CRATS), tired, worn out and scared stiff.

On the morning of May 6th we gathered our gear and prepared for another attack on the enemy who was dug into fortified positions. We broke down our night laager positions, packed up the barbwire and metal mats used to cover our night defensive positions, emptied sandbags and loaded our gear into the tracks. Then we jumped up onto the track to move out.

We rode our tracks through relatively open fields with hedgerows and tree lines breaking up the landscape. In the distance we could see artillery strikes hitting the enemy positions. That is where we would be headed. We moved onto an open field where we were told to dismount and prepare to attack in line toward a tree line perhaps a half a mile or so away. Artillery was still striking the tree line, tearing up trees and earth with huge explosions and filling the air with smoke and debris. The artillery stopped, which was our signal to advance. The company formed into squads and platoons and made a line, our typical attack formation. We walked straight toward the enemy—a full frontal assault, which seemed to us the only formation that Captain Glory knew how to execute. Of course this made all of us upright targets for the enemy. From our perspective, we believed it was idiotic for us to attack frontally in a straight line, making it easier for the NVA to fire machine guns at us, sweeping laterally side to side. We were taught in our infantry training not to attack frontally, especially standing up, but rather to go around the flanks of the enemy to get at his flanks and rear. We were also to advance under cover using the terrain to protect us. But, of course, Captain Glory remained behind us a safe distance away. He had us approach frontally standing straight up firing as we went and, of course, taking casualties along the way. But in the end, with our massive firepower, we would overrun the enemy. At least that was the theory. Unfortunately for us it didn't always work that way, and often we were sitting ducks in the middle of a battlefield with no cover fighting a dug in enemy. We only found out how many of the enemy survived the shelling when they opened fire on us as we approached their fortified positions. Most of the time, we could not even see the enemy until we walked up on their bunkers. By that time it, of course, was too late.

As always, my stomach was in my throat as we walked alongside the tracks in a line. When we began receiving enemy fire, the tracks opened up with their 50s with devastating fire directed at the wood line. We could not see the enemy but we knew he was there in the tree line in fortified positions. As we got closer we began firing all our weapons at the tree line. The massive fire, with the whole company firing every weapon as we advanced, tended to keep the enemy's head down, giving us a chance to advance. Eventually we overran the enemy positions.

I approached the tree line that had been chewed up by the artillery. However, most of the covered bunkers remained essentially intact. I could see several covered bunkers with a trench connecting them together. Typically in such a situation, you could only see a few yards to either side of you as you approached the tree line. The closer you progressed to the tree line, the smaller your field of vision.

There were two soldiers on either side of me firing into the bunkers. As I carried four to six grenades I used these quite frequently to clear out any holes or bunkers. Better to be safe than sorry as I had seen too many enemy pop out of spider holes after our troops passed and shoot them in the back. Throwing grenades from further away was a good opportunity to kill anyone in the bunker before I got any closer. However, unlike other soldiers, I did not "cook off" the hand grenade by holding it two seconds before throwing it. Some of the veteran soldiers did as they had seen the enemy throw grenades back at them, but I was more concerned that it would go off in my hand before I got rid of it. I reasoned that it was made by government contractors who may have had a bad day and cut the fuse too short. So we continued to advance toward the bunker being careful to stay down low just in case. We were sure there were enemy in the bunker waiting for us to get close. I advanced to within hand grenade range, pulled the pin on one of my grenades, yelled, "Fire in the hole," a warning for everyone near me to get down, and threw the grenade into the opening of the enemy bunker. As I threw the grenade, I "hit the deck," which was SOP. To my shock, as I was dropping to the ground, I saw my grenade coming back out of the bunker toward me. I had time to think, "Oh shit," then the grenade blew up directly in front of me!

The explosion threw me back, knocked off my helmet, and blew away my rifle and some of my gear. I also think it knocked me out, but for how long I don't know. The real shock was when I came too and could not see! I thought I was blind forever. I felt blood on my face and eyes and along with everything else was hurting everywhere. As I was feeling myself to see where else I was hurt, someone came along and grabbed my arm and asked if I was OK. I said I didn't know except I am blind. He said we have to get out of here, and then asked if I could stand. I said I would try. My legs were a bit wobbly, but I stood up; however the loss of my eyesight was what scared me the most. I could see light but not much else, and it hurt to open my eyes. The battle continued all around us with lots of noise and explosions. The trooper led me away and we went crashing through the brush falling several times as I could not see.

We arrived at a track where a medic took over and the troop who led me there left. I don't recall his name or even where he came from but I was sure glad someone was around to help guide me back to our tracks. Being blind in a battle is a death sentence.

I sat down leaning against one of the tracks while the battle continued. The medic poured water over my face, checked my eyes and gave me a quick look over, and said I would be OK. He wiped the blood off my face and placed a bandage around my eyes. He said not to take it off as my eyes could be damaged further. I asked if I would be blind, and he said it is likely only a flash blindness and that it did not look serious. He said to just keep my eyes shut until I got to the hospital. I was not sure if I believed him as medics always told you that you would be OK even if they didn't believe it. He said the other wounds were superficial and that he had to go, but I would be dusted off as soon as the next chopper came in for the wounded. Then he moved on to other wounded.

As I was leaning against the track, I could hear several other wounded being brought in and placed around me. The sun was punishing and the heat of the track was burning against my back. Periodically

I would lean away from it; but I stayed where I was so that I would not be run over by another track.

I don't know how long I was there, but while I was thinking the worst about my eyesight several machine gun bullets ripped across the track just above my head. I was hit by several splinters from the rounds coming from the track armor (it was aluminum). I immediately forgot about my eyes and hit the dirt and began crawling around the track treads and under the track. One of the other wounded crawled alongside me as we took shelter under the track. Several rounds hit around us and on the track treads and side. We stayed there for a while until someone yelled for us to come out as the medevac chopper was landing.

I was then led to the dust off chopper, and sat down on the floor while other wounded were loaded onto the chopper. It was a short ride of perhaps fifteen or twenty minutes to the base camp. I didn't know it at the time, but we were flown to the 45th Surgical Hospital in Tay Ninh.

When we arrived at the Tay Ninh Hospital, I held on to the arm of one of the medics who led me into an air-conditioned building where he sat me down on the floor and told me to wait. The building was cold and I was freezing as I only had on my flak vest with no shirt. Obviously I was not used to air conditioning.

Someone came along and asked me a few questions, looked under my bandages, and told me to wait. Later someone else came along and gave me a drink of water but it likely had a sedative in it. I believe he also tagged me as he tied something to my flak vest. Obviously there were many other wounded that needed more attention than I did. At least that was good news. I must have dozed off to sleep because I don't remember much clearly after that. I vaguely remember being taken into another room and lying on a cold metal table but not much else.

The next thing I remember was waking up in a cool ward under blankets. I still had bandages around my eyes but I could at least see some light through the bandages. I remember having to go to the bathroom really bad. I called out for someone to help me go to the bathroom, and to my surprise a women came to my bedside and asked what I needed. I told her I had to take a leak really bad. She laughed and that made me feel better. I had not seen a female since leaving the USA.

She led me by the arm to an outhouse and told me that my chart said that I was to keep the bandages on until a doctor examined my eyes. My right eye felt like it had gravel in it and was very uncomfortable. Generally I felt like an old man when I moved. The female nurse was very nice and talked to me as she walked me back to my ward. My left eye recovered and I could see fine, but my right eye was still swollen and hurt like heck.

Sometime later that day, a doctor or medic came around and told me I was very lucky as the grenade hit me in the nose, took out a chunk of flesh and cut my right eyelid. He believed it only grazed my cornea. He also said my eyesight should recover in a few days, but that I had to take it easy and not touch my eyes. He gave me some pills and I went back to sleep.

After a few days in the hospital I was sent back to my unit base camp by jeep. My right eye still hurt and was still swollen, so I was placed on light duty and restricted to our company area in Tay Ninh Base Camp. Later my eyesight got better, and they removed the stitches in my right eyelid. It hurt like hell to have the stiches removed, and I was scared to death the medic would poke me in the eye with the tweezers. I stayed in base camp a few days and then was to be sent back to the field as our company was engaged in battles and needed every man. Several others who had been wounded were in our base camp recovering, and the first sergeant was sending us all back saying we could have light duty in the field. Light duty in the field meant we could ride on the tracks and did not have to go out on ambush, but otherwise we did everything everyone else did. There were just too few us in the field and they needed everyone who could fire a weapon.

I continued to have trouble with my right eye for some time as I had difficulty focusing. This was not a good thing for an infantryman, but they needed me so badly they didn't care. After many complaints to my lieutenant and the doctor who came to the field periodically, I was eventually fitted with glasses. I have worn glasses ever since. The eyesight in my right eye kept improving for many years afterward until my late fifties.

Odds of Being a Casualty

A post war analysis of killed and wounded showed that there were several factors which determined the probability of being killed or wounded. These factors were the following:

- Location in Vietnam
- Dates of Service
- Grade/rank
- Military Occupational Status (MOS)
- Unit assignment

As it turns out, I hit on all of these categories as an enlisted infantryman with an MOS of 11Bravo (enlisted light weapons infantryman). Some 73% (in 1968 some 90% of causalities were 11B infantrymen) of all battle deaths were suffered by this MOS. This is logical when one considers that at the time I served, the US Army had some 350 different MOS types including 11Bravo infantrymen. Consider that only one in ten who served in Vietnam was in a "maneuver unit" in the field. This category included: armor and mechanized soldiers, artillery, drivers, radiomen, mortar men (11C MOS), combat engineers, helicopter flight crews, officers, and finally enlisted infantry (11 Bravo MOS). My estimate is that less than half of those serving in these capacities were 11Bravo or enlisted light weapons infantry. Thus 11Bs represented only around 5%–6% of those who served in combat in Vietnam. It has been estimated that there were never more than 40,000 soldiers of all types in the field fighting the enemy, even at the peak of the war in January 1969. This month represented the highest troop levels in the Vietnam War where some 549,500 USA troops of all services were in the theater. 1968, while I was in the field, was the worst year for casualties, numbering some 14,589 battle deaths or 30.9% of the total war. May 1968 the worst month with 2,444 USA killed and 7,602 wounded, including me! Over 86% of those who were killed in the entire war were enlisted men of a rank E-1 to E-9. I was an E-4 grade. The 25th infantry division had the most battle casualties of any army Unit in Vietnam with 34,484 casualties during the war. The mechanized infantry took some of the highest casualties since they covered much more ground than regular infantry and were used to rescue other units. Our location in III Corps in 1968 took some of the highest casualties, second only to I Corp where the marines operated and had higher casualties. The rate of army maneuver battalions killed per average annual operating strength for the periods I served was as follows:

- April–June 1968..............123.8
- July–September 1968.........79.7

These statistics tell only part of the story as they include only those killed in battle! If wounded were included, these statics would be many times higher. The above analysis excludes the wounded, which had a ratio of 6.4 wounded for every soldier killed in battle.

The time I served in Vietnam was during the years with the highest battle casualties. As stated earlier, 1968 alone accounted for almost 31% of all battle deaths for the entire war (14,589). 1969 was the second-highest year for battle deaths with 9,414. Together these two years accounted for almost 51% of all battle deaths for the entire war. Thus the time you served in Vietnam made a significant difference in your odds of being a casualty.

Arc Light B-52 Air Strikes

Almost the entire time I was in Vietnam there were air strikes from the massive B-52 bombers in our Area of Operations (AO). While I was in the field I recall these happening twice a day. You could hear these from twenty miles away and feel the earth shake from the explosions. Sometimes we were so close to these air strikes that you could see and feel them when the bombs impacted. On one occasion we were sweeping an open field mounted on our tracks moving toward a wood line perhaps a half a mile away. As usual we were told nothing about the mission. As we entered the field we were told to hold up and dismount.

We did as ordered not knowing what was going on (typical situation for us). Once we were on the ground we were told we needed to holdup here as B-52 strikes were up ahead.

We had taken up defensive positions around the tracks in a U-shape with the tracks facing outward in case of enemy assault. We took up positions on the ground not very concerned about attacks or the B-52 strikes which we assumed would be far away. About a half an hour later we saw the B-52 bombs hitting less than one click (one thousand yards) or a half mile away. To us it seemed like it was on top of us! You could see the massive explosions from the bombs and actually see the shock wave coming toward us. We all got down very quickly and took cover. I got behind the berm I was leaning against. This was far too close to our position from our perspective. We had never been this close to a B-52 bomb run. I watched until the shock wave hit us then got my head down and opened my mouth and held onto my helmet. The noise from the explosions was terrible and the blast threw chunks of debris flying in all directions including ours. The earth shook like an earthquake. It seemed to me it would never end. Fortunately they were dropping bombs away from us, because if it was toward us, I would not be here to tell the story. Of course, at the time, we had no clue where the bombs were going to hit. You could not hear nor see the planes, just the bombs hitting constantly for a very long time. It was scary as hell, and I thought "Thank God I am not an NVA." I prayed that they would not drop bombs on us.

After the bombs stopped no one was anxious to move just in case more bombs would fall. It was obvious to everyone that someone had screwed up. We were far too close to the air strike and we all knew it. Once again it seemed that everyone and everything was out to get us. We all just looked around at each other not saying anything and trying to clear our ears. We stayed there perhaps a half to three quarters of an hour waiting for the dust to clear. I assume our CO also spoke to someone about the close call. Of course no one ever explained to us what had happened or why. After all we were simply enlisted men expected to do what we were told, no questions asked. After a while we were told to mount up as we were moving out. Everyone was asking each other, "What the f——k was that!" indicating a close call, at least from our perspective.

Soon we mounted up and continued moving toward the tree line in front of where the bombs had exploded. As we moved through the woods we encountered more and more trees which had been knocked down by the blasts. Soon our track could go no further due to the knocked down trees. Apparently we were to sweep the area for enemy which based on what we saw was idiotic. No one or anything else could live through that bombing. But we moved ahead on foot climbing or trying to go around the downed trees and debris. After going through increasing destruction we came upon a scene of utter desolation as far as we could see. There were bomb craters back-to-back some thirty to forty feet deep and perhaps fifty yards in circumference. The area was devoid of any vegetation, just dirt and debris throw up everywhere anyone looked. We walked about the bomb craters for a while until someone finally realized we were going to find nothing. Then we were ordered back to our tracks, which had returned to the field we had crossed in a defensive circle. We mounted up having accomplished nothing at all and moved out on the tracks to sweep another area on our way back to our night laager position. We never heard another word about this screw up, and I am sure no one ever reported it to anyone higher than our battalion, nor was anyone likely held accountable. Just another day for the infantry where we all believed no one gave a damn about what happened to us or how we were used. We were expendable in the eyes of the army and at the mercy, not only of the enemy, but of our own side. Mistakes by our officers and support personnel ended up killing and maiming us.

B-52 Ark Light Strikes

B-52D Stratofortresses were massive bombers which could carry in excess of 35 tons of bombs. A typical bomb load could hold 108 500-pound bombs inside its bomb bay and 24 750-pound bombs on its wings. They flew to Vietnam, Laos, and Cambodia from Anderson

AFB in Guam to drop their load. They bombed from high altitudes so you could not see them coming. A three-plane cell of B-52 bombers could destroy everything in a three square kilometer area (almost two square miles) in one bombing run. In 1968 B-52's conducted 1,800 sorties a month over Vietnam, Laos and Cambodia. Many of these bombings took place in our area of operation (AO) or the adjoining Ho Chi Minh trail leading into our AOs. They were so accurate that they were allowed to bomb within 1,000 meters of friendly troops!

"Volunteered" to Become a Helicopter Door Gunner

May 9–10

While I was in the hospital one of the wounded men in my ward told me that the helicopter unit in the 25th Division was looking for soldiers to "volunteer" to become door gunners. I thought anything was better than being out in the field fighting. This was my chance to get out of the infantry. I viewed being a door gunner as a real step up from walking around and living in the bush fighting about every day. Remember, I was only out in the field for two weeks and I had been blown off my track by a short round, hit in the back with an enemy .51-caliber spent round, crushed by an APC, and blown up by my own hand grenade. That plus we had been in a firefight with the enemy every day I was in the field. It sure seemed to me that volunteering to be a door gunner was a cake walk job compared to the two weeks of hell I experienced fighting in the mechanized infantry.

When I got back to Alpha Company area to convalesce after being released from the hospital (Mash unit), I reported to our new company clerk who I had not met before. After reporting in with the company clerk, I turned to the top sergeant who was sitting in a desk on the other side of the room and said, "Top, I want to volunteer to become a door gunner." He looked up at me and smiled. He said nothing for a moment and then replied, "Well, that's great. You and every other grunt in this unit would like a cake job like that. Just because you were wounded doesn't give you the right to get out of this unit. Why, we have men who have been wounded two and three times and are still humping in the boonies. You need to pay your dues before you get a job in the rear, son." I said, "But I understand if you volunteer you can get the job." He laughed and said, "You can volunteer all you want but you're not getting out of this unit. There are only two ways out of Alpha, in a body bag or on a stretcher! So stop wasting my time and get out of here." With that he went back to doing his paperwork. I was crushed. I thought for sure when the army asked for volunteers and you volunteered, you automatically got the assignment. So I went back to my hooch depressed and dreading going back out to the fighting. I felt that my odds of making it out alive were slim to none given what I had been through in two weeks.

Stateside "Top" Sergeant Fragged

May 10–11, 1968

For those soldiers in the infantry who were not severely wounded enough to be evacuated out of country to Japan or other hospitals outside of Vietnam, they were returned to their units in base camp. For slightly wounded soldiers they were often treated by medics in the field and continued on with their duties. In our unit we were so short of men that you had to be hurt enough where you could no longer function to be evacuated out of the field. We even had medical officers come to the FSBs to stitch-up wounded men, change bandages, treat illnesses, and do medical evaluations all in an attempt to keep soldiers in the field, rather than have them go back to base camp for treatment. We were that critically short of infantry.

In my case I was one of the wounded who was not wounded badly enough for evacuation, but hurt too bad to return to duty in the field. I needed to fully recover my eye sight and eventually required glasses to correct my vision (the only long term result of my wounds I still have today, plus ringing in my ears). For wounded soldiers like me we were released from the hospital as soon as possible to make room for the newly wounded soldiers. Thus we were sent back to our units in base camp. There we would recuperate, go for outpatient treatment at the base camp medical facility and pull light duty. Light duty typically meant manning the perimeter bunkers at night to pull base security and do various light duty jobs around the post. Some of the more seriously wounded men did nothing at all except to recuperate in our base camp area until well enough to go back to the field.

In our company, our top sergeant, the most senior NCO in our company, did all he could to let the wounded men recuperate in peace and to get them off of any duties which were not absolutely necessary, such as guarding the perimeter if fit enough. He did not call for formations or any other "chicken shit" army regulations. We could dress anyway comfortable to us (e.g., no shirts or helmets) so we could recuperate faster and be as comfortable as possible in the heat and weather. At base camp we were able to sleep in cots and stay out of the weather in wood framed hooches with screens to keep out the bugs and tin roofs to keep out the rain. We also got to eat real army chow in a mess hall complete with picnic style wooden tables and benches. This was a real luxury for field infantrymen. The rest of the day was ours to spend how we wanted except for those who had duties.

About this time our top sergeant was rotating back to the States and a new top sergeant came to replace him. As there were so few of us left in the base camp, some simply said goodbye to the top and others ignored his leaving. He was always respectful to me, so I think I was one of the men who said goodbye to him. Most of us met the new top when the old top was showing him around the company area. At the time I didn't think much of the change since the top sergeant mostly operated out of the base camp and not in the field with us. The new top sergeant was obviously fresh from duty in the states and, as it turned out, full of the only way he knew, which was stateside regulations. He would quickly learn that this was not how things worked in Vietnam! At first light on his first day in command we were awakened by him coming into our barracks kicking our bunks and yelling for everyone to "get your asses up and into formation, now!" I guess this was the "Stateside way" of showing everyone who was boss. Everyone stumbled out of bed wondering what was going on. We looked like a raggedy bunch of mercenaries with a variety of uniforms none of which were regulation, flip flops instead of shoes and with perhaps half the men even carrying their weapons. Most of the men had bandages or slings on their bodies or were walking with the aid of canes. None of the men was in any shape for field duty. Some not even suited for bunker guard duty as they could not hold weapons with their arms in slings or walking on crutches. There were about fifteen or so recovering wounded men in Alpha Company base camp at the time.

The new top started out dressing us down, saying something like "I have never seen such a raggedy bunch of soldiers in my twenty-five years in this man's army. You call yourselves soldiers? Look at you, you sorry-ass excuse for United States soldiers," and so on and so on. Then he told everyone that he was having a new formation in 030 minutes and that everyone was to get into full uniforms and gear and report for inspection. No one could believe it. Many of us didn't even have full uniforms as much of our gear was either destroyed when our tracks were blown up or it was left in the field when we were "dusted off" (flown by medical evacuation helicopters to the nearest Medical Evacuation Unit). Most of the men, including myself spoke up that we were all wounded, didn't have all our gear, and that we were on medical light duty and never had to go to formation before. It didn't matter to the new top. He said, "Fall out and be back here in 0030 minutes in the most complete uniforms and gear you have, then we will get you the rest of your gear so you can look like soldiers." There was a lot of grumbling between the men. I heard several talking about how "this shit is not going to stand" and "we will show this son of a bitch what it means to be wounded" and "fuck this shit, I am not putting up with stateside chicken shit from some fucking lifer" and so on. I was not very happy myself and thought that this guy needs a reality check.

Thirty minutes later a few wounded men were lined up in formation. Some others purposely wandered in late. No one, not one wounded soldier, showed up with a full uniform or his field WEB gear. The only soldiers dressed in full uniforms with their weapons were the handful of company house cats (armorer, supply sergeant, company clerk, Sierra Bravo, and cooks). It was an understanding of the wounded men that none of us was going to show up with our uniforms and gear even if we had them. Most everyone carried a rifle which was loaded with a magazine. Some of the men even chambered a round in case the new top inspected their weapons. It was against base camp rules to chamber a round unless you were on the perimeter or under attack. Seeing this motley crew assemble in defiance of his orders the new top flew into a rage. Yelling at us and once again dressing us down. No one except for the house cats either paid much attention or looked worried in the least. After all what was he going to do to us, send us back to the field? All of these men had seen combat and we noticed that our new top sergeant did not even have a CIB (combat infantryman badge which is only awarded to soldiers who had been in combat). Some of these men, like our Serra Bravo, a large Hispanic soldier had been wounded three times. In our division soldiers wounded three times with at least forty-eight hours in the hospital were allowed to be assigned to other duties outside the infantry. All of the wounded were veterans of fierce fighting and not feeling very well at the moment.

With little choice and lots of threats the new top sergeant warned, "Tomorrow will be different. Anyone not showing up in full uniforms and gear will be given an Article 15!" An Article 15 was a company punishment short of a military court-martial administered by the company CO or, in some cases, the executive officer (officer second in command of a company) when the CO was not available. Then he dismissed everyone and walked off. Again several of the men made comments like "We will see about that" and "This son of a bitch needs to learn his lesson." Later that evening or early the next morning while everyone was asleep, I awoke to an explosion of a hand grenade very close to my hooch. I woke up grabbing my rifle, chambered around, and grabbed several hand grenades out of the crate of grenades I kept by the side of my bed. Several of the other men did the same as we hit the floor and tried to figure out what was happening. At first I thought enemy sappers had gotten into our company area because it was a hand grenade and not a mortar or rocket, but one of the other guys in our hooch thought someone had fragged (thrown a hand grenade under the top sergeant's hooch) the new top sergeant. Almost immediately we heard someone calling for a medic and others milling around outside. So we pulled on our boots and went outside. By now we all realized someone had fragged the new top sergeant. As we did not have a medic, someone got the company jeep while others were pulling the wreckage of the hooch off the unfortunate top sergeant. As it turned out, he was alive but bleeding from several fragmentation wounds and in shock. Several men carried him into the jeep, and they took off for the evacuation hospital not too far from our company area. As the men were carrying the now wounded top sergeant to the jeep, I heard several men say, "Now you will see how it feels to be wounded!"

Anyway, the top sergeant never returned to our company. Either that day or the next, some officer from the brigade came around and asked each of us questions about the incident, but of course nobody knew anything about anything. Nothing ever came of the incident, and no one was ever accused of the fragging, nor was anyone punished. The next day we were told by the XO (executive officer) that there would be no more formations. Things went back to normal. I don't recall when a replacement top sergeant came to Alpha Company, but I believe it was after I was back in the field. No one ever heard another word about the old top sergeant or how he fared from the fragging. However, from what I saw, his wounds were not life threatening. He likely was shipped out to some "house cat" company where his military chicken shit would be accepted. You can be sure that he did not go back to a line or infantry unit.

New Company Commander Takes Over Alpha

May 10–May 12, 1968

I was recuperating from my wounds back in Alpha Company base camp when we got the news that our company commander, the hated Captain Glory, had left and a new company commander had assumed command. The rumor back in camp was that Captain Glory had more or less gone a bit off his rocker when his RTO was killed by either an RPG or mortar round. Apparently this was too much for Captain Glory, and he either asked to be relieved or was relieved, or it was his time to rotate anyway. I never did get the story straight. Most of us thought that Captain Glory was crazy anyway, and for sure he did not give a damn about how many of us got killed. We knew nothing of our new CO but anyone would be better than Captain Glory.

As it turned out our new captain was very different from Captain Glory. His name was Captain Henry Montgomery. Unlike his predecessor, he was not as aggressive nor was he as reckless with our lives. Apparently he cared more about his men than making a name for himself or getting promoted. According to Lieutenant Colonel Neilson's diary notes, he states, "During my 6 months in command I had 8 Captain line company commanders. Montgomery served the longest under me and was a soldier's soldier. Of the eight, he was the most careful of his men's lives and the hardest one to convince that I really wanted him to put the men of A Co. in danger's path." This rebuke by the lieutenant colonel is a testament to how different Captain Montgomery was to Captain Glory. Believe me, we all appreciated having Captain Montgomery as our new CO. Even though we had some very difficult battles ahead of us and we had many of our company killed and wounded after Captain Montgomery took over, he was a far better officer caring for his men than Glory. I served under Captain Montgomery for the duration of my time in the field (until September 13, 1968), unless he was on R&R as in the case of the battle of Tay Ninh or absent for some other reason.

Massacre on Nui Ba Den Mountain

May 13 and 14, 1968

Nui Ba Den Mountain

Nui Ba Den Mountain, or the Black Virgin Mountain, was a unique feature on the mostly flat area around Tay Ninh. It towered 3,232 feet over the plain of Tay Ninh providence. It was honeycombed with NVA tunnels with the Americans on the top and around the base of the mountain. The top of the mountain was a fortified American communications camp. There were bunkers around the perimeter and several buildings, a water basin to catch water, generators and a communications center. At the base of the mountain there was the Rock Crusher which was basically a quarry used by the Americans to line roads and culverts with gravel and rock. Our unit helped to guard the Rock Crusher and the roads which ran by the mountain. To the west of the mountain was French Fort or FSB Santa Barbara, up Route 4 guarding the way to Cambodia. At the base of the mountain running along-side the road to French Fort was a banana grove which made an ideal hiding place for enemy ambushes.

While the men on "light duty" who were recovering from wounds were preparing to return to the field with our unit, the outpost on top of the Black Virgin Mountain, or Nui Ba Den, was attacked and overrun by NVA troops the night of May 13, 1968. The next day as we were to proceed to the field to join our unit, we were quickly gathered together and told we would be part of a task force to "take back the mountain." As we were all on light duty, none of us felt up to being dropped by helicopter into an enemy held fortified outpost where our soldiers were "wiped out" the night before! We would also be going into battle with a temporary task force, where we did not know anyone and had no idea of how we were being supported. Many USA soldiers had been killed around the Black Virgin Mountain, and it had a very bad reputation with our unit.

In spite of our complaint to the executive officer that we were still on light duty, he ordered us to the landing strip where we would be helicoptered onto the top of the mountain. We were told we were to load up on trucks in five minutes and take only ammo and water in preparation for a battle. We all scrambled to get our gear ready and loaded up with bullets, grenades and LAWs for blowing bunkers, plus the necessary two canteens of water.

We were driven to the Tay Ninh landing strip on deuce and a half trucks where we unloaded. Some of the men in our company still had wounds bandaged and even arm slings. We joined a group of soldiers who already were forming up in eight men groups ready to board Huey helicopters to drop us off on the mountain. None of us wanted to go and thought this was going to be a very difficult "hot LZ" (a helicopter landing in the middle of a firefight). We were formed up near the end of the line of troops waiting their turn to board the choppers (HUEY helicopters).

Fortunately one of the officers saw our sorry state, and he held us back until they ran out of helicopters. If we had gone, we would have been in the second wave or second group of soldiers to be dropped into the fight. As it turned out, the NVA had abandoned the USA Outpost after killing almost everyone on top of the mountain. Later I met one of the soldiers who was on top of the mountain during the NVA attack. He told us that all night long the NVA were killing soldiers who were hiding in the rocks and bunkers around the outpost. He said they strung up some of the soldiers on poles and cut their balls off. He said he crawled around all night from rock to rock, taking pot shots at the NVA whenever he saw one in the open. He survived because he kept moving all night and the NVA were never able to find him. The next day he came out from hiding when the relief helicopter task force landed to reclaim the outpost. Fortunately the NVA had pulled out before the relief helicopters landed.

CHAPTER IV

Back in the Field

May 14 or 15, 1968

I was sent back to the field on a resupply truck where we met up with our unit which had established a night laager off the road. I hardly knew anyone from my squad, as most of the men I met initially were either wounded or killed. Besides I had only been with these men for two weeks before I was wounded. I believe it was at this time that I joined up with two replacements, George, our APC driver, and Tracy who liked to man the .50-caliber machine gun. Both were draftees and good guys who, like me, didn't want to be in Vietnam and just wanted to survive and come home.

The first day back with my squad, we went on a sweep in a jungle area. We were told that we would be assaulting an enemy base camp. I was not looking forward to such an assault on a fortified enemy base. We swept the first day and found little evidence of an enemy base camp or the enemy. Our squad was sent out on ambush that night; again we saw nothing. The next morning we loaded up, broke down our night laager, and moved out. After heading down a road, we turned off and headed into the jungle or thick woods for a sweep of a suspected enemy base camp. I was walking right point on a three-man point. Here three men would walk point in a line with a squad following each and the tracks behind, if the terrain allowed. I believe we were operating somewhere in the jungle near the Cambodian border at this time. It was hot and humid in the jungle, and it was difficult to see more than a yard or two. The jungle is very dark, even in the day, as the overlying canopy shades the forest.

I was walking slowly, following along-side a trail, being very careful not to get on it as I was aware it could be mined. The jungle was thick on the sides of the trail, so I had to hack my way through the undergrowth. It was worth it, though, not to get blown up on a trail. I could not see much of anything except more jungle in front and on the sides of me. I could not even see the point man to my left but I could hear him cutting through the jungle. As I followed the trail which looked like it had been well used, I saw something up ahead which looked out of place. I stopped. The column following me got down on the ground as did I. Then I moved slowly forward and there in front of me, not ten feet away on the side of the trail, was a five-hundred-pound bomb sitting upright! I froze, afraid that if I moved I would step on a wire which would blow the bomb. I turned around and made a fist, indicating for everyone to stop and not move. Then I mouthed to the man behind me, "A big bomb!" With that the soldier started crawling backward and passed the word down the line. I carefully began to back up, watching every move for a wire which would set off the bomb. After I joined the rest of my squad about twenty yards from the bomb, the lieutenant came up and asked what was going on. I explained that it was a five-hundred-pound bomb booby trap. The lieutenant said he didn't believe it, and said, "Show me." I looked at him like he was nuts and said, "Lieutenant, I'm not going anywhere near that thing. It will kill us all if someone triggers the bomb!" He said, "Fine, where is it?" I pointed straight ahead. With that he motioned for the platoon sergeant to come forward, and they slowly worked their way toward the bomb. I began to move backward, and a couple of troops followed me as we got down as far away as possible. I had seen what a five-hundred-pound bomb could do, and I didn't want anything to do with it!

A short time later the lieutenant and sergeant returned walking upright and said, "Let's go, it is just a bomb casing"! Then someone else took the point and I melded in with the rest of our squad toward the front of the platoon. A short time later, we came upon an abandoned enemy base camp with lots of bunkers, fighting holes, trenches and jungle buildings. It looked as if the enemy had left a few days ago as the jungle had not reclaimed the area. We searched the entire area and bunkers but found nothing of value. So we destroyed the buildings and pissed in the wells, then left to rejoin our track, which we left behind as they could not go through the jungle.

Soldier Run Over by Tank

May 14–15, 1968

We were to proceed in line with the rest of the company and advance across an open field of rice paddies, to attack the NVA who were suspected to be dug into the tree line. The tree line was to be hit with mortars from our mortar platoon who used large 81 mm mortars mounted in the back of their APCs and supporting artillery, typically 105 mm cannons. We were also to be supported by M-48 tanks most likely from the "black horse" regiment, since the enemy position was supposed to be a strong one. We were to attack in a frontal formation firing as we went in a standing position. Take the objective regardless of our casualties.

After the artillery barrage had lifted and while the dust and smoke were still masking the NVA wood line and bunkers, we set out in line firing as we went. About halfway across the rice paddy field, we were taking casualties and heavy fire. After several RPGs were fired at our tracks and tanks, we all hit the dirt and got behind the dikes. While the infantry was hunkered down behind the rice paddy dikes, the tracks and tanks began to back up, firing as they reversed. They were trying to get away from the RPG rockets. Unfortunately one of the men from our company who was behind a dike was run over by a tank backing up from the wood line! It was not a pretty sight, and there was not much left to put in a body bag. The M-48 tank weighed some fifty-two tons combat loaded, so he never had a chance.

I learned a valuable lesson that day: always be aware of where the track and tanks were in my area. If they were shot at with RPG rockets, they would quickly back up to get away from the rockets, regardless of who was in back of them.

Army Ants Defeat the Enemy

May 15

We were sweeping a jungle area for the enemy. Our APCs were doing their best to follow us through the thick jungle. The driver and track commander manning the .50-caliber were both getting beat up by the vines and branches. Then there were the ants who made nests of leaves in the trees, hornets and other stinging insects who were mad as heck when their nests were disturbed and took it out on these troopers. We were out in front, hacking our way through the jungle. I was still having trouble seeing out of my right eye. When I needed to see clearly, I shut my right eye and looked only out of my left eye. I was walking right point to the far right of our unit. Two other soldiers were walking center and left point leading the way for others to follow. The jungle began to thin out a bit and walking was easier. I became very cautious because this was likely where the enemy could build a base camp. I guess I was out front of both other point men because I saw a recently used trail. This could only mean one thing, the enemy was close by. I called back to the next troop in line to be careful and that I had come across a trail. He passed the word along to the lieutenant. I went much slower and the tracks following us likewise slowed down and everyone was on edge. I crept forward and thought I saw a camouflaged bunker. So I got down and watched for perhaps half a minute. Then I saw other bunkers in the distance and motioned for the next man in line to come up. I pointed to the bunkers and to what I perceived to be a tree line. He passed the word along to the lieutenant. The lieutenant said to go forward a bit but be careful. So I crawled up on my belly to see if I could get closer to the bunker staying behind cover as much as possible. Nothing happened but something didn't feel right. Then I realized that the jungle was quiet except for a low crunching sound. I had never known the jungle to be quiet and never heard this sound before. I did not want to move so I just stayed where I was and watched and listened. My sixth sense kicked in and I was not going to go forward until

I was sure it was safe. After a couple of minutes our platoon sergeant crawled up to where I was and whispered, "What's up?" I pointed to the bunker and what looked like more camouflaged bunkers and a fortified fighting trench. The jungle is shades of gray and looks like dusk. Plus the heavy vegetation blocks and distorts your view. I also showed him the path I had been paralleling. Of course we stayed off the path because of booby traps and ambushes. He stared at the bunkers and fortified fighting positions and acknowledged with a nod of his head that he too saw them. Then I whispered in his ear, "Notice how quiet it is?" He listened and his eyes got bigger as he too realized something was wrong. Then I said, "Do you hear the crunching sound?" He listened and nodded his head in acknowledgement. I looked at him and turned up my palms to indicate "What is it?" He shrugged his shoulders indicating he did not know. Then he said, "I think it is empty." I looked at him and nodded my head to the side, indicating I am not so sure. I didn't want to go any further forward. I guess this took all of a minute or so but it seemed much longer. The other guys just stayed down waiting for us to move or something to happen. The sergeant then whispered in my ear, "Let's move up to that large tree," pointing to our right front. I looked at him and he indicated for us to move out. So we went forward crawling on our bellies keeping low and making as little noise as possible. As we got near the tree something did not look right about the jungle in front of us. It looked like it was moving, like when you watch TV and the pixels are moving. The platoon sergeant saw it also. I whispered into his ear, "What the fuck?" He looked straight ahead and didn't say anything. The men in back of us were not thirty feet behind, waiting to see what we were doing. No one was anxious to get caught in an ambush.

When we concentrated we could see that, yes, something was not right. The trees, ground and everything else was moving, and the crunching sound was definitely coming from the enemy base camp. However, there were no other sounds and the base camp appeared empty. I was getting afraid, and I did not want to go any further. The more we looked, the more unusual was the jungle. It was like it was alive. Another soldier then crawled up to us and whispered to the platoon sergeant, "The lieutenant wants to know what you have found." We pointed to the moving forest ahead. At first he too did not understand what he saw, but he recognized something was not right. Then the sergeant said, "Let's move up a bit," pointing to another large tree. This time the three of us moved up to the large tree crawling on our bellies as quietly as possible. As I was crawling, I noticed more large ants than usual crawling around, and some of them were biting me. Not wanting to make noise, I kept pushing ahead. When we reached the large tree I noticed there were ants over all of us. The others noticed it also and were trying to get them off as they were the biting type. Then it dawned on us. The moving jungle was billions if not trillions of ants! They were swarming over everything in their path and eating the leaves of the trees, which is why they looked like they were moving. We got up on our knees from this position and could see trails and trails of ants marching in columns into the enemy base camp. Following the ant trails, you could see how they blended into a single moving mass which eventually overtook everything we could see in front of us. We realized that no one could live with billions of biting ants intent on eating anything they came in contact with. So we swatted off as many of the ants as we could and took off to the rear. When we reported to the lieutenant, he couldn't believe there were that many ants. But as we all had many large biting ants still hanging onto us, he took our word for it.

We all got out of there and went back to the road. Everyone had had it with biting insects by that point in time, and no one wanted to move into an area infested with swarming army ants. I don't know what the lieutenant told our captain, but I am sure he questioned our story. However, it was true! We concluded that the enemy base camp had recently been taken over by the swarm of army ants, and they did the only thing that they could—retreat. So in the end, the army ants attacked and took over the enemy base camp. Not being an expert in ant types, I am not sure if these were actually "army ants," but they sure acted like an army.

New Battalion Commander

May 15, 1968

Not that we knew it at the time, but Lieutenant Colonel Neilson assumed command of our Battalion. Of course we never found out about much of anything beyond our company. It was rare that we ever saw any officer higher than a captain in the field. For the most part, field grade officers (majors and above) avoided being with us in the field. They flew over our unit in helicopters, out of the line of fire. Most nights they returned to secure base camps and a hot meal and shower. They did not share the same burdens as the line infantryman, and thus had no feel for the ordeal that combat and patrolling every day and two out of three nights "outside the wire" on LP or ambush, had on us.

Tay Ninh Stand Down

May 18–20, 1968

Our company and, I believe, the Battalion was ordered back to Tay Ninh Base Camp for a retrofitting, reinforcements and a stand down. So we broke down our night laager position, loaded up on our tracks and preceded to Tay Ninh base camp. After all of the fighting we had been in and our many casualties, we needed a rest and to get new equipment to replace what had been damaged or destroyed. This was called a "stand down." At our base camp we got to take showers, get clean clothes, trade in our equipment which was damaged or worn out, get supplied with new tracks to replace the ones we had lost, and generally stock up on everything and prepare to go out to the field again. Generally we took the time to get our equipment and gear in order. Apparently (per Lieutenant Colonel Neilson's diary) there was a Command Management Maintenance Inspection, but I don't recall it ever impacting us. Generally we were left alone when in base camp during the day and only pulled perimeter guard duty at night. This was easy duty for us, since we sat in bunkers and not much happened. The only time we were called upon to do something was if the base camp was attacked. This was the case the evening of the twenty-first.

Attack of Tay Ninh Base Camp

May 21, 1968

While we were in base camp supposedly to take it easy and have a break from battles, the NVA decided to attack our base camp. We were in our company area when we heard rockets and mortars hit the base camp and then all hell broke loose around the perimeter. Rockets and mortars were common in Tay Ninh base camp two or three times a week. But ground attacks were rare. After the firing began we heard a huge explosion. It was much bigger than any rocket or mortar attack so we knew the enemy had hit a supply or fuel dump. As it turned out it was one of the base camp's ammo depots. Having experienced this in the field we immediately went to defensive posture. In our camp we only had bunkers to protect us from indirect hits from mortars and rockets. Direct hits would likely penetrate the basic sandbag bunkers we had for protection. We had no fighting positions inside of the base camp so we had to make do with what we had. Mostly we gathered in ditches and waited to see what was happening. I had a case of hand grenades under my bunk so I took as many as I could carry, grabbed ammo belts and headed for the nearest ditch. No one organized our company into a fighting unit, nor gave us any orders whatsoever. So everyone just hunkered down and waited to see if the enemy overran our perimeter. This was likely as the perimeter was manned mostly by house cats that were not used to fighting and were poor sentries at best.

We did not have to wait long when someone in our company opened fire on some sappers. Sappers are enemy experts at sabotage, infiltration and blowing things up behind enemy lines. It was too close to throw hand grenades so most of the fire was from M-16s and M-60s which in close quarters was bad enough. As it turns out we killed a sapper in our company area that was carrying a satchel charge (explosives in a satchel for blowing up large objects). He never had the opportunity to use his satchel charge before being killed. His mistake, which cost him his life, was crawling into an infantry company area.

We stayed on the alert all night in our company area, but we had no further contact with the enemy. However, there was firing all night long throughout Tay Ninh, especially around the perimeter, and several more rockets and mortars hit the camp. Fortunately no rockets or mortars hit our company area. None of us knew anything about what was going on around us so we simply stayed put and guarded our company area.

Next morning we were called together and told we would be mounting our tracks and patrolling the base camp for enemy. We had no idea of the size of the unit which attacked our base camp, but we found out later that it had been a small ground attack to distract our attention along with rockets and mortars. The real purpose of the attack was to infiltrate sappers into the base camp and blow up key installations. One such target was obviously the ammo depot. We never learned what the other targets were although usually they were the airfield, fuel dumps and the headquarters. As the VC/NVA had many civilian spies working in Tay Ninh, I am sure they knew exactly where each of these were located and had "paced them off" (by counting steps from a known object) for use in aiming rockets and mortars.

As we drove around the camp in our APCs, we did not encounter any other enemy, although we saw the destruction they caused and some bodies of both NVA and our soldiers. According to Lieutenant Colonel Neilson's diary, the NVA destroyed an artillery ammo dump, several cannons, and killed six of our men. Several others were wounded. In the end we killed six sappers inside of Tay Ninh. There was no count of how many were killed outside the wire.

We thought the attack was all over, and we returned to our camp to get ready to go back to the field. Later, though, we learned that several soldiers were shot within the base camp that morning. Apparently some of the sappers were still alive, but no one knew where they were hiding. Later that day someone saw a sniper shoot at another soldier.

Apparently he had climbed up on top the PX (Post Exchange building, a merchandise store for soldiers) and was taking pot shots at soldiers who unknowingly were walking within his sights. He was quickly killed by some of the troops. After this excitement in the base camp we loaded up and moved out of Tay Ninh and toward the Rock Crusher at Nui Ba Den Mountain. Each time we passed by Nui Ba Den Mountain we fired our weapons at the mountain as it was full of tunnels manned by the NVA. It was a good time to test fire weapons and possibly shoot up some NVA.

Aircraft hit by mortar at Tay Ninh

Rock Crusher at Nui Ba Den Mountain

May 22, 1968

The Rock Crusher was a small outpost and quarry at the base of Nui Ba Den or the Black Virgin Mountain. We often guarded the combat engineers who worked at the quarry mining stones to build bridges and roads. It was usually a good assignment as you could take a bath and wash clothes in a nearby stream, with relatively clear water runoff from the mountain. A few men at a time would bathe while the rest of the platoon would guard against enemy attack. Our unit had many attacks by the NVA in and around the Rock Crusher. We had many killed and wounded fighting there so it was a dangerous assignment, especially since there were so few of us at any one time guarding this outpost. Fortunately I never was personally involved in a major enemy assault while pulling security for the Rock Crusher. That said we often had small arms fire and snipers shooting at us many times when we were at the Rock Crusher or driving around Nu Ba Den. We likewise had many battles in this area since it was considered Indian Territory (enemy territory). Later, down the road on Route 4 while attempting to clear the road to French Fort, our platoon was almost wiped out. But that is another story.

The problem with Nui Ba Den Mountain was that it was honeycombed with caves that the NVA/VC had used for years to hide and store weapons, ordinance and ammunition. On top of the mountain was a communications installation which was recently attacked and overrun. The enemy used these caves as staging areas for attacks.

We would often accompany the combat engineers when they loaded up their trucks to haul rock to construction sites. Our job was to provide security in the event that they were attacked along the road or at the site. We would ride in front, in-between and at the rear of the column of trucks, if it was large enough and if we had enough APCs. Other times only one or two tracks would go with the convoy while the rest stayed and guarded the Rock Crusher camp.

Other times, such as this day, we would have a test firing of our weapons where everyone could fire their weapons at the mountain to check out if they were working properly. This included some of the heavy weapons such as the heavy mortars. Then we would move on to other sweeps or road patrols.

Award of the CIB

May 22, 1968

The combat infantry man's badge or CIB is one of the most coveted of all awards in the US army. It is awarded only to those who have been in front line ground combat for at least thirty days. It was first authorized in WWII to distinguish those army infantrymen actively engaged in ground combat. It is one of the few awards which can be worn on both dress uniforms and fatigues. In the army everyone recognizes those wearing CIB insignia over their left breast pocket. The insignia is a wreath around a rectangle with a rifle inside. A star at the top indicates being in combat in two wars (such as Vietnam and Korea) and two stars at the top indicates being in front line infantry in three wars (Vietnam, Korea and WWII).

On May 22 I was awarded the CIB as I was in front line combat for thirty days.

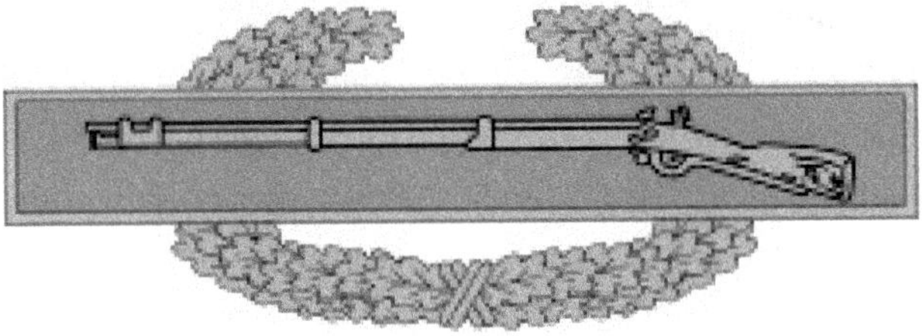

Combat Infantryman's Badge

ARVN in French Outpost Run Away

May 23, 1968

As we made our way down the highway away from Nui Bad Den Mountain, we moved to support B Company which was engaged with the enemy. While we were proceeding down the dirt road, we were halted by perhaps ten to twelve ARVN troops running away from their heavily fortified outpost. They were yelling "VC," pointing to their outpost they abandoned and running away with their weapons. It was obvious to us that the South Vietnamese or ARVN had abandoned the outpost without a fight. They had simply run away when the NVA approached. This was my first experience with "our Vietnamese allies." I would find out later that this situation was common with the ARVN who were worthless in a fight, especially if they faced the hard-core

NVA soldiers. Several of our old-timers wanted to shoot the ARVN as they ran away, but the lieutenant told them to stand down.

The outpost was an old French fortified concrete bunker with firing slits surrounded by many rings of thick interlaced barbed wire. The outpost was half buried in the ground on a hill giving the defenders a 360 degree sweep of the surrounding area. If there were four USA soldiers in the bunker, they could have held off a company-sized NVA attack.

We came to a stop on the road which was just to the left of the road on a hill. Obviously the outpost was placed there to guard this section of the road. We were then ordered by our CO to take back the fortified outpost by attacking it with our APCs and infantry. We all knew then it was going to be a heck of a fight as the NVA were now in control of the fortified outpost and they did not run.

We formed up in a line off the road to attack from three sides. We used the APCs to mow down the barbed wire while all of us fired at the gun embrasures, hoping to keep the NVA from firing machine guns and RPGs (rockets) at us while we attacked. The 50s were all firing at the outpost pouring devastating fire into the gun ports. With all that firepower I thought that surely no one could be alive in the outpost. The APCs approached the outpost with the infantry following slowing behind. We were all getting tangled up in the many strands of barbed wire even after it was mowed down. All of a sudden one of the APCs was hit by a rocket and was blown up not twenty feet from the outpost. By this time some of our men had managed to get close enough to the bunker to throw in hand grenades and Willie Peter grenades (white phosphorus grenades) which were devastating. Just to be sure no one was left alive, several more hand grenades and WP grenades were thrown into the outpost. My squad was still making its way through the barbed wire when one of the other squads entered the outpost. They were most careful of the white phosphorus, which was still dangerous because if it got on you it would burn a hole through you until it burned itself out! They fired a couple of more shots into the bunker and what was left of the NVA soldiers, likely more out of caution and adrenalin from the fight than necessity. It appeared that only perhaps a platoon-sized NVA unit of 30-40 NVA soldiers had attacked the outpost and left perhaps half their number (eighteen to twenty soldiers) to occupy it after the ARVN ran away. During that firefight we lost one track, one soldier killed from the APC which was blown up, and several others wounded—all because our allies, the ARVN, ran away.

To make matters worse, while we were dusting off our wounded and dead and getting ready to move out, the ARVN who ran away came smiling down the road holding their guns by the barrel over their shoulders (this is the unprofessional way they carried their arms) smiling and waving at us. They were met with stern faces and menacing glares with several rifles and machine guns pointed their way. Seeing the approaching ARVN, the CO ordered us to mount up and move out quickly. He very quickly recognized that there was going to be a bad international incident. The ARVN were very lucky that day because we moved out so quickly or they too might have been killed.

We then proceeded toward the rubber plantation where there was a firefight in progress.

Fighting in the Rubber Plantations

May 23, 1968

After the firefight at the French Outpost we proceeded to support a fight in one of the rubber plantations in our AO. Apparently B Company was engaged with the enemy in the rubber plantation and we were to go to help. It was not unusual for us to be engaged in a firefight and then be pulled out and go to another fight to help out another unit in trouble. Often this was one of our sister companies or a "Leg" or infantry company. By the time we arrived it was late in the afternoon—a very bad time to begin a firefight. At night in enemy territory they had all of the advantages. They knew and prepared the battlefield and they had planned how they would fight and when and where they could bring in reinforcements. They also prepared how to escape if they wanted to break off the fight.

A typical small firefight in "the rubber" would start with us sweeping a road, protecting "Rome plows" (large Cat 9 bulldozers with a sharp blade which could cut down large trees), or sweeping the rubber plantations themselves. We would receive fire or be ambushed from the area of a rubber plantation and we would subsequently attack. Almost always the enemy selected the time and the place to fight. We would move through the rubber plantation where trees were lined up in parallel lines. We would come upon fortified fighting positions or sometimes foxholes where the enemy was dug in. We would kill the enemy and move on while we took casualties ourselves. Often the enemy would draw us into an ambush where they were waiting with RPG rockets to blow up our tracks. They also used mortars to kill us as we advanced. If the enemy could cut off some of our troops they would move in for the kill. Or if they had a large enough presence they would attack us and try to close with us to neutralize our air and artillery support. Due to the US Military restraints we rarely could call in artillery because it damaged the rubber trees. Apparently the US government had to reimburse $100 to the owners of each tree we destroyed. Of course we were more interested in saving our skins than in saving Uncle Sam $100. The NVA seemed to know this and used the rubber plantations to lure us into fights. When the enemy had had enough they broke off contact. If they were winning they reinforced their initial troops with additional troops and firepower. Typically they hit us with mortars when we approached their positions or when they wanted to disengage. When they disengaged they would hit us with mortars and leave behind troops whose role was to keep us occupied while the main body faded away back to their base camps in the Iron Triangle or Cambodia.

Visiting a Friend in the Air Force at TSN Air Base

May 25, 1968

After the battle in the rubber Plantation we moved into a night laager position just outside of Tan Son Nhut Air Base (TSN). A night laager was a temporary position where we made a circle with our tracks and built bunkers in between each similar to how the wagon trains formed to fight off Indians in the Old West. If we had a bulldozer available we would dig in each APC and construct a fence barrier in front of the track to explode RPG rockets before they hit the APC. As we had an extra .50-caliber machine gun on our APC we installed this in the bunker we built. We carried Marston Mats (a corrugated steel mat used to construct airfields) which we carried on the sides of the tracks to cover the position then filled sandbags and placed them all around and on top of the fighting bunker. Two of us typically manned this bunker unless short staffed (often) where only one of us was available.

This was the first time I was close enough to the perimeter wire of TSN Air Base to be able to plan on going over the wire to visit a friend who I knew from High School. I knew he was in the Air Force and was stationed at TSN. The perimeter fence in TSN was manned by Air Force personnel who had no clue about guarding perimeters. Without our company outside the wire it would have been very easy for NVA sappers to infiltrate the base and raise havoc, which they did several times blowing up planes and other valuable military material.

That evening after filling sandbags and preparing for the night I worked out with my Squad to cover for me while I sneaked through the barbed wire and fence and into the TSN Air Base. That night I took only my M-16 with me and crawled under the barbed wire just to the left of a guard tower. The wire was lighted with spot lights, but I stayed in the shadows. Looking back, this was idiotic as I very likely could have been shot by the Air Force guards. Given all I had been through, though, it didn't seem like much of a challenge. Everything is relative I guess. I slowly crawled through the wire until I came up against the perimeter fence, which was probably 10' high and lined with razor wire (a sharp type of barbed wire). I crawled along the fence until I found a depression where I could slip under and pushed my way under the fence. Once inside I simply brushed myself off (I was rather muddy) and proceeded to walk through the base. It was a very large base with many buildings and Air Force personnel all around. I saw some Air Force enlisted men standing near a building and went up to them and asked if anyone knew my friend. I did not know his unit or where on the base he was, but the airmen were so impressed that I crawled through the wire to see him, they took me all over until I found his Quonset hut. Everyone in his hut wanted to hear about being in the infantry, and they gave me food, beer, anything else they thought I could use. Their hut was even air conditioned. We had a great time, and it was like being in another world far from the infantry. After spending a few hours with the Air Force soldiers, I had to return to my unit before it got light. So I left most of what they gave me behind, as I could not carry it back with me underneath the fence and barbed wire. On my return I simply took the same route as before, crawling under the fence and the wire. The only time I was cautious was when I approached our company night laager position. I knew that the infantry would certainly see me, so I had made sure that my squad alerted everyone close that I would be coming through the wire. I returned to my squad with no one the wiser.

Author outside the wire of TSN Air Base, Saigon

Zippo Flame Track

May 26–27, 1968

We sometimes operated with an APC which was armed with a Flame Thrower instead of a .50-caliber machine gun. This was a fearsome weapon shooting a stream of fire (Napalm) perhaps 150 meters. We called them Zippo tracks after the Zippo lighters the soldiers of the Vietnam era carried (often to burn down villages). The first time I recall seeing them in action was when we were in a firefight being held off by the enemy holed up in a wood line with covered bunkers and trenches. Every time we approached the wood line, we were thrown back by automatic fire and RPGs. After a while of getting nowhere and being mostly pinned down, we saw two Zippo tracks rolling up to the right of our position. Everyone was told to open up on the enemy to keep them down so they could not shoot the Zippo tracks with an RPG. Obviously they would go up like a firebomb. Everyone opened up with suppressive fire while the two flame tracks moved up to firing range with the wood line.

When the flame tracks opened up with the stream of fire, everything it touched burned ferociously. After shooting out all of its fuel, the Zippo tracks retired. The brush and everything else kept burning. We stopped firing, and it appeared that we were receiving no more enemy fire. Thick black smoke was coming from the fire and you could not see anything. We waited for a while, then we were ordered to move out toward the wood line. Fires were still burning. We approached very carefully expecting the enemy to jump up and shoot at us at any time. When we got close to the wood line we could clearly see the trench and bunkers where the enemy had been hiding. The vegetation was burned off and you could see several NVA bodies in the trenches. We could not get very close as the fires were still burning and smoke continued to block our view. We threw grenades in the bunkers just in case, but did not receive any fire from the bunkers. Apparently the fire, or lack of oxygen, had killed them all, or they simply retreated when the Zippos opened fire. Either way they were either dead or gone. With the fires still raging we moved back to our tracks, mounted up and moved out. We did not search the enemy base camp further that day.

I recall several other times where the Zippos were used to clear our perimeter when we were setting up a night laager or in a Fire Support Base. However, our company did not have Zippo APCs permanently assigned to us. I believe that they were assigned to a battalion or brigade platoon with four APCs in the platoon, but we rarely operated in field sweeps with more than two. When we operated with the Zippo flame throwers everyone moved away from them as no one wanted to be near them when they got hit. I never saw a Zippo track hit by an enemy RPG while I was in the field. Nor did I hear of one being hit. Nevertheless everyone stayed away from them when in contact with the enemy.

We had them support us a couple of other times, one of which I snapped a picture of two NVA on fire running out of a bunker or fighting trench when the Zippo opened up on them. I was very close to the two enemy soldiers when they came running out of the flames on fire. They didn't last but a few seconds and burned to a crisp. We called them Crispy Critters. The stench of burning flesh was terrible. Napalm was really nasty stuff and a hell of a way to die.

One other time when we were under attack in a FSB (perhaps Rawlins), the Zippos were used to fire at the enemy, but this was on the opposite side of the defensive perimeter from where our squad was facing. I did not see them at night when they fired as I was too busy firing at the enemy in front of our position. However, the next day we saw where they had turned the attackers into Crispy Critters who were attacking that side of the defensive perimeter. Bad luck to attack directly into a Zippo Flame thrower track. I would not have liked to be them.

We saw several other crispy critters in our sweeps who had been hit by Napalm dropped from planes. Typically a large area was burned out. If the enemy was caught in the open, in trenches or bunkers when they were hit by Napalm the result was the same, Crispy Critters.

Zippo Flame Tracks

Officially termed an M132A1, it was an APC which carried 200 gallons of Napalm. The flame thrower had two spheres, one holding the Napalm and the other holding compressed air used to shoot the Napalm. It could shoot a stream of flame some 150 meters (almost 500 feet) at maximum velocity and range for approximately thirty-two seconds before running out of fuel. The glow-plug igniters on the flame tracks were often faulty, so the operators carried Zippo lighters and a can of lighter fluid just in case. The operators often jerry-rigged a coat hanger with a rag soaked in lighter fluid, lighted it with the Zippo lighter, and used this to ignite the Napalm stream coming out of the nozzle. The flame platoon members carried a Chemical MOS and were in quite a bit of danger when we were engaged. The enemy was very afraid of the flame tracks, and so they would focus on blowing them up with RPGs.

The flame track was recharged by a deuce and a half support truck which carried the Napalm and had an air compressor to recharge the flame track's air tanks.

Second Battle of Xom Binh Dong

May 26 and 27, 1968

With Captain Montgomery in command, we were in the same night laager position outside TSN Air Base near the end of the runway. We were set up across Highway 1 near the village of Xom Binh Dong in a three-company laager. This area had been the site of a major battle in the Tet offensive of February 1968. So many of the enemy had been killed and the bodies quickly buried on the battlefield that the area stank from decaying flesh.

On the evening of May 26 around 10 p.m. we began receiving small arms fire, and then a ground attack with mortars and rockets hit our position. A Company, as usual, was the first to be hit in the perimeter. At the time we were on alert and had built bunkers in between the APCs. We had also used bulldozers to dig in our tracks to protect them against rockets and constructed fencing in front of each. I was on top of the bunker we constructed when the attack began. I jumped inside where we had a .50-caliber machine gun and fired my M-60 and assisted as the loader for the machine gun. One of our other troops fired the .50-caliber as the attack began.

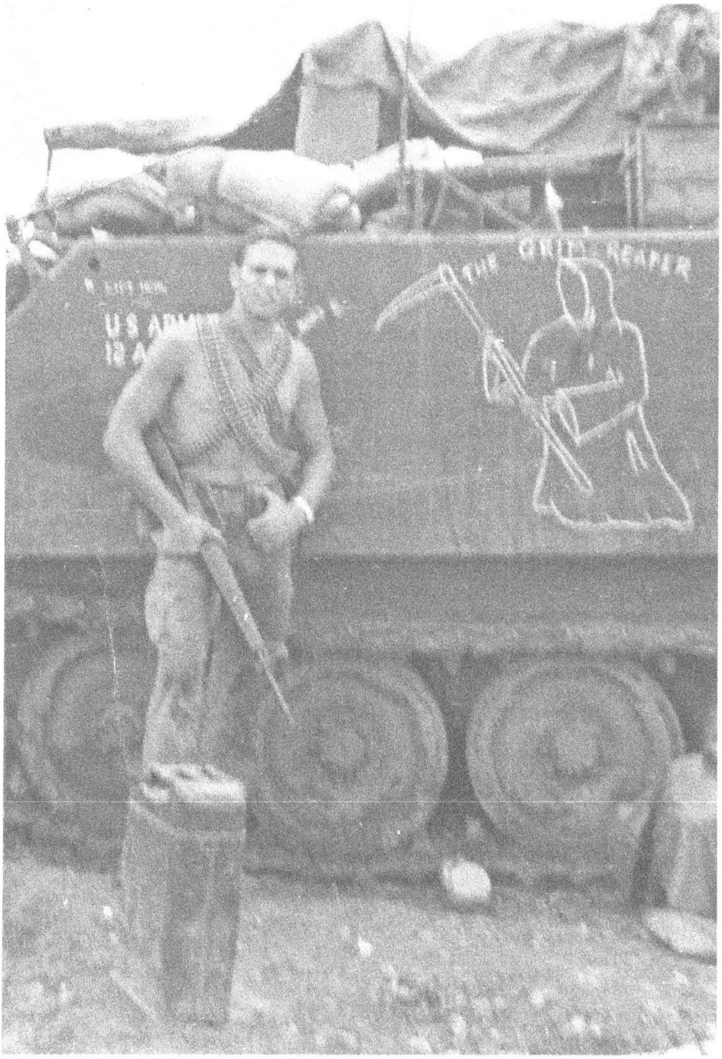

Author with Track 3-2 Grim Reaper

We saw several of the enemy approaching our position, but they were either killed or retreated when we opened up with the .50-caliber machine guns. As soon as the attack began, our men opened up with mortars, artillery and helicopter support. This massive firepower drove the enemy back. Since we were dug in, none of our squad was wounded. While there were rockets fired at our perimeter, none was fired at our track or bunker. The attack went on for most of the night with none of the enemy breaching our perimeter. The attack slacked off around 4 a.m. but we were all on alert and ready for another attack by the enemy.

At 6 a.m. the NVA attacked our position again. Company A and the HQ Company were the object of their attack. Once again we fought them off with machine guns, rifles, mortars, artillery and gunships (helicopters). This attack was bigger and more determined than the prior one in the evening (at least in our sector). During this attack several of our APCs and bunkers were targeted by the enemy. According to the after action reports, our company lost two tracks with two others damaged. Several of our troops were killed and several wounded. I do not recall the number of the enemy who attacked us but they would have likely been at least a reinforced battalion to take on three mechanized companies. From where I was in my bunker it looked like hundreds of enemy coming at us all at once. I thought for sure we would be overrun! No one in our squad was killed and I do not recall if anyone was wounded. Our APC was not hit nor was our bunker although several rockets were targeted at us. Per Lieutenant Colonel Neilson, during the battle B Company had moved out and attacked the NVA from the south. The battle raged on until around 2 p.m. at which time the enemy pulled back. While we had casualties our side of the perimeter was never breached. We were lucky as our side of the perimeter took the bulk of the attack. We were all exhausted by the end of the battle. We dug in again even though we were dead tired because we expected the enemy to attack us again. Fortunately they did not. Apparently they had had enough as did we!

The next day helicopters took out the dead and wounded and flew them back to the hospitals. We spent the morning picking up enemy dead and weapons from the battlefield around our perimeter.

I recall picking up lots of bodies in front and around our APC and bunker. They came very close to overrunning our position. Some of the bodies were only fifteen to twenty feet from the bunker where I spent the night. There was a bulldozer which dug a huge pit in front of our defensive perimeter and we placed the bodies on the back ramp of our APCs and then drove them over to this ditch and dumped them in on top of the other bodies. Some of the other squads tied the enemy bodies to a rope and pulled them behind the track like gladiators, then dumped what was left into the ditch. There must have been a hundred dead in the trench. The whole battlefield and especially the trench stunk like rotting corpses and decaying flesh. In Vietnam, with the extreme heat, bodies rot within hours and begin to smell very badly. After we moved the dead NVA bodies into the trench the bulldozer covered it over with earth. I remember one foot sticking up out of the trench when the bulldozer was finished which we used for target practice for the next few days. We also gathered up many weapons, rockets, Bangalore torpedoes, and ammunition from the dead left on the battlefield. I got a couple of weapons but they were later lost when my track was blown up. We also gathered up some NVA helmets and web gear and some other items from the dead. The excess ammo and weapons no one wanted were taken out to a ditch outside the wire and blown up with C-4 explosive. As I recall we stayed in this position for several days but no further attacks came.

Sweeping a Village for Enemy

May 29–30, 1968

After enemy attacked us at Xom Binh Dong, our unit was given a supporting role to help out units engaged in Cholon (the Chinese section of Saigon). Fortunately we did not have to go to support this battle. After this we did a sweep of a village with B and C Companies while we had the easy job of blocking an enemy retreat to the north. No contact was made and we had a relatively easy day. That night we returned to our night laager position and waited for an attack which did not come.

The next day we did a three company sweep of another village. A typical sweep of a village was conducted as follows:

Sweeping a Village

We would move out of our night laager before morning light, around 4 a.m. We would travel to the village which we were to sweep and position our soldiers around the village on all sides. We would move as quietly as a mechanized unit can move (not very quietly), staying far enough away from the village so as not to alarm them prematurely. Then we would all lie down hidden behind rice patties, or in the hedgerows, or jungle with rifles pointing toward the village. This way we could capture anyone who tried to enter or leave the village. The enemy often moved into such villages at night and departed at dusk.

At first light we would move into the village at one end. With several companies surrounding a large village, one or two companies would sweep a village from one end while the other companies blocked anyone from exiting or entering. Sweeping a village involved entering every house, hooch building and bunker. In the typical village, every house or hooch had a bunker for its occupants. If it was an NVA occupied village, they had tunnels and fighting positions protecting it. We would group all of the people in the village together and place them under guard. Mostly villages were full of women, children and old men. Any young men were either VC/NVA or deserters from the ARVN army. ARVN interpreters would accompany us and question the civilians trying to find out about the enemy or if there were any arms or enemy in the village. We would look in every basket, grain storage, bunkers and hooches looking for arms or evidence of the NVA.

Often we would take away any young men and send them to Saigon internment camps for further questioning. If we found any arms we would confiscate them and then more of the occupants would be detained. If we were fired upon, the APCs would move in and we would attack and often destroy the village by running over the buildings with our APCs, tanks and Rome plows if accompanying us. We would also burn down the villages, throw the rice on the ground and piss and pour oil in the wells to contaminate them. With a fortified village, we would use C-4 satchel charges to blow up masonry buildings and bunkers.

Sometimes we would encounter unusual situations in attacking villages. One time in particular I recall we were fighting in a village going house to house, bunker to bunker and tunnel to tunnel killing the enemy. I was with two other men and we had just finished killing several NVA housed in a building with bullets and grenades. I was carrying an M-60 machine gun that day. The M-60 was a preferred weapon in villages as it could easily shoot through walls whereas the M-16 bullets, being of lighter caliber, were often deflected in going through walls. As we turned a corner we came upon a small fenced in courtyard in-between several hooches. Inside the courtyard was a very angry water buffalo with menacing horns. Immediately the water buffalo came charging at us. The fence was made of sticks, as were the hooches, so they were no protection against the beast. Being primed to any movement with our adrenalin flowing, we fired first and quickly. All three of us opened up at once on the water buffalo, and he dropped dead just a couple of feet from where I was standing. Frankly I did not think he was going to drop before he ran over me! It just reaffirmed once again that everything was out to kill us in Vietnam.

We completed the sweep and found no enemy. Our company was then tasked with moving out at 4 p.m. to establish a night laager position. This was always my least favorite time of day. We were vulnerable when we set up, and it was hard work building bunkers and digging in the APCs for the night, often only to break everything down, load it on the tracks and do it over again the next night.

Guarding the Hoc Mon Bridge

May 30–31

This day we were assigned to guard the Hoc Mon Bridge which is on the Highway 1 about 5 or so miles northwest of Saigon. The bridge had recently been rebuilt out of cement after the original bridge was blown up in the Tet Offensive of 1968. We had a platoon-sized group guarding the bridge and I was stationed on the Saigon, or south side, of the bridge in a fox hole. We were on the side of the bridge where the current was running down toward our position. It was late at night when all traffic was stopped due to the night curfew. We had starlight scopes and were able to see a large log with tree leaves floating down the river toward the bridge. As this was highly unusual, we called into our platoon leader (who as I recall was an E-6 lifer sergeant who I threw in the river, but that is another story) and informed him we were going to toss a few grenades in the river. He agreed and we snuck out of our fox hole and waited until the "log" floated near the bridge. Then we both threw grenades into the river. They exploded about the same time (three seconds) with muffled bangs and a geyser of water each. Then we threw in a couple more just to be sure. We then saw a couple of bodies dressed in only shorts floating up to the surface and shot them several times as they floated by down the river. Obviously they were NVA sappers (demolition troops). However, there was no secondary explosion from their satchel charges and they continued to float down the river. We crawled back into our foxholes and the rest of the evening passed without incident. At night you did not want to move around much as you could be shot by a sniper if you were seen. We stayed low in our fox hole. The next day there were no bodies nor did we find any evidence of the bodies we both saw and no satchel charge bags.

Hoc Mon Bridge Claymore Mine

It was late one night after midnight when we saw a NVA sapper sneaking up on our position without a weapon. We were once again in the same foxhole with claymore mines strung out in front and to the side of our position. We quietly called into our platoon saying that we had sappers in the wire, and we were going to blow a claymore mine. They asked us to hold up to notify everyone to keep their heads down, and we said "hurry up." They got back with us immediately about the time the NVA sapper had almost reached the claymore mine. He was engaged in turning around the mine toward our position when we ducked down low and hit the electrical trigger. The blast lit up the night and made a tremendous explosion. It was the first time I believe I ever triggered a claymore mine, and it was shocking as to how much the blast lit up the night and the noise it made. That evening there were no other incidents, but we were all expecting an attack. It kept us up all night, and we were all very nervous and wide awake. The sergeant asked us if we were sure we saw a sapper, and we assured him we did. Everyone was on alert as a sapper attack often preceded an attack by NVA infantry.

The next day there was no evidence that a human had been in the blast area, as the mine apparently disintegrated the NVA sapper. The staff sergeant asked us several times if we had really seen anything or were just fooling around. We assured him we saw the sapper, but as there was not even a trace, he was skeptical.

Hoc Mon Bridge Tower

As was often the case when we were in a fixed location the "bom de bom" girls (prostitutes) would arrive to see if we wanted a good time. At the Hoc Mon Bridge (on the side north of Saigon) there was an old partially destroyed guard tower. It was a tall stone guard tower perhaps two and a half or three stories high with the roof partially destroyed from the time of the Military French occupation. What was important is that the roof was destroyed on the side facing away from the bridge but the back half was partially intact (later this will come into play). The inside of the tower had been burned out or destroyed so the only way to get to the top was by a not so safe ladder on the outside of the tower. It was a long climb to the top.

At the top of the tower there was an intact wooden floor (except for a stairway hole) approximately four and a half feet below the sides of the stone tower walls. On top of this French guard tower was a one-man portable radar installation, which was used to warn us if an enemy attack was coming from the downside of the river from the bridge. The radar set peered over the top of the stone wall toward the open swamp area. The radar operator was a big old guy who was very friendly and was happy to have company, especially infantry who could protect him from an attack. Apparently he was stationed there for some time. He also had a ready supply of beer and other goodies we normally did not have in the infantry. I believe he was in the engineers but I am not sure.

Portable Radar Set

The radar was a type AN/PPS-4 Portable Radar set. This radar set was supposed to be able to detect moving individual enemy and other targets up to five thousand meters away. It was also able to detect sound. It sat on a tripod which was about four feet high. The radar set was an eighteen-inch or so round canister which sat on top of the tripod. The entire set was about five feet high. The radar set faced outward toward the enemy.

Sometimes in the early evening (before curfew and sometimes after) we would climb to the top of the tower and drink beer and party with the radar operator and the girls. Early one evening we were involved with the "girls" when the roof of our tower suddenly exploded. Needless to say the radar operator was not at his radar station at the time nor was he concerned about the radar. I was likewise engaged and not paying much attention to anything to do with the war or guard duty. Fortunately for us, the RPG rocket had passed through the open part of the roof rafters and had exploded outwardly away from where we were lying on the floor. Needless to say it scared the hell out of us but fortunately we escaped with only splinters in our backsides and a bit of a concussion from the explosion. Then all hell broke loose with firing from everywhere, although we didn't stop to see from where or by whom. We quickly exited the tower as we thought another round would be on its way and this time we may not be so lucky! I for one quickly shot down the ladder (in a couple of jumps) getting splinters in my hands and hitting the bottom of the ground very hard. I was the first one down, followed closely by the radar operator who almost fell on top of me and hit equally hard. The girls came down a bit slower, but not by much.

Unfortunately when I hit the bottom of the ladder I realized I forgot my rifle at the top of the tower and the radar operator forgot his as well. There we were stuck at the bottom of the French tower in the middle of a firefight with no weapons. We could have climbed back up in the tower to retrieve our weapons but frankly, with the threat of an RPG blowing up the tower again, that was not a good idea. In the end we stayed where we were, hugging the bottom of the tower with the girls, and waited to see what happened next. Fortunately there was enough firepower from our platoon to scare off the NVA, and they did not press the attack. Later when things slowed down, we went back to the tower to retrieve our weapons and gear and never told the staff sergeant what had happened to us. We spent the next day with the medics getting splinters removed from our backsides, which encouraged us to stay on the ground from then on. As I recall, the radar operator left shortly thereafter as the French tower was unsafe and the radar did not give us any warning. Of course he was not paying attention, so I don't know how he explained this to his commander.

Platoon Sergeant Thrown into the River

After the incident with the watch tower, the platoon sergeant got on my case even more than he had in the past. We had received a load of beer and everyone was drinking. Once again he started picking on me and giving me shit since I was a "no good" draftee. He went on and on, so I responded that he was a "looser lifer who couldn't make it on the outside." He kept getting more and more worked up and talking about how he would kick my ass, how he had beat up better men coming up through the ranks. The standard lifer bull shit about the good old days. Then he said, "I should throw you in the river and give you a good dunking." I told him something like "I wouldn't if I were you or you will wind up in the river with me!" With that he started coming toward me. He was about my size but a bit heavier since we all had lost about 20% of our body weight in the field. As he approached me he went to grab me, but I quickly grabbed his arm and, bending down, hoisted him up on my shoulders in a dead man carry. He couldn't do much of anything with his feet off the ground except grab me around the neck. As soon as I had him up on my shoulders, I jumped into the river. Unfortunately it was deeper than I thought, and he kept my head under water in a vice grip. I tapped his arm indicating that I wanted him to release my neck just like in wrestling, but this was no game. He would not let go, and I could not breathe under the water. I needed to get out of his grip or drown, which seemed to be his intention. I couldn't do much in that position under water except break away, which I did by pulling at his arms while slipping my head out from his vice grip around my neck. When I came up, I was grasping for air! In getting out of his headlock I had pushed him away from me so I was several feet away when I broke the surface. He started coming toward me right after I broke the surface, but I was ready for him and stepped back and got into a boxing position with fists clenched. He was in deeper water than me so I was higher than him and on firmer ground. I started cursing at him, calling him a son of a bitch among other choice words as soon as I could speak. He stopped when he saw me in a boxing position and glared at me but did not approach. Then he said, "You're going to get it and I'm going make sure of it." Still mad as hell from him trying to drown me I said something like "I'll be waiting if you try you son of a bitch!" With that I got out of the water as did he. He went stomping off toward his track and one of my squad men grabbed me by the arm and said, "You better get out of here. I think he is getting his gun!" With that we retreated to our track which was on top of the bridge, while all of this took place in an open area next to the river. As soon as I got back to my track I grabbed my M-16 and chambered a round holding the gun across my lap with finger on the safety switch. Everyone in my squad grabbed their weapons and we all sat around waiting to see what happened next. No one liked the platoon sergeant as most of us were draftees and he was a *lifer* who didn't give a damn about us. After a while nothing happened. The platoon sergeant must have cooled off or someone calmed him down. After that incident he backed off on leaning on me, although he continued to be an ass to me along with everyone else. Not long afterward he was either killed or wounded. I don't remember which but in either case he was out of our unit never to return.

Set Up in Graveyard

June 1–2, 1968

After sweeping another village our platoon set up that night in a graveyard. This was not unusual as graveyards were usually on high ground and thus we could set up there without being in standing water. Furthermore, we liked them because the grave stones sheltered us from incoming fire. The mausoleums also offered us shelter from the rain. Digging in foxholes was another matter. But we did so anyway.

This night I went out on an ambush with two new replacements. After we had traveled about 1000 yards we set up in a thicket of bushes about 50 feet off a well-used trail. We set up six claymore mines (each of us carried two on ambush) around our ambush with four facing the trail and the other two facing other directions. One of the new men began to take off his boots, and I whispered for him not to remove them. This was in case we made contact and had to move out quickly. Just after we left the wire and we were alone, I stopped with the two new men and explained to them how we were going to operate on the ambush. I told them to forget what the sergeant had told them and that all we were going to do was to watch the trail. If we saw anyone, we were not going to move or make a sound, nor were we going to blow the ambush. I told them that the NVA often let a couple of people lead the unit so that they would be hit first. Then the main body of the enemy would move up later if it was safe. I told them that, with three of us, we would be overrun and quickly killed if we blew an ambush on almost any size of enemy formation. Then I said, "If you blow this ambush, or make any noise to attract the enemy, you're going to die, because the first thing I am gonna do is shoot you because you will have gotten all of us killed! Understand?" Both looked at me wide-eyed and shook their heads in understanding. Both were nervous as heck so I led the way to the ambush site. Getting to where you were supposed to set up an ambush was extremely difficult with a map that was not detailed and a compass, neither of which you could see at night. Nor we were going to use a flashlight to see and let the enemy know we were there. This made calling in mortars for support very dicey since you could be a hundred yards out of position and your own mortars could land on top of you. This is why I almost always moved to our alternative location before calling in mortars on the enemy, unless I was far off from the known position where the mortars were zeroed in.

We arrived at our ambush site around 9 p.m. and set up our claymore mines and settled in for the night. We were behind a slight rise in the ground covered by thick vegetation. I set up far enough from the trail so that if anyone came our way we could blow the claymore mines and run like hell away from the ambush site. We called in our "sitrep" (situation report) letting our platoon know that we were set up. After that all we would do was to respond to inquiries by squeezing the hand set twice to acknowledge we received the message. We all stayed awake listening to the many sounds of the jungle at night. Around 1 a.m. we heard voices coming down the trail. They were rather noisy and not paying attention to being quiet. We also heard their gear banging, so we knew that these men were likely new troops who assumed they were in friendly territory. We did not have a starlight scope but could see five or six men moving down the trail talking softly. I grabbed the arm of the new soldier next to me and kicked the boot of the soldier facing the other way. I indicated to them to be quiet by putting my finger to my lip. It was very dark, so if we made no noise the enemy would never know we were near.

We let the first group pass and I indicated to the new men to sit still and wait. Sure enough in a couple of minutes we heard a much larger group moving up behind them. I estimated that this group was a platoon of perhaps thirty to forty-five men as they were walking three or four abreast. Far too large a group for us to tangle with! They passed by and the two new men indicated they wanted to move away from the area. I shook my head and waved my hand indicating for them to stay down and be silent. Then a few minutes later, a larger group of enemy came down the trail. This group could have been a company-size group of perhaps 100 or more soldiers, walking in a loose formation of three or so abreast. With our heads buried in the dirt and hands covering our mouths, we were panicked not to make a sound. It is very hard not to cough or breathe heavy when you are trying not to make a noise. Even your heart beating sounds loud to you. You are sure the enemy can hear you breathing! Once again we waited for them to pass. Then a few minutes after that, another platoon-sized formation of enemy, walking three or so abreast, passed by us. We were scared stiff and doing all we could not to breathe too loud or move a muscle. This was the closest I had ever come to so many enemy soldiers! Every bone in my body wanted to get out of there immediately, if not sooner. But I realized to move would mean certain death.

After this last group passed we waited about fifteen minutes, listening for any sounds of more enemy coming or having left someone behind. I indicated we would wait a bit longer just in case. We waited another ten minutes, just to be sure. Then I indicated we were to retrieve our claymore mines quickly and split. I motioned with my finger on my lips to be quiet, but that gesture was certainly unnecessary. I wanted to leave the claymore mines so we could move faster, but I knew the damage they could do if used against us. Furthermore, I wanted them to protect us in our alternative position, just in case.

One of the soldiers motioned to the radio, indicating if he should call in what we saw. I shook my head no, and indicated to just hurry up and retrieve the claymore mines. After that we moved away from the area as silently and quickly as possible. Our alternative position was perhaps three hundred yards from our current position, and I wanted to be there and set up before we called in mortars, again just to be safe. Of course, this is not what we were supposed to do, which was to blow the ambush and/or call in mortars while staying in position—good luck with that! After we got in our new position and quickly set up our Claymore mines, I grabbed the head set and reported what we had seen. I told them I estimated "two zero, zero to two five zero" men in several large groups moving down the trail. I also told them that they had passed us a few minutes ago (I stretched the truth since it was more like a half an hour plus), and that we were moving to the alternative position. The soldier manning the net (radio network) for our platoon was very excited and asked me to "say again number of NVA" (repeat). I said, "two zero, zero to two five zero." With that I assume he called the mortar platoon and set up a fire mission. He came back on the radio a couple of minutes later and asked, "Are you in alternative position?" We responded, "Affirmative." Then he said, "Roger, keep you heads down."

A few minutes after that, we heard the sounds of mortar tubes and then a dozen or so loud explosions from our prior ambush position. When we came back into our camp the next morning, the lieutenant wanted to know all about the ambush and enemy. He asked why we waited for them to pass before we called in a mortar barrage. I simply looked at him in disbelief and said we didn't want to make any noise. I wonder if he really believed we would have stayed in that position and called in mortars so close. No one made a big deal about it, and no one ever followed up with us.

According to the diary of Lieutenant Colonel Neilson he states that "B Company AP (Ambush Patrol) let 85 VC in 5–7 groups pass by during period 0030–0430."

He goes on to note "Rec'd ML. Sent ML letter." I assume this is an abbreviation for some type of letter of disapproval! Sitting in a secure rear area with soldiers all around, I guess it makes sense for three lonely men to attack "85" or more enemy (more like a couple of hundred in our situation), a half a mile from any friendly support! Since this notation in the diary happened about the same time as the incident we encountered, it is perhaps the same incident. Although it was a fairly common occurrence, so it could be two separate incidents. Either way I heard nothing more about it from anyone. Best of all, I am here today to tell the story, which would not have been the case if we blew the ambush.

Night Ambush

A night ambush typically entailed three to four men going out perhaps ½ to 1 click (a click is a 1,000 meters or 3,281 feet), and setting up to ambush the enemy as he passed by. Apparently this was not the way night ambushes were to be executed. Army SOP was to send out squad-sized units comprising eleven or so men led by NCOs or lieutenants on ambush. Sometimes a platoon-sized ambush was set up but these were rare. Only once do I recall going out on such a mission, and I do not think it was led by our lieutenant. Officers simply did not go outside the wire (defensive positions) at night. Likewise, rarely was an ambush led by an NCO (SGT or higher). Mostly we went out on ambushes with three to four men. Considering that at the time I was in the field our squad had only four to six men out of an authorized eleven men, we could not afford to spare more than three men to go out on an ambush. Three or four minimum were required for defense of our sector of the defensive perimeter, one manning the .50-caliber machine gun on the track, two in the bunker we built on the side of our track, and often one or two for a listening post (LP) outside the wire every second night. We were constantly far below our authorized strength, so the few men we had carried multiple jobs for a normal squad.

If we were watching a trail, two soldiers would face the trail looking both ways while the third would face the opposite side so we would not be surprised by the enemy. We would set up two claymore mines facing the approaches and center of the trail, and then at least one or more facing the opposite direction in case of an ambush by the enemy. We carried a radio with us and sent in "sitreps" (situation reports) in the form of two clicks on the radio handset so as not to make any sounds talking. We would only respond to queries from the Platoon radio by squeezing the hand set twice. If we made contact or if we wanted to call in mortars from our mortar platoon, we would speak very quietly when the enemy was far enough away. The coordinates for an ambush site were pre-established, so you had to find exactly where you were supposed to be at night with no GPS and only a compass and a lousy map to guide you. If you got it wrong, you may get killed by your own men who would not be expecting you to be in the wrong place. Furthermore, as the mortars were to be used for close-in support, if you were too close to where they hit, you would be a casualty of "friendly fire"! You also had an alternative site where you were supposed to relocate after you sprang an ambush!

Once in a while we would carry the M-14 rifle with an Infrared Scope (could detect heat such as people) set to be used as a night sniper scope. We had all been trained on the M-14 so we all knew how to use one. The M-14 was big and bulky compared to the M-16 but it was much more accurate and its bullet has much more stopping power (heavier bullet). The only drawback of using an M-14 rifle during an ambush patrol is that the noise and muzzle flash would give away your position. Being in Indian Territory with three to four men a half mile or so from your own troops is not a good way to survive. So while I saw enemy through the M-14 Infrared Scope and the Starlight (night vision scope which glowed green) several times during an ambush, I never fired a shot at the enemy, even though I am sure I could have killed several of them. What we would do was to move to our pre-defined back-up position and then call-in mortars where we had been. We simply did not trust our own mortar men or artillery to not drop rounds on top of us. We moved away first then called them in pretending that we were still in the ambush site.

The concept of the ambush was that you would spring the ambush on enemy troops who were amassing for an attack on your night laager position and break up the enemy attack. In practice, with three or four men, if you sprang an ambush of an attacking enemy, who presumably was grouping in force, you would spring the ambush and very quickly be killed yourself. Knowing this, no experienced soldier in their right mind would spring an ambush on a large number of troops unless they had a death wish or no other choice. The majority of ambushes which were sprung were on small groups of the enemy walking down trails or those who came too close to the ambush set up. One had to be cautious as the enemy typically had small groups walking in front of large formations. So you didn't want to act unless you were sure they were alone. The real purpose of the ambush with so few men, not explained by the officers but obvious to us, was to warn the night laager of a pending attack. Of course, the three or four men who blew an ambush would be killed, but the sacrifice would have paid off by warning the main body of troops of the pending attack.

An ambush or multiple ambushes, in the case of a multi-company night laager or Fire Support Base (FSB), would be sent out every night. To the infantryman that meant that about every third night you went on a night ambush in addition to your other duties. Of course with only three or four men most of the time, you were expected to stay up all night and be on alert. A very difficult challenge when you were exhausted from the day's fighting or slugging it out through the jungles and rice paddies.

Second Purple Heart

June 3, 1968

I am not certain, but it is possible that this incident took place a couple of days earlier. With so many wounded and killed, the medics sometimes reported the wrong dates. As I was considered a walking wounded (more like limping wounded), I am sure that submitting my Purple Heart was a secondary concern to the medics. I did not receive my orders for my second Purple Heart or my first for that matter until months after the actual wounding. For the purposes of continuity, I will use the date published on my Purple Heart award as the date when I was wounded as described in this summary.

We packed up and moved out of our night laager position in the graveyard on our tracks. We were on the move by 8 a.m., well aware that we would likely meet up with the enemy who was known to be in our area in force. We were patrolling in the area west of Tan Son Nhut Air Base. We were told that day we would be working with ARVN troops in a combined operation. We had zero respect for the ARVN as they would run when in battle, and we believed many of them were working secretly for the enemy. We discussed this with our squad and decided we would make sure we kept an eye on the ARVN, especially if we were in contact with the enemy. Our plan was to tell the ARVN they were to keep in front of us at all times, and we would make sure someone was always behind them, just in case. We simply did not trust them at all and did not want to work with them, especially if they were behind us.

We came to a relatively open area which abutted a heavy wooded area. This is where we met with the ARVN troops. Our squad was assigned five or six ARVN soldiers who were to sweep alongside of us and fight if we encountered the enemy. This made us even more nervous as we were told that the ARVN were to walk in-between each of us. None of the ARVN spoke English and we could not speak much Vietnamese so communication was a problem. We were sure the enemy was around and moving across an open area. This made us all the more nervous. To us this seemed like an ideal position for the NVA to ambush us if we ventured too close to their camp. We were not to be disappointed nor surprised when we encountered the enemy. Using sign language and what little Vietnamese we spoke we told the ARVN they were to walk in front of us. They were not to get behind us or we would shoot them. We did this via sign language and by walking in back of one of our soldiers and another soldier lifted his rifle and made motions and saying, "Bang-bang we kockadow you" ("kill you" in Vietnamese)! They got the message, and I am sure our message did not endear them to us. However, they kept in front of us even when the enemy opened fire on us as we crossed the field. Of course once or twice I saw them look back only to see our squad looking at them sternly letting them know that if they ran we would shoot them. It did the trick, as none of them ran or got behind us.

Alpha Company in battle with track destroyed by an RPG

As we proceeded across the field walking in front of our tracks, the ARVN soldiers were doing as they were told, walking ten feet in front of our squad. It was raining, which turned the open field into muck. This was fortunate for us because the mud helped to deaden the enemy mortars. We were cautiously moving toward a wood line spread out in a company and platoon line formation. We all were very aware there was a large enemy formation in our area. Even the ARVN sensed the NVA were in the area and they too moved very cautiously. About halfway across the field, we began taking enemy mortar rounds. When the first round exploded, everyone hit the dirt and tried to get under cover. When I hit the ground there was a slight depression in front of me, so I immediately began low crawling toward the depression. At the same time the mortars hit, the enemy opened fire with long range machine guns. Our APCs and everyone else opened fire with every weapon on the wood line. We could not see the enemy, but we knew they were dug in the wood line. Within a few seconds, as I was crawling toward the depression, an enemy mortar blew up just off to my left and rear. The explosion blew me to the side, and it felt like someone had kicked me hard and jumped on my right foot, painfully twisting my ankle. Mud and debris fell on top of me and I was consumed in a swirl of smoke. I was conscious and knew it had been a near-miss mortar, but I was unsure how badly my leg and foot had been hit. I just stayed that way for I don't know how long, hoping that all of my body parts were still intact. Gradually I felt around; my ankle and foot were aching, but were still in place—good news. I was hurt but I did not know where, other than my ankle felt like it was twisted or broken, like in a bad fall. I felt around some more. While my lower leg and ankle were very sore, there seemed to be no blood. I had no clue as to why it hurt so much. I could not move around too much since we were taking extreme fire from the wood line. In between firing my weapon, I pulled up my leg and felt my foot through my boot. Then I discovered that the heel of my boot had been blown off completely, and the bottom of my foot was bleeding! I did not want to move my leg too much, to see how badly I was hurt, because the slight depression I was in did not provide me with enough cover, and the enemy was sweeping the field with machine gun fire. I stayed like that for a while, not wanting to call a medic, as I knew I was not badly hurt. The only real pain I felt was my ankle. The cut on my foot did not hurt much, so I did not think the cut was too bad. I did notice a chunk of mortar in the shape of a perfect pyramid with a base about one inch square and about one inch high near my foot. When I picked it up it was still hot so I dropped it immediately. This was the chunk of shrapnel from the mortar which had surgically removed the heel of my boot and sliced a cut across the bottom of my foot! Later I picked up the triangle shaped piece of shrapnel from the mortar and carried it through the battle. I wanted to keep it as a souvenir of how lucky I was once again. Unfortunately some time later I lost it when my track was blown up, along with several enemy rifles and everything else I had, which was not much. It would have been a nice souvenir for me to keep, like the .51-caliber bullet which hit me in the back. I lost that one also when my second track was blown-up.

Gradually the mortars stopped and our tracks began to move up across the field where we were prone. They opened fire with the 50s, laying down suppressive fire. Everyone, including myself, began to return fire toward the wood line. I was carrying my M-16 rifle. At the same time, our mortar platoon began counter fire against the enemy mortars, and they stopped after that. When our squad began to move out, I looked at my foot and saw I had a cut across the heel of my foot which was bleeding. The cut was like a sharp knife had made a straight cut across my heel, cutting my sock. I did not try to bandage the cut as it was not bleeding too badly, and I did not want to be left behind. However, what really bothered me was my ankle, so I hobbled along in the mud trying to keep the weight off of it. I went limping along like that, trying to keep up with my squad and the ARVN who had moved ahead of me along with our track. I did not want to be left behind, so I did my best to catch up to our track.

As we approached the wood line, our platoon slowed down and I was able to catch up to our track. It was sitting off from the wood line providing machine gun support to other squads while they attacked the bunkers. I limped up to the back of the track and climbed on-board, as I knew I would not be much help limping around during a fight. This way I could shoot from the top of the track and provide support in case the enemy popped up out of a spider hole. The battle continued for the rest of the afternoon with the company cleaning out the bunkers. I do not recall how many NVA we killed or how many men we lost or were wounded. After the battle the ARVN went on their way. I assume they met up with the rest of their company. Anyway we did not see them again after the fighting died down.

When the firing concluded, Tracy or George called the medic over to our track to take a look at my foot. The doc said I was lucky and had a million-dollar wound. He helped me to take off my boot, washed the mud off my foot with a canteen, and put on antiseptic, which burned like hell, and bandaged the cut. He said there was no metal in my foot and that it had been a clean cut. He said it probably should be stitched-up but he did not have time now, and besides, with the mud, he needed to be sure it did not get infected before he closed it up. I showed him the pyramid shaped shrapnel from the mortar, and he shook his head and smiled. He wrapped some supporting bandage around my ankle and told me to take it easy and ride the track until we got back to our night laager. By that time, my ankle had turned black and blue and was swollen. Then he went off to help other wounded.

That night we set up in a night laager position and were not attacked. The doc visited with me and changed my bandages and put more antiseptic on my cut. He told me then that he though it may be better to see if it closed up itself and not stitch it up. He spoke to our lieutenant and had me relieved of any duties other than guard duty on the .50 caliber. He told me to keep off my foot and ankle. As it turned out I never did get stitches and the wound healed itself. At the time the biggest problem I had was that I only had a single pair of boots. Thus I could not walk around with one boot even if my ankle was better. Later that day the medic came over and tossed me a pair of boots. He said, "Just change your bandages daily, put on this shit [antiseptic], keep your ankle taped, tie your boot laces up tight, and try to stay off your ankle, and it should be fine"! At the time I didn't think about where he got an extra pair of boots as we had no resupply of such items in the field. Later one of the guys told me the doc had taken the boots off one of our guys who had been killed. He told the lieutenant, "He doesn't need them any longer." I didn't like wearing the boots after that but I had no choice. One odd thing about the boots was that one of the boots had one of the drain-hole screens missing. Later this would prove to be a real problem as the leeches constantly crawled through this small hole in the bottom side of the boot and got onto my foot through my sock. As a result my boot was often full of blood where the leach got to my skin and was crushed by my walking. So when I took off my boot water and blood would come out for months to come until I finally got a new pair of boots.

The next day, our company again went out looking for the NVA but fortunately we did not make contact. We swept with our tracks and so I was able to stay off my ankle manning the .50 caliber. Even though you stood up in the track manning the .50-caliber machine gun, I was able to balance on one foot and keep my weight off the wounded ankle. My ankle felt better each day I stayed off of it. It also saved me from going out on patrols or LPs. Tracy, who often manned the .50-caliber machine gun, took my place walking with the squad.

As I did not receive my Purple Heart award for perhaps a month after this incident, I had forgotten that I was even put in for the medal. However, after receiving my third Purple Heart award, I sure was thankful to the medic who put it in for me since with three Purple Hearts you could get an assignment out of the infantry. It is interesting to note that I actually was hurt worse my first day in the field when I was blown off of my track by a short round from our own artillery, suffering a concussion and bruises as a result.

Personal Items

We kept our personal items in duffel bags for clothing and in .50-caliber ammo cans. These we left in our tracks on top of the ammo which was carried inside the track lining the floor. I had no clothes other than those on my back plus an extra pair of socks, a field jacket, waterproof poncho and liner, a light weight camouflaged blanket. So I had little spare clothing in my duffel bag, as did most of the others. No one that I recall had extra boots which was a real problem due to our boots being wet all the time. I solved this problem by drying out my boots (for a few hours anyway) on the exhaust pipe of our diesel track. The boots stunk like diesel fuel but at least they were dry for a while until I went out on patrol or LP or stepped in water and mud which was everywhere. We used the .50-caliber ammo cans, which were water proof, for any personal items we had. I had a pen, writing paper, tooth brush, tooth paste, sometimes a disposable shaver and shaving crème, camo sticks, goggles (used to protect against dust when driving down the roads in the dry season), and above all military issue insect repellent. We also used an M-16 ammo can, a smaller version of a .50-caliber ammo can, for our cleaning tools and supplies for our weapons including rubbers (prophylactics) to place over the barrel of our guns to keep out the water.

We had air mattresses but they got holes in them quickly so they were really not very useful. We also had tent halves whereby two people could make a tent by snapping the two shelter halves together. Most of us did not use these as they afforded zero protection from mortars and they were always soggy, moldy and wet. We only used them when we were in fire support bases. Most of us had a "fanny pack" as opposed to backpacks which were in short supply. All of us had our own personal gear which we customized and scrounged together.

Walking, crawling, and cutting our way through jungle, moving through swamps and streams, going through elephant grass, pushing through thickets and woods, not to mention being in battles, all took a toll on our clothes and equipment. We all walked around with ripped and worn out clothes and often no extra boots! As we rarely had extra clothes, we wore the same clothing every day and night. Sometimes we had extra clothes and were able to wash them, but really only in the dry season when we had a stand down or were in base camp (both rare). The way we were supplied with clothing was interesting. Periodically when in a Fire Support Base (FSB), a helicopter would bring out a net of used but clean clothes, and drop them in the middle of the FSB. Everyone was told to send a few men to the area to get new uniforms while others stayed on guard. We never had a crowd anyplace in the field as we never wanted more than a few men at a time in any one place, for fear the enemy would drop mortars or rockets on us and kill a large number of men. We would go over to this area and try to pick out shirts and pants which fit us or at least we could wear. For a long time I did not have a shirt, just my pants and a field jacket when I got cold. Usually we were only allowed to have one set of each until everyone took what they needed. All of these uniforms were used and many had been repaired. Typical of the army was that everyone in the base camps (house cats) had two or more sets of uniforms and boots. But we in the infantry, who needed them more than anyone, were always given used clothes and were often short of a change of clothes. Boots were also distributed in much the same way, but much more infrequently. They were also used. We assumed they were taken off the dead or when the house cats rotated back to the States.

In the field we did not wear underwear as it would rot off. So we only wore shirts, pants, boonies hats or helmets, and socks. Of course, we also carried two dog tags with our name, rank, serial number, and blood type, in case we were killed or wounded. It was a myth that you took one dog tag and kicked the other in-between to two front teeth of our soldiers when they were killed. The truth is that when there was a body of one of our soldiers (sometimes there was little or nothing left), we would place it in a row with other dead soldiers and someone would place ponchos over the bodies. After the wounded were evacuated and after the firefight was over, the dead would be loaded onto helicopters who would take them away to a morgue. We buried only the enemy dead and only when we killed them near our FSBs or night laagers where we intended to stay. Otherwise we let them lie where they died.

First Eagle Flight

June 5, 1968

Prior to this point the mechanized infantry in the 4/23rd operated with their APCs during operations. However, due to the rain and flooded rice paddies, we were confined to operate on the roads. On June 4 we were told that tomorrow we were going to be dropped into a swamp and search for the NVA who were operating in this area. Apparently we were so short on infantry that the Battalion was forced to use mechanized infantry, who typically operated with APCs and armor. We had never trained for helicopter assaults. I had only been on a helicopter once before, and that was on a "dust off" flight to the hospital when I was wounded. I was just getting used to operating as mechanized infantry, and now I was to be dropped from helicopters into a potentially "hot LZ." A hot LZ is when you are dropped into a landing zone and the enemy is expecting you, and opens up on the helicopters and the infantry as they are unloading from the helicopters. Needless to say I was not happy about walking around all day in a swamp with my sore ankle and injured foot. Amazingly it never did get infected, so I guess the antibiotic cream the doc gave me was powerful medication.

We were ordered to "saddle up" and to take only ammo, weapons and water, since we were going to be operating in a swamp and any extra weight would work against us in the mud. To an infantryman you could never take enough water or ammo so I took plenty of both plus my usual four to six hand grenades. I also took along some C-Rats and hazoline pills (water purification tablets which made the brown water taste terrible) as you never knew how long we would be out. We were led to an open area and waited for the Hueys (helicopters) to arrive. In a short time we saw 10 helicopters approaching. They were in two parallel lines of four helicopters each and two gunships (helicopters with multiple guns and rockets who did not carry troops), one on each side. Since most of our squads only had four to six men and two stayed back with the APCs, the driver and one to man the .50 caliber, we loaded two or more squads into each helicopter. Typically a Huey helicopter can carry a crew of four, two pilots and two door gunners, plus eight fully loaded infantry. In Vietnam, with the high humidity, eight loaded troops were about all they could safely carry. There were about seven or eight of infantry on the helicopter I boarded. With all of the helicopters, we had about half of a significantly reduced company available for the assault. Typically a group of ten "slicks" (Huey helicopter which carried troops into battle armed with two M-60 machine guns on each side manned by a door gunner) in two columns would carry a company of eighty or so men into a landing zone to conduct sweeps and surprise the enemy.

We climbed on board the Hueys which were hovering a foot or so above the ground. As they had no doors we placed our feet on the skids and jumped on board. We sat on the floor while the door gunners sat by M-60 machine guns on either side. Then we took off with the front of the Hueys leaning forward and gaining altitude. It was refreshingly cool as we gained elevation with the air flowing over us. It was a nice break from the stifling heat and humidity at ground level. It was like we were in another world. When you looked out over the country side it looked lush and green broken only by the fields of rice paddies and small villages and a few roads now and then. The most striking feature was just how many bomb craters there were everywhere. The country looked like Swiss cheese. Occasionally you could see a mile wide and two mile long string of bomb craters with nothing left except huge craters and debris indicating a B-52 bomb strike. Soon the detached feeling of watching a movie began to fade as we quickly began to drop altitude in anticipation of being dropped off in the swamp. The ground came up very fast as the helicopters came in two rows to drop us off and get out of there in a hurry.

The chopper (helicopter) dropped very quickly. As we approached the clearing on the ground, the door gunners opened up, firing M-60 machine guns at the wood line. This was a precaution in case the NVA were waiting to ambush us. Not that it would do a lot of good, as we found out later, if the NVA were in prepared positions. We jumped off the helicopters as they came in for a landing. The helicopters kept their noses up while landing with the tails down as they hovered a couple of feet off the ground. I jumped out and landed in the mud and knee high grass. The ground looked a lot closer when we were in the helicopters. I was on the side of the chopper facing the wood line so, as soon as others joined me, we started forming up into a line. The helicopters never really stopped; they just dropped us off and then took off as quickly as they landed. When the troops jumped out on each side, the helicopter hovered back and forth sideways. The tail of the chopper also had a tendency to sway back and forth, which was really dangerous. With all of the blades of the chopper spinning and the helicopter moving, not only side to side, but front and back and rocking, I was very cautious of getting near the blades of the helicopters. When I jumped off, I got down as slow as possible so as not to get hit by the blades. Once you jumped off the helicopter, the backwash from the rotor blades blew water and debris all around and pushed down on you. It was not a good feeling knowing that the chopper could crash or be blown out of the air on top of you any moment. I just wanted to get away from the helicopters as low and fast as I could. After all, if the NVA ambushed us, they would be shooting rockets at the Hueys and they would crash on top of us!

I jumped off the Huey, landing on my good leg and keeping off my wounded ankle. This helped, and I walked all day long with the other troops without too much trouble. When you are nineteen years old, you heal fast! Minor issues like flesh wounds and sprained ankles are not major issues when you are more worried about being left behind or being shot. I was more concerned about stepping on a mine or walking into an ambush, so most of my thoughts were focused on these concerns not my ankle.

While disembarking from the helicopters, one of our soldiers, fortunately not from our squad, had jumped off on the opposite side of the Huey and tried to run around the back of the chopper to join the rest of his squad. As he ran around the back of the chopper, the back of the helicopter swayed toward him, and he was hit in the head by the rotor blade. He was killed instantly! The helicopters continued to get out of the field as quickly as possible. We then moved rapidly to the wood line while the medics took care of the body. Fortunately there were no NVA waiting to ambush us because we would have been sitting ducks.

We swept the swamp and found evidence of enemy base camps. Leading out of one of the base camps there was a trail through the grass. It was recent, so we followed it. We came to an island in the middle of the swamp, hemmed in with thick vegetation; we spread out and moved in cautiously. I was crossing through a swollen creek, holding my rifle over my head to keep it out of the dirty water. As I moved forward, I looked up and saw an NVA soldier pointing his rifle at me. At that instant, I stepped into a hole or off a ledge and went under water. I didn't even have time to hold my breath. I thought as I came back up I would be killed by the NVA soldier. I clicked my safety off my gun and pushed up off the bottom bringing my gun up so as to be prepared to shoot. To my relief when I broke the surface of the creek, someone had killed the NVA who was lying dead where he had aimed his rifle at me. I never did find out who shot the enemy soldier who had me in his sights!

The Good Word – "Enough of these swamps, let's go back," says Captain Henry Montgomery (left) of Memphis, TN. The Tomahawks were in search of enemy weapons caches.

Tropic Lighting News, Captain Henry Montgomery in swamp

After I moved to the other side of the creek, there was intense firing of AK-47s, M-60's AND M-16s. The sides of the creek were wet and slippery, so I had to hang onto brush to pull myself out of the creek. As I got to the top of the creek sides, I saw several of our men assaulting the island in the middle of the swamp. Hidden on the island, several of the enemies were firing at our men as they moved across the open swamp. I immediately opened up on the island and began to move forward towards the island. As usual I could not see any enemy or their muzzle flashes. They were not shooting toward me, but rather toward the men assaulting from my right. At the same time, one of our guys was dropping M-79 grenades on the island. The assault was over very quickly. I arrived at the island to see two of the enemy dead in shallow foxholes and evidence of a small enemy camp. No one else seemed to be shooting at us as we swept through the base camp. As we moved to the other side of the island, we saw two of the enemy running through the swamp grass attempting to get away. They were quickly cut down by troops who had circled halfway around the island. We searched the

NVA and collected a knapsack full of documents. These were turned over to our officers for review by the Intelligence branch. The bodies were left where they died. We continued to move through the swamp the rest of the day which was exhausting and miserable. Toward the end of the day we moved into a field and were picked up by helicopters. Everyone bent down low before approaching the helicopters to land. We viewed helicopters as yet another danger to infantry troops. Again it seemed to us that everyone and everything was out to kill us, not just the NVA. We loaded up and took a short ride back to our night laager position where our APCs were dug into defensive pits.

Hot Landing Zone (LZ)

June 7, 1968

That night I would have been on either a night ambush, a LP (listening post), or pulling perimeter guard duty on the .50 caliber on our track or the one in our bunker. We had two .50-caliber machine guns but were only authorized one. We got the other one by taking it off one of our platoon's tracks which had been blown up. We never turned the machine gun back into the armory, and no one ever asked for it. But then many of the other squads also had two 50s which were retrieved from blown up tracks, a common occurrence. The officers either pretended they didn't know or didn't care about returning extra weapons to the armory, as everyone appreciated the extra firepower. You can imagine how dead tired you would be by nightfall after walking all day in the jungle, or swamp or rice paddies, or being in a firefight. Then, though exhausted, you would have to either set up a night laager position, digging holes and filling sandbags, or to go out on a night ambush, or LP, or stand guard. The next day, with only hours of sleep, you would get up and do it all over again. Then on top of this we never got enough to eat. "C Rats" (C rations) were enough to keep you alive, but not by much. This is why we were so thin and exhausted all of the time. The compounding impact on your body and your outlook to go through this day-after-day and then to be in firefights with the adrenaline flowing, drained you of all your strength and stamina. This is what the military calls the thousand-yard stare of men who have been in combat too long. All of us had had it after about a month . . . then to think you had to do this every day for a year. Not an encouraging prospect for survival.

The next day, we went out on another "Eagle Flight" on the choppers. We were told we were going into a suspected enemy camp site, and we could anticipate a warm reception.

After boarding the choppers we took off and went up into the cool air, with the wind blowing into and around the chopper. It was cold when you only had on a flak jacket, as we often did. In a short period of time, we saw an open break in the forest. The door gunner pointed down to the clearing and motioned five minutes by holding up his hand with fingers extended. As normal, we flew high to keep away from small arms fire, then we dropped very fast onto the landing zone or LZ. Everything seemed normal until we got within about twenty feet from the ground. I was in the second chopper on the right hand side of the eagle flight. All of a sudden, all hell broke loose with machine guns, AKs, mortars and RPGs shooting at us as we were landing. Immediately the door gunners opened up firing at the wood line. Then the chopper directly in front of us, which was just slightly lower, kept going and hit the ground! It had been hit by ground fire or an RPG and crash landed. Fortunately it was low to the ground, so everyone survived with injuries. At that point, all I wanted to do was to get out of the chopper and get on the ground. You were a sitting duck landing on a chopper with no protection at all. We were still moving and going down, and I was hanging out on the struts of the chopper so I could dismount quickly. When we got within what I thought was five to six feet above the ground, I jumped out. Turns out that the grass was about shoulder-length high, and we were more like ten feet from the ground. It also turned out that the grass was growing in mud up to your knees. Of course jumping from ten feet drove me into the mud up to my thighs. I was stuck solid in mud! I couldn't move my legs at all. So here I was in the middle of a killing ground with machine guns and enemy firing all around us and, just for good measure, they had mortars and RPGs zeroed in exactly where we landed. I could hear and see the bullets mowing down the grass all around me, but no matter how hard I tried, I could not pull my feet up out of the mud. I leaned forward as far as I could to keep a low profile, while trying desperately to extract my legs from the mud.

After what seemed an eternity, someone came by from in back of me, moving slowly through the knee high mud. I yelled for him to help, and he came over. After a lot of grunting and pulling, I finally pulled free from the mud. I was exhausted fighting the mud, and yet I knew we had to get out of the killing zone and move to shelter in the hedgerows. We continued to move forward, but did not want to fire our weapons since we could not see anything, and we knew our soldiers were in front of us. We yelled curse words and other profanity as we moved forward so none of our troops would shoot us, thinking we were the enemy sneaking up from behind. No gook could curse like American soldiers.

The bullets continued to cut down the grass above our heads as we moved forward, as close to the mud as possible. Moving like this was exhausting, trying to keep low and yet pull your feet out of the mud, which is pulling back at you every time you lift a foot. Besides that the grass was elephant grass, and it cut you as the leaves were very sharp. We moved toward the sound of M-60 and M-16s firing which have a very different sound than AKs, which have a scary crack-crack sound. We found a trail that someone else had made through the elephant grass and continued forward toward the shooting. Finally the grass was less thick and the mud not as deep. We were getting closer to the wood line. We got down on all fours and crept forward very carefully. Then we saw a slight rise where our men had set up a fighting line and were firing against the enemy, who was dug into fighting positions and bunkers. While we were struggling through the grass, two gunships, which had accompanied us on the Eagle flight, were firing rockets and mini guns into the tree line where the enemy was located.

We crawled up to the slight rise and began to fire into the tree line looking for muzzle flashes of the enemy. The enemy machine guns were easy to spot as they threw out a tremendous amount of fire with green tracers (our tracers were red). We could see some others in our company maneuvering around the left sides of the tree line trying to get behind the enemy fighting positions. In our position we were pinned down and could not move in any direction without drawing a tremendous volume of fire from automatic weapons. So we stayed put digging in as best we could while returning fire.

Some of the enemy positions were as close as twenty-five to thirty yards away from where we were pinned down. Too close for artillery or mortar support. There were perhaps ten of us in this position with the rest of the company spread out on the edge of the clearing. I had no clue where my squad was or the rest of our platoon for that matter. I didn't know the men who were firing alongside of me although I recognized a couple from our company. We stayed in this position returning fire for perhaps an hour waiting for something to happen or someone to give us orders. Then someone saw one of the other troops on the left hand side of the tree line motioning for us to get our heads down with hand signals. We all knew what that meant, either artillery or an air strike coming in real close! We stopped firing and put our heads down and held onto our steel pots hoping the artillery would not land on us. I had bad memories of what artillery could do to a human. I wanted to be someplace else, anywhere else in fact.

Less than a minute later the world crashed around us, explosions and dirt and chunks of whatever being thrown all around and on top of us. The artillery was hitting very close to us, way too close for comfort! We just kept hoping and praying for no short rounds to fall on us. The artillery barrage kept up for about ten minutes then everything was quiet. No shooting on either side. All of us where just glad it was over with, but no one moved just in case. Then we saw troops on our left side, which was the only side we could see from our position, moving forward toward the tree line firing as they went. So we too got up and began firing and moving toward the enemy positions. The artillery had chewed up the enemy's defensive positions. Vegetation, logs, parts of bunkers and bodies were thrown about, with craters and caved in bunkers. In front of us the closest bunker took a direct hit and all that remained was a crater. No bodies or anything else. We heard firing all around us but apparently no one I saw was hit. We spread out and fired or threw grenades into several more fighting positions and bunkers. I saw a bunker which was untouched and threw in a grenade, yelling, "fire in the hole" then hit the dirt. I looked inside but it looked abandoned so I moved on to keep up with the troops sweeping the fortified enemy position. There were several enemy bodies and parts of bodies spread around so there had been perhaps a couple of squads or a platoon of enemy facing our company. It was difficult to tell how many of the enemy we faced as many got away when it was apparent to them that they were about to be overrun. They always had a well-planned exit strategy and multiple routes to escape. I finally met up with my squad near the end of the enemy's encampment. None of them were wounded or killed. The company sustained six wounded in the engagement and we lost one helicopter. After that we searched for documents and weapons and then moved to another field where we were picked up by the choppers and returned to our night laager position with the tracks.

Eagle Flights and ARVN Soldiers

In speaking with some of the door gunners who rode shotgun on the Eagle Flights, they told us about numerous situations where they literally had to "throw the ARVN" infantry out of the helicopters when they landed in hot LZs, which were landings where the enemy was firing at you. They said they were under orders to toss out any ARVN soldier who refused to jump out of the chopper at the LZ. They said they did so even though they had to stop firing their M-60 machine guns and thus endangered their own lives. One told me that they were carrying an ARVN mortar squad and that several of the ARVNs would not get out of the helicopter. Not only did they throw them out but one of the door gunners dropped a mortar base plate (a heavy metal base plate weighing twenty-plus pounds depending on the type of mortar) on top of one of the ARVN soldiers they had thrown out of the chopper! No soldiers I know who came in contact or had to fight with the ARVN respected them as fighting men. In fact we all knew that if we Americans left Vietnam the tough NVA would overrun them in no time, which is exactly what happened.

Another Eagle Flight with Contact

June 8, 1968

Upon returning from the firefight, we had our usual C-rations and settled in for the night. Fortunately we had an uneventful night and got some sleep. Next day we ate C-Rats for breakfast and then boarded the slicks or choppers for another Eagle Flight. We landed in the LZ without incident. By now we were getting the hang of operating from helicopters. Under fire it does not take long to learn quickly how to survive. Once we landed everyone dismounted and quickly moved toward the wood line. Then we began to sweep the area in a clover leaf search pattern. A few hours later we made contact with an enemy squad in an encampment. When we approached they opened fire and we hit the dirt and spread out. It was apparent that we were not up against a large force as there were no heavy weapons such as machine guns. Two platoons worked their way around the sides and back of the enemy while our platoon kept them pinned down in front. Once in position the platoons charged the enemy positions from three sides. The enemy was in foxholes and trenches with minimum cover. With overwhelming firepower they were quickly overrun and killed. We took no prisoners as the enemy chose to fight to the death. We counted a half dozen bodies. It is likely that some escaped before they were surrounded. In addition we captured several weapons and documents. No one was killed on our side nor was anyone in our platoon wounded. After searching the camp and destroying rice and other provisions we moved out to another LZ to be picked up by the slicks and returned to our night laager position.

Mounted and Un-mounted Patrols

June 9–12, 1968

The next three days we spent making mounted and un-mounted sweeps of our AO (Area of Operations) and conducting night ambushes. We remained patrolling in the area around TSN Air Base. On the night of the 12th TSN received rocket fire once again but we did not see anything. During this period a culvert covering a stream over a road was blown up, forcing the engineers to spend the day repairing it.

I am not sure if this was the exact date, but we had an incident on ambush when we set up to protect another culvert from being blown by the NVA sappers. This night three of us went out on an ambush with a starlight scope. This was a most advanced and secret night vision scope which enabled us to see in the dark. It was like looking through a fish tank with a green light in it. We were perhaps a thousand or more meters from our night laager position. We set up in the woods overlooking a road where a culvert made up of three large corrugated pipes four- or five-feet in diameter were used to cover over a stream. This culvert apparently was a favorite of the enemy to blow up and then set up booby traps and snipe at the engineers when they came to repair it the next day. During the day our mortar platoon had zeroed in on the culvert with 81 MM mortars. Our job was to call in mortars if we saw anyone mining the bridge. Then we would get away from the area and go to an alternative site until morning when we could safely enter our company perimeter. You did not want to try to re-enter the company defensive perimeter at night or you would likely be shot by your own men. Thus we always had an established secondary position where we would move after blowing an ambush,

After a few hours I was taking my turn at the starlight scope when I saw movement on the side of the road. I shook the other two men with me on the ambush and told them to be alert. One of our ambush team alerted the mortar platoon to be ready to fire via radio. We were hidden in the woods two hundred yards or so from the road where the stream ran through the culvert. I saw three sappers setting up explosives on the bridge. I handed the scope to one of the others so he could see and then I took it back to assure we hit the sappers at the right time. Two of the sappers were on the road while the third was setting charges in the culvert pipes. I could see them plain as day. I waited until all three were on top of the road and I told our radio operator to call in the mortars. I took only a few seconds and the mortars arrived dead in the middle of the road! I don't know how many mortars hit but I think they shot four of them. It was quite a series of explosions. With the first hit all I saw was a flash of light and then I was blinded through the starlight scope and saw nothing further. After the mortars stopped one of the others took a look through the starlight scope and said he could see nothing. After that we reported a direct hit and told our command post we were moving to the alternate site. We stayed in that position all night until morning when we carefully returned to our night laager position where our company had set up.

The next day we investigated the area and found where the mortars had hit. All of them landed in the middle of the road, right on top of the three enemy soldiers. We found a few scraps of web material, very little blood and nothing else. It was clear that the three sappers had disintegrated in the massive explosions of the 81 mm mortars.

More Enemy Killed in the Swamp

June 18–19, 1968

For the next few days we were airmobiled into another swamp. It was dirty, wet, and generally lousy trudging through the swamps. You could see the leeches swimming after you trying to get into your clothing. They would be about two to four inches long swimming through the water. They could swim about as fast as you could walk through the water and mud knee high. So it was impossible to get away from them. Once they got on you they would shrink to one to three inches and fill up with blood. Whenever we got to dry ground, we would drop our drawers, open our shirts, and light up cigarettes to burn them off. Everyone helped each other burn them off. If we could not light up cigarettes due to the rain and wet, we sprayed on "bug juice" which would force them to let go. But cigarettes were better for getting them off of your skin. If you pulled them off, you would get an infection which got much worse in the putrid swamp water. I hated the leeches. They were disgusting, hanging off of you, and they got all over your body. Especially annoying was when they got on your balls or tried to climb into your ass. It was not unusual to have twenty or more of them just from walking around in the swamp for a couple of hours.

When we came upon islands (or more accurately high ground not under water) in the swamp, we would often find evidence of squad-

or platoon-sized enemy camps. We found several of these which were recently occupied, and in some of these we found weapons, ammunition, mines, and documents. These we either carried back with us or destroyed in place. We also destroyed any bunkers we found. We could sometimes see where the enemy retreated through the swamp grass as we approached. Obviously they were nearby. On one of these sweeps, where we approached an island from three sides, a squad of five or six enemy soldiers bolted out the back side of the island as the main part of our company approached. My squad was in the frontal assault with the bulk of the company. As we approached the island, we heard automatic weapons firing from the rear of the island. The squad of enemy who were trying to escape was cut down by our soldiers who had circled around the sides of the island. We killed all of them and incurred no casualties ourselves.

After another exhausting and filthy day in the swamps, the helicopter came in to retrieve us and return us to our night laager position. When I got back to our night laager, I tried to avoid getting trench foot and ring worm, which everyone had to some degree, by changing into dry socks. Since we only had a single pair of jungle boots, and these were wet all the time, it was impossible not to get some form of trench foot.

More Weapons Caches

June 20–22

We got a break from the Eagle Flights and went out on sweeps with our APCs. This way, at least, we stayed out of the swamps. We made several mounted and un-mounted sweeps of suspected enemy base camps and generally continued looking for the main body of NVA which were supposed to be in our area. Frankly it was fine with me if we never found them. We also dismounted and searched stream beds and high ground for the enemy. We found another larger enemy base camp of perhaps a company size, with gear, food, cooking supplies, and enemy weapons, mines, rockets, grenades and ammunition caches. Once again the enemy had cleared out as we approached. We saw several of the enemy retreating and fired at them at long range with our 50s, but I don't think we killed any of them. After these sweeps we returned to our night laager and set out on ambushes and pulled LP and guard duty at night. It was common for the NVA to fire some rockets and mortars at our night laager position during the night, just to get even and see if they could kill a few of us. Most of the time they wounded or killed some men in the initial bombardment, but by the second round everyone had taken cover. For the most part we stayed under cover most of the time. Many of the wounded or killed were support troops, such as artillery, who did not dig in like the infantry.

We Lost another Lieutenant and Sergeant Due to Arrogance

June 23, 1969

The next day we went out on another Eagle flight (helicopter landing) this time in a rice paddy surrounded by hedgerows and with a large swollen stream running through the area. The swollen stream was perhaps ten yards wide with a slow moving current. We were operating in a company-sized sweep of the area, but the platoons were separated conducting a clover leaf sweep of the area. A clover leaf sweep had three or four different platoons moving forward to the side coming together in overlapping circles at the top of the cloverleaf. The name "clover leaf" was named because the sweep looked like a clover leaf from the air.

In the area we were covering we came across the swollen stream. Walking besides the stream we found evidence that the enemy had camped in the area and had built fortified fighting positions and trenches. We were on guard for booby traps and for any signs of the enemy. We were all aware that the NVA set up mines, booby traps and ambushes whenever we entered his territory. At this time we had a brand new platoon lieutenant and also a new platoon staff sergeant fresh from the USA. The way we operated with new lieutenants and

NCOs was to listen to them when we were not in combat or if they asked us to do something reasonable. However, in combat or if they told us to do something we knew was stupid, we try to persuade them that it was wrong. If that didn't work, we just did not do it, or we did something different when out of their sight.

At this time I was the acting Squad Leader. There were only four of us left so, with the most experience in-country, I was the ranking leader. At this time Tracy and George were in my squad. These were still the two men I was closest with in Vietnam. Both were draftees and both only wanted to go home in one piece. Unfortunately, later on both were severely wounded. Tracy was with me that day, but George was not. He was our track driver, and as such, he stayed back with our track pulling maintenance. Soldiers didn't last very long in our company.

We were walking about fifteen feet behind one another on the side of the stream watching very carefully for booby traps and signs of the enemy. We had been sweeping the rice paddies and hedgerows all morning. Then the new lieutenant came up to us and told us to go into the swollen stream and search for tunnels and weapons. We told him that was not a good idea, as the NVA sometimes put booby traps in the streams where you could not see them. As I was arguing with the lieutenant, the new platoon sergeant came up and told us to go into the stream. I told him that that was bad idea, and that it was dangerous enough being on the side of the stream. We could get ambushed too easily and there were sometimes booby traps in the streams. He told us to go into the stream anyway and to follow orders. I told him I wasn't going to do it because it was a stupid order and could get us killed for nothing. At that the new lieutenant went bonkers and said I was disobeying a direct order and that I would be court-martialed. I told him, "I don't care. What are you going to do, put me in LBJ! That would be better than this!" LBJ was the name of the army jail in Vietnam, called Long Ben Jail or LBJ for short. It was also an infantryman's insult to the president Lyndon Baines Johnson (LBJ). The lieutenant said, "You're on report. I will handle you when we get back to camp." I said, "By the way, Lieutenant, aren't you supposed to lead the way." Then he looked at me with a look that could kill and said to my squad, "Follow me!" They looked at me and looked at the sergeant and lieutenant and just shook their heads. They didn't say anything, but their message was clear. They were not going either. So the lieutenant said, "You're all on report." Then he and the sergeant stomped away and got into the stream.

We moved away from the stream, far enough that if a grenade went off we would not be killed. Then the new sergeant took the lead with the lieutenant following behind and some other soldiers he got to follow behind him. Sure enough, about twenty minutes later we heard the sergeant yell that he found a wire and that he was going to follow it and disarm the booby trap. With that my squad got down behind the rice paddy berm, knowing what was likely to happen next. Amazingly the sergeant found the booby trap which was a clear fish line attached to a grenade (one of ours as we found out later) and somehow disarmed it, perhaps by inserting a pin into the grenade. Finding a booby trap was extremely difficult, especially under brown moving water. We all assumed that the sergeant and lieutenant would get out of the stream, as now they knew it was booby trapped. I also believed that this would vindicate us for refusing to go into the stream. Finding the booby trap before it killed someone was a real stroke of luck. In Vietnam you didn't want to push your luck too far. To our amazement, the sergeant and the lieutenant stayed in the stream and continued on like nothing happened. We were shocked, as we knew better. The troops behind also knew better and wanted to get out of the stream. They were falling back, letting the sergeant and lieutenant get further ahead. I told my squad, "These guys are fucking nuts. They are going to get someone killed. We are going to move farther away from the stream." And we did.

Sure enough, about ten minutes later, the sergeant yelled, "Found another one! I am going to disarm it." The lieutenant said, "Go ahead but be careful!" Everyone else in the stream got down and moved to the side, seeking some cover. The new lieutenant just stood in the middle of the stream like the fool he was. A few seconds later, there was the loud explosion of a grenade. BOOM! I looked at my squad with the knowing look of "we knew it; they pushed their luck and got themselves killed!"

With that we hurried over to the stream and saw the sergeant with part of his head blown off, and the lieutenant with severe wounds to his head. Some of the soldiers following behind the new lieutenant were in the process of pulling the wounded men out of the stream bed. The other soldiers in the stream were getting out of the stream bed, climbing out as fast as they could in case someone else hit another booby trap. We were walking parallel to the sergeant and lieutenant, but a distance away. My squad and I jumped in to help pull the wounded men out of the stream. I helped carry the wounded lieutenant out of the stream bed. He was in a bad way. Frankly, I didn't think he would make it. I believe the sergeant was in worse shape. One of our medics was on the spot as soon as we pulled the lieutenant and sergeant out of the water, and he started giving first aid to save the lieutenant. Fortunately, only the sergeant and lieutenant were blown up by the grenade booby trap.

It didn't take very long for the medevac helicopter to arrive, and we loaded the lieutenant and sergeant onto the helicopter. The lieutenant was still alive, but was making that guttural sound when men are dying. I don't think he made it! While I didn't help with the sergeant, it appeared to me the sergeant was likewise not going to make it. Off they went and we never heard about them again. The captain was on the net with our platoon RTO who was keeping him up to date on what was going on, but I don't know what he told him. No one ever asked me what happened. We did not speak to the CO much as he rarely ever spoke directly with us about anything.

After that, no one else got into the stream. The other squads just followed our squad as we carefully continued sweeping our side to the stream. We found nothing and saw no one and fortunately did not find any more booby traps. In the afternoon we were picked up by helicopters and returned to our night laager Position with our tracks. No one ever said anything to my squad or me about being "on report" or anything else about the incident. Tracy, George and the other couple of men in our squad, new replacements, talked about what happened. We all agreed we would not follow stupid orders from new sergeants and lieutenants if it meant we were going to get killed for nothing.

Ambush and the Giant Leeches

June 24, 1968

After sweeping all day it was once again my turn to go out on ambush. It was raining all day and, like everyone else, I was tired, hungry, cold and wet. We used C-4 to heat up some C-Rats and black coffee. Then it was time to get our gear in order and to be briefed on the ambush site and intelligence which was almost never accurate or useful. As usual we took a radio, pop-flare and starlight scope with us in addition to the extra Claymore mines and grenades we always carried on ambush. I was to lead an ambush of two new men who just joined our platoon. I was not thrilled to have only two rookies with me, but as usual we were severely short of men. With new men, they would be so afraid that at least they would not fall asleep, and perhaps I could catch some extra sleep which was badly needed. The only caution with new replacements was to warn them never to blow an ambush or we all would be killed for sure. Before proceeding outside the perimeter I checked their gear and made sure they carried plenty of grenades and claymore mines, in addition to ammo and extra water. I also checked to make sure that they carried nothing extra, such as food, and nothing that made any noise. I also sat down with them and told them what to expect and to stay close to me and do as I did. I also told them my usual warning, which went something like this, "You are never to make any noise if we see the enemy, nor are you to shoot or blow a claymore mine unless I do so first! If you do, I guarantee you will die because I am going to shoot you myself for getting us all killed! Do you understand me?" Typically new replacements would look at my eyes and see I was dead serious, and then they would shake their heads in understanding with wide-open eyes.

Our orders were to proceed out about one click from our night laager position and set up the ambush on the high ground in an open field. This would give us a field of vision to the surrounding tree line where the suspected enemy would be marching. It seemed like a decent spot to me since the field was a large open area surrounded by forest. Thus we would not be too close to the wood line, and we could see someone coming a long way away. According to the map, (maps we had were very unreliable), a small stream ran through the middle of the field. It did not look like much of a stream so we figured we could hop over it and try to keep dry as much as possible. We were cold and wet so we took along our field jackets and ponchos, and wrapped our poncho liners in plastic to keep them somewhat dry. We left our helmets with our tracks and wore fabric "Boonie hats" so we could hear better at night and make less noise going through brush and jungle. We also checked the radio to make sure it was working, and I verified the password with the men manning the perimeter where we would go through the barbed wire surrounding the perimeter. I didn't want anyone to think we were sappers going through the wire.

We left the wire, checking with the men in the bunkers one last time, letting them know we were going out and when they could expect to see us return. We always returned from ambush in the dark so that if any enemy were around they would not see us moving around outside of our defensive positions. Coming back through our wire at night was a scary experience, since you never knew if everyone had got the word that you were coming in. There were just too many itchy fingers manning the perimeter that fired first and asked questioned later.

We proceeded to follow the azimuth we were assigned, navigating as best we could when it was pitch dark and raining. There are no lights in the boonies so you only see by starlight and moonlight if the sky is clear. When it is raining, it is very dark and you cannot see but a few feet in front of you. This has its advantages since the rain masks a lot of noise and it blinds the enemy as well. Of course from our standpoint, not bumping into or seeing any enemy was the ideal situation. We did not want to meet up with the enemy a half a mile from friendly lines with only three men.

We were, of course, soaked for the most part, in spite of our ponchos. But at least some of our upper bodies were dry. Even in the tropics it is cold at night, especially when you are wet and tired. We proceeded out into the middle of the field, trying to keep our bearings without the use of a flashlight. It is difficult in daylight to follow a compass heading in the woods, much less at night when you can't see or use any light for fear of being spotted by the enemy. We finally came to the small stream indicated on the map. As usual, the map was dead wrong, and the small stream looked more like a canal to us. It is likely that it was swollen by the rain, but it certainly was not a stream. In the dark it was unclear how deep the canal or stream was, but it looked a lot deeper than a stream. We walked along the sides of the now large stream or canal, looking for a place to cross. I didn't like being out in the middle of a field near a large canal but I did not know how we would get across the canal. I decided to call back and to see if we could go to an alternative ambush site. I silently as possible put my head underneath the poncho and whispered our situation to our command net. I was ordered to go to the prescribed ambush site because intelligence was certain we would see a troop movement in the wood line. I responded with single word "bullshit!" But cut off further argument as I did not want to risk talking anymore in that exposed position. I wanted to get across the canal and get to safe ground under cover. Besides there was no place to set up for the night in the immediate area since the field was flooded in several inches of water.

I looked around and thought I saw an area where the water seemed to be running slightly faster indicating shallows. The water was running slowly since the area was flat so there was no fear of being washed away. I just didn't want to get more wet or cold than I already was. So I began to cross the canal or flooded stream. I waded about halfway across with the other men guarding me. I went up to my knees and then to my waist. The water was freezing cold, but at least my chest and blanket were keeping dry. As I got within a few feet of the opposite shore, I stepped in a hole and went up to my chin. I was so mad at getting a cold dunking and being ordered to cross the "small stream," and generally pissed off anyway, that I bellowed out "FUCK" as loud as I could! I am sure anyone within a quarter of a mile heard it. The two men I was with were terrified and didn't want to cross the stream. I motioned impatiently for them to come over, but they did not seem to want to cross. After what seemed like a quarter hour, but more likely a minute or so, they came over one by one. Both had somehow missed the hole and got wet only halfway up their chests.

After that we found a dry area which was elevated above the rest of the field by a couple of feet and covered in thick vegetation. We scanned the area with the starlight scope and saw nothing but woods all around. So we set up our claymore mines around us with several extra facing the wood line where we most likely thought the enemy could emerge. Then, as we were close enough to where we were supposed to be, I called in to command to whisper quietly that we were set up. After setting up the ambush site, I handed the starlight scope to one of the new men and indicated for him to keep looking around since we did not know from where the enemy could emerge. Next it was personal time to get the leeches off of us using only bug juice since we could not use matches or lighters. Most of the leeches that were on us were on our legs, chest and backs. These were some of the largest leeches I had seen. I really hated being eaten by leeches so I wanted them off of me as soon as I could settle down. We took turns getting the leeches off one another's backs with one of us watching through the starlight scope at all times. One of the replacements kept indicating a big leach was on his back and wanted help. I pulled up his shirt expecting to see several of the large leeches. It was dark, but on his light skin I thought I saw a snake on his back! Instinctively I slapped it away with my hand. To my amazement the snake didn't move! It was anchored into his back. Then looking closer, I saw it was a giant leach. I had seen some large leeches in Vietnam but never one the size of a small snake. It must have been two feet long! We sprayed it with bug juice, using up a whole bottle, but it would not let go. I didn't know what else to do, so I told the other replacement to pull on it while I cut it in half with my knife. He gingerly grabbed the slimy leach and pulled it tight while I cut it in half. It was difficult to cut, as it was rubber-like, and I only had a small pocket knife which was not very sharp. Eventually I managed to cut the leach in half, however it still would not let go, and the head remained in the replacement's back. At this point in time there was nothing more we could do, so the replacement soldier spent the night with the leech's head imbedded in his back.

Of course all of my gear was soaked and I did my best to wrap up in my cold wet poncho and poncho liner. During the night nothing happened except for more leeches crawling up on us. After spending several uncomfortable hours at the ambush site and seeing nothing, it was time for us to return to our night laager. So we packed up our gear and mines and headed back the way we had come. It was still dark, but since we had just traveled this route a few hours ago, we had little trouble finding our way back. On the way we managed to ford the swollen stream as before without falling into another hole and only getting our chests wet midway.

When we returned to our night laager I had the new soldier immediately report to the platoon medic. Apparently he, too, could not get the leech's head to let go of the soldier's back. He also felt that the leach had been in long enough where it had infected the soldier. So the next morning the new soldier was dusted off to the hospital where they surgically removed the leech's head, gave him a bunch of shots, and disinfected the wound. He had light duty for a couple of days while the hole in his back healed. Everyone was amazed at the size of the leach. Even though it was cut in half, it was still an impressive size.

Surrounding and Searching a Village

June 25, 1968

Typical of our missions was to surround and search a village for enemy, weapons, and enemy documents. This day we surrounded a village called Xom Go May. We arrived outside the village at 5 a.m., just before light. We first moved in with dismounted infantry and surrounded the village. No one was supposed to be moving after dark or early morning. If anyone was trying to enter or exit the village, they would likely be enemy. Often they were collecting taxes, food, or manpower, or just terrorizing the population. On this day we did not see anyone entering or leaving the village. So at dawn we called in the APCs and then went about searching the village for enemy or enemy contraband. We would sweep through the village searching baskets, hooches (Vietnamese houses made of mud and straw), storage bins, haystacks and bunkers. Then we would gather all of the people together in the center of the village to be interrogated by South Vietnamese accompanying us. On this search of the village, we discovered no enemy or military supplies and took no prisoners, but something seemed suspicious.

We all felt that the villagers were hiding something. Our Cho Hoa (NVA soldiers who had surrendered to our side and later joined our units as guides and interpreters) questioned several of the villagers and indicated to us that he believed they were cooperating with the NVA. We were all frustrated with being fired at by snipers, which was an almost daily occurrence especially when running the roads and being injured or killed by booby traps and mines, so we were not friendly disposed to these villagers. Tracy, George and a couple of others in our squad had swept a small shrine with a cement or plaster Buddha in it. So we decided we would take it and use it on the front of our track like decoration on the front bow of a ship. When we entered the shrine and began to take the Buddha several of the old ladies started jabbering and falling on their knees. We simply pushed them out of the way and took their Buddha for good luck. We used the water deflection plywood on the front of the APC to tie up the Buddha and drove away with it. We drove around like that for a while until, sometime later, when our track was blown up, the Buddha went along with it.

Sometime later, during another unrelated sweep through a small village which seemed friendly enough, Tracy and I were going through one of the larger village hooches. The villagers were not hiding from us and seemed friendly enough. We entered this hooch and there we saw a beautiful Vietnamese girl sitting on a bed, or more like a simple weaved elevated platform, with a picture poster of an American model hanging on the wall. We had never seen good-looking women in any of the villages we had swept previously. We were stopped dead in our tracks. We sat down next to her and used sign language and what we knew of Vietnamese to try to talk. She was very friendly, and we stayed like that for a while talking. We totally neglected our duty to search her hooch and the village in general. After a while, we heard the lieutenant call for everyone to form up as we were moving out. I recall this incident, since it was about the only time we saw a good-looking women in such a small village in the middle of nowhere in Vietnam. Most of the time the only people left in the villages in the countryside were the very old and very young. They looked like death warmed over, all wrinkled with black teeth.

Air Mobile into NVA Camp

June 26, 1968

Once again our company was airlifted via choppers into a swamp. We spent a few hours moving through the swamp, searching the high ground and jungle outcrops for enemy and his base camps. After spending the morning searching, we found nothing of interest. Trudging through a swamp with leeches, bugs, mud and grasses was exhausting. But as usual, the army wanted to get their due from us for the combat pay we were receiving, so they sent in choppers to transport us to another part of the swamp. Thus we moved into an area of the swamp where choppers could hover but not land, and we jumped on. We were transported to another part of the swamp and disembarked. After searching the area for several hours, we came upon a small enemy base camp. Here we found living quarters for perhaps several platoons or an understrength company of men. While we found no enemy there at the time, there was plenty of evidence that they had left in a hurry. So quickly, in fact, that they left behind weapons, ammo, grenades, mortars, rice, cooking gear and other military items. We searched the area for the enemy but found no one. Then we gathered up the weapons, ammo, mortars, and other gear, and destroyed the base camp and food. We did this by burning everything we could find and throwing the rice on the ground. When we had oil from our APCs, we would also pour it down the wells to poison them. This time we did not and simply threw in as much garbage as possible and urinated in the wells. After an exhausting day, we moved out into another area of the swamp and the choppers picked us up. We flew back to join our tracks in the night position and began to prepare for the evening of ambushes, LP and guard duty within the wire.

More Sweeps and Trang Bang Village

June 27–28, 1968

We spent the next few days operating with our tracks sweeping the area around our night laager position. We would move out in the morning, sweep the area for the enemy or base camps, and then return to our night laager positions in the late afternoon. At night we would pull ambushes, LP, and guard duty inside the wire and generally fortify our night laager position in between. On June 29, we moved with our track into Trang Bang. Trang Bang was a village on Route 1 leading from Saigon to Tay Ninh. We often encountered enemy in the surrounding area and had firefights while patrolling Route 1 protecting convoys. In this sweep we condoned off the village and worked with popular forces who interrogated the local populace in the village. This time we found nothing, but the PFs took away several suspected VC or NVA who were of military age in the village. Later we mounted our tracks and moved into another night laager position.

ARVN Draftees

It is interesting to note that in the USA we were eligible to be drafted at the age of eighteen years old immediately upon graduation from high school. In practice most of the men drafted had just turned nineteen, as was in my situation. The Vietnamese in the south only drafted men who were nineteen years or older. In fact, many of the South Vietnamese avoided the draft and hid from the government troops. Others deserted once they had the chance. Anytime we encountered young men in villages or anyplace else they were either draft dodgers, deserters or the enemy. The NVA went into villages in the south and simply pressed into service anyone, men or women, who could help them to transport supplies, dig trenches, tunnels or, if physically able, incorporate them into a fighting unit. They took men and women as young as fourteen years old.

Chinese Soldier Kia in Ambush

June 29, 1968

We set out to set up an early morning ambush with several platoons taking part in the ambush. This was unusual and the only time I recall we ever set up a large ambush. This night, our whole platoon, which was operating at half strength of around twenty men, set up a late night ambush. Apparently someone had good intelligence of enemy movements in this area. We left after midnight from our night laager and moved out to the ambush site. I do not recall if our lieutenant led the ambush or our platoon sergeant. Either way, it was most unusual for our lieutenant or platoon sergeant to go out on ambush with us. It took us about an hour to locate the trail where we set up an ambush site. We went perhaps twice as far from our night laager as our normal ambush—perhaps two thousand yards. We set up a classic L-shaped ambush where most of the platoon set up on one side of the trail while a machine gunner and three to four others set up across the trail, forming an L shape. In spite of everyone's effort to be silent, twenty or so men made a lot of noise walking through the heavily wooded or jungle area. After setting down in the ambush position, we set out claymore mines. I found cover perhaps fifteen to twenty feet off the trail behind a log with a somewhat unobstructed shot at the trail. At least I thought I had a somewhat clear shot to the path, as it was pitch dark and mostly we felt our way around. Our squad set out two or three claymore mines just off the path, facing away from our men at the L-shaped end. I did not want to be on the L-shaped end of the ambush and worked my way into the middle of the side of the ambush. My squad was next to me with about four to six feet in between each of us, just far enough apart where you could touch someone's arm on either side of you. Several hours later, nothing happened and some of the men dozed off. You heard men snoring lightly or breathing heavy, then someone would wake them up and it would stop until the next person dozed off. I, like everyone else, kept dozing off as we were all dead tired. The jungle animals and bugs made quite a racket, so it masked most of our sounds unless you were very close.

After a few hours, likely around 4 a.m. or 5 a.m., we heard the enemy moving toward us down the trail. I heard our soldiers click off the safety switches on their weapons. It was very loud, and I was sure the enemy heard the noise. However, the enemy was talking and making a lot of noise moving down the trail. This worried me, because usually if they made that much noise there would be a lot of them. I hoped that this was not the case since there were only twenty or so of us. I had never triggered an ambush before, even though I had seen enemy. I was deathly afraid to trigger an ambush, not only because we were always vastly outnumbered, but also because I was afraid of our own mortars and artillery falling on top of us. I hoped someone knew what they were doing this time.

We were told to keep our heads down and wait for the ambush leader to fire his claymore mine. Then everyone else was to fire their claymores, keeping their heads down and staying behind cover. Next we were to open up with all rifles until told to stop. I heard the enemy walking past my position and held my breath, hoping they would not hear me breathe. It seemed like a lot of enemy troops were passing me. I am sure my mind was thinking the worst, that we would be overrun. All of this happened in seconds while I waited and waited. Then a loud "boom" broke the silence followed instantly by all of the other claymore mines exploding. After that, everyone opened up with their weapons. I went through several clips, firing on full automatic, before I heard the order to cease fire being passed down the line. By that time you could not hear much of anything. But the slacking fire indicated for everyone to stop. We stayed in position until the word passed not to fire as our own men were going to check out the ambush site for anyone living. I stayed put with my rifle on the ready, the safety position on fire. We heard perhaps one or two of the enemy making gurgling sounds, which were those of a mortally wounded man. We heard a very loud single M-16 shot fired and assumed our men had found someone alive, but no more shots were fired. This would have been a mercy killing as the mortally wounded enemy soldier was too far gone to help.

We stayed in that position for perhaps another hour, waiting to see if anyone else came along the trail. A couple of our men put out claymore mines while others dragged the dead off the trail. I hoped no one else would show up, since I felt we were very lucky not to have run into a larger number of enemies. At dawn we were told that we were moving out and to dismantle our claymore mines. This was a dangerous time since, if the enemy was near, we would be very vulnerable. As dawn broke, you could see massive amounts of blood and guts spewed all over the killing zone along with enemy gear, shredded rifles and packs. Everything and everybody looked like it went through a meat grinder. We estimated that there were perhaps fifteen to twenty of the enemy in the column, but they were so chewed up that it was hard to tell. A claymore mine at close range wipes out anything in its path. We were told to quickly police up weapons and gather up any documents we found as we were moving out. Around us there was nothing left to pick up. Then one of the soldiers told us that there was a Chinese soldier among the dead. We all wanted to see him so we quickly walked to the head of the ambush site where two or three enemy soldiers had been shot but not hit badly by claymore mines. Their bodies were mostly intact. The Chinese soldier had on a khaki uniform like the other soldiers, but he had on better boots and web gear and was much larger than a Vietnamese soldier. In fact, this soldier was bigger than most of us since he did not look like he had been in the field very long.

We took everything of value and left the dead where they fell or were dragged off the trail. Then we made a quick exit back to our night laager base camp. While I was in the field we had heard that one of our other platoons or companies had a similar incident where they triggered an ambush and they found a Russian or Eastern European soldier among the dead enemy. Obviously these were advisors from China, Russia and the Eastern bloc.

Volunteered to Spend Night in Ruff-Puff Compound

June 30, 1968

We were driving down a road passing through a small village with a "Ruff Puff" (Regional Forces) Compound at the far end. We called the Vietnamese Regional Forces Ruff Puffs because they were known to run off and not defend their village if the NVA or even VC attacked them in force. The Ruff Puffs had a fortified compound, likely left over from when the French occupied this area. In driving through the town, Tracy, George and I noticed there were a couple of good-looking women hanging out near what we thought was a local bar hooch. After we set up in our night laager position outside of the town, the captain asked for volunteers to stay in the Ruff Puff compound and to provide sitreps (situation reports) throughout the night. I assume the captain wanted to know what the Ruff Puffs were doing at night so he wanted some volunteers to monitor them.

When our platoon lieutenant asked for volunteers, the three of us volunteered. As we never volunteered for anything in the past, the lieutenant asked, "What's up with you guys that you want to volunteer?" I replied, trying to be serious, "Well, Lieutenant, we are turning over a new leaf and want to be good soldiers." He didn't buy this one bit and replied, "Well, I will tell the captain, but I know you guys are up to something." With that he moved off to report back to the captain. We all laughed to ourselves and got ready to go to the compound. George did not want to go, but Tracy and I insisted he join us. After a while our platoon sergeant walked over to us and said, "I don't know what you guys are up to, but the captain said since no one else volunteered, you're going to the Ruff Puff compound, so saddle up and take the platoon radio!" Then he added, "You are to send in sitreps every half hour, understand?" We nodded our heads. Then the platoon sergeant added, "No screw-ups, you hear. Now get going!" We took off for the Ruff Puff compound at the other end of the village.

We arrived at the compound which had masonry walls surrounding it with broken glass on top. Inside the Ruff Puff compound there were several masonry buildings which made up the compound. They had a chow hall and sleeping quarters, along with a small HQ or administrative building. We were greeted by an interpreter who spoke broken English and who obviously knew we were coming. He indicated we could set up for the night anywhere we pleased, and suggested a small cement elevated platform near the front gate where we could observe the village. So we did as he suggested and set up on the cement platform. Once settled, George called in to notify our company that we were set up for the night. It was beginning to get dark and Tracy and I had other plans. We wanted to sneak into town and see if we could meet the girls we saw when driving through the village. After all, we had been out in the boondocks for months and had not been with a woman during that time! Tracy was a real good-looking Romeo and was always on the look-out for women.

Tracy and George with author

When we told George that we wanted him to stay with the radio and call in sitreps (situation reports) while we went into town, he went nuts, saying, "I'm not gonna stay alone with a bunch of gooks. If you're going, so am I!" We said, "Someone has to stay with the radio, so you take the first shift, and we will be back, and then you can go." He didn't buy this at all, even when we did our best to reason with him. He wasn't buying what we were selling, and he knew there would be no second shift. He complained to the end. Finally Tracy and I gave up and just started toward the gate with George yelling at us all the way.

The gate was a combination double wood door with barbed wire on top. We motioned that we wanted the gate opened, and the Ruff Puffs guarding the gate opened it and we walked out into the town. None of the Ruff Puffs said anything; they just watched us go through the gate. Of course we took our rifles and gear.

So we walked into the town (more like a small hamlet) and located the bar, which was the only hooch in town with lights besides the Ruff Puff compound. We walked in, and for a moment everyone stopped and looked at us. It is likely that in this hamlet they had never seen American GIs up close. Certainly not coming into their bar at night. They probably thought we were there to raid the place or conduct a sweep and search. Anyway, when the two of us moved to a table and sat down, people seemed to calm down. But they were still watching us to see what we were going to do. We called over one of the girls and, with our hands, said in Vietnamese that we wanted beers (bam de bam or something like that as I recall). One of the girls brought over the beers, and we started talking to her using what little Vietnamese we knew (which wasn't much) and pig English. More or less we got along. Everyone in the bar was still very curious about us. Since several of the patrons were young men, they were likely either VC or draft dodgers. We stayed in the bar for several hours and got a bit tipsy. We even bought a round for the patrons who were still in the bar when we left. Everyone seemed to be enjoying themselves, especially Tracy and me. Looking back on this, it was probably very stupid, as we could have easily had our throats slit, but perhaps the VC enjoyed themselves and left us alone because we bought a round of drinks for everyone.

After that we went stumbling and singing back to the Ruff Puff compound where the guards opened the gates and let us in without saying a word. They simply smiled at us and nodded as we walked through the gate. George was highly pissed at us because we had been away for several hours. He had to call in sitreps every half an hour while we were gone. Both Tracy and I fell asleep and George stayed up most of the night calling in sitreps. George tried to wake us up, but we kept falling asleep when it was our turn to call in sitreps. I guess we missed a couple because the next day, when the company came to pick us up, the captain bawled us out personally, which was unusual. I guess he figured out we were up to no good, as both Tracy and I were hung over and looked the part, standing not quite upright on the side of the road. We never volunteered again and were never asked. It was the only time we ever had any fun in the field.

Airmobile Ap Tay Village

July 1, 1968

Earlier this day B Company had swept the bridge and stream near the village of Ap Tay. They found bunkers, 122 rocket parts, grenades, an enemy sampan (like a large canoe), and other evidence of recent enemy activity. After they departed, we were air-mobile into this area around 5 p.m. to sweep the area once again. This was a rather risky set up for us as we went in at dusk and were not at all familiar with the area or what we would find. Eagle flights were bad enough in the daytime but at night they were down-right scary. After a few hours we found nothing, and the choppers were called in to lift us out to rejoin our tracks in our night laager position. Some unfortunate troops were left behind to set up a night ambush at the site. Fortunately it was not my squad and we returned to our track at the night laager.

The troops left behind for the ambush spotted two VC in the open and a helicopter was called in who killed both of them. Fortunately there were no USA casualties.

Company Ambush Patrol and Surprise on LP

July 2, 1968

Apparently our platoon-sized ambush worked so well a few days before that the lieutenant colonel decided to try sending out two companies to set up different night ambushes. Apparently intelligence had gotten wind of a large enemy formation in the area, and we were set out to "ambush them." It seemed to us that "ambush them" meant putting us out in the boonies as bait, daring the larger enemy force to attack us! Then when they attacked we could use our overwhelming firepower to kill as many as possible. At least that was the theory. Unfortunately, unlike a FSB or night laager there was no opportunity for interlocking support between units. For support we had untried and untested artillery registered around our position. In a tight situation the artillery would have to be adjusted while we were under attack. Keep in mind that we were on an "ambush" so we did not register our artillery rounds nor spend any time preparing. We simply moved into a position at night and waited for the enemy to run into our ambush. Basically we were the bait for the enemy and thus expendable for the greater good. It was dusk by the time we arrived at our proscribed position. We set up as quickly and best as we could in a tight company perimeter, hastily uncoiling and putting up a triple stack of concertina wire, flares and mines. We did not have time to dig in proper night bunkers nor dig in our tracks. Some of the men dug foxholes while others did not as they were too exhausted. This was a very vulnerable position to be in should the enemy attack in force. We were all very anxious since we felt very isolated and unprepared for defense of our position, having moved into this location so late.

I was on a listening post (LP) perhaps twenty-five yards outside the wire with one other soldier and a radio. We had set up some trip flares ahead of our position then crawled back behind a small rise in the earth. We were scared stiff to be so exposed so we both tried to stay alert. Sometime late in the evening or early morning hours, the flare went off in front of our LP. This shocked us since it was perhaps fifteen feet in front of our position. We never heard the enemy sneaking up on us, nor did we see a thing in the pitch dark night. When the flare went off, the enemy jumped up and ran! We saw three of them clear as a bell in the light of the flare. Not wanting to be caught outside the wire in such a vulnerable position when the enemy attacked, we jumped up also and began running for our track on the perimeter. We immediately started yelling, "Don't shoot, coming into the wire,

Americans" over and over. It took us about twenty seconds to cover the ground back to our track, jumping over the three strands of concertina wire, ripping a gash in my leg in the process. As soon as we got near our APC, everyone opened up on where the trip flare was still burning. We were just glad to get back inside the wire. We thought an attack was imminent, as sappers often preceded an infantry attack.

Almost immediately, numerous large and small mortar explosions from our side began to hit around our perimeter. This was to kill any enemy who may have been massing for an attack because we were on our own if they did. There were a lot of artillery and mortars fired that evening. According to the Lieutenant Colonel Neilson's diary, there were sixty 4.2-inch mortars and eighty 81 mm mortars fired around our perimeter. That is a lot of ordnance fired in a very small area. The next day we did not find any enemy bodies. It is very possible that the NVA were planning to attack us, but the assault was broken up by the massive mortar barrage we launched at them. We will never know why they didn't attack us. Either way, we were relieved to get out of there the next morning.

July 4th: Real Fireworks

July 4th, 1968

On July 3 we moved our battalion down Highway 1 to a position on the west side of the road opposite of Gate 51 of Tan Son Nhut Air Base (TSNAB) on the northern edges of Saigon. The next day, July 4, we conducted sweeps as normal and then continued to set up our defenses. That evening every rifle and mechanized company in our immediate area began to shoot off Star Clusters in all different colors. Others shot off their rifles. All of this was strictly forbidden by our brigade and battalion commanders. We had been told that "there would be none of these fireworks" earlier in the day, but it was done with a wink and a smile. So no one paid much attention. As far as I know, no one got in trouble. It was quite a display of fireworks.

Running the Roads

July 5–6, 1968

After our July 4 "unauthorized celebration," we swept roads to keep the enemy clear for convoys in and out of TSN Air Base. Typically this involved running down the roads with engineers to assure that they were not mined during the nighttime, then setting individual tracks and squads up alongside the roads at several mile intervals. This was lonely duty as we knew we were exposed if we were hit (attacked) by a platoon or larger group of NVA. We would set up a small perimeter and dig in with everyone on the lookout for enemy. If we saw anything suspicious, we would open fire on them and call the other tracks to come help. Since they were far away we were essentially on our own until help arrived. Frequently we were shot at by snipers and did not know where the rounds were coming from. Fortunately, most of the snipers we encountered were not good shots. The biggest danger we often faced was from mines in the road and claymore mines strapped to trees, which were command-detonated by an enemy soldier as we passed by. Since we sat on top of the tracks to protect ourselves from mines, a large claymore mine could kill or maim a whole squad. This happened several times to tracks in our battalion, but fortunately never to us. At the end of the day we would have to wait until the last convoy passed our position, and then we would fall in behind the last vehicles and return to our night laager position. When it was getting dark and we were alone and exposed, sitting on the side of the road with four to five men was a scary position. We knew that the enemy was always watching us and yet we could not see him.

I do not recall if this incident happened this day. However, early one morning we were heading down a road to clear it of enemy and mines before a convoy came through the area. It was not unusual for us to proceed down a road to watch for mines and enemy. It was, in fact, unusual for us to have engineers attached to us who could clear roads. There were simply too many roads to clear and not enough time. So they used us as guinea pigs to proceed down the roads first. Of course if the roads were mined, our track would hit them. Similarly, if there was an ambush they would attack us, especially being a single track with only four to six men.

We were proceeding down the road at perhaps 20 mph when someone yelled, “Mine!” I saw it about the same time, sticking up in the middle of the road. I was carrying an M-60 machine gun at the time. Our driver (George), who was driving with “lateral extensions” on top of the track, let go of the laterals, which locked the treads. I half dove and half was thrown off the top of the track, along with everyone else except the driver and track commander who was manning the .50-caliber machine gun. I landed very hard on my chest and stomach. As I had bullets for my machine gun wrapped all around my body (we carried around 800–1,000 rounds crisscrossed across your body), when I hit the dirt the bullets dug into my skin and was very painful. Being thrown off of a track which is around six feet high and moving at 20 mph is not a pleasant experience. As it turned out, the “mine” in the road was not a mine at all, but a fake placed there by the enemy to look like a mine! It did exactly what he wanted to accomplish, by having our track stop short and throw everyone off to the ground. Upon inspection, the “mine” was a piece of track from an APC buried halfway into the road with a wire leading into the woods. Coming down the road, it had the appearance of a command-detonated mine. Once on the ground we all crawled for ditches, thinking that we were going to be ambushed. But there was no ambush and indeed no enemy. They were just messing with us, hoping someone would get hurt or killed by the track stopping so quickly. No one was seriously hurt, but we all had a lot of bangs and bruises from being throw from the top of the moving track.

Driving Tracks with Laterals

Laterals were two straps that looped around the two laterals levers which controlled the APC tracks. If you pulled them back, the track would move; if you let go, the tracks would stop. By pulling one side, the track would turn right or left. The driver sat on top of the APCs to protect himself from mines and had a metal extension which he used to push down on the gas pedal. Tracks have no brakes; they just stop rather quickly when the tracks are locked.

Two Men Wounded By Our Own Mortars

July 7, 1968

Our company was assigned to block the road from enemy trying to escape from a rubber plantation that was being swept by B and C Companies. Typically we would arrive at our location at sunrise and take up positions behind cover, or dig in and wait for the enemy to be driven toward us. This was called the hammer and anvil. One company, the hammer, would drive the enemy toward the blocking position company who acted as the anvil. Usually the anvil position was the best part of the operations since you had the chance to dig in while the enemy was driven toward you. The companies acting as the hammer had to push into the enemy and drive them out of their fixed position, a much more dangerous job.

Unfortunately on this day as we were waiting for the enemy to be driven toward us, we received mortar fire. Two men were wounded as a result. As it turned out, the mortar fire was from our own mortars section. We were once again hit by our own men with a short round. Since many times the artillery and our mortars fired over our heads, a short round would land on us. Fortunately no one in my squad was injured. The two men were from another platoon in our company.

Large NVA Base Camps and Ordinance Cache Discovered

July 9 through 13, 1968

We swept areas north of the small village of Dau Tieng and discovered several large NVA base camps. We destroyed many bunkers, buildings, a kitchen, and various other enemy facilities. We poured oil and pissed in the wells to poison them and took whatever materials and supplies the enemy had. We continued to sweep the area and then moved into a rubber plantation. We continued to find evidence of large enemy units in the area. Our recon platoon saw several of the enemy and called in artillery fire on them. Later we found fresh graves in one of the base camps.

On July 12 our platoon was sweeping an area five miles southeast of Tay Ninh and north of Dau Tieng off of Route 19. The area was a heavily wooded area with thick undergrowth. Once again I was walking right point. As I was walking just off a well-worn path (we usually did not walk on the paths as they were often booby trapped) I was watching the ground very carefully for wires indicating a booby trap. We knew we were close to the enemy base camp so I was extra cautious.

We continued to move forward seeing more and more evidence of the enemy. Soon we came across a large enemy base camp which had very recently been occupied. Fortunately no one was in the camp nor did they leave anyone behind to defend it. That in itself was unusual. In the camp we discovered a very large cache of ammunition, grenades, CHICOM (Chinese) claymores of the same type they used to blow us off the top of our APCs, satchel charges (large explosives contained in a satchel for blowing up bunkers), anti-tank mines, 82 mm mortar rounds and Bangalore torpedoes (used to blow up barbed wire when assaulting a defensive position). I have a picture of the ammo cash where we are loading up some of the ordinance into duffel bags to take away from the base camp. We also made the *Tropic Lighting News* on August 12, 1968. As usual we destroyed everything in the base camp as best we could and then moved on to our night laager position.

Outside the wire in our night laager position we dug a large hole and placed the captured ordinance in the hole. One of the men placed C-4 (plastic explosive) in the hole, ignited it with a blasting cap and ran for cover. Everyone in our perimeter took cover. There was a massive explosion and it blew a huge crater in the ground.

The next day we returned to the base camp to see if any of the enemy had returned. But we found no one. That night we moved from our night laager to a more secure Fire Support Base with a battery of artillery from the 7/11 artillery unit. Typical of a FSB there was usually at least a company and more likely several companies of Mechanized

Infantry guarding the artillery. The artillery in turn provided fire support for our local sweeping operations and those of nearby units.

Life in the Infantry

It is an understatement to state that life in the infantry in Vietnam was the most difficult time of my life. Every day was a challenge just to survive the elements without the constant fear of attack, snipers, booby traps and mines. As I mentioned several times, our outfit was always far short of the manpower in which we were supposed to operate. Generally our platoon and company had half or less of the allocated T/O (table of organization) strength. With our platoon's T/O of forty-plus men we frequently operated with 20 or less and often without an officer or platoon sergeant. Our company was always short of officers and NCOs not to mention the infantry men themselves.

Almost every day we were in the field or on the road conducting sweeps of the areas or engaged in firefights with the enemy. We were sent out in company, platoon or squad formations to find and engage the enemy. The enemy almost always began the fight by killing or wounding some of us because we were going after them in their territory. When they did not feel they had the upper hand they simply disengaged and melted away into the jungles or their Cambodia safe havens. It was not unusual for us to come across a company or battalion of NVA in prepared positions while making a sweep. We were grossly outnumbered and outgunned until we brought in artillery or airpower to "get us out of trouble." In the meanwhile we were sacrificed so that additional support troops and firepower could engage and kill the enemy.

A typical day began around 5 a.m. where we had cold C-Rats to eat and perhaps a cup of black coffee when we could heat up the cup with C-4 explosive. We only lit the C-4 when no snipers were around due to the flame which you can see for a long way off. Then we would have some of the men on guard while the others began to breakdown our night laager position un-filling the sandbags which we filled the night or day before, taking down the barbed wire, undoing trip flares, claymore mines, and Marston Mats and loading up everything into our tracks. Then we would head out on patrol either via helicopter or on our tracks or on foot. After marching or patrolling all day we would begin to set up a night laager position about 4 p.m. and begin to "dig in for the night." This took a couple of hours of hard work to dig in our tracks (sometimes with the help of bulldozers in larger FSB or when artillery was present), set up defensive fighting positions, setting up three strands of concertina wire outside our perimeter, registering our weapons with ranges, setting up trip flares, and C-ration cans with stones in them to make noise if the enemy tried to sneak up on us, set out claymore mines and building a fence in front of our track to explode RPGs. Many times when I knew we were going to be attacked I dug a shallow trench the size of a grave underneath our APC and drove the APC over top of the position. Then I laid my poncho in the trench and got in to sleep. That way, when we were attacked, at least I was safe from mortar rounds, but not RPG rockets, and could crawl out of the trench and get into a fighting position quickly. This of course was typically only one night in three unless we were under a threat of imminent attack. After setting up the night laager position we quickly ate some C-Rats (the one hot meal a day was a myth) and prepared to go out on an ambush typically with three men or go outside the wire on a listening post. We were always hungry as you might imagine running around all day and night with little sleep. The "listening post" was a position outside the barbed wire which ringed our night laager position in front of the squad where two men stayed all night. You would report any movements via Prick 25 radio and call in "sitreps" or situation reports during the night. The idea was that if you were being attacked or infiltrated these men would be first to know and of course be killed and thus warn the others inside the night laager perimeter. It was not enviable positions to be in if you were attacked or the enemy was sneaking up on you. Basically you were caught between the enemy and your own men both of whom would be shooting at each other! This is why as infantry you were always exhausted. Couple this with the lack of proper food and diet plus the daily fight to survive in this environment, and even the fittest of men were ground down both mentally and physically. We were like zombies most of the time struggling just to put one foot in front of another and haul around our ammo, water and sometimes packs if we were going out for an extended period without our tracks. Usually we did not carry much beyond ammo, grenades, claymore mines, LAWS, water, a poncho and box of C-rats.

We were constantly hungry, as a box or so of C-rations a day was not nearly enough to keep us fed. When we killed the NVA soldiers, many of them carried bandoliers of rice in a canvas sling around their chests. It was around four feet long and two and a half inches in diameter. Apparently this is what they could live on for a week. When we had a chance we would take these off the dead NVA and use the rice to make a meal. We would cook the rice in water using our steel pots or helmets and heat it up with C-4 explosive. Then we would add whatever C-rations we had to the mix and we would have a sort of hot stew. It beat plain C-rations. But of course we could only do this when we had set up for the night and could light a fire. Being near a fire at night is always dangerous as the enemy can see you a long way off and will often give you a present, such as a mortar, or use you for target practice with a sniper rifle.

In addition to being used as bait to draw the NVA into battles where our superior fire power of air and artillery could annihilate them, we constantly fought the elements. In addition to enemy activity and booby traps/mines, almost every day we lost men to the elements or disease. There are 103 different types of snakes in Vietnam, 100 of which are poisonous, scorpions, army ants who devour everything in their path, bees, termites, nits, multiple types of biting insects, and leeches, the heads of which often caused infections in the stagnant and polluted swamp water. Then there was Trench foot or emersion foot, from being wet constantly, jungle rot where the skin falls off your lower extremities, ring worm, bronchitis and pneumonia, falls resulting in broken bones and sprained ankles, cuts from the jungle grasses, especially elephant grass which cut like a paper cut, poison bushes, attacks by jungle animals (deer, tigers, rats and other jungle animals), and even attacks by domesticated animals such as dogs and water buffalos.

In spite of trying to keep my feet as dry as possible, in the wet season your feet were almost always wet. This invariably resulted in every one of us getting trench foot during the rainy season. The only thing that was different was the extent of the trench foot each of us had. The same is true for ringworm and other water borne infections. During the months of June and July in the height of the monsoon season, which started in late May and began winding down in early November in our area of operations, while tugging through the swamps, jungle, streams and flooded rice paddies nearly every day, I developed a severe case of trench foot. My skin would come off in my sock when I took my boots off. If I rubbed my feet, the skin would come off in my hand, exposing raw flesh. It became too painful for me to walk, much less go back into the disease ridden water and mud.

The thing that eventually got to even the strongest and bravest men was that you were constantly tired, hungry, physically miserable, and always under life-threatening stress. Then, add on top of that, almost every day someone you knew or was in your unit was killed or wounded. You loaded them up on the helicopter dead, or got up thinking that every day made it more likely that your turn was next. Then doing the same thing over and over again every day until your number came up! The constant fear and stress, without a break, just pounds you into the ground, and you became a walking zombie. That is where the description of an infantryman in combat of having a thousand-yard stare comes from.

Battle in an Enemy Base Camp

July 14 and 15, 1968

We set out early in the morning looking for the estimated regimental-sized NVA unit who was occupying the base camps in the areas we were uncovering. We were operating on the northwest edge of the Boi Loi Woods. This was an area where we always seemed to encounter the enemy. Sooner or later all of us knew they would stand and fight. But only when it was to their advantage and when they were ready and prepared. This was typical of how we operated. We would send out groups of men searching for the enemy and find nothing but evidence of his presence or sometimes base camps. The way we found the enemy was when they were in prepared positions waiting to ambush us when we stumbled into their trap. Then we would have a battle on our hands which often resulted in many of our soldiers wounded and killed. When we called in heavy air and artillery support the main body of the enemy would disengage in an orderly fashion via prepared escape routes while a remaining force would tie us down giving the majority of the enemy time to escape.

Fortunately for our company, the recon platoon and B and C Companies stumbled into the enemy ambush as they were approaching his base camp. We had been sweeping in an area away from the camp, so our company was not directly engaged initially. We saw the smoke from the air strikes and artillery but we did not receive any direct fire. Then we were moved into position to support the other companies in the battle. It was estimated that we were facing a regimental-sized enemy force of NVA regulars. We stood off watching the airstrikes and artillery do their worst to the enemy base camps. Frankly I felt lucky that we were not under that intense bombardment. I hoped that it would kill all of them, so we did not have to go in bunker by bunker to kill off the survivors but I knew that that was wishful thinking. It appeared to us that the other companies in the battalion were heavily engaged in the fighting. The battalion was unable to penetrate the enemy fortified base camp in spite of several attempted assaults. The enemy was too well dug in and had too many soldiers for us to make much headway. Likewise they had numerous heavy weapons, including RPG anti-armor rockets, to destroy our lightly armored aluminum tracks.

Our squad did some firing at the enemy, and they fired back, but apparently we were on a nominally defended part of the base camp. However, we did not assault as there was too many artillery and air strikes in progress for us to move in. Letting the airstrikes and artillery do its job was fine by us. That night we formed a defensive perimeter with the other companies not far from the enemy base camp. We were not happy about being so close to such a large enemy force. We dug in deep and stayed up all night on alert expecting an enemy assault. Knowing how many perimeter breaching weapons the enemy had made us all nervous.

Fortunately the enemy did not attack during the night. Apparently they had been severely hurt during the fighting and air and artillery attacks the previous day. Next morning we formed into a multiple company assault line and proceeded toward the enemy with our tracks and all weapons firing. When we reached the enemy bunkers and trench lines we were shocked by the massive complex and how large some of the bunkers were. Our squad came upon massive trench lines connecting bunkers with curves to protect against grenades and direct hits by mortars and artillery. We cautiously moved in and around each bunker checking each one out as we came upon it. I believe that this was the complex where we found the underground hospital, made up of a large room, perhaps twenty feet by thirty feet. It was complete with beds, medical operating equipment, supplies (some from the USA courtesy of Jane Fonda or "traitor Jane"), kerosene lamps and numerous bloody bandages. It was apparent that there were many severely wounded and enemy killed, although all of the wounded and dead bodies had been removed the evening before. Sweeping through the camp we found the evidence of many killed and wounded blood trails and bloody equipment. We also found more enemy ammo and ordinance scattered throughout the base camp. We also came upon a huge bunker full of heavy weapons equipment, RPGs, heavy 82 mm mortars and other ordinance in the middle of the camp where we were searching. What was surprising was how few bodies and body parts we came across, given the massive amount of air and artillery strikes which hit the base camp.

We spent the balance of the day searching every bunker and trench and gathering up all of the weapons, ordinance and documents we could find. I believe that it was in this enemy base camp that we discovered a three-quarter ton US Army truck which was perfectly operational sitting in a bunker. We couldn't figure out how they got it in the bunker as there were no roads around at all and the base camp was in a heavily wooded area or jungle. As we could not move it, we blew it in place with a satchel charge. Then we destroyed everything else with C-4 and satchel charges, and by running over bunkers with our APCs and spinning the tracks. As was our SOP, we pissed and poured oil down the wells so they could not be used again by the enemy.

Once again we made the *Tropic Lighting News* August 12, 1968, edition. For once I got my picture in the newspaper, although you cannot see me very well as the picture is of me riding on a track far in the distance. The next day our Battalion again went searching for the enemy but made no contact.

That evening we were brought together by our platoon lieutenant and told that tomorrow we would have a "special mission" to assault a NVA POW (Prisoner Of War) camp which was holding several of our captured soldiers. Apparently several Special Forces soldiers were being held captive including a Major. We were told that no mention was to be made of the mission over the radio. Likewise no ambushes would be sent out that evening to prevent one of us being captured and disclosing the mission. This was good news to us. We were to have radio silence throughout the mission and there was to be no talk of a POW camp. We were going to head down a road and at a certain command all of the tracks were to form up and make a mounted assault from the road toward the enemy POW camp. We were to be very careful not to kill any American POWs, but that we were to kill all of the guards as quickly as possible so they could not kill the POWs. We were all excited about attacking a POW camp and getting back some of our guys.

Assault on an Enemy POW Camp

July 16, 1968

Our field strength on the day of the assault was down to 496 men in the battalion or 55% of our allocated strength. The next day at dawn we were loaded up on our tracks and moved out quickly. We were going to attack with two companies. We headed down Route 9 (a twenty-five-foot-wide dirt road) northeast of "Check Point 36," a Y intersection of Route 326 near the infamous Boi Loi Woods. The POW camp was according to our intelligence, to be located in the Boi Loi Woods area. After proceeding down the road we arrived at the reported location parallel to where the enemy POW camp was located. At the proper command the two companies turned off the road and proceeded to make a full mounted armored assault on the suspected POW camp. A mounted assault was highly unusual as we were sitting ducks on top of the tracks and furthermore we needed to be on the ground to protect the track from enemy RPG fire. However, this enabled us to move very rapidly through the jungle to the POW camp.

A mounted armored assault crashing through the woods and brush as far as the eye can see on either side of you is quite a sight. We felt like we were in a WWII charge. Best of all we were going after an Enemy POW camp to rescue some of our fellow soldiers and kill any enemy we found. We all had heard stories of how badly our soldiers were treated by the enemy and how they tortured anyone they captured. We would take out our revenge on any of the guards we found. We had visions of a barbed wire enclosure with POW cages holding our men just like you see in the movies.

We crashed through the woods and moved as fast as our APCs could go over the terrain and through the woods and brush. For the most part the terrain was flat and reasonably dry (remembering it was the height of the rainy season and even high ground was wet and muddy) with trees spread far enough apart for our track to negotiate so we were able to move very quickly toward the suspected POW camp. Much to our disappointment, when we arrived at the suspected POW camp, we found only a small enemy compound with few abandoned buildings. There was no sign of POWs, nor even that the enemy had been in the area recently. Everyone was disappointed, as our blood was up for a fight to save our POWs and kill their captors.

Tank Stuck in the Mud and Destroyed

July 17 and 18, 1968

We sometimes were accompanied by M-48 Medium Patton Tanks on our missions. Less frequently we had M-60 Tanks attached to us for operations. We were always glad to have this additional firepower with us on missions. On this day we were operating with several M-48 Patton tanks. It was the height of the monsoon season and driving off roads was hazardous to both APCs and especially the heavier tanks. Whereas a combat loaded APC weighed some 2.25 tons a Patton Tank weighted forty-seven tons or over twenty times as heavy. APCs with their aluminum armor and sealed hulls could actually float and drive through water which we often did, so they were much more able to negotiate wet rice paddies and mud than a tank.

This day we were sweeping an area looking for the enemy in the vicinity northwest of Dau Tang. We were crossing a muddy field with waist high scrub foliage which was in between wooded areas. Our Track 3-2 was operating between two tanks, one on either side of us. As we were crossing the field the tank on our right side began to bog down in the mud. As it tried to move forward its tracks sank deeper and deeper in the mud. The driver tried to back up but he only managed to dig the tank in deeper. I was walking along side of our APC providing ground protection and searching for the enemy as we advanced. When the tank became stuck the sweep came to a halt. We had been through this drill before. When a tank was stuck in the mud one of more of the APCs would hook up two lines to the tank and pull on it while the tank reversed its tracks. Normally we could pull a tank out of the mud if we lined up several APCs in a row and they all pulled at once as in a train.

As we were the nearest track we hooked up our APC to the tank first and then a second APC hooked up to our track to give it extra pulling power. The tracks and tank were hooked together by thick braided steel towing cables. These towing cables were hooked onto towing hooks welded on the back ramp of the tracks. They in turn connected to towing hooks on the rear of the tank body. Both tracks gunned their engines pulling forward while the tank tried to move backward out of the mud. Both tracks pulling together could not budge the Tank. By this time it had sunk deeper into the mud and now it was stuck up to its turret. We linked up two more tracks for a total of four in a chain to pull the tank out of the mud. This time when we pulled, one of the cables snapped from the tension! Fortunately everyone stayed clear and no one was hurt by the breaking steel tow cable. If you were in the vicinity of a breaking cable you could be killed when it broke. Armor is very dangerous even when not in combat due to the sheer size and weight of the equipment and vehicles. Next we tried placing all of the cables we had to connect the four tracks and the tank together. With several cables on each track, we believed that the cables would not break and thus we could pull the tank free from the muck. This time with all four tracks pulling in tandem and the tank spinning its tracks trying to back up, the tank hardly budged. However, when the tracks increased their pulling the three tracks in front actually pulled so hard that our track was lifted off the ground, suspended between the three pulling tracks and the immobile tank. After a few minutes of pulling as hard as they could the back ramp on our track was pulled completely off the back of the track! No one had ever seen this happen before. In essence the entire back of the APC was a ramp and when it was pulled off the entire back of the track was open to the elements. After this we gave up on trying to pull the tank out of the mud. It was obvious to everyone that it was not going anywhere without some additional assistance.

By this time it was late afternoon. There was no way that a tank retriever and/or bulldozer could be brought to our position before nightfall to dig the tank out of the mud. Thus our officers and the tankers decided that we would set up a night laager position to protect the tank until morning when help could arrive. The location where the tank was stuck was far from ideal as we were in the middle of a small open field surrounded on all sides by heavily wooded areas. It would be relatively easy for the enemy to sneak up on us and assault us from all sides. We would never see him coming. Furthermore, we had only a half-strength company and a few tanks to set up a perimeter. Thus we had insufficient men to adequately protect ourselves in such a set up.

Nevertheless we were ordered to dig in and establish a perimeter around the tank. Our squad took up a position to the front of the tank which was stuck in the mud. I dug a fox hole to the left of our track while the rest of our squad was to my right surrounding our APC. There were only four of us in our squad at the time, Tracy, George myself and one other soldier. We also dug in our APC as best we could and erected a chain linked fence in front of our track for protection against RPGs. We did not have time to dig another bunker, surround it with sandbags and cover it with Marston Mats or sometimes called PSP mats and sandbags as usual. We simply did not have the time before it got dark. The rest of the company dug in as best they could around the

Tank in a defensive perimeter. We also put out concertina wire, flares and claymore mines as was our standard procedure for night laager defensive positions. As usual it rained most of the day and the sky was very dark. You could see and hear almost nothing because of the cloud cover, rain and utter darkness of the Vietnam nights in a wooded area.

We all were on a 100% alert because of the precarious location of our defensive perimeter. I was alone in my foxhole trying to stay warm and as dry as possible. Even though it was in the seventies at night we were very cold because we were soaking wet with cold rain hitting us. My foxhole was all mud with a few sandbags surrounding the top. It also had a couple of inches of water in the bottom and was fairly shallow. It was impossible to dig a proper fox hole as the ground turned into muck a couple of feet down. A crouching foxhole with sandbags and my poncho as a cover is a better description of my foxhole. In the early morning hours, 2:30 a.m. per Lieutenant Colonel Neilson's diary, I kept looking out in the rain from under my poncho to watch for enemy sappers. I could hardly see a few feet in front of me. All of a sudden, not fifteen yards from where I was dug in, an explosion lit up the sky. The tank was hit by an RPG rocket. I instinctively opened up with my M-16 at the location where the RPG was fired. At the same time, a couple or more RPGs were fired into our perimeter, and the enemy opened up with small arms and machine gun fire. Immediately the entire perimeter of our defensive position opened up at the wood lines surrounding our position. With everyone firing, it was impossible to know what was happening. I knew we were under attack but did not know by how many enemies nor where they were attacking. I kept my head low and fired toward the only point of reference I had, which was where the RPG had been fired. I did not see nor hear any enemy soldiers including the one who fired the RPG. All I saw was the flash and the noise of the rocket and the subsequent explosions against the tank.

About a half an hour later, helicopter gunships arrived on scene. They began firing at the wood line around the perimeter. We could not see anyone that we were firing at, just woods. We found out the next day that an ambush sent out from one of the other platoons had been walking in the wood line outside our perimeter, and our own helicopter spotted them and fired rockets and mini guns. Two of our company soldiers were killed and three others wounded. We always seemed to pay for others mistakes! My personal estimate is that about a quarter of all casualties in our company were caused by our own side!

Tank stuck in mud and hit by RPG

Picture is courtesy of Lieutenant Colonel Neilson's diary and the 25th Infantry Division Association.

After a while, fire discipline was established within our perimeter. There was an occasional firing, likely at ghosts, but no attack by the enemy. It was a long night waiting to see what would happen next. Because we were spread so thin on the perimeter, no one ventured out of their foxholes. I believe the tank crew had stayed in foxholes and so I don't believe that any of the tankers were killed. No one moved around much that night because they did not want to get shot by our own men or snipers, who were likely covering us from hidden positions in the surrounding woods. Dawn did not come soon enough for us that night. At dawn some of the men began to take stock of what had happened. We found out that our new platoon's sergeant, who had arrived only the day before, was hit directly by a rocket while outside of a foxhole. He had been completely incinerated by the explosion of the rocket. The only evidence we found of him was a small bloody piece of his web belt and trousers, perhaps five inches long by three inches wide shaped like a right angle triangle. I believe he was listed as MIA because we could not find enough of his body. He had lasted one day! No one else in our platoon had been killed or wounded. Likely because we all stayed in our foxholes and bunkers and did not move around.

We inspected the area where the enemy had fired the RPG which blew up the tank stuck in the mud. We found it was less than twenty yards from the tank. The enemy couldn't have missed at that distance. He had hit the tank in the turret which was the only part sticking out of the mud. One shot and the tank was destroyed. The turret had a small hole melted through the armor only a couple of inches in diameter. It was amazing to us that an RPG could penetrate such thick steel armor so easily! No wonder our 26 mm or approximately one-inch aluminum armored tracks were blown up so easily by RPGs.

From this point on our Track 3-2 operated with no back ramp. We did our best to hang a poncho on the back where the back ramp had been. But it did little good and everything we had got full of mud and rainwater. We conducted sweeps and forded irrigation ditches and even one time forded a small stream where our track went across on the bottom but got the interior soaked with water. But the APC kept going. When we got into firefights with the enemy our track driver and commander were fully exposed from the back to small arms fire. They had zero armor in between them and the outside if an enemy got behind our track. Fortunately we were very careful to protect our track and men so no enemy ever got behind our track. Track 3-2 was later destroyed by an RPG in a later engagement. The fact that our track was not removed from our unit and replaced with new equipment speaks volumes of the state of our replacement system when not even a major piece of armor was replaced or repaired. The result was that we went into combat with defective and inadequate armor placing more of our troops at risk.

M48A3 Patton Medium Tank

The M48A3 Patton tank was a 47+ton monster tank which weighs up to 60 tons combat loaded, which carried a 90 mm cannon and both a .50- and .30-caliber machine gun. The cannon could fire HE rounds to destroy tanks or penetrate enemy bunkers. It could also fire canister rounds which were devastating to enemy soldiers caught in the open. It had a crew of four including a driver, gunner, loader and tank commander. It had armor ranging from 120 mm of frontal armor to 12.7 mm thick. It could travel at 30 mph. It was approximately 10 feet 2 inches high, 12 feet wide and 30.6 feet long. It was driven by an 810 HP turbo diesel engine. The tanks also had a million candle power Xenon light on the turret which could light up enemy positions. It also was a good aiming point for RPGs so I rarely if ever saw one used in the field. They could take on any Soviet or Chinese Tank fielded by the NVA.

Battle in NVA Base Camp

July 18 through 21th, 1968

According to Lieutenant Colonel Neilson's diary our Battalion field strength at this time was 493 men, little more than half of our authorized strength of 907.

After evacuating the dead and wounded by helicopter, we gathered up our equipment, loaded up the tracks and tanks, and moved out. We left the blown-up tank in the mud and moved on to reinforce B and C Companies who were in a firefight with the enemy. They had apparently made contact during sweeps where Rome plows were clearing the sides of the roads to prevent ambushes on convoys. Of course we did not know this at the time only that we were going to reinforce our sister companies who were in a firefight with the enemy. We were told very little about any operation by our platoon lieutenant and sergeant. Later that day we linked up with B and C Companies.

We arrived in time to see jet airstrikes and massive artillery strikes on the enemy base camp. Most of B and C Company infantry had withdrawn from the battle ground to let the airstrikes and artillery do its job. That night we set up a night laager with the other two companies near the enemy base camp which was still being bombarded. We were all nervous about an assault which was inevitable the next day. We had heard that several of our men had been killed in the days fighting. We put out LPs but none of our platoon went out on ambush. We all stayed on 100 percent alert that evening as we knew the enemy was next door to our defensive position.

Early the next morning, we formed up in a line and conducted a multiple company attack on the enemy base camp. It was a large base camp well defended with fighting trenches and bunkers with overhead cover. By this time we were becoming very familiar with enemy base camps and fortifications. We had a great deal of respect for the enemy who could withstand attacks by air strikes and artillery and still come out fighting. Fortunately the enemy had had enough from the attacks and air strikes the previous day and had made an orderly withdrawal. Again a standard operating procedure for the enemy when he believed he could not win or had incurred too many casualties. They only stood and fought when they thought they had a defensible position or could win. Otherwise they withdrew to a pre-planned safe area. Many times it was in Cambodia where we were not allowed to follow. We found some enemy weapons, ammunition, military supplies, gear and ordinance. They did leave some of their dead behind. As usual we destroyed the base camp and polluted the wells.

The next day our company made a mounted sweep into the area of the suspected enemy POW camp. We found nothing but the abandoned and destroyed "camp" with little evidence of anyone having been there since we visited last time. As it was getting late we returned to our night laager defensive position near the enemy base camp joining up with our sister companies.

The following day we were assigned road security detail, whereby we swept the roads for mines and ambushes. We continued to move up and down our sectors of the road until the convoys passed our position and then we fell in behind them and went on to join the rest of our company. Later we were ordered to a FSB to protect an artillery unit for the night.

Tracy and George WIA and Evacuated

Sometime during one of these battles our driver, George, and Tracy, who was manning the .50-caliber machine gun in the APC turret, were both wounded. Our track was hit by an RPG rocket and severely wounded both George and Tracy. Both were flown out by medevac helicopter and neither returned to our unit. We never heard what happened to either one which was typical. We just never saw or heard from them again. In our squad we were a team for just a few months. I missed them and never even got to say goodbye because I was off at another part of the battlefield. They were just gone when I returned, along with our track which had been destroyed. I never even knew their last names as we called each other by nick names or simply first or last names in the field. After Tracy and George I was never close to anyone else in my squad or Platoon with the exception of our Artillery Observer who often patrolled the bush with me. Unfortunately he too was killed in the battle for Tay Ninh in late August.

Another Battle for an Enemy Base Camp

July22–24, 1968

The next day we were improving the defenses of the artillery FSB anticipating we would be there for a couple of days. But no such luck. We were told to "saddle up" and move out to support the rest of our battalion which was engaged in another fight with the enemy in a fortified base camp. We arrived at 12 p.m., and along with supporting tanks and the 1/5th Mechanized Infantry, we assaulted the base camp. Our battalion B and C Companies continued to press the attack on their sector. There was a massive artillery barrage on the enemy and, according to Lieutenant Colonel Nielson, some 250 rounds of 155 mm huge artillery shells and 450 rounds of 105 mm shells were fired into the enemy base camp. By any measure, this is a significant amount of artillery on a relatively small area. I believe in this battle I picked up a relatively new Chicom machine gun. This machine gun was to help me later as a bribe to obtain a highly coveted billet going to Australia for R&R.

As I recall, the artillery busted up the base camp pretty thoroughly by the time we attacked. This day I used our Remington trench shotgun most effectively as we were fighting in trenches. I used the shotgun by pointing it around the corner of a trench and firing several rounds at the enemy, who was around the corner. It was most effective at keeping them back while one of the other guys tossed a couple of grenades around the corner. We found many bodies of the NVA and equipment and weapons scattered about. We entered several of the damaged bunkers, many with overhead cover which had been caved in by the artillery, and found bodies and some documents. We turned these over to our lieutenant as we could not read them since they were in Vietnamese. At this battle I took some North Vietnamese money with Ho Chi Minh on it and North Vietnamese stamps off of a dead NVA soldier. I mailed these items home for safe keeping shortly after the battle, so I still have them to this day. I also picked up an AK-47 magazine vest which holds three thirty-round magazines and a NVA helmet, which we called Rama of the Jungle helmets after a 1950s television show of the same name, where the key actor wore a jungle helmet similar to the NVA helmets. I lost these when my track was blown up. However, I was able to hold on to a Chinese machine gun by having our resupply vehicle deliver it to the armorer in base camp. The armorer kept our captured weapons in a conex shipping container with our names on them.

We found many tunnels in this complex as we had throughout our AO. One of our smaller men but among the bravest was a "tunnel rat." This soldier stripped to the waist, took only a .45-caliber model 1911 handgun and a flashlight and went into the enemy tunnels by himself! These tunnels, while extensive in size and extent, were very small and claustrophobic. They were purposely made small to accommodate the Vietnamese who are small people compared to American soldiers. The average Vietnamese was about five foot high and weighed around 100 pounds. On this occasion the tunnel rat went into a tunnel and emerged about an hour later one hundred yards away, dragging a dead and bloody NVA soldier. Apparently he had encountered the NVA in the tunnel and shot him dead. I later went into some of the larger tunnels myself, but only after the battle was over, to see what was inside. I never entered one if I thought they would be occupied. Like I said tunnel rats were very brave soldiers! This situation was repeated numerous times in different locations as we found many tunnels throughout our AO. After the tunnel rat emerged from the tunnel complex one of our officers decided that we should use CS gas or tear gas to drive out other soldiers hiding in the tunnels. Several CS gas grenades were tossed into the open entrances of the tunnel complex. This would both drive out the enemy and contaminate the tunnel for some time. My squad and I moved away as we did not have any gas masks and didn't want the CS gas on our skin as it burned, especially with the heat and sweat. We saw several hidden openings where the CS gas escaped from the tunnels. We expected to see some enemy emerge and we were prepared to shoot them as they popped out of these hidden holes. However, we did not see any enemy emerge from the openings in our immediate area. I do not recall if any enemy were routed out of their tunnels by the gas in other places in the enemy base camp.

We destroyed whatever we found and then moved into a night laager position. The next couple of days we swept the area north of the enemy base camp and found many other fighting positions but no enemy soldiers. Then we were ordered back to the area around Ton Son Nhut Base Camp. Apparently they were expecting a major attack and needed us to help protect the base. We set up northeast of the Base Camp. We never were allowed into the Base Camp for some reason, always outside the wire. I guess it was so we could attack the enemy or be attacked, before the enemy reached the Base Camp.

Cu Chi Tunnels

Today the Tunnels of Cu Chi are a tourist attraction. At the time few on the American side understood the extent of the tunnel complexes in the Cu Chi area, even though hundreds of tunnels were uncovered. By the end of the war the NVA and VC had some 200 miles of tunnels in the area where we operated stretching from Saigon to north of Tay Ninh. In the Iron Triangle the tunnels were massive and were used in the 1968 Tet offensive to move men and materials to the outskirts of Saigon undetected. The ground in this area was ideal for digging tunnels. It was a dull-red colored laterite clay which was very stable for tunneling. It was hard as brick and seemingly impermeable. The earth was sticky in the tunnels and it did not crumble. Likewise it was not particularly impacted by the amount of water it absorbed. In this densely vegetated area the roots of the vegetation served to further strengthen the tunnels almost like reinforcing rod does in cement. Interestingly in the fall of 1967 a Korean Infantry unit found an NVA document describing in detail the use and construction of the tunnels. This document described how to build the tunnels in exact detail. For example they were to be no higher or wider than 1.2 meters (just under 4 feet) and no smaller than 0.8 meters (slightly more than 2 1/2 feet). They were also to be constructed in a cone shape to protect against bombs and artillery.

These tunnels were used by the VC and NVA, the vast majority of enemy soldiers we fought after TET 1968 to live, eat, store supplies, move troops and equipment, as hospitals, and as fighting positions. With the concealed openings they could pop up behind or in the middle of USA troops moving through these areas or use them to hide and retreat without detection above ground. In the area we operated we constantly were facing the enemy using these massive tunnel complexes to attack, maneuver and hide from us. On a few occasions we did toss CS gas grenades down the tunnels to smoke out the enemy but usually without success.

Duel with a Machine Gun and Attack by Armored Vehicle

July 22–24

Lieutenant Colonel Neilson's Diary on Manpower

Field/Base Camp
A Company 105/54
B Company 88/87
C Company 117/59

From this report you can see when even if the numbers of troops in our company, A Company, reflected 159 soldiers versus an authorized level of 188 for line companies, only 105 or 56% were actually in the field available for combat. This is why we were always short of fighting troops, operating with about half the number we should have had.

This day we were attacking a fortified NVA village across an open field. We had another company with us who had tanks attached to them. They were off to our left as we approached the NVA fortified village. There were woods all around us as we moved across a large open area. As we approached the wood line perhaps three hundred to four hundred yards away we began receiving rocket and automatic weapons fire. Our company moved into a u-shaped position since there was a heavily wooded area to our left and front. To the right side the open area continued for a long way until it too ended in a heavily wooded area. I do not know our location except that it was in the general area in which we operated.

As the fire began to intensify we remained in this u-shaped position with our platoon on the left side. Far to our left was another company attacking the same wooded area but perhaps four hundred yards away from our position. They had one tank attacking alongside of the APCs and infantry as they advanced. Of more concern to us was a rather accurate machine gun hidden in a bunker off to our left. It was this fortified bunker complex and machine gun which was hitting our company with accurate and heavy machine gun fire. While the APCs returned fire with their .50-caliber heavy machine guns, we positioned ourselves against a large dike perhaps three feet tall and fortunately thick enough to stop the machine gun bullets of the enemy.

I had a LAW with me as did the other soldier who was stuck behind the dike with me. After a while by peeking over the top of the dike we could see the enemy machine gun firing at us from a covered bunker. I thought we were close enough that I could hit him with my LAW. He would periodically fire at us to keep our heads down and not allow us to advance further toward his bunker and the fortified line. Once in a while we would crawl to a different spot and shoot a burst at his bunker and the trench line where we were taking fire. I doubt we hit anyone at that distance as we never saw anyone, only the muzzle flashes from their weapons. I told the soldier with me that I was going to pop up and quickly shoot the LAW at the machine gun bunker. It was a difficult shot as it was some two-hundred-fifty yards away from where we lay hidden behind the dike. I told him to move away and fire a burst at the machine gun and trench line to distract the machine gunners attention. Then I would pop up and fire. He moved away crawling behind the dike some twenty-five meters from where I was positioned with my LAW. In the meanwhile I popped off the covers, extended the LAW which popped up the sight and prepared to quickly fire at the bunker. My thought was I would have time to fire the rocket and get down before the enemy saw me and directed fire at my position. In this I was to be proved very wrong.

When my partner opened up at the wood line, I popped up as planned and quickly took aim at the bunker. At the instant I was depressing the firing mechanism the machine gun fired a series of well-aimed shots directly in front of where I was, hitting the top of the dike. I involuntary reacted by falling backwards just as I squeezed the firing mechanism on the LAW. It went off with a loud boom, and I fell behind the dike for cover. By falling backward, the front of the LAW pointed toward the sky and not the bunker. I peered over the top of the dike just in time to see my round hitting directly in front of the other company's tank which was attacking the tree line. With the explosion so close it looked to us like I had hit the tank with my wild LAW round! Fortunately the tank began to back up out of the smoke of the explosion. He obviously thought that the enemy had fired an RPG at him from the bunker and trenches to his front. He immediately opened up with several rounds from his 90 mm cannon at the bunker and trench line.

By this time my partner in crime had crawled up to my position with a wide-eyed look on his face and an expression of "What the fuck!" I must have had an "oh shit" look on my face also. Both of us just looked at each other and finally, not knowing what else to do, I simply shrugged. Later we both agreed that we would say nothing to anyone about almost blowing up one of our own tanks.

However, this situation did nothing to stop the machine gun and fighting positions from shooting at us. It may seem strange now, but we were so enraged by this machine gunner who was so personally trying to kill us both that it was getting us really mad. Our blood was up, and we were determined to kill him first! We needed more firepower and a more accurate weapon, so we both wanted to use our 90 mm recoilless rifle. The problem was it was in the back of our APC which was about fifty to seventy-five yards away from us. The APCs were staying back, keeping their distance because the enemy had fired RPGs at our position. So no one wanted to move any closer with the thin skinned APCs. We all had seen what an RPG could do to the APCs and the men inside.

Like I said, my blood was up and we were determined to kill this son of a bitch before he killed us. I remember not being afraid for one of the first times ever, just very angry and determined! It became personal, like we were the only ones engaged in the fight. In fact I was so focused on killing this machine gunner that I didn't think about anyone else in the battle. So I said I would go back and get the 90 mm recoilless rifle. Remember this was a bulky and heavy weapon and we needed a round to shoot it. Normally a two-man team manned this weapon. So I told my partner to open up on the machine gun position and trench line while I ran back to our track to retrieve the weapon. With that, I slung my M-16 over my shoulder and took off running zigzag across the open field, bent over to present the smallest target possible. When I ran up to our track, the driver and squad leader manning the .50 caliber looked at me like I was nuts. I ran behind the track for protection, and opened the door and yelled to the track commander who had squatted down inside the track to question what I was doing. I told him we were going to use the 90 mm to kill the fucking gook shooting at us. I asked if he could see where the machine gunner was located, and gave him some additional points of reference to focus his firepower on the bunker. He smiled and said he would cover me. Problem was, no one else was around so I had to carry both the weapon and a single round at the same time. I got myself ready to run the gauntlet back to our position and yelled for the track commander to lay down suppressive fire at the machine gun nest. I also grabbed a couple of bandoliers of M-16 ammo while I was inside the track. Then I grabbed the track commander's leg so he would come down into the track. I told him I was ready to go, and he said "Good luck" and opened fire at the bunker. I got out of the track and took off running at a crouched position, carrying the clumsy 90 mm in one hand and a single round in the other. It was not easy, as both the rifle and round were difficult to carry while running. I guess they were shooting at me when I ran back across the field, but I don't remember any shots coming close. It was like I was in a dream and not in the middle of a battle. I skidded into the dike at a full run. My partner pointed out that since I had almost killed a tank, he should take the shot with the 90 mm. He received no argument from me. We moved about twenty-five yards away, crawling alongside of the dike to confuse the enemy as to where we were. Then I loaded the 90 mm and closed the chamber. I told my partner we were ready and to wait until I crawled away to open fire. I moved further down the dike about twenty yards, and when we made eye contact, he popped up and fired at the enemy bunker. All the while our TC was firing directly at the machine gun position, keeping their heads down. .50-caliber rounds coming at you at hundreds of rounds per minute is not something to look forward to, especially if you have to expose yourself to fire back.

My partner delivered a 90 mm round directly into where we thought the machine gunner was located. It created a large explosion along with lots of dust, flying debris, dirt and smoke! We thought for sure we had killed the son of a bitch, along with several of his buddies. When the smoke cleared, we peaked over the top of the dike, looking for signs of death and destruction. What we saw was that some of the foliage and trees had been blown away revealing the black slit of the bunker. But the bunker seems to be untouched! About that same time the persistent enemy opened up on us again, hitting our dike just to reaffirm that he was alive and well, challenging us to kill him before he killed us. This made both of us even angrier, and it further personalized this battle.

There was only one thing we could do, and that was to go back for more ammo. The TC was watching us. Lying down behind the dike I motioned with my hand and arm that I was coming back to the track. He knew that I wanted him to lay down suppressive fire, and so I waited for him to load a new belt of ammo into his .50 caliber. With that I once again ran across the field to our track and retrieved two rounds this time. I carried one in each arm and ran back to our position behind the dike. Once again we crawled to a new position behind the dike, signaled the TC to open fire with the .50 caliber while I did likewise with my M-16. The second shot seemed to go directly into the bunker and blew it up! Just to be sure, my partner placed another round into what was left of the bunker. This was a direct hit, as the enemy did not return fire. In the end, we had won our battle with the enemy machine gunner.

We were considering what to do next, wondering if we should return to our track and form up with the rest of our platoon, or wait for them to start moving. We didn't have to wait long as we heard a lot of extra firing, and the tracks on our side of the U-shaped position began moving toward the opposite side of the perimeter. At first we did not know what was happening, but very quickly we saw a large group of enemy approaching our company with what looked like an armored vehicle. We had never seen an enemy armored vehicle, although we had heard they had them operating in our area. With our blood still up from killing the machine gunner, we ran to join the attack. This was our first chance to get even for blowing up so many of our tracks. At last we had an opportunity to kill an enemy attacking us with armor.

We both ran for our perimeter to join in shooting at the attacking enemy with the armored vehicle. As we joined our company, most of our tracks had begun to pull up in a line and were firing at the approaching enemy and armor with their .50 calibers. Likewise, several of our men began to fire LAWs at the armored vehicle which was leading the enemy assault. I grabbed a LAW from the back of our APC and I too fired at the armored vehicle. Unfortunately, not one of the many LAWs fired at the armored vehicle hit it. However, the combined weight of the .50-calibers from our entire company hitting the vehicle seemed to be blowing it apart piece by piece. The 50 or so enemy soldiers who were foolish enough to attack our company were all quickly killed or shot to pieces, mostly by the .50-caliber machine guns, but also by our other automatic weapons. They never got closer than three hundred to four hundred yards before they were shot to pieces! As it turned out the armored vehicle was a WWII French four-wheeled vehicle mounting two .30-caliber machine guns. At least that is what it looked like to me from three hundred to four hundred yards away. In either case, this was the only time we were attacked by an armored vehicle while I was in the field. Later our helicopters reported that they had destroyed several tanks and armored vehicles near the Cambodian border, but I never saw them or was involved. I believe this happened during the battle for Tay Ninh, but I am not sure.

Enemy in the Haystack and Faulty Grenades

Later that day we assaulted the enemy village again. For some reason we did not have artillery nor air support, which was unusual. This time our combined companies were more aggressive as the enemy force had been hurt by our attacks that morning. Our squad and platoon were on the left of our company nearest the beginning of the village as we moved forward. In front of our squad, there was some type of large structure which looked like a small barn with a large opening on the bottom floor and a smaller opening in the second story. This was an unusual building for Vietnam as it was larger than most building we saw in the countryside. The village was a typical village with small huts on both sides of a dirt road, or more appropriately a wide path. Our company approached the village from the right side and our sister company approached from the left. We were moving toward the village on the right side, sweeping left toward the road. Some of our company was engaged, as was our sister company, but far away from where we were moving toward the village. When we came within perhaps two hundred yards or so of the small barn, a NVA soldier opened up on our squad with an AK47 (it has a distinctive sound you will not forget). We all hit the dirt, and I was able to get behind a small dike along with the other three men in my squad who were on the ground with me. I don't recall the reason, but we were out ahead and to the left of our APC and exposed. We all returned fire, and a couple of the squad began to maneuver to the left and right so we could get around the sides of the building. I stayed in front of the building firing at the top opening where I saw muzzle flashes. There seemed to be only one or two enemy firing at us and not all that accurately. When the enemy shifted to shooting at the other men moving to the sides of our dike, the soldier I was with decided we should move in closer to get within grenade range. Unfortunately no one in our squad had an M-79 grenade launcher or a LAW. We all carried M-16's and one of the men had an M-60 machine gun. We jumped up and ran to the next dike which was perhaps twenty-five feet away. The NVA apparently did not notice us or they were occupied shooting at others. We leapfrogged again and moved closer. This time the enemy saw us and opened fire. However, the dike was high enough where they could not hit us until we rose up to shoot or move. Once again we seemed to be isolated from the rest of our platoon fighting an individual battle against a couple of enemy in the small barn.

We maneuvered as a team to get around the sides of the building while keeping the enemy busy by firing at them from different angles. Our M-60 kept their heads down most of the time, enabling us to maneuver in short bursts of movement. I guess they had some type of protection because the M-60 was hitting inside of both openings and did not seem to kill the enemy. I never did see either of them, but I did see muzzle flashes coming from the top opening in the structure. After maneuvering for perhaps an hour, I had moved up close enough to lob a grenade into the building. I could throw a grenade a long way and fairly accurately. I signaled to my squad I was going to throw a grenade and wanted them to all fire at once into the opening. When they opened fire, I threw a grenade into the bottom opening of the structure and quickly got down. Nothing happened! Apparently it was a dud hand grenade. In all my time in Vietnam, I had never even heard of such a thing much less experienced it myself. So I moved to another location twenty yards or so along the dike. Then I signaled to open fire for cover. I tossed another hand grenade into the same opening and got down fast! That one did the trick, blowing up both hand grenades and apparently penetrating the top floor, killing the enemy and blowing out some of the buildings sides. As with all of the rural villages in Vietnam the building was nothing more than mud, wood, sticks and straw. Anyway we did not receive any more rounds from that building, and we moved on down the street.

Our company had moved into the village by the time we joined them and were mopping up small pockets of resistance. One of our leaders, I believe it was our platoon sergeant, told us we were going to burn down the village and destroy everything in it. This was standard procedure for us when we encountered an enemy-occupied village. There was a hay stack near where we were sweeping the village. It turns out that it was not a stack of hay but rather a stack of pot or marijuana. Anyway our company began burning down the village. I grabbed some straw or dried marijuana and used it to light up a building. I ran back to that hay stack twice to get straw to burn down buildings in the village. On my third time running back to the hay stack, I was shocked to see two very bloody dead NVA who apparently were hiding under the stack of pot in a shallow hole! Someone had killed them in-between when I was running back and forth getting pot to burn buildings. Once again, someone was looking out for me as the two NVA could have easily shot me when I had my hands full of pot hay, not once, but twice! After that I always shot into hay stacks when passing by them. Anyway, we burned the village and it smelled like a pot party on steroids.

Our company discovered several tunnels in the village. CS gas was used to gas the enemy and clear out the tunnels. As I did not have a gas mask with me, since I rarely carried one in the field, I stayed away from the tunnels which were being gassed. I heard later that several NVA were flushed from the tunnel and shot when they emerged. But I did not see this myself as I was busy burning the village.

Shortages in "A" Company

An example of how we were constantly short of supplies and equipment in our unit Lieutenant Colonel Neilson reported in his diary of August 11, 1968, the following shortages in Alpha Company:

- Helmets-1+
- Vests-22 (author's note: flak vests)
- Prot. masks-28 (author's note: gas masks)

Being in battles so often and going out every day and many nights through the jungle and heavily wooded areas played havoc on our equipment and clothing. Clothing especially would get chewed up and ripped by the barbs on the vines or elephant grass which could cut like a razor. Handling barbed wire and crossing through it daily would often rip clothing. So it was not unusual to walk around with ripped clothing most of the time. When we lost a track (typically blown up by a mine or RPG rocket) we lost all of our personal gear (clothing, boots, soap, shaving gear, letters, etc.) plus the additional weapons, cleaning equipment, mechanical tools, shovels, picks, sandbags, barbed wire, steel mats for bunker covers, ammunition, grenades, C-4, food (C-rations), water/drinks, tents, poncho liners (blankets), and everything we used. The only thing we had left was the clothes on our backs and what we carried on our person. Considering I went through some five tracks in five months one can understand why we were constantly short of equipment and gear. Ammunition, food and water were typically supplied every few days by resupply CH-47 Chinook helicopters. They would typically sling a cargo net full of supplies underneath their bodies so that they could quickly release these in the middle of our night laager and be on their way. When in FSBs we were also supplied by truck convoys.

For weeks at a time we went with filthy ripped up clothes because we could not get sufficient replacements. When they did come, used and recycled clothes and occasionally boots were dropped into a big pile. Of course when it was raining the clothes were soaking wet by the time we retrieved them. Boots were much more difficult to obtain, and much of the time I had only one pair of boots, which made keeping your feet dry impossible. This resulted in severe cases of emersion or trench foot. For several weeks I operated with only one set of boots, socks, and a field jacket when our track was destroyed. I did not even have a shirt, which made living outdoors difficult as it got cold at night, especially when you were wet all the time. You would think that the army leadership would make sure the "fighting men" who lived in the field would have all they needed before giving extra uniforms and boots to soldiers operating in the rear who lived in hooches. It was especially infuriating for us to see Field Grade Senior Officers coming to the field in starched uniforms and shined boots landing in helicopters and then quickly returning to their base camps, while we rotted in the field. It certainly reinforced our feelings that no one gave a damn about us.

More Sweeps and Road Patrols

July 25–28, 1968

We spent the next few days sweeping the area and on road security duty. We captured an enemy soldier in one of the abandoned enemy base camps we discovered during one of our sweeps. We conducted road sweeps to open the roads and continued to patrol them to assure no convoys were ambushed or mines planted in the roads.

When we operated on the road and went through small hamlets and villages, the kids would often come to the sides of the road and yell, "Hi, GI," with their hands out for food and treats. We would sometimes throw them chocolate bars or C-Rats we didn't want, especially Lima Beans which was inedible for most of us. Sometimes I would pretend I was "pulling the pin" on a hand grenade and throw a can of C-Rats at the kids. They all knew what a hand grenade was so they would scatter. One brave one would run back and pick up the can of C-Rats. One of the days we were "running the roads" I saw a young boy in a hamlet selling loafs of French bread. I jumped off the track and bought a loaf of bread from this youngster. Then I jumped back on our track and we took off down the road. As we proceeded down the road, I took a bite of the loaf of French bread. My mouth went on fire as soon as I bit into the bread! I spit it out and washed my mouth out with water, but it still burned inside my mouth. Apparently the little rat of a kid had poured battery acid on the bread he sold to me. We turned the track around in an attempt to find the kid, but he was long gone—so much for being nice to the kids. Once again we felt that everyone and everything was out of get us in Vietnam!

After running the roads on the evening of July 28, we set up a new FSB which later became to be known as Fire Support Base Rawlins, one of the larger FSBs we operated out of while I was in the field.

Running the Roads

Running the roads was a typical operation for the mechanized infantry in our Battalion, especially in the rainy season when it was difficult for our APCs to operate off roads due to the mud and water. During the time I was in the field we ran the roads from Saigon to our northern most outposts in French Fort near the Cambodian border. Most often we ran the roads near French Fort and the Rock Crusher quarry in Nui Ba Den Mountain to various construction sites, from the HQ Base Camp of the 25th Division at Cu Chi Base Camp, and down Route 22 and Route 1 to Ton Son Nhut Air Force Base. When we were north of Tay Ninh City or out near the Rock Crusher we would often be accompanied by engineers with mine sweepers who swept the road on the first runs of the day for mines. Most often the engineers who came with us were from the 65th Combat engineering Battalion. On one of these runs we were ambushed and one of the engineers riding on my track was captured by the NVA.

We would typically leave our night defensive position at daybreak running down the roads. A typical day for us was up at 5 a.m. and on the roads by 6 a.m. then sweeping roads or out-posting along the road until 4-6 p.m. at which time we would return to our FSB or night laager. Where the foliage met the road we would be very careful to avoid ambushes. We were also alert for any mines which were either planted in the road, on side of it, or strapped to trees. The roads were all dirt and thus with heavy military traffic became potholed and this made it very difficult for us to detect mines. We typically moved out in a single formation as the roads were very narrow so that each track would follow in the tread tracks of the APC in front. This way if the first track passed a location and did not hit a mine the tracks behind would be safe. For this reason the first track was the most dangerous position and thus this duty was periodically rotated to spread the risk of mines.

As we cleared sections of the road a squad with an APC would drop off at a defensible location on the side of the road, dismount and set up a defensive perimeter. We would also sweep out beyond our perimeter to see if there was any evidence of enemy or booby traps. Periodically we would move our position and run down the road to assure that it was still clear and to catch any enemy who might be trying to plant mines or set up ambushes as we passed by. Often we had helicopters overhead on the initial run to watch out for ambushes and mines. Sometimes the mines were command detonated. This means they were triggered by wire controlled by an enemy hiding on the side of the road. Occasionally you could spot the wires which brought the tracks to an abrupt halt! No one wanted to hit a mine with an APC. The drivers steered the track by sitting on top and driving with lateral straps so that they had a chance of survival if the track hit a mine. They would be blown off the top rather than killed inside the track.

A typical convoy consisted of fifty to one hundred heavy deuce and a half and five-ton eighteen-wheel semi-trucks.

POWs Killed by Crazy Sergeant

July 26, 1968

One day while making sweeps, we captured two healthy young men who did not have identity papers and were almost certainly enemy soldiers. They had no uniforms, but were well built and in good physical condition. Our interpreter, a Kit Carson Scout, was convinced they were North Vietnamese soldiers after he had interrogated them. He would know since he was a NVA soldier previously. A Kit Carson Scout was a NVA soldier who had surrendered and changed sides, volunteering to work for the Americans and ARVN as a scout. The one who accompanied us was very helpful in recognizing enemy booby traps, trails, hidden weapons caches and base camps. Unfortunately he was killed in one of the fights with the enemy who was defending their base camps. We never got a replacement for him, which was unfortunate for us.

We rarely took prisoners, but when we did they were almost always captured when we made sweeps and never in battle. I do not recall us ever taking a prisoner in a battle. Most of the time the NVA we encountered did not surrender and we did not look kindly on any enemy who had killed or wounded our men so enemy prisoners were rare. Conversely we never thought about surrendering ourselves. In fact I was more afraid of becoming a prisoner of the NVA or VC than of getting killed. I had made up my mind that I would not be captured nor surrender no matter what. I always had extra hand grenades just in case. The way we handled prisoners was to cover their heads with sandbags and tie their hands behind their backs. Sometimes if on patrol we would also tie a rope around their necks and tie them together this way. They could walk with us but did not know where they were going nor could they lead us to step on a booby trap on purpose.

The two enemies were taken back to an open field where we were told to wait for a helicopter that was bringing in an officer to interrogate them and take them away. We set up a defensive perimeter, basically a circle of tracks similar to a wagon train in the old west movies, while waiting for the helicopter to arrive. Shortly afterward we heard an M-16 open-up on automatic fire. We looked around to see what they were firing at around the perimeter. At the time we didn't know what had happened. Later we found out that the crazy sergeant who had been guarding the prisoners had killed them both. He claimed that they tried to take away his rifle. This would have been difficult since they had their hands tied behind their backs. No one bought this story. When a REMF Major arrived on his helicopter, he was furious that his prisoners were shot. Apparently our captain protected the sergeant because nothing ever came of the incident. I heard later that, after the sergeant claimed he shot the prisoners as they attempted to take his weapon, he stared at the major with a look of evil in his eyes and his finger on the trigger of this M-16 rifle. Knowing this soldier, I wouldn't have pushed things much further myself.

Everyone in our company, me included, was cautious of the sergeant who was guarding the prisoners. He was known to be a bit crazy. He was one of the longest-serving members of our company. I don't know how long he was with our unit, but he was an old-timer with more than three months in the field when I arrived. He was known to be very brave, not afraid of anything, and had several Purple Hearts. I heard he charged a machine gun bunker by himself several times. As he was not in my squad, I had never seen him in action myself. Apparently he went off his rocker during a battle in a village when he tossed a hand grenade in a bunker under a house and it was full of children. It killed or maimed all of them, and this deeply affected him psychologically. Apparently he was married and had young children himself. After that he was never right. He was quiet most of the time, stayed alone and did not speak much to anyone except to give orders. In combat he was brave and aggressive to the point of foolhardiness. Some believed he wanted to get killed! No one wanted to cross him or get on his bad side, so most just kept away from him. It was said he hated the enemy with a passion and just wanted to kill as many as he could. He probably should have been taken out of the infantry and given help, but in 1968 this just didn't happen.

What had actually happened, as we heard from the rumor mill, was that the sergeant was taunting the enemy soldiers, hoping they would do something to give him an excuse to shoot them. Apparently he could speak enough Vietnamese to get his message across. One of the enemy soldiers must have been a very hard core NVA soldier and possibly an officer or just stupid, because as the sergeant got in his face, he spit at the sergeant. That was all the excuse the sergeant needed, and he shot them both on the spot!

This was the only time I knew of where our company had killed enemy prisoners outside of a battle, where one of the enemies may have wanted to surrender; but in the heat of battle you cannot take a chance. Especially with an enemy like the NVA, who did not play by our rules, and tortured and mistreated our soldiers when captured. I never heard of any torture by our soldiers, other than to tie prisoners to a pole and soldiers patting them on the head not too lightly as they passed by. Our prisoners were typically flown out of our company area as soon as a chopper was available, so we did not see many prisoners nor did we take many while I was in the field. I only remember the two who were shot, and one other who was tied to a pole while awaiting evacuation, and perhaps a couple of others. All of whom were captured during sweeps, not one during a battle.

I did hear stories about the ARVN who tortured their captives by dunking them in barrels of water to the point of almost or sometimes drowning them. Likewise I had heard they cut them up with knives when trying to extract information from prisoners. There also was a rumor going around that our brigade colonel, Colonel Wolf, who we all thought was crazy aggressive, at least with our lives, had thrown a prisoner out of the chopper in an effort to get one of the other prisoners to talk. Most of us would have liked to see him shot up or killed! I never saw him in the field with the troops, only flying around in his helicopter, far above where we were fighting. Another rumor about Col. Wolf was that he threatened another prisoner with a .45 pistol. When he would not talk, he shot him in the head, with the bullet going through the front Plexiglas of his chopper, almost killing his pilot. But these were only rumors, and I don't know how true they were. That said, Col. Wolf was universally hated by the men in the field. In fact I have seen our own men in a fight take a shot at Col. Wolf's chopper during battles. I heard that once he was shot down, and they found M-16 bullet holes in his chopper. This rumor I tend to believe.

Almost Ran Over by a M-48 Tank

July 28, 1968

We moved into a new area to set up a new Fire Support Base, called FSB Rawlins. This time we were met by bulldozers of the Combat engineers to help us dig in and build the FSB. Sometimes we would operate from one of these for only a day and sometimes for days at a time. Then we would move on to another FSB or night laager. While a FSB was a much larger and semi-permanent field base, a night laager was typically set up with only our company and typically for as little as one evening and at most a couple of days. A FSB was set up in an open field or one which was cleared by bulldozers. This was to give the defenders a clear field of fire against attacking enemy. Typically a company or two of mechanized infantry would provide security for the bulldozers clearing the area and for the artillery setting up their guns. Sometimes we also had tanks assigned to us for additional security in clearing the area and setting up the defensive perimeter. Bulldozers would dig in our APCs and tanks in a circular perimeter with the artillery, ammo dumps and command centers located in the middle of the perimeter. The mechanized infantry with our APCs and tanks would man the perimeter defenses. We would dig a bunker between each APC and Tank position which was manned by infantry with machine guns. Then we would set up barbed wire, flares and claymore mines in front of each fighting position. We would also set up a fence in front of our APCs to explode RPGs fired at our positions. The result was a somewhat circular position, depending on the ground, which looked very much like an Old West wagon train setting up at night to protect against Indians.

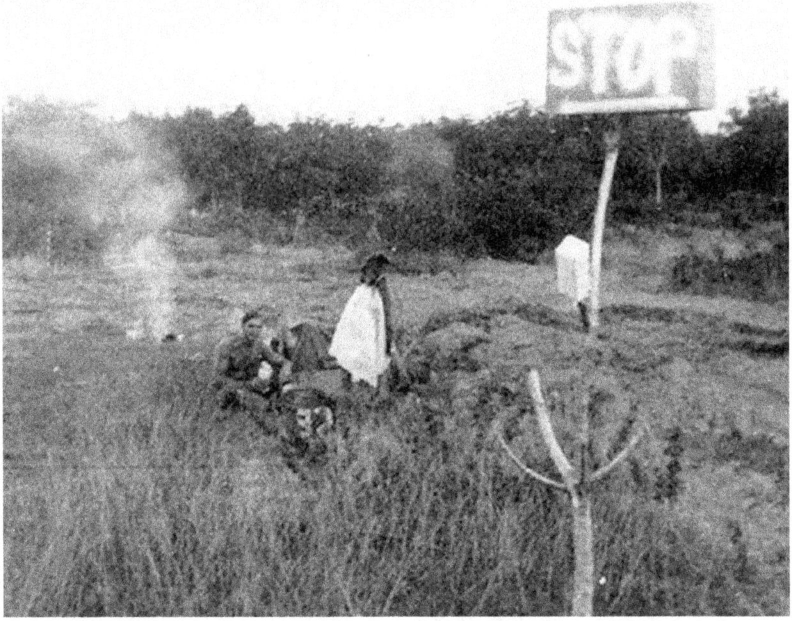

Author with stop sign—almost run over by M-48 tank

It was raining as usual when we moved into the area to provide security and set up the perimeter defense for the new FSB. After digging our defensive bunker and setting up the barbed wire, trip flares, and mine defenses and the protective sandbags and fence for our track, we were exhausted. I slept on the ammo cans and C-Ration cases in the track. The next night I set up a tent which I rarely had and don't recall where I got it, in back of our fighting position on a dry piece of ground. I thought I would get a good night's sleep for a change. After my turn at guard duty I retired to my tent and wrapped up in a poncho liner. Sometime in the middle of the night I woke up to the sound of a tank moving right next to me! It was unusual for a tank to move at night but for some reason the tank was ordered to move to the other side of the defensive perimeter. Unfortunately my tent was set up in the tanks path. As they did not use lights at night and it was pitch dark and raining, the tank driver did not see my camouflaged tent in its path. I was startled awake by the closeness of the tank and reacted instantly. In the infantry we slept lightly and awoke instantly, ready to react to whatever. I quickly sensed the tank was almost on top of me so I rolled to the right, taking my tent with me, and crawled away just as the tank came within a couple of feet of where I had been sleeping! The tank went by me, never seeing how close it came to running me over. I spent the rest of the night curled up in my poncho in our defensive bunker just in case the tank came back. The bunker had water in the bottom and was not very comfortable for sleeping. The next morning I saw just how close I had come to being crushed by the tank! The tank tracks were only a couple of feet away from the edge of my tent. So in order to get a dry night of sleep or at least with rain not directly falling on me, I set up my tent again. This time I placed a stop sign in front of my tent on a pole. I made it out of an empty carton of C-rations and painted "STOP" on the front, then placed it on a pole I cut down outside the perimeter. I had a good night's sleep that evening in between guard duty.

Fire Support Base

A Fire Support Base or FSB was a semi-permanent self-contained and self-defended artillery base from which infantry and mechanized infantry companies operated. It was positioned to support other FSBs, infantry night laagers, and other military installation in the area. This was so each FSB could give interlocking fire support to other FSBs in the area. The infantry operated out of these FSBs to make sweeps and set up ambushes to locate and destroy the enemy using the FSB artillery for support. The infantry, especially the mechanized infantry, guarded these FSBs with their APCs and large pierced steel reinforced sandbag bunkers dug in between each APC. The APCs were dug in behind a berm of dirt. Often tanks would also operate out of the FSBs and guard them at night with their 90 mm cannons and occasionally with search lights.

The FSB contained a battery of six 105 howitzers and sometimes larger 175 mm guns along with a platoon of three or four 81 mm mortars, if mechanized infantry, and/or 60 mm infantry mortars.

Once I recall a FSB had an 8-inch self-propelled cannon inside. I recall this vividly since I was going out on an ambush with three other men silently going through our surrounding barbed wire. As we passed near the muzzle of the cannon it fired over our heads almost knockings us down and knocking off my helmet. I couldn't hear a damn thing; my head hurt from the concussion and my eyes had been flash blinded. Needless to say we stumbled back to our company area and did not go out on ambush. Someone had failed to tell the artillery that we were going out of the wire in front of their position! After that no one in our company ever went out through the wire on ambush or LP in front of those cannons.

The FSB was set up in a circle with an approximate three-hundred-yard circumference. Around the perimeter, at approximately fifteen-foot intervals, dug-outs would be carved by bulldozers for APCs. These dug-outs would have a berm of dirt pushed up in front, along with a cyclone fence to protect APCs from incoming RPG rockets. In-between each of these track dug-outs, there would be a bunker built to house the infantry squad with an M-60 or two machine guns within. Circling the entire perimeter would be a triple pyramid of concertina barbed wire, complete with trip flares and command-detonated Claymore mines. Typically there would be a guarded and fortified entrance with bunkers and gates for resupply by vehicles coming by road. Often FSBs would be located off of roads on which we ran convoys or which ran next to the various rubber plantations in our area of operations.

In the center of the FSB there was a command center and artillery control center along with sandbagged tents for cooks, communication, medical, and administration. Sometimes there was a prefabricated tower inside the perimeter manned with anti-personnel radar. Most of the supplies for the FSB were brought in by Chinook helicopter, a two-bladed workhorse helicopter for carrying supplies and troops. Sometimes larger artillery would be brought in by the Sky Cranes or CH-54 Tarhe helicopters. Once I saw one of these Sky Cranes carrying a Chinook helicopter which had been shot down by the enemy to our base camp in Tay Ninh.

A FSB had to be set up very quickly, so that required a lot of work by everyone involved, including the combat engineers, artillerymen and infantry. This is because they were prime targets for the enemy who would take every opportunity to attack a FSB and over run it if possible. So we needed to be prepared to fight off an attack the first night we set up. There was a lot of effort in building bunkers, filling sandbags, setting up the defensive perimeter and setting up mines and trip flares. After working all day building the FSB, we were dead tired. Then we had to pull guard duty, go out on ambushes to break up enemy attack formations, and man LPs (listening posts) outside the wire.

Poisoned By Our Cooks-The Hot Meal Myth

July 29–31

US Army propaganda and reports to higher-up officers indicated that we had several hot meals in the field every week. This was nonsense when it came to front line infantry. Consider first that we would often arrive at a location at dusk 5 pm, have to build bunkers and dig in our tracks (to protect them from RPG rockets), put out barbed wire, flares and claymore mines, and get ready to defend our position at night. When we returned to an established FSB, things were easier and we had a higher chance of getting a hot meal, but often from leftovers of the FSB artillery cooks. We were also supposed to get beer and soda that came in cases which we stored inside our tracks. Needless to say it was very hot inside the tracks. We sometimes would get ice delivered to our night laager, when established, or a FSB, but by the time we arrived, most of it melted even though it was buried underground for most of the day. It was a wasted effort as we rarely got cold anything.

When we did get a hot meal, it was often warm at best and not very nourishing. It was delivered to the FSB, almost never to a night laager, in large green thermos cans via helicopter. We would then rotate going to the chow lines in squads so that we always had people on the defensive perimeter and never had too many people in one place, to guard against enemy mortars and rockets. We would line up and be fed with paper plates since no one carried mess kits in the field. There was no place to clean them in either case, so they would have simply made us all sick. Paper plates in driving rain made whatever we were fed soggy, and it was difficult to hold the food when the paper plate bent at the edges. By the time we got back to our bunkers or tracks, much of the food we did get was soggy or, worse, washed off the paper plates. The senior officers in charge did not live under such conditions, reinforcing our belief that no one gave a damn about us. I guarantee if one general had to live like us for one week, things would have changed dramatically. Mostly we survived on C-rations which we carried on our tracks. We heated them with C-4 in the cans they came in or in the cup we had at the bottom of our canteen. My favorite was spaghetti and meatballs, but we only got one can of these in a case of C-rations. The worst was lima beans with some kind of inedible meat chunks. These we gave to the Vietnamese children as we drove through villages. Most of the C-Rats we ate were packaged in the 1950s. The meat had a quarter inch of yellow fat on top which we ate as we were starved. We filled our canteens with brown water, which was disinfected with horribly tasting brown pills which were supposed to kill all known water-borne bugs and bacteria. We often received Kool-Aid in our packages from the real world (USA), but back in those days they did not contain sugar. It made the water very sour tasting, but anything was better than the foul tasting brown water we received. The fact is that the average GI in the infantry lost 20% or more of his weight after arriving in Vietnam. Remember we were in excellent "fighting trim weight" upon arrival, so we didn't carry much if any additional weight when we arrived. Basically we were all thin and underfed, considering the number of calories we burned every day, and going with only a few hours of sleep day in and day out.

This day we were served undercooked chicken by our cooks. I believe this happened at FSB Rawlins, but we moved around so much I am not sure. We were always hungry, so we all ate the chicken. It tasted foul, but we were all so hungry we ate whatever we were given. Fortunately we were in a FSB where there were Artillery soldiers with us who had their own food. Later that evening our entire company began to get sick from food poisoning. I was so sick, all I could do was throw up. I was incapable of doing much defending and felt like I was going to die. Other soldiers got so sick, some were dusted off that evening to go to the hospital. No one from our squad was dusted off, but we had a rough night of it. If we had been attacked, we would have been overrun as most of the men were incapacitated from severe food poisoning. The next day we did not go out on our normal maneuvers, but had an unofficial "stand down" giving the men time to recover. There was a lot of grumbling about our cooks. I heard several men say they were going to drop a grenade in the cook's food coolers next time they came out to the field. Based on these threats, which the officers took seriously as threats in the infantry were not idle, we did not have another hot meal for a long time. The cooks would not come to the field for well over a month to deliver us hot food. They were afraid and justifiably so.

After this I could not eat chicken for some thirty plus years, then only if it was fried to a crisp and never boiled. I still don't like chicken and eat it only when necessary.

Weapons I Used

While in the field as an infantryman, I used a variety of weapons. For the most part I preferred the M-16 since it was light, flexible, I could aim and fire quickly, it had excellent firepower, I could carry lots of ammo, and it was an accurate rifle. I also carried the M-60 machine gun when our squad needed extra firepower, but I did not like carrying it on un-mounted sweeps. Riding on top of the track I often used the M-60 for extra firepower, and I did not have to lug it around all day. You could also link the 100-round ammo belts together and keep firing from the top of the track. At night in our bunker alongside the track, we used the M-60 or two since we had two on our track. We also procured another .50-caliber machine gun from a blown up track, and for a while we used this in our bunker along with the M-60. This in total was quite a lot of fire power. We also had an M-14 with a mounted infrared night scope for sniping at the enemy. I carried this on several ambushes but never used it as I was afraid to give away my position with only three of us half a mile from any other friendlies. We did use the starlight scope, which in those days was a bulky night vision scope which showed up everything as green, like looking through an algae-green fish tank. But these were very useful in seeing the enemy movements at night. We used these on ambushes and for perimeter defense, giving us the ability to see in the dark.

At one point in the summer, we were fighting in enemy base camps. On our track we had a Remington 12-Gauge Pump Trench Shotgun. I used this very effectively when fighting in the trenches and bunkers of the enemy base camp. However, once I was caught in the middle of an open area by the enemy and, due to the range of the shotgun, it was useless. So I decided that the benefits of using it in the trenches did not outweigh the downside of having a useless weapon out in the open. I carried lots of hand grenades everywhere we went since we were always fighting the enemy who hid in fighting trenches, bunkers and had many tunnels. We had two types: the old pineapple-type from WWII and Korea (MK2 grenades) and the newer round-type called the M-26. Sometimes I would use a Willie Peter M-34 or white phosphorous grenade, but only when we wanted to clear out bunkers or tunnels. I did not carry these on un-mounted sweeps as I was deathly afraid of one of them being hit by a round and exploding! White phosphorous was really nasty as it burned through anything (including metal) that it came in contact with, until it burned itself out. One time the backsplash from an aircraft bomb hit our bunker line, and one of our troops got a small amount on his boot. It burned right through his foot before they could get his boot off to cut it out! Some of our troops "cooked off" grenades by counting to three before throwing them in a bunker so the enemy could not throw it back out. I never wanted to "cook off" one because I did not trust the armaments factory to get the fuse timing right every time. They were supposed to go off after four to five seconds, but I did not want to take a chance. I used the time to get down, but one time the enemy did throw one back at me. In addition to these grenades we had CS gas grenades. I did not like to use them since we did not carry our gas masks with us the majority of the time. In fact it was rare that everyone had a gas mask for use in our company at any one time. We did use these several occasions in tunnels we found, but I never personally used one as I did not want to get gassed myself. So I simply moved away from where they threw the CS gas grenade in tunnel openings. We used smoke grenades for signaling purposes, especially when trying to identify landing areas for helicopters. You used different colored smoke and then communicated with the helicopter crew as to which color you were using to identify yourself. The enemy also used our smoke grenades to lure helicopters into an ambush pretending they were US soldiers.

We also carried LAWs (one-shot disposable anti-tank rounds that replaced the WWII bazooka) with us when we thought we would encounter enemy bunkers. But mostly we left them on our tracks until we needed them and then went back to retrieve several for blowing up bunkers. I heard several men say that they fired some and they failed to explode (including Tom Foster), but this never happened to me. On our track we also had a 90 mm recoilless rifle which was one heck of an infantry weapon. But it was blown up along with our track in the summer months. We did not use it much because we only had a handful of artillery rounds to fire. I only recall having used it perhaps three times in battles. I shot it once and acted as the loader two other times. I also fired the "blooper" or M-79 grenade launcher. This was a single barrel weapon which fired a 40 mm shell up to 400 meters. It could also fire a canister round for close in fighting. Normally the soldier who carried the M-79 also carried a .45 pistol. Some of our guys could put the 40 mm grenade shell through a window at 200 meters! One time I saw our grenadier (an infantry soldier who carries the M-79) hit a running enemy in the head at 180–200 meters! It killed both him and his companion—quite a shot. The shell went slow enough at 75 meters per second and was large enough that you could watch it travel to its target. I used these several times in battle as we had more than one on our track. But I did not like carrying it as a substitute for my M-16 or the M-60.

For blowing up bunkers we carried lots of C-4 explosive and used it frequently to blow up enemy base camps. We also had satchel charges, which was essentially a canvas bag full of C-4 with a built-in fuse that could really blow up bunkers and houses. The only mines we used were Claymore mines which were anti-personnel mines. They were devastating to the enemy. In base camp I carried a .45 pistol but not in the field. It was too heavy, not very accurate except at close range, and I would rather carry more ammo and grenades.

One time we somehow got hold of a portable flame thrower which you could carry on your back. Unfortunately I do not recall which battle I used the flame thrower. However, when one considers I used it only once for about ten seconds and never used it again, this is understandable. The flame thrower was not from our track, so apparently one of the other squads got hold of the thing. This was an upgraded type that the army used in Korea and WWII (designated the M2A1-7). It was a heavy, bulky device weighing just under 70 pounds fully loaded with three cylinders, one carrying compressed gas and two carrying two gallons of napalm each. There is a hose and a trigger mechanism with a nozzle on the end for directing the fire. It had an igniter on the nozzle end which created a flame, and when you pressed the trigger, it shot flaming napalm about forty yards to the target. Napalm is essentially jellied gasoline which sticks to everything and everybody it hits and burns ferociously.

I recall that we used it in a rather small firefight. It was likely when we were sweeping the roads or near the rubber plantations. We were always getting into skirmishes in these areas. There were not too many enemies and someone suggested we hit them with the flamethrower. I thought it would be cool to shoot as I had never used a flame thrower before. This would burn away the camouflage from the fighting bunkers and flush out the enemy.

The damn flame thrower was both heavy and bulky. It kept twisting on my back as I moved along and caught on every branch and vine I came in contact with. As I moved toward the enemy, it dawned on me that this was a really bad idea. Finally we got near where we thought the bunker was located. I didn't want to get any closer. Then the really bad news, you had to either stand up or at least expose the top half of your body in order to shoot the flame thrower. One of the guys lit the flamethrower with a Zippo lighter since the automatic lighter apparently did not work very well or we didn't know how to use it. With that and wanting to get this over with, I propped myself up on one leg kneeling and fired the flame thrower at the tree line. As soon as I fired the flame thrower, bullets started coming our way. Apparently the enemy did not take kindly to flame throwers. Fortunately the flame thrower only lasted a few seconds and then it ran out of napalm. A few seconds is a long time when people are shooting at you! Napalm is really bad news as it burns at 3,000 degrees, hot enough to melt steel. Furthermore it emits deadly carbon monoxide and sucks all of the oxygen out of the air. So it is really a bad news way of killing the enemy. The spray really made quite a fire and, even with the vegetation being wet, it burned everything it touched. After that we got the heck out of there, crawling away. I couldn't wait to get rid of the flame thrower. This was a really bad idea on my part. The fire continued to burn for quite a while, but we did not receive any more fire from the enemy. As I recall we didn't find any crispy critters or mortally burned enemy, but the flames had apparently scared them off. As we did not have any way to refill the flame thrower, our platoon never used it again while I was in the field. Either way, I wanted nothing more to do with it ever again—so much for volunteering.

In our FSBs and night laagers we used trip flares which were essentially flares connected to a camouflaged string with a pin so that if someone tripped over the wire the flare would go off. We also had starlight and illumination flares for signaling and illumination around our base camps at night. The only time I recall setting these off was on the Fourth of July as a celebration.

Philippine APC Abandoned

August 1 or 2, 1968

We were sweeping roads near the rubber plantations on Route 13 or 14 to the east of Tay Ninh. We received a call for help from a Philippine Combat Construction team to report they were under attack by the enemy. They had been repairing a bridge and had some excavating equipment doing work with two APCs guarding them. Our platoon raced off down the road to help. When we got near the construction site, we met the Philippine combat engineers loaded on one of the APCs retreating down the road toward us. They stopped near us and were pointing down the road. They spoke to the lieutenant who determined that they had apparently left their equipment and an APC behind. This was bad news for us because we would be up against an APC with a .50-caliber machine gun. We did not know how many enemy we would be facing, but our lieutenant told us to proceed quickly. We moved out while the Philippine combat construction team stayed behind us. Apparently the lieutenant wanted to attack the enemy before they had time to destroy the equipment or get away with the APC. We proceeded up the road less than a mile and saw the construction equipment where the Philippine team had abandoned it. We raced forward, firing our 50s just in case. However, when we arrived there were no enemy, and the APC had been driven off the road and appeared to be stuck in a ditch. The .50-caliber machine gun was gone but it appeared that no other equipment had been blown up or stolen. We searched the area but found nothing, and we did not receive any enemy fire. The enemy had just disappeared taking only the .50-caliber machine gun and, we assumed, all the ammo they could carry. There could not have been too many enemy soldiers, or they would have stayed and fought with us, especially if they had the APC with the .50-caliber machine gun. We pulled the APC out of the ditch and got it back on the road. We carried towing cables with us on each track, so towing an APC was standard procedure for us as we were always getting stuck in the monsoon season. About the time we pulled the APC onto the road, the Philippine combat engineers returned. They were very grateful to us for helping them and invited us to come visit them in Tay Ninh where they would throw us a party. They were very friendly. The Philippines claimed they had been attacked by a lot of NVA soldiers, but we doubted it had been more than a handful. They did not want us to leave them and asked if we would accompany them back to Tay Ninh base camp where they were based. We drove with them part of the way then returned to our night laager position.

Sometime later when we were on a stand down in Tay Ninh base camp, a few of us went to see the Philippine construction company. They had a really nice area in the base camp with better food and accommodations than we did. They also had their own generator for electricity and better all-around facilities. Several of the construction crew recognized us when we pulled up in a jeep and they invited us for a cookout. The food was excellent, much better than the lousy food we had at our company mess hall. So we drank beer and generally had a good time with them. Periodically we would see them doing construction work on the roads when we were driving by on road sweeps. We never had the occasion to visit with them again.

Ambush Resulting From Kid Stealing Camera

August 3, 1968

This incident did not happen to my squad nor did I see it happen but it happened in our company. It was a further warning to all of us never to let our guard down, and beware of the kids who often flocked around us looking for C-Ration leftovers. You will recall my brush with acid in my mouth from a kid who sold me bread laced with battery acid.

While running the roads we were sitting ducks. We were vulnerable to snipers, mines, ambushes, RPGs, and claymore mines strapped to trees and command-detonated. We called our APCs "rolling coffins" because so many of us were killed or wounded while riding on them.

After sweeping the road by clearing it of mines and often running into ambushes, we would set up on the side of the road for hours. Then we would periodically run back down the road to the nearest APC to assure the roads were still clear. When we set up on the side of the road, we would have to wait for the last convoy to pass our position until we could head back to our FSB or night laager position. While we were guarding the roads, we typically had only four or five men in our squad. Not much of a presence to defend ourselves if the enemy wanted to attack us. Since we were almost always outnumbered and the enemy decided when and where and how to attack us 80% of the time, we were at a severe disadvantage when they decided to attack us. Often times we would patrol out a few hundred yards from our APC positioned on the side of the road, to make sure no enemy was waiting to ambush us. Other times we would open up with a .50 caliber into any heavy brush or jungle near to the roads. If we received any fire, we would usually take off as we knew we would be outnumbered and in a dire situation if the enemy chose to attack. He typically only attacked when he thought he could win his objective and then get away with a well-planned route if he had to break off contact.

While we were on the side of the road waiting for a convoy to pass, we heard discussion over the net or radio about one of our tracks reporting some KIAs. We knew this was trouble but we did not know what happened. After the convoy passed, we returned to our FSB Buell. At our FSB we heard what happened from some of the troops involved. Apparently one of our APCs had set up outside of a small village. Several kids came around asking for candy or C-rations or whatever handouts they could get. The soldiers gave them some C-Rations and were generally playing around with the kids. While the GIs were distracted, one of the kids stole one of the soldier's cameras. He was seen but took off toward the village running. Two of the soldiers immediately ran after him to retrieve their camera. A few minutes later some shooting was heard. The remaining troops jumped in the track and slowly moved into the town where the kid and the soldiers ran. In an alleyway they saw the two dead soldiers who had been stripped of their weapons, ammo, and other gear. No one was around so the remaining soldiers quickly picked up the bodies and took off down the road. Eventually they linked up with the rest of their platoon and later returned to the FSB. We thought it sounded like an enemy set-up to ambush our soldiers by using kids as bait. This further reinforced our opinion that everyone and everything in this country was stacked against us.

C-4 Stomped By Replacement

August 4–8, 1968

One evening our squad, of perhaps five to six men, were in a night laager on FSB Rawlins sitting around on ammo cases or other props to keep us out of the mud. As usual it was raining very heavily. We were all tired, cold and wet and wanted to get some warm food and black coffee in our stomachs before we headed out for ambushes, LPs or guard duty that night. Earlier that day we had received a new replacement soldier who had joined our squad. Even with the replacement, our squad was at half strength. We were always glad to have replacements as they could help share our numerous duties, and it was one more gun to help in a firefight. That said, no one got very close to replacements as they didn't last long in the field. We lit a couple of chunks of C-4 plastic explosives, which we used for heating up our C-Rats and coffee. The C-4 would burn very hot, even in the rain and mud, so it was excellent for heating up food and drink. Unfortunately, it was also a highly explosive compound we used for blowing up bunkers or other enemy fortifications. You could set it on fire or bang it around, but you could not heat it and bang it at the same time. Unfortunately no one told this to the replacement soldier. We were all too tired and hungry and miserable to think about much of anything, other than putting some hot food in our bellies. After each person heated up their C-Rats and coffee, the normal procedure was to simply let the rapidly burning chunks of C-4 explosive burn themselves out. Unfortunately, this time the replacement soldier stood up, and to the shock of everyone around, began to stomp on the C-4! Everyone yelled "NO" and "STOP" at the same time they all dove away from the C-4 and soldier. Everyone thought he was going to blow himself up and some of us with him. Fortunately it was so muddy that when he stomped on the C-4, he drove it into the mud and it did not explode. Seeing our reaction he did not attempt to stomp it a second time, thus avoiding a catastrophe! Once again proving why replacements did not last very long in the field.

Mortar Round in the Fire

August 4–8, 1968

One morning before dawn our company was in a FSB providing night protection to the artillery units and operating out of the base. We were getting something hot to eat after pulling guard duty, ambush or LP all night long. As usual we were tired, muddy, wet, hungry and generally miserable from a cold and wet night. We had just started heating up our C-Rats and coffee as best we could in the rain and mud. There was a fire or two started around the FSB where the artillery men burned the artillery casings, C-Ration boxes and other garbage in pits to dispose of it. Since we were cold and wet it was not unusual for the infantry in our unit to gather around the fire pits to try to warm up from a cold night. All of a sudden we heard a large explosion similar to incoming mortars. We all dove for our bunkers or tracks and got ready for an attack. It was not unusual at all for the enemy who was always watching us to drop a few mortars on us especially if they saw a group of soldiers together. Many times a mortar barrage preceded an attack by the NVA to kill as many of us as possible and keep our heads down while the infantry charged our position.

This time it was not an enemy attack. Rather some fool had thrown either a live mortar round or artillery shell in the debris to be burned. It was obviously a mistake but a very costly one indeed. The explosion killed a couple of soldiers and terribly wounded several others. Many of the wounded had all manner of debris penetrate their bodies in horrible wounds. Helicopters were brought to take out the dead and wounded and fly them to the hospital or morgue. I added yet another thing to avoid, fire pits in my goal for self-preservation.

Rome Plow Falls into Tank Trap

August 4–8, 1968

We often guarded the Rome plows which knocked down the trees and vegetation on the sides of the roads we patrolled. The plows stripped the vegetation so it would deny the enemy cover to spring ambushes and conceal themselves when planting or detonating mines in the road.

Rome Plows

Rome plows were enormous Caterpillar D7E bulldozers which had a very large 4,600-pound stinger-shaped blade with a sharp cutting blade mounted on one end of the plow. The cutting blade was designed so it could cut a three-foot tree in half and knock it down. The cutting edge was sharpened at least once a day during operations. The name Rome

Plow came from the fact that the bulldozer blades were manufactured in a small town in Georgia called Rome. Thus the name Rome plows. Fully combat equipped the Rome plows weighed 52,600 including the blade. For protection against mines and booby traps, the bulldozer had an armored cab with steel protecting-bars and a fully reinforced roof to protect the driver. The machines seared off all trees and vegetation six inches above ground and, using the blade which was pitched to the right at an angle, piled them up for later burning. Between 1968 and 1969 they cleared some seventy-eight square miles of vegetation adjoining roads and for fire support bases. Typically they cleared three hundred to four hundred meters of vegetation on the sides of roads where they were deployed. They were very effective in clearing heavy vegetation and trees. Much of the clearing in our area of operations was done on the roads around the Michelin Rubber Plantation, Ho Bo and Boi Loi woods, and Iron Triangle areas. Typically we would sweep an area to assure there was no enemy close by before the Rome plows began their clearing operations. As a result we got ourselves in several small firefights with the enemy who was either trying to blow up the plows, snipe at them, or simply get out of the area before they overran their positions.

The Rome plows would knock down the trees and push the vegetation into piles well off on the sides of the roads. The roads were dirt roads often the size of a single or one way lane of a US highway. They had just enough space for a large vehicle such as a tank or five ton truck to drive along. There was not enough room for two such vehicles to pass each other going in opposite directions. As there was no road shoulder you would find yourself in a ditch if you ran off the road. They were often pot marked and were very muddy during the rainy season. Conversely in the dry season driving down the road created huge dust bowls especially with a convoy or company of armored vehicles. We all wore masks and goggles during the dry season to keep out the dust. We looked like we were all in dust bowls in the dry season and were full of mud in the wet season. Remember we had no way to take a shower or bath other than if we were lucky enough to be able to stop to bathe in a bomb crater. Thus we were constantly dirty which caused skin and infection issues.

Typically we would ride along side of the Rome plows with our APCs riding parallel to them fifty to one hundred yards away in the woods depending upon the terrain. We would also sweep the area out front and to the sides of where the Rome plows were stripping the land of vegetation and trees. This way we could break up any ambushes by the enemy and would hopefully discover or more likely hit mines before the plows hit them.

This day while we were guarding the Rome plows, one of them fell into an enormous tank trap with an explosion. A tank trap is a huge ditch approximately fifteen-plus feet deep with ninety-degree walls on four sides and perhaps 30 feet square. It is covered by logs, brush, and covered in dirt with vegetation planted on the top. The one we found was also booby trapped with a small mine. A person or even a light vehicle could pass over it and never know there is a hole underneath. Of course a tank, or in this case a Rome plow, was heavy enough to break the logs and fall into the trap setting off the booby trap. When we arrived on the scene, the Rome plow driver was standing on top of the roof of his cab seeking a way out of the hole. Fortunately the mine did no damage to the Rome plow or to the driver, thanks to the heavy construction and armor of the bulldozer. The enormous machine was sitting upright in the hole completely surrounded by fifteen-foot straight walls. There was no way to get the Rome Plow out of the hole without digging it out.

We set up a perimeter to guard the Rome plow and did some additional sweeps into the surrounding area to make sure we were not going to be attacked by the enemy. Once that was done, one of the other Rome plows began to dig a very large and long ramp down to the bottom of the hole where the trapped bulldozer was sitting. It took the Rome plow quite a long time to grade a ramp down to the bottom of the tank trap. We all were amazed at how the NVA could dig such an enormous hole by hand. We knew it was done by hand because you could see the shovel marks on the sides of the hole where they dug it out.

As it was getting to be late afternoon, everyone was anxious to get out of there before nightfall when the enemy would surely sneak back to the area and shoot RPG rockets at the trapped Rome Plow and our APCs. We had learned this lesson the hard way with the tank stuck in the mud. Anyway before nightfall the combat engineers finally were able to drive the Rome plow out of the tank trap via the ramp. Then we accompanied the Rome plow back to our night laager position. I do not recall if they were loaded on trucks to drive back to the night laager position or if it was close enough for them to drive as they moved slowly. Either way, we got back to our night laager with both Rome plows without interference from the enemy.

Platoon of Enemy Women, Soldier Tied to Tree

August 4–8, 1968

On one of our road clearing and protection of the Rome plows missions we were called away to support one of our sister units that was engaged in a firefight in a fortified village. Apparently the village was not far from where we were because we came under fire very shortly after arriving at the location of the village. It was a typical small village off one side of the road with perhaps a dozen or so mud, straw and timber huts. However, the NVA had dug a rather large defensive ditch in the front and sides of the village, from where we were receiving heavy fire from automatic weapons.

Apparently the other units, which might have been one of the platoons from our company, had been ambushed moving near the village. Several of their soldiers had been killed and several others wounded. They had pulled back and were laying down fire when we arrived. We also learned that the enemy had tied one of our soldiers to a tree as bait. But apparently he was already dead before we arrived. The company commander in charge wanted us to retrieve the body tied to the tree and the other dead bodies. None of us thought it was worthwhile getting shot just to retrieve our dead, especially since it was obvious to all that this is exactly the trap the enemy had planned for us.

We advanced slowly forward but received far too much automatic weapons fire, and some RPGs were fired at our tracks. Fortunately, they came close but none hit their mark. We tried to advance several times, but we were forced back by heavy fire. In particular there was one enemy machine gun position which had a fortified bunker with overhead cover. They were most effective in their fire, keeping us from moving forward. After several attempts at trying to knock out the key enemy bunker, a Rome plow showed up on the scene. The driver volunteered to push earth in front of the plow and to provide cover for us while we walked behind this huge machine. We in turn would protect the driver and plow from infantry attacks as they moved forward. The bulldozer pushed up a huge pile of dirt and trees well over the top of the plow and almost covering the top of the cab. We walked behind the bulldozer and the large protecting mound. When the enemy saw what was coming, they opened up on the bulldozer with everything they had. It did no good at all since the huge pile of dirt and trees simply absorbed the machine gun fire. They even fired an RPG at the plow, but all it did was to explode against the dirt and tree mound. The Rome plow kept moving forward. We fired at the trench line behind the machinegun bunker to keep the other enemy down, as did our APCs who were hanging back due to the possibility of RPG rockets. Soon the Rome plow pushed the mound over the enemy machine gun bunker and keep going, effectively destroying the bunker and burying everyone inside. Then he kept on moving toward the trench line. That, plus the firepower of our APCs, broke the enemy resistance, and they withdrew as always when they were overpowered. However, they left behind a squad or so of soldiers to cover their orderly retreat.

By the time we had moved up with the Rome plow to the trench line, all of the enemy soldiers in the trench were either dead or dying. We shot up and down the trench line and threw hand grenades in the cut outs (which the enemy dug for protection when a grenades were thrown in the trench), clearing out any enemy who was still alive. At the same time, other units operating with us had cleared out the rest of the village of enemy and were searching for documents and weapons. We went into the ditch to recover weapons and documents. To our surprise, we found out that almost the entire trench line of 15 or 20 enemies were women NVA soldiers! It appeared that we had been fighting a platoon of enemy women soldiers. They fought as hard as the men and did not give up. They were also dressed exactly the same, carried the same weapons, and until we inspected them closer, they looked exactly like all of the NVA soldiers we had been fighting previously.

They were not local Vietcong (irregulars) but regular NVA soldiers from North Vietnam.

Later we saw that the enemy had tied a dead black soldier to a tree, taunting his comrades to come get him. We never did find out if he was alive or dead when the enemy had tied him to the tree. As usual no one told us much of anything, either before or after a battle. The Rome plow continued through the village, mowing down the entire village in less than an hour. Nothing remained of the village after we left, just piles of dirt and rubble where the village had been. After the battle we moved back to our night laager position moving out before dark.

Large Base Camp Discovered

August 9, 1968

We were on a combat sweep to the east of a large rubber plantation, which was likely the Michelin Rubber Plantation. We had been in many firefights and battles in the rubber plantations as there were several large ones in the areas we operated within. Surrounding this rubber plantation was a thick wood or jungle area called the Crescent Forest. As we swept through this area, we came upon some camouflaged bunkers. We approached these carefully, as they could be manned with enemy. Fortunately the first one or two we found were empty, but they were obviously new and had recently been occupied. This made us more cautious, as we knew the enemy was near. We advanced further into the area. As usual, I was on the right point position. In a thick wood or light jungle where you could walk (unlike a thick jungle where you had to cut a path with jungle axes) in somewhat of a line, we operated with three men out front of the main body of troops. This way we covered a larger area so we could find the enemy. Of course the point men were the first to get killed, as they would walk up on the hidden enemy positions. The reason I walked right point was that I believed it was better for survival to be on my own rather than be with the main body of troops. My rationale for this was twofold. First, I did not want to be blown up by a careless trooper who walked into an enemy mine. I walked very carefully, watching every inch of ground where I stepped.

I was terrified of stepping on a Bouncing Betty mine, which would bounce up around three feet and blow off the lower part of your body. I had seen first-hand what these mines could do and wanted nothing to do with them. Secondly I figured that if I were the enemy, I would ignore the point man and wait for the main body of the enemy before I opened up on them. This way I could kill as many as possible before they had time to react. Meanwhile, I could hide or crawl away as the enemy would not be concerned with one soldier. This worked out well for me on many occasions. While I was cut off from the main body of troops, few of the enemy paid attention to me and I was able to either get behind cover or crawl away. I also carried four to eight hand grenades so that if anyone came close to me, I would throw hand grenades around me, keeping them at bay.

As we moved forward, I let the rest of my platoon know we were walking into a fortified enemy camp. A couple of them moved up to join me moving forward. We had no idea of the size of the base camp as the first bunker I found was small, indicating a forward lookout position. We moved slowly and cautiously forward. We were expecting any moment that the enemy would open up on us. We could not see any other bunkers or trenches as they had been well camouflaged. As we moved forward, we heard someone from our platoon on the left yell that the camp appears to be abandoned. We still were cautious. As we moved forward, we came within perhaps five to eight yards of the bunkers and fighting trench line before we saw it. If it had been manned by the enemy, we would have all been killed for sure.

Apparently the enemy had decided not to fight this day and pulled out in a hurry, leaving much of his supplies and ammunition behind. Perhaps this was a storage and midway camp and was only guarded by a few men. Typically the enemy would have fought for the position if there had been sufficient men to man the bunkers and defensive perimeter.

In either case we came upon one of the largest caches of weapons, equipment, and ammunition we had yet found. The camp was full of all sorts of offensive weapons and gear including: ammunition of all types, Chinese claymore mines, hand grenades, mortars, RPGs, Bangalore torpedoes, and automatic rifles. We also found lots of bags of rice. We spent the rest of the day destroying the rice and burning down the base camp. We also used satchel charges of C-4 explosives to blow up the many bunkers and tunnels we found. We carted off all of the documents, weapons, ammunition, mines, Bangalore torpedoes and anything else of value to the NVA. Later these were destroyed outside the wire of our FSB in the biggest explosion I had ever seen besides a B-52 strike!

The Iron Triangle

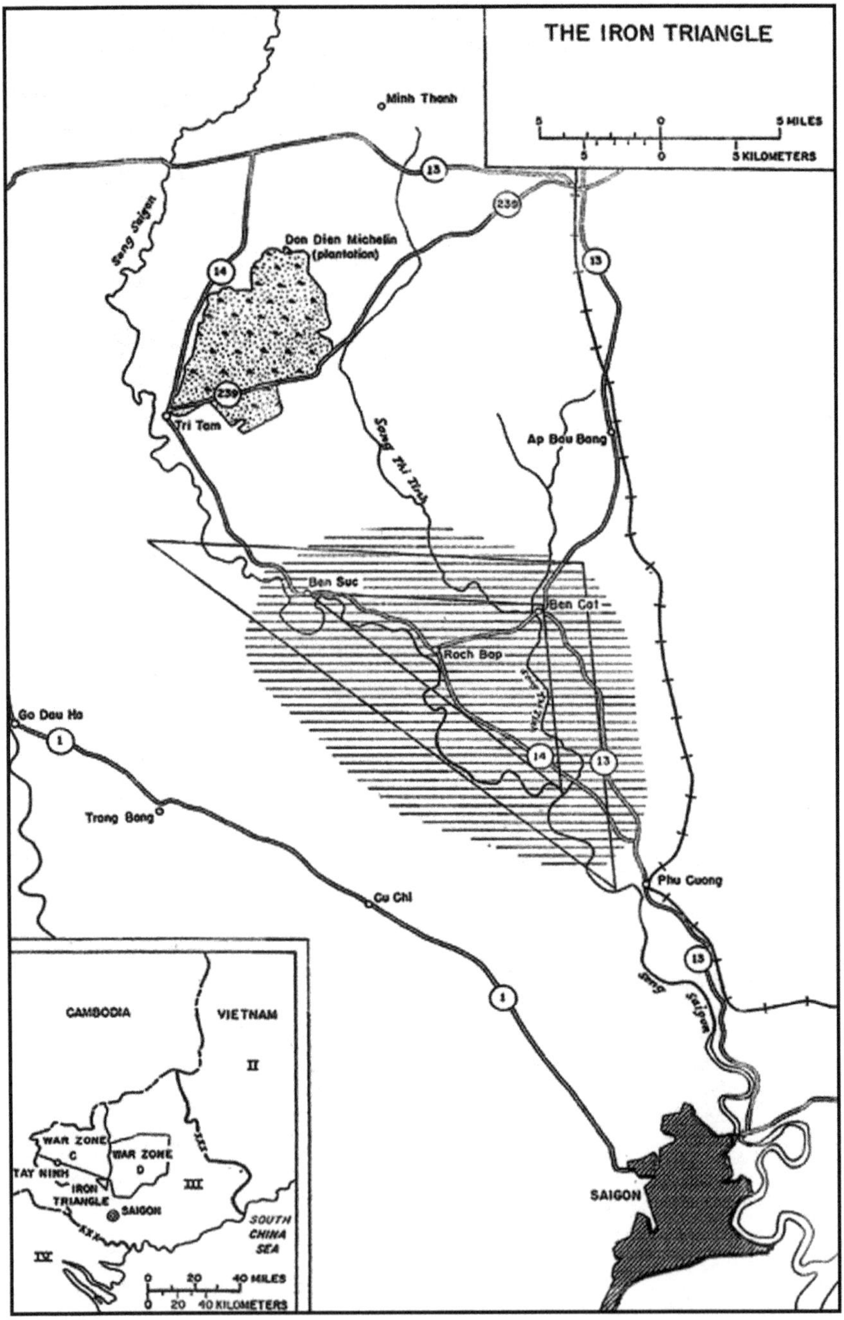

The Iron Triangle was an area of some 60 square miles 35 miles to the north west of Saigon. It was used as a staging area for enemy troop's intent on attacking Saigon. Some have called it a dagger pointing at the heart of Saigon. It was generally defined by the Saigon River to the southwest, the Thi Tinh River to the east, and the Than Dien forestry reserve to the north. Its corners were located by the villages of Ben Cat, Phu Hoa Dong and Ben Suc. All of these villages were found to be enemy strongholds that supplied men and material to the enemy. Later they were abandoned and the villagers resettled out of these areas. The area was like a human mole hill full of enemy bunkers, tunnels and fighting positions. The triangle was chocked full of enemy supplies and storage rooms, all of which were heavily protected by bunkers, mines, spider holes, fighting positions, and booby traps. Ever since WWII it had been a refuge for anti-government and communist insurgents. Thus they had decades to tunnel and build up fortifications. There were numerous battles in this area throughout the war and especially in the later years of the war. We often fought in the Iron Triangle and the Michelin Plantation to the northwest and on Routes 13 and 14, which pass through this area. We were in for a fight anytime we penetrated into this enemy stronghold. The Triangle is a mix of jungle, marshes, swamps, open areas with rice paddies, and dense forest. Outside of Routes 13 and 14, which pass through the fringes of the Iron Triangle there are no other roads, only foot paths and ox-cart paths. The area generally lies some 40 or so meters (131 feet) above the water table, but it is crisscrossed with swamps and marshes, making it difficult for armored vehicles to navigate in certain areas. Thus it is an ideal location for the enemy to hide and prepare for assaults on the populated areas and trigger ambushes on the roads around the Triangle.

Rest and Recuperation in Vung Tau

August 10–15

After serving four months in Vietnam, every soldier was eligible for an in-country R&R (a so called Rest and Recuperation or Rest and Relaxation leave) of three days. You could go to either China Beach or Vung Tau on the coasts. Both were considered secure areas. To me I didn't give a damn where I went, as long as I was out of the fighting. Every day you were out of the field was another day to live and another day toward your DEROS (Date Eligible to Return from Overseas) date when you could go home. I was asked by our Sergeant if I was interested in going on R&R to Vung Tau, and I jumped at the chance. I was told to be ready to go the next morning. I was ready that moment, but I had to pull duty with everyone else. Getting ready to go for me meant grabbing my rifle and gear and hopping on a helicopter. We had nothing else in the field that we would need for R&R. The next morning when the resupply helicopter came in, I jumped on and was flown back to Tay Ninh base camp. I hitched a ride from the runway back to Alpha Company where I reported to our company clerk, who had already cut orders for me to go on leave. I went back to my hooch where I had a decent set of jungle fatigues, a razor, toothbrush and some toothpaste. I then went over and took a cold shower. We had a limited amount of water stored in 55 gallon drums suspended in the air which we used as a shower. The water was always cold, except in the dry season when it heated up. You took a shower by sprinkling water on you, then turning off the water, lathering up with soap and then quickly washing it off. Either way it felt good as we had no showers in the field and were wet all the time during the monsoon season anyway.

Then I hurried back to my hooch, got dressed and left my rifle with my gear, which was the only time we were not allowed to take our weapons. The company clerk was kind enough to give me a ride back to the airport to catch a ride to Vung Tau. The only thing I carried was a small bag with my shaving supplies as I had only a shirt, pants and boots from the field with me, wet as always. I didn't care—I was going on leave. The way we got around in Vietnam was to go to the airfields and then catch any aircraft with room flying to where you wanted or near to where you wanted. No transportation was arranged, and it was strictly first come, first served, with the NCOs and officers going first of course. For enlisted men, we got whatever rides we could grab. The bad thing about this was that you only had three days, travel time included! So you didn't waste time getting to Vung Tau or it ate into your leave time. I hopped a C-47 Caribou airplane, which is a two engine cargo aircraft made for short take offs and landings that had just landed with supplies. There was a group of us who got on quickly and sat down in the web seats along the sides of the cargo aircraft. Some men sat on the floor. The pilots wanted to get off the ground quickly in Tay Ninh as they were frequently mortared by the enemy while landing. So we loaded up while the plane was unloading and then it immediately turned around and took off. The aircraft could take off from very short runways so we were up in the air in a flash. This plane was only going to Cu Chi so I would have to get another plane to go to Vung Tau, which was south of Saigon on the South China Sea.

The ride to Cu Chi was probably only fifteen minutes by air. Yet when we went on the roads it was always a challenge, as we were frequently attacked running the roads. At Cu Chi I was able to hop another flight to Tan Son Nhut Airfield where I got another flight to Vung Tau. The flight time was less than a half an hour if we had gone straight, but I wasted half a day getting to Vung Tau. On arrival you were essentially on your own. No one was there to help you. You just walked off the plane and hitched a ride into town with any military vehicle going that way.

Quickly I went to one of the bars looking for drinks and women of course. After a while I met up with a local Vietnamese woman, and she and I went back to her room. We didn't make much money as an E-4; with combat pay and overseas pay, I believe we made about $240 a month. The conversion rate on the currency was about 100 piasters to the dollar so even in the inflated GI R&R areas, living was cheap. Of course the food was not good either, and every meal consisted of rice and more rice. I couldn't eat most of the stuff they served, so I ate a lot of rice, French bread, and some meat they called beef, but more likely pig or dog. Anyway it was better than C-rations, and you could eat all you wanted if you had the cash. They also had coke that was cold—a real treat, even if they likely stole it from the US Army.

After two and a half days of shacking up with this Vietnamese woman, it was time for me to leave or I would not make it back to my company on time. Of course the time had gone too fast, and I didn't want to go back anyway, especially back to the fighting and living like an animal in the field. The room I was staying in had a wall three quarters the way to the top. Another bar girl had the room over the wall. It was in the afternoon, and I was talking about having to go, and the girl I was with was trying to talk me out of going. I guess we were talking loud because over the wall I heard someone call out, "Esher, is that you?" I was shocked that someone in Vung Tau would know who I was from my voice. So I replied, "Yes, who are you?" From the top of the wall one of the soldiers whom I had gone through AIT (Advanced Individual Training in Tigerland) was looking over the wall with a big grin on his face! Sure enough I recognized him and we had a good laugh. Today I do not recall his name, but he shipped out with me and was one of the guys who went AWOL with me before we left for Vietnam from Oakland Army Base. I had not seen him since we were assigned to different units after processing from the Repo-Depot in Vietnam.

Apparently he was assigned to the 4/23rd Mechanized Battalion but in another company. He told me he had just arrived in Vung Tau and his unit and ours was in "deep shit," which meant heavily engaged with the enemy. Then he said, "I wouldn't go back now if I were you!" I thought this was good advice, and so I decided to stay a little longer than I was authorized. This is called AWOL, or Absent With-Out Leave. Anyway, I didn't really care, as what were they going to do—send me to LBJ or the military jail in Long Ben, Vietnam? To the infantry, jail was better than the field and fighting. You got to eat three meals a day, live in a building, work eight hours a day and, best of all, no one was trying to kill you! So after that the four of us hung out together for the next day or two. Then I thought I should go back before they came looking for me. I thought I would simply tell them I had difficulty getting rides back to our unit.

Anyway when I got back to my unit the top sergeant gave me hell and didn't buy my excuse for a moment. He had been around the army too long to be fooled. Anyway I was not the first soldier who took a few extra days, so he sent me on my way to the field with the resupply vehicles within hours after I reported back to my company area. I barely had time to grab my gear before the vehicles left for the field. Nothing ever came of my few extra days. The company was so short-handed they were just glad to have anyone come back.

Picture in the Tropic Lightning News

August 12, 1968

The only communications we had with the outside world or outside of the army in Vietnam beyond the infrequent letters we received from home was the Tropic Lightning News of the 25th Infantry Division. Our battalion was in the news quite frequently, since we were in many battles and found many enemy base camps and weapons caches, but I was never in the news except for this one time. In the picture you can't really see my face, but you can see my track and our squad riding on top of it. I sent this picture home to my parents with an arrow indicating where I was in the picture. I was in the third track in the column sitting on my lawn chair on top of the APC. The picture taken was of our company making a mounted sweep in the Bo Loi Woods. It was taken on July 14, 1968, when we were engaged in numerous firefights with the enemy in this thickly wooded area. We also found a huge base camp and ammo cache during these battles.

Prelude to the Battle of Tay Ninh

August 16–17, 1968

For us the so-called Battle of Tay Ninh started early. In the late afternoon of the sixteenth of August our company was sweeping an area in the rubber plantations. We had been on a stand down that morning but it had been cut short as we were told to move out around 2:30 p.m. As it turned out we apparently were looking for a large formation of NVA in one of the large rubber plantations nearby. We swept the area assigned to us for several hours and saw a few isolated enemy soldiers but no main body of troops. We exchanged fire with them but as I recall we didn't find any bodies. We returned to our FSB around 7 p.m. to prepare for night defense.

That night an ambush patrol from one of our units spotted a large formation of NVA soldiers moving toward Tay Ninh. Fortunately our night in the FSB was a quiet one with no enemy sighted or attacks. In hindsight this was the prelude to the Battle of Tay Ninh as the NVA moved troops and supplies into position to attack the city. Country-wide the numerous attacks by the NVA, which included Tay Ninh, would come to be known as the August 1968 Offensive.

Ten-Day Battle of Tay Ninh

August 17–27, 1968

The battle for Tay Ninh began with an attack on Tay Ninh, Nui Ba Din Mountain, and FSB Buell among other locations in and around Tay Ninh City. FSB Buell sat astride the main approaches to Tay Ninh from the north about 4 or so miles outside of the town. There was a major battle when the NVA attacked this base camp. Our company was at FSB Rawlins that evening, and we waited all night for the anticipated attack which did not come. The next morning at dawn we set out to sweep the road. After sweeping the road, we were told that our sister company had made contact in Tay Ninh, and thus we were directed to support them in the battle.

We rolled down the road toward Tay Ninh. On the way into town we could see smoke and hear a firefight near the Cau Dai Temple complex. As we rolled down the road, we saw what appeared to us to be a group of Cau Dai monks in long robes moving rapidly away from the Cau Dai Temple complex on the sides of the road along with some civilians. As I recall there was forty or fifty monks or perhaps more. We continued to roll toward the battle, and we did not pay too much attention to them. We assumed they were civilians trying to get away from the fighting. As we rolled by the monks on the sides of the road, some of them lifted up their robes and began firing AK-47 machine guns at us! We were surprised, as we did not expect monks to be firing at us! However, we reacted instantly and opened fire from the top of the tracks while continuing to move down the road. I was riding on top of our track holding my M-16 in the ready position facing outward. I immediately opened up on some monks shooting at us at point blank range! It was mass confusion with monks running every which way trying to get away from our fire, while others were shooting at us. It looked to me like only some of the monks were shooting at us while most were running away from the firing. This all happened very fast. When some of our tracks opened up with .50-caliber machine guns, it was devastating to anyone in their path. However, we were moving rapidly down the road so most of the guns missed the monks before we were out of the ambush zone. I heard our track commander yell at our driver to "run them over," and he immediately headed into the monks on the side of the road. All this happened in less than a minute, and there were a lot of dead monks, or NVA disguised as monks, on the side of the roads. The majority got away by running away from the roads or hiding behind anything they could find. I don't know how many were killed and who was an NVA soldier hiding under the robes and who was a monk. However, most of our troops were battle hardened and did not shoot monks who did not have guns if they could help it. We never stopped during this ambush, but kept rolling down the road toward the Cao Dai Temple complex where the heaviest fighting was occurring. The Cau Dai Temple complex was huge, encompassing many acres. As it was by far the tallest building around you could see it from a long way off.

As an interesting note, after the battle I sent a post card of the Cao Dai temple home to my parents. On the back I wrote, "*Believe me nothing over here looks this good! The priests are probably hiding guns under their robes. PS: We got ambushed by this place (VC dressed like priests).*"

We moved in to support our sister company which was engaged in a firefight at the Temple complex. There were lots of NVA all around the temple complex and in the outskirts of the city which was more like a town. Our platoon did not fight in the Temple complex, but rather we fought around it in the fields and open areas on the outskirts of town. We found out later that the army or South Vietnamese political leaders would not allow us to use artillery on the Cau Dai Temple Complex. This restriction was in spite of the fact that the NVA had taken it over and were using it as a defensive position. Once again, better to have some of us killed and wounded than to damage their Temple!

The battle lasted for several hours with very heavy fighting. We knew we were up against a large number of professional NVA soldiers who were well trained and well equipped. We lost several tracks, and many men were killed and wounded in the brief battle. Later, when it was getting to be dusk, we moved out and moved into a night laager defensive position with another company (B Company I think) on the outskirts of town near a bridge. Fortunately we were not attacked that night.

Company Takes on Two NVA Battalions

Battle of Tay Ninh August 21, 1968

In the book *Armored Combat in Vietnam* by General Donn A. Starry, he mentions a battle which sounds familiar to the ones we fought. On page 132 he states, "*On 21, August a mechanized infantry company took on two North Vietnamese battalions and for more than an hour held its own. After suffering heavy losses with one officer left alive, the company was forced to withdraw under cover of supporting artillery.*" The company General Starry is referring to is more than likely our company (Company A). That said we were more like half of a company as we operated most of the time at half strength. During this battle we operated with even less manpower. According to Lieutenant Colonel Neilson's diary of 21 August he states, "*At 1600 contact initiated 1KN NW* of *CP T. Co. A (4/23) hit. Lt Blake, platoon leader and Lt Russell, FO both KIA; 5 others wounded. Withdrew and put in air strikes. Reinforced with 51st ARVN. Laager vic. Old airstrip w/A Co. 1/5 and A Trp. ¾. A Co. and B. Co. 4/23 Inf defend FSB [not stated but probably Rawlins which was not too far away]. Lost 4 APC. 20 BC.*" Author's note: BC referrers to "enemy killed or body count," KIA and WIA referrers to USA casualties. Lost four APC means that we had four Armored Personnel Carriers or APCs destroyed, likely blown up by RPGs. Our track or APC was not among the destroyed as I manned the .50-caliber machine gun during the battle that evening. Apparently, given the information above, on this day we had the last two of our three remaining officers killed. Unfortunately the officer I liked the best,

Lieutenant Russell, our FO, was killed this day. By the end of the battle of Tay Ninh we only had one officer left commanding what was left of our company and four APCs remaining. Thus I am quite sure both officers are referring to the same incident which involved our company. I was one of the fortunate survivors of this battle escaping with no wounds. But my chances of not being killed or wounded were getting slimmer and slimmer by the day! Watching my fellow soldiers killed or wounded every day it seemed certain that it was only a matter of time before it was my turn again.

We spent the next week fighting the NVA mostly in the rubber plantations and along the roads. We were constantly moving from one location to the next searching for the enemy. We would get into fierce firefights, and we would kill many of the enemy and they would kill and wound many of us. We lost a bunch of tracks in these fights. Every day there were less and less of us and less tracks.

This whole battle was like a blur as it all mixed together with us fighting with the enemy almost constantly. But I do remember certain incidents which stand out from the rest. I remember one incident where our platoon was running down a road and we were ambushed by a large number of enemies on the side of the road running next to a rubber plantation. We charged into the ambush on the side of the road and into the rubber plantation. We immediately lost several tracks to RPGs and had a bunch of men killed. Our charge into the enemy broke up the ambush and we killed a lot of enemy mostly with the .50 caliber machine guns. They started retreating through the rubber trees as we fired at them. We didn't follow them too far into the rubber plantation, but after a few minutes of fighting we retreated back to the road. There was still a lot of enemy milling around sporadically firing at us. At the time I did not think they were running away because they were too organized in the way they retreated, almost like it was preplanned. I believe they wanted us to follow them into a trap. Fortunately our remaining lieutenant saw it the same way and we did not take the bait. We broke contact and did not follow the enemy further into the rubber plantation. We took off back down the road the way we came. Fortunately our APC was not hit but we too lost one of our men in our squad to machine gun fire. I don't recall his name as he was a replacement. I think we were down to just four of us by this time. Every day we thought it was going to be our last. The place where we were ambushed had bunkers dug in behind the rubber trees which had been knocked down. I remember firing the .50 caliber through the rubber trees at the enemy as we moved toward them. It was a most confused fight with firing going on all around us. The .50 caliber machine guns made all the difference as the enemy did not have heavy weapons. We also knocked over a lot of rubber trees which as I recall someone told us afterward the USA government had to pay the plantation owners $100 each.

Similar Enemy Trap with Disastrous Results

In reading about the history of this battle many years later in the *Illustrated History of Armor, The Vietnam War* by James A. Arnold (pages 97–101) a similar incident occurred with disastrous consequences for the US mechanized infantry unit involved. It happened on August 22, 1968, during the battle of Tay Ninh. A small mechanized infantry unit of the 1/5th was searching for the enemy in the Ben Cui Rubber Plantation. The US mechanized infantry unit comprised nine APCs with thirty-five soldiers. Operating near this team was a recon platoon who observed hundreds of enemy soldiers advancing rapidly toward their position. They did the smart thing and retreated, reporting the enemy location. The other mechanized unit (essentially an understaffed platoon with a couple of extra tracks) decided to stay and fight in the rubber plantation. James A. Arnold in his book describes what happened next: "Six APCs deployed forward, with a reserve of three vehicles. For thirty minutes wave after wave of enemy soldiers swept forward into the assault. They fell in heaps before the Americans' machine guns. But some got close enough to fire rocket grenades from their RPG2s and RPG7s. The first tracks burst into Flame."

The American commander decided to stay in his position so as not to abandon the men whose vehicles had been hit. This decision was to cost him and his men their lives. The enemy continued to charge the remaining APCs and men with overwhelming manpower. In the end all twenty-eight officers and men who remained in place were killed. The reserve unit decided to retreat and lived to fight another day.

As I read this story of the battle, it reminded me of how the enemy tried to lure us into the rubber plantation in much the same way. But fortunately we did not take the bait and I am here to tell the story.

An Enemy Assault and Human Wave Attacks on FSB Rawlins

August 21/22, 1968

After heavy fighting for yet another day we returned to FSB Rawlins, to provide additional night defensives for the FSB along with B Company. We were exhausted from the fighting and mentally strained from all of our casualties. We retreated from the battle at dusk and arrived back at our FSB later in the early evening. At FSB Rawlins there were a couple of tanks and two of our mechanized infantry companies guarding the perimeter. These tanks were sometime attached to our company for sweeps and often they resided at the FSBs. It was always nice to have a tank accompany us as they could blow up the enemy bunkers with their 90 mm guns and for attacking enemy they could fire canister rounds. Typically we operated with the ¾ Cavalry or 3rd Squadron of the 4th Armored Cavalry, who would attach a couple of tanks to our unit for certain battles.

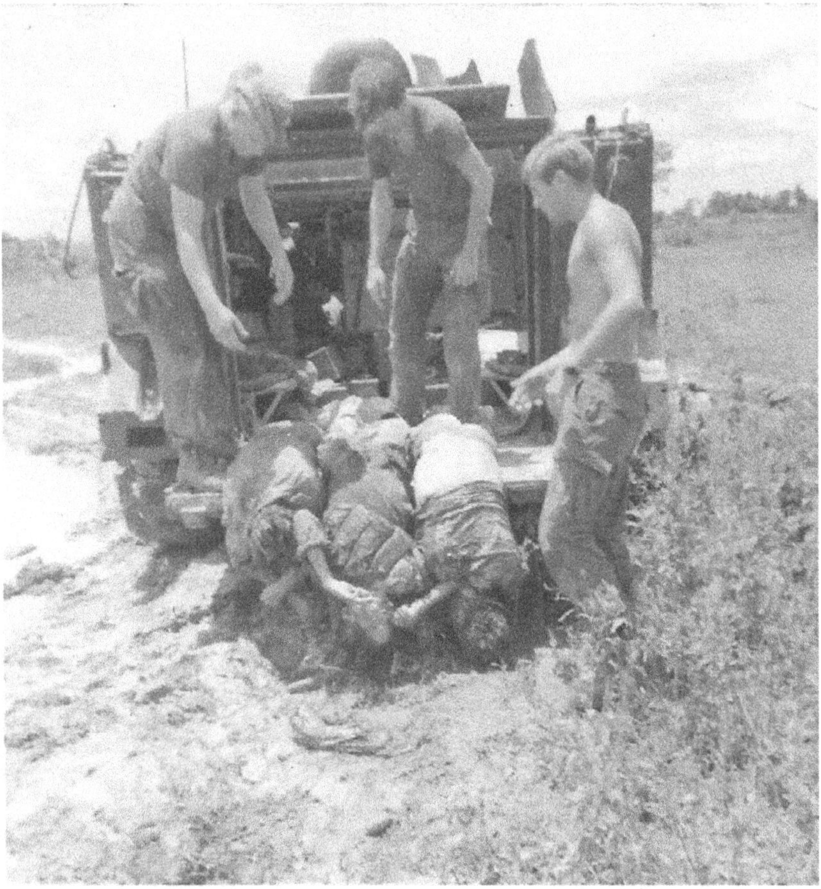

Dead enemy from human wave attack on FSB Rawlins

We had been fighting every day and some nights for several days. We were outnumbered every time we got into a firefight. The enemy was definitely on the offensive, and we were reacting to their moves. What made no sense to us was that we had so few men and vehicles left that to go out looking for the enemy when he was all around us seemed absurd! We all knew deep down that sooner or later the enemy would come to us and it was not going to be pretty. They knew we were taking heavy casualties and getting weaker and more worn down every day and night.

At the FSB everyone was expecting an attack. The enemy had attacked some of our other FSBs so our turn was coming. The only question was when. Sure enough they hit us this night. When the attack started I was pulling guard on top of our APC behind the .50-caliber machine gun. I was dead tired barely keeping my head up as with most of the other men on the line. We had all been fighting for days and were exhausted almost beyond our ability to function. The attack began just after midnight with a mortar barrage inside of our perimeter. This alerted everyone to a pending attack so we were all ready when they began charging our perimeter. Almost immediately our artillery and/or mortars began falling outside of our perimeter on the suspected enemy formations. The attack began while the mortars were still dropping on our positions. Fortunately none came close to our track so I opened up with our .50-caliber on top of the track, and our squad opened up with our M-60 machine gun in our bunker. The enemy hit our defensive line at several points at the same time. I don't recall who opened fire first, but the perimeter opened fire all about the same time. As soon as the attack began, our men shot off parachute flares which lit up the battlefield. In front of us we saw human waves of enemy charging toward our position. We mowed down everyone who we saw in front of our position! I was going through bullets so fast that the barrel was heating up and the brass casings piled up all around the copula. One of the guys in our squad kept getting me additional boxes of ammo, and I was loading them into the gun as fast as I could. He would not get up on the track to help as he surely would have been shot off.

We had a couple of RPG rockets shot at our position and many others fired at APCs on our side of the perimeter. You could see them coming at you. They looked like balls of fire shooting directly at you even if they were close. Several of the tracks were hit and exploded due to the ammo and ordinance inside. They often exploded and were very dangerous to be around when they were hit. I recall a couple of close calls with RPGs. One came very close, but fortunately it went in-between our track and bunker just missing our protective fence in front of the track. Another went high over our position. I could feel the heat of this one as it passed overhead, but I was too focused on firing at the infantry attacking our position to worry too much about it. I believe I killed both of the shooters since you automatically traverse the machine gun on where the rocket was fired. I was frightened during the battle, but was more focused on killing the enemy, especially when he was charging directly at you!

After what seemed like a short time, the enemy attack faltered in front of our position. It was a good thing because my machine gun barrel became so hot that the rounds started going wild out of the barrel. When the barrel heated up too much, it expanded and the bullets no longer went straight as they did not fit tightly in the barrel. We were supposed to replace the barrel before it got this hot, but replacing the barrel of a .50-caliber machine gun was not an easy task, especially when the enemy was shooting at you. Basically you had to stop shooting, get out asbestos gloves, get in front of the machine gun, exposed to the enemy, and try to twist a hot barrel off, which was difficult since it had expanded. Needless to say I was not going to attempt this in the middle of a battle. So I kept on shooting with the bullets going in a circular motion toward the enemy. The bullets were still deadly if they hit anyone. Anyway I called for my loader to get me the spare 50 barrel, and the two of us kicked aside the shell casings which had piled up so high on our track. It was very difficult taking the barrel out of the gun when it was so hot. My hands got slightly burned, even with the asbestos gloves! Anyway we had so much adrenaline that we changed the barrel and were back in business quickly. However, the enemy had shifted his attack to other parts of the perimeter. Nevertheless, we continued to fire into the woods just in case. The battle lasted on and off until almost daylight. I believe that at some point in time a Spooky gunship joined the battle, but I could be confusing this with a similar attack back in April/May. When it fired it looked like a solid stream of red coming out of its guns. It was devastating to the enemy if caught out in the open. Especially devastating were the beehive rounds, which were antipersonnel canisters of flechettes or darts fired at point blank range into the attacking enemy by the tanks and 105 mm howitzers. These canisters would simply mow down and disintegrate anyone in their path.

We had a lot of dead enemy in front of our position, with a couple of them coming within a few yards of our bunker and track. The artillery, mortars, and tanks were firing along with the machine guns, and the noise and volume of fire was incredible. The attack was stopped in its tracks by the volume of fire. We found out at dawn that the enemy breached our wire where they blew up several tracks with RPGs. I believe this was in the B Company area, but I am not sure. We lost a lot of tracks in this attack, and many men were killed and severely wounded. Our company lost four more APCs in this attack but as I recall no tracks were hit on either side of our squad. We were lucky that the enemy missed with the RPGs they fired at us. No enemy got past our side of the defensive perimeter but they came close, right up to our tracks and bunkers.

Next morning we dusted off our dead and wounded. Then we policed up the enemy equipment, weapons and dead bodies, burying them in a mass grave outside of our perimeter. I also collected a couple more guns and an RPG-7 from the dead enemy on the battlefield. One of them, an AK-47, looked as if it was brand new out of the box. I believe this was one of the guns I traded for a pass to Australia. According to Lieutenant Colonel Neilson's diary our two companies lost four APCs in this battle. My recollection is that several more APCs and artillery pieces were destroyed in this attack. But no tanks were lost. It is possible that the additional APCs lost were from the ¾ Cav. who was with us during the attack. I do not recall anyone in our squad being a casualty. Once again we were very lucky.

Ambush of a Large Convoy of Trucks

August 25, 1968

Another incident I remember during this battle was that a large convoy of 100 or so vehicles was ambushed on the road running supplies and ammunition to Tay Ninh Base Camp. Once again the ambush took place on the sides of the road near one of the rubber plantations. Apparently a lot of vehicles were destroyed and many of the soldiers on the convoy were casualties. We were directed to go rescue them but we were ambushed before we got within sight of the convoy. Fortunately we fell back quickly before the enemy could do much damage to our understrength platoon. This resulted in a long drawn out fight with the enemy, which was obviously prepared to fight us off. Once again they were dug in on the sides of the road in and around the rubber plantation itself. This time we waited for supporting artillery fire. But every time we tried to advance the enemy fought us off. This went on all day long, artillery firing at the enemy, and then we would advance only to be pushed back each time. Of course every time we advanced we lost more men and tracks. Finally we gave up and retreated back to our FSB exhausted. We never did get to the convoy which was attacked by the NVA. Little by little we were becoming less and less of an effective fighting force. We did not receive any replacements during the entire ten-day battle that I am aware of in our company. We were just ground down day by day fighting an enemy who vastly outnumbered us.

We went back to this site of a battle for several days and never did succeed in overrunning the dug in enemy. Finally we were told they were on the run and had abandoned the position. We didn't believe this for one minute. They were certainly not on the run. At best they were making a fighting withdrawal to some pre-arranged defensive position. We were under no illusions as to the battle hardness of the NVA regulars we were fighting. We were exhausted and worn out from fighting. As far as we were concerned, if they were withdrawing we should let them go as we were not in any shape to pursue them.

However, this was not to be as we were ordered to chase the enemy into the jungle and woods. As a result we got into running battles with the rear guard of the enemy troops. Each time they would hold us up and we would call in artillery then advance only to be held up again. We did this for a couple of days and then returned to our FSB at night. Every time we returned there were less and less of us. Soon our company was more like a reinforced platoon rather than a company. During these battles our acting company commander and several of our platoon Lieutenants were wounded and the next senior in line would take over. We went through all but one of the platoon lieutenants, either killed or severely wounded. The remaining lieutenant who took over the company didn't really have much of a company left to command. We had about half of our men killed or wounded and as I recall we only had four APCs left in our company. Our track was one of the casualties. There were only three of us left from our squad by the end of the fighting. When we pulled into our FSB, we only had four tracks left, and they carried the entire remainder of the company on top. Normally a track could hold only about eleven or twelve men riding on top. So there were perhaps 45–50 or so men left of our entire company. When Captain Montgomery returned from R&R on August 27, his company and equipment were essentially gone!

The Third Offensive

The battle of August 17–27 has been called the Third Offensive by historians. This offensive involved major attacks in Da Nang and Tay Ninh areas plus numerous rocket and mortar attacks on cities and US and ARVN Bases around Vietnam. In our Area of Operations this attack by the NVA was called the Battle of Tay Ninh. It involved some ten days of heavy fighting where we were both on the offensive and defense. In our area the US ARMY fighting men were outnumbered 8:1 by the attacking NVA and VC soldiers. The NVA made up over three quarters of the attacking force, with local Vietcong units making up the balance. The attackers were all battle hardened veterans with a local knowledge of the terrain and with their "safe areas" which we were not allowed to bomb or attack and support bases nearby in Cambodia. Our defending 1st Brigade was led by the aggressive Colonel Wolf who seemed not to care about how many casualties he incurred on our side as long as we killed lots of the enemy! Our severely under strength 1st Brigade comprised approximately 2,000 fighting soldiers backed up by 1,500 support personnel, facing an attacking enemy some 16,000 strong. For example our Battalion, the 4th of the 23rd, was authorized some 42 officers and 865 enlisted soldiers for a total of 907 men only 546 of whom operated in the three "line" or fighting companies. The other 361 were HQ and support soldiers. In the line companies we operated at half strength or less almost the entire time I was in the field. Of course most of the half strength was of infantrymen who took the majority of the casualties. During this battle our company was essentially wiped out as a fighting force with only a reinforced platoon and one officer remaining. The 1st Brigade was authorized to have some 160 APCs and 15 M-48 tanks. But as with the soldiers we were always short on armored vehicles.

The attacking force of 16,000 soldiers was comprised of the veteran 5th and 9th Vietcong and North Vietnamese Divisions. For our side the 1st Brigade comprised the 1st Battalion, 5th Infantry Mechanized; 4th Battalion, 23 Infantry Mechanized; 3rd Battalion, 27th Infantry; 2nd Battalion, 34th Armor; and the 2nd Battalion, 22nd Infantry. For ten days the battle raged on over an area of some 1,500 square kilometers. The battlefield included many types of terrain including; agricultural land, open fields, rubber plantations, forest, jungle, roads and cities. Movement of armored vehicles in the jungle and rice paddies was severely restricted due to the monsoon rainy season and subsequent standing water. At the end of the ten-day battle the 1st Brigade had lost 81 killed and about 400 wounded, almost a quarter of its combat soldiers. Historians have said that for these ten days of fighting the American units involved engaged in a running battle that saw examples of every kind of large scale combat experienced in Vietnam. There were ambushes, battles of maneuver, fixed battles against defensive positions, and human wave attacks.

For the three major enemy campaigns of 1968, Tet in February/March or the First Offensive, Mini Tet or the Second Offensive in May and the Third Offensive in August, the NVA and VC forces lost somewhere between sixty thousand to eighty thousand men killed and many times that number of wounded. For the five week period before and after the Third Offensive it was estimated by the US Military Command (MACV) that some 20,000 enemy were killed. The USA troops also suffered during these battles with the highest weekly casualties of the war.

New Brigade Commander Arrives At Rawlins FSB

August 27

We were at Rawlins FSB repairing our gear, fixing up our defenses from the attacks the prior days, policing the battlefield outside and inside our wire and burying the dead NVA soldiers in a ditch made by the bulldozers. According to Lieutenant Colonel Neilson's diary on the 26th Lieutenant Colonel Wolf was relieved of his command and was replaced on the twenty-seventh by Colonel Fair. Of course at the time we knew nothing of this nor would we have cared since we were exhausted! According to Lieutenant Colonel Neilson's diary Colonel Fair arrived by helicopter at Rawlins while we were cleaning up from the battle. The FSB was in a sorry state due to the death and destruction of the battles the night and days before. According to Lieutenant Colonel Neilson's diary, he states of his first meeting of Colonel Fair when he arrived at FSB Rawlins via helicopter:

"Major Don Starnes, BN XO, alerted me by radio that the NEW BDE CO was inbound to Rawlins about ten minutes before he arrived. I first saw him on the helicopter pad, dressed in heavily starched jungle fatigues and spit-shined boot and no doubt determined to make a name for himself.

He must have viewed me as the sorriest looking, dirtiest, and most disheveled lieutenant colonel he had ever seen. I cannot imagine what must have gone through his mind when he looked around the FSB.

There were bodies and parts of bodies on the wire and in front. A bulldozer was digging a trench outside the perimeter where we intended to put the enemy remains. There were piles of expended .50 caliber brass near every track. Guys were exhausted and either asleep where they dropped or trying to clean up. Nobody had a shirt on except me.

He walked around a while, and it was easy for me to see he was appalled at what he saw. First he told me I could not bury the remains without properly identifying them, as that was against the Geneva Convention. Next, he wanted me to mount the troops up and pursue the long-departed

NVA. I told him, "Yes, sir, as soon as we get resupplied with ammunition." He nearly exploded. He sternly informed me I had twenty-four hours to shape the mess up or I was out of there.

He next visited nearby FSB Buell defended by 2/22, their perimeter had been breached, and conditions were far worse. Later, their BN CO, Alex Hunt, told me he got the same treatments, only Alex had no bulldozer and no plan to bury the enemy.

That night TNBC got rocketed, his hooch took a near miss, and he got a frag in the butt. Welcome to RVN, Col Fair! After that he was a prince, a great BDE CO to work for and eventually became a lieutenant general."

This illustrates the aftermath of a battle and also how out of touch some of the senior officers were with the men in the field. Arriving after a battle in starched fatigues with spit shined boots while there were dead all over the place, many wounded still waiting to be helped and front line soldiers too exhausted to move did not play well with the troops. Then to compound the situation he wanted us to mount up and pursue the enemy! Not only were we low on ammo, but the survivors were exhausted and in no condition to pursue anyone. Besides, the enemy was already long gone having retreated to his safe areas after a bruising battle. Apparently no one paid any attention to the new CO's orders as we buried the enemy dead in the ditch. There was no way of identifying them even if we gave a damn to find out as most carried no ID or dog Tags. Besides they smelled so bad and the flies were so thick that if we had not buried them quickly we could not have stayed in the FSB for long. I do not recall ever seeing this new Colonel nor even Lieutenant Colonel Neilson at the FSB. Frankly we didn't give a damn about senior officers; we were more concerned with staying alive and getting through the day and night.

Engineering Convoy Ambushed

August 28

Typical of the types of security duty and ambushes we had experienced occurred on August 28. A Platoon from B Company was pulling security for the Combat construction engineers. A mechanized infantry platoon is typically comprised of four APCs and twenty-five men. However at this time there were likely much fewer men and only two or three tracks. Typically they would meet the Engineers at the Rock Crusher quarry at Nui Ba Den Mountain and escort them to the construction site to do road repairs. Then they would pull security while the engineers made the repairs to the roads/bridges and then escort them back to the FSB for the night. Then the APCs would return to their night laager to pull security or go out on ambushes. This day the platoon from B Company was protecting the Construction crew and vehicles while they repaired a culvert. Culverts were simple bridges over streams. They were constructed by placing three or more large three foot or more diameter corrugated pipes in the stream, then fixing them in place with rock and finally paving over the top with compressed soil. The roads in Vietnam were made of compacted soil and were not paved in our area. While this was going on the security platoon would sweep the roads and surrounding area to make sure the engineers were not attacked during construction.

Later this day, while the convoy of construction vehicles and escorting APCs were returning to their night defensive positions, the enemy ambushed them. Typically the enemy would mine the road with command-detonated mines and would fire automatic weapons and RPGs at the vehicles as they came into the ambush zone. This time our company was returning to our night laager position, and we were following close behind the Engineering convoy. When the enemy sprung the ambush, they immediately blew up a crane and dump truck with mines and RPGs. The escorting platoon of APCs immediately attacked the enemy on the sides of the road, and our company attacked from the rear. At about the same time we had helicopters overhead attacking with rockets and machine guns firing at the enemy positions. Soon afterward our artillery began hitting the enemy. The combination of this firepower quickly broke up the enemy ambush and the enemy retreated. Likely they retreated via a well-planned path of retreat, which was the enemy's modus operandi for such attacks, taking their dead and dying with them.

As our primary responsibility was to escort the remaining construction vehicles to their night laager, we did not pursue the enemy;

as it was getting near dusk, this would have been a foolish and likely fruitless adventure. So we took our dead and wounded, loaded them up on the remaining vehicles and continued down the road toward our night laager. The entire ambush likely lasted no more than 20 minutes. The rest of the time was spent gathering up our men and gear and loading up for our trip back to base camp. We lost one large crane, a dump truck, and one engineer killed and another wounded. We found only two enemy dead but likely there were more as we saw blood trails. It was common practice for the enemy to drag away their dead after a battle. They likely had many times more wounded than dead as our own statistics were for every one of our soldiers killed, six to seven more would be wounded, about half serious enough that they would be evacuated out of country and never return.

Opening Roads After Battle of Tay Ninh

August 31–September 4

After the battle of Tay Ninh, our company spent time getting resupplied with men and equipment lost in the battles. We mostly pulled duty opening roads which had been closed due to the heavy enemy activity. The western portions toward the NVA base camps in Cambodia and the Ho Chi Minh Trail of Routes 22, 26, and 4 leading to French Fort were key roads we opened during this period. We also escorted construction units and Rome plows who were clearing roadsides or repairing bridge culverts blown up by the enemy. During these road sweeps we had to watch for mines and ambushes. We were often shot at by enemy hidden on the sides of roads. They typically fired small arms fire at us as we passed by and occasionally they would shoot an RPG-7 rocket trying to blow up our APCs or the equipment we were escorting. To clear mines we often had combat engineers with mine sweepers to locate and detonate mines in the roads and bridge culverts. At night we would pull our usual ambushes, LP and general FSB defense in our bunkers and APCs. On the fifth of September our platoon of twenty-two men went to French Fort to defend the artillery base. We were to be stationed at French Fort for a week.

Banana plantation going toward French Fort viewed from track

French Fort

September 5–13, 1968

As an understaffed mechanized infantry platoon, we had been dispatched to camp Saint Barbara, which we called Santa Barbara or more frequently French Fort, on August 5 to relieve the platoon from C Company. They had been there a week previously to guard the fort from ground attacks. A platoon from different companies rotated this duty every week or so. French Fort was an old French outpost which was taken over by the Americans. It was essentially the last American outpost on Route 4 before the Cambodian border (XT272680). It was a square-shaped fort with high dirt berms surrounding it. Built into the sides of the berms were fortified bunkers. It was surrounded on all sides, except for the access road in the front of the fort, by an extensive barbed wire and mine field. It was an artillery outpost for Battery A, 2nd BN, 32nd ARTY of the 23rd ARTY Group. Work to expand the fort to accommodate Battery B after Operation Yellowstone had begun in December 1967. It was occupied on February 20, 1968, by Battery B. On April 24 and 25, Battery B moved from French Fort to Tay Ninh and was replaced by Battery A, who occupied the Fort. The battery had 175 mm guns and massive 8-inch howitzers, which were some of the largest howitzers in the USA arsenal at that time. The only redeeming feature was that the fort had a mess hall where we could get hot meals in the evening. This was a big benefit to infantry as we rarely got meals of any type except for C-Rations. Of course since the fort had been there so long, the enemy had it zeroed in, so anytime they felt like it, they would toss in some mortars. This was a daily occurrence while we were stationed there. This made going for meals in the mess hall dicey, especially if there was a major mortar attack. Several times while we were guarding the perimeter there were major mortar attacks where the enemy walked mortars up and down the camp several times. The fort was surrounded by 20-plus years of concertina wire in row after row of wire obstacles. Integrated into this barbed wire barrier were booby traps, mines and trip flares. It seemed to us like it would be very difficult for the enemy to get through this barrier in any mass. That said, enemy sappers did penetrate the wire, and thus we had to be on constant vigilance to watch for them. The only path through the barbed wire was the entrance gate accessed through a single road just wide enough for a large truck to pass. This is the gate we guarded with our APCs. The Artillery also had a "quad 50" which was a two and a half ton truck with four .50 caliber machine guns mounted on its flat bed with a defensive deflector shield. The artillery men thought that French Fort was their most dangerous assignment in our area. We thought it was a real easy duty and looked at it as a reward and break from the day to day infantry fighting and trudging through the swamps and jungle. Anyone of us would have gladly traded places with the artillerymen.

French Fort's primary function was to support infantry operations and guard the border and highway from an NVA assault on Saigon from the safe havens in Cambodia. It was thought that the NVA headquarters in the south COSVN (Central Office for South Vietnam) was located a few miles inside Cambodia, not far from this location. In fact that was confirmed after the war. Supplies came through this area, both from North Vietnam via trucks and later an oil pipeline, and from Cambodia via the port of Sihanoukville (Kompong Som). Both supplied the NVA and supporting VC with plenty of arms and supplies. Just over the border, where we were prohibited from bombing or pursuing the NVA, they had huge training and supply depots. This is where they headed when they broke off contact if we were winning or they drew upon reinforcements when they were attacking us.

At French Fort we had been cut off from supplies as the NVA had closed down the road since the fifth of September. They had been shooting mortars and rockets at the fort for several weeks. French Fort is located on Route 4, approximately nineteen miles from the Cambodian border. Route 4 runs from Tay Ninh to the Cambodia border near the Mimot Plantation, which lies on both sides of the border. It lies to the West of the Fishhook area of South Vietnam near Nui Ba Den or the Black Virgin Mountain. The NVA controlled the Cambodian Vietnam border and through it ran the Ho Chi Minh Trail.

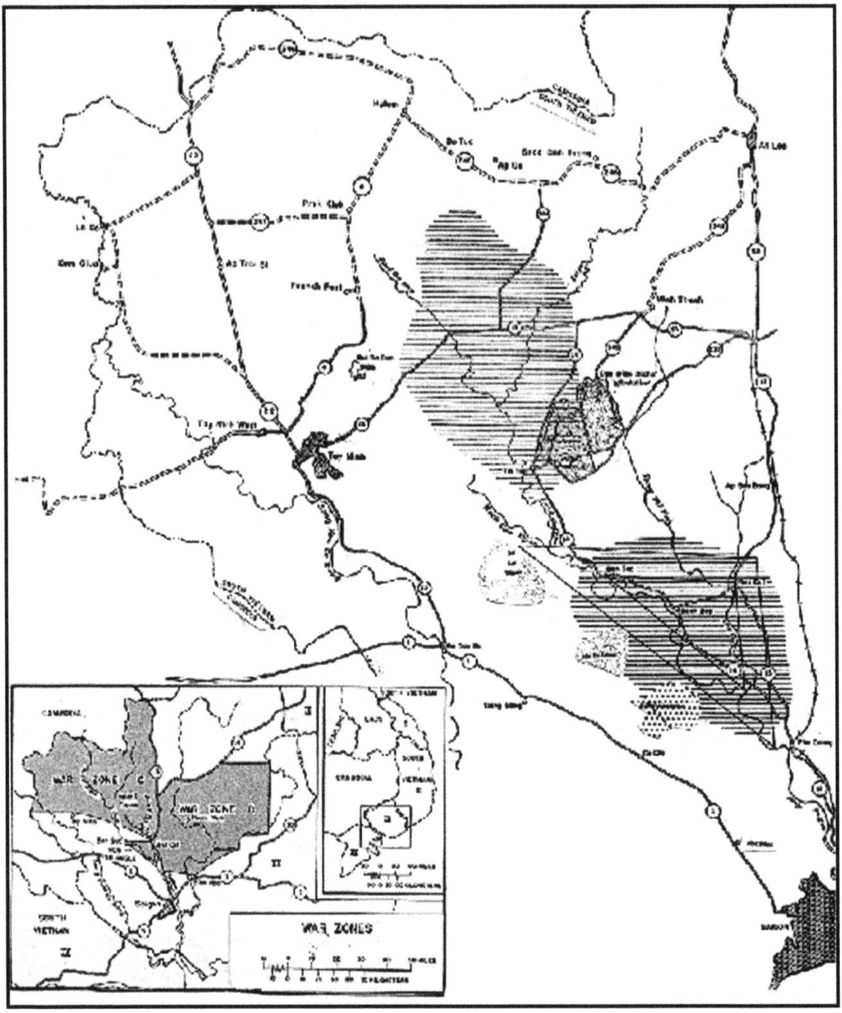

Location of French Fort off Route 4 near the Cambodian border.

Ho Chi Minh Trail

The Ho Chi Minh trail was a series of hundreds of miles of different routes the NVA used to smuggle arms, ammunitions, fuel, supplies and soldiers into South Vietnam. There were hundreds of thousands of soldiers guarding and repairing these transit routes. These were in addition to the millions of soldiers who traveled to the South from the North over decades to fight and support the wars with first the French and as of late the USA, ARVN and its allies. They even buried an oil pipeline running parallel to the route to supply the trucks, tanks, and other military vehicles guarding and traveling south. It truly was a "highway" which was repeatedly bombed by the USA Aircraft, including B-52 Bombers, or Arc Light raids typically staged twice a day during this period of time. It also included the trails leading to the South Vietnam border from the Cambodian Port of Shihanoukville.

We were guarding the single entrance to French Fort which was perhaps two hundred yards from the road sandwiched between multiple rows of barbed wire and an extensive minefield of over two hundred yards deep. It was considered the only way an infantry assault could attack the Fort as it was surrounded an all sides by the barbed wire and minefield defenses considered impregnable at that time. Nevertheless, with our four APCs and less than 20 soldiers, we were considered the rapid response defensive unit in the event of an attack as we could quickly bring firepower to any area of the fort with our .50 caliber and M-60 machine guns. We were stationed at two bunkers facing the road at the entrance to the fort. Next to us was the Quad 50, an awesome weapon. The firepower it could deliver was devastating, especially against infantry where a single bullet could go through many bodies, not to mention steel with armor piercing bullets.

For a week or more we had been cut off from the road due to the heavy concentration of enemy troops in the area. We had been unable to be resupplied by Route 4 as the NVA ambushed anything which moved on the road. The artillery outpost had to be supplied exclusively via helicopters which were fired upon by surrounding machine guns, small arms and mortars when they dropped off their supplies. Retrieving the supplies was very dangerous as the NVA would drop mortars on the fort whenever we were resupplied.

One evening while guarding the front gate we heard an explosion to the left side of the fort in the barbwire minefield. What was strange was that no one opened up on the minefield. We heard a lot of yelling and being the rapid response task force it was our job to go investigate and defend the position. We ran with our weapons and grabbed extra ammo, grenades and LAWs, in case it was sappers trying to penetrate our defenses. We assumed one of them had hit a mine. When we arrived at the side of the berm, some of the artillery soldiers were saying that they were our men in the mine field and not to shoot! We didn't know what to think as someone would be crazy to venture into the mine field, especially in the dark. About this time someone brought up a starlight scope and verified that there were three Americans in the minefield. Apparently two were down and one was standing. I do not recall what unit they were from, but I do not believe it was our unit. In either case, apparently the three had set off to set up a listening post of some kind and somehow got mixed up and wound up in the barbwire minefield! This would have been very difficult to do unless you went over the side of one of the berms, as the only place to exit the fort safely was via the entrance road, which we were guarding. No one bothered to tell us that a scouting parting was even going out of the wire. Again typical of the mess in Vietnam where people who needed to know were not told. It appeared that one of the troops had stepped on a Bouncing Betty mine, blowing off his lower legs and severely wounding one other troop. The third soldier apparently was either unhurt or only slightly wounded but afraid to move even to give assistance to his buddies. He was frozen in place! At this juncture there was little anyone could do to help them as there was no way to safely extract them from the mine field. In fact, they had penetrated almost to the middle of the barbed wire minefield before setting off a mine. That itself was a miracle!

Several times during the night we could hear the survivors calling for help. The only thing anyone could do was to tell them to keep quiet and not to move until daylight when a helicopter could try to extract them. They stayed in the mine field, not moving all night. I believe the second wounded soldier lived through the night but was in bad shape. I don't know if he lived or died of his wounds afterward. The first soldier who hit the mine was killed instantly, as his legs had been blown off. The third soldier stood up all night, frozen in place. At dawn a helicopter arrived to try to extract the two survivors. The only thing they could do was to lower an extraction rope with a harness to the standing soldier. As soon as the helicopter showed up, the NVA saw what was happening and began to mortar the minefield where the soldiers were located. The standing soldier was too afraid to even lie down and could only crouch. The helicopter naturally took off when the mortars began falling. A short while later, the helicopter came back and dropped the harness to the surviving soldiers once again. This proved most difficult as the soldier would not move, even to grab the harness. Eventually the helicopter maneuvered the harness to the soldier, and he hooked it around the wounded man. He was hauled up and deposited back in the fort directly without even being hoisted up to the helicopter. Then the helicopter came back for the unwounded or slightly wounded soldier who was likewise deposited in the fort. Then the helicopter took off rapidly to get away from the mortars. The KIA soldier was left in the minefield at least during the time we were stationed at the fort. No one thought it made sense to venture out into the mine field to recover the dead especially with the enemy all around us waiting for someone else to venture into the minefield.

Being at the front entrance to the fort, we would stand on top of our tracks and quickly try to spot the white puffs of smoke which indicated the presence of a recently fired mortar tube. Then we would quickly duck in the track or bunker before the mortars hit. We would call in artillery strikes on the site of the mortar and then try to adjust the fire via the radio while ducking the mortars as they rained down on the fort.

The mortars were so frequent that only two of us at a time would go up the road to the artillery mess hall to limit casualties when an enemy mortar barrage landed in our area. One time another soldier and I were walking up the road to the main fort area to go to the mess hall. Just then an enemy mortar strike began to be "walked across" the fort. There were drainage ditches with small culverts of corrugated metal on both sides of the road. When the mortar rounds began to hit near us, we both jumped into the left hand side ditch. The ditch was perhaps three feet deep with no cover. As the mortar rounds began getting closer I tried to crawl into the corrugated metal drain pipe. Unfortunately the pipe was very small only 2–2.5 feet in diameter and it was most difficult to squeeze into. My partner kept pushing me further into the pipe as he wanted to get undercover. As I moved further into the pipe I saw two red eyes looking at me and then a very large rat (the rats in Vietnam were huge) getting very agitated that I was crawling into his space. At the same time my partner was pushing me to get further into the pipe the rat was threatening to bite me! It was a most unpleasant situation since I could not bring my weapon to bear on the rat as it was squeezed by my side and I could not move. Anyway the mortar barrage walked past us exploding several rounds on the road and neither of us was wounded, only sprayed with dirt and debris. I recall having a most difficult time trying to crawl backward out of the pipe with my partner pulling on my legs and the rat running around in the hole.

Another time half of our platoon was off guard duty lying in wooden bunks or sitting around cleaning weapons in the large sleeping bunker. The sleeping bunker was a large bunker which was perhaps four times the size of the two bunkers at the front of the fort entrance where we parked the tracks. It was built into the dirt walls of the fort and covered with dirt and sandbags. The entrance was an L-shape to prevent mortars from going directly into the bunker. It had sandbags all around the entrance. It was made out of large planks of wood with huge 12" × 12" sized supporting beams to support the massive weight of the earth and sandbags above and around the bunker. Unfortunately some of the dirt had come away from one of the upper sides of the bunker exposing only the wood and a thin layer of dirt. On this occasion we were being mortared. No one was overly concerned as we assumed we were safe inside the bunker. A mortar would explode outside and would normally not penetrate a bunker. They were used to kill personnel and destroy things above ground. On the other hand, a rocket was designed to penetrate bunkers and armor. This time the NVA scored a direct hit on the top rear side of our bunker where the earth was the thinnest. It must have been one of the larger mortars as it blew out the side of the bunker wall. The explosion blew a hole in the bunker wall, throwing shrapnel, splinters, wood, dirt, debris, dust and cordite into the bunker. Several in our platoon were wounded, and all of us were shaken up by the explosion. Fortunately most of us sustained only minor wounds of shrapnel and splinters which were later pulled out by the medics. A couple of our men were seriously wounded and had to be medivacked to the hospital, although I don't think any-one died. Of course this further reduced our manpower in the platoon to the point where we now only had around 18 or so men, with our lieutenant and an E-6 acting as platoon sergeant and one other buck sergeant. All of the squad leaders were SP4, including me. A normal full strength Mechanized platoon has around forty men including a platoon lieutenant and platoon sergeant with four squad leaders (E-5 sergeants). Promotions to E-5 almost never came to our unit, even though we were in those command positions. It seemed that most of the promotions went to the house cats because they were regular army, whereas many of us were draftees. The army didn't really care much about draftees one way or another.

A couple of days later I was eating a C-Ration in the right-hand bunker near my track. All of a sudden the quad 50 opened up along with the 50s on top of the tracks. I jumped out of the bunker and asked someone what was happening. One of the men on my track said "gooks in the wire"! I looked out over the top of the bunker wall and could see nothing but dirt and flashes from where the .50-caliber rounds were hitting. Someone yelled, "Cease fire," and the 50s stopped firing. When the dust cleared we could see nothing at all but an empty road in front of the fort. The lieutenant decided that we should go investigate and see if there were any bodies from the firing. My squad was "volunteered" for the task. The road leading to the Fort was mined on both sides and covered by perhaps 10 layers of barbed wire obstacles with mines in-between. The only way to approach the fort was directly up the road into the mouth of our eight .50-caliber machine guns, four on the quad M-50 flat-bed truck and one on each track plus four M-60 machine guns. We did not relish walking down this road with no cover and no place to go, other than straight ahead or back, with mines on each side. If this were an ambush, we would be sitting ducks caught in-between our machine guns and those of the enemy. Should the NVA decide to mortar us, we would likewise be sitting ducks out in the open with no place to run. Slowly we moved down the road, ready to shoot at anything that moved on the other side of the road. As we approached the main road, we heard several people excitingly speaking Vietnamese. We hit the dirt and, with weapons pointed at the ditch on the other side of the road, yelled for them to come out! To our utter shock a bunch of kids no more than ten to twelve years old got out of the ditch with their hand held high in the air. We told them to stand in the middle of the street with their hands up. With all that firepower leveled at them, not a single one had even a scratch on him. Apparently when the 50s opened up, they all took cover in the ditch and did not move. All of the rounds sailed over their heads. Apparently they were thinking of coming to the fort to sell something. This in the middle of us being surrounded by the enemy and cut off. Lots of incidents like this made no sense in Vietnam. Anyway we told them to go home and never come near the fort again. I believe they learned their lesson as no one even came down the road the remainder of the time we were at the fort.

Another day I was on top of the track trying to locate the source of the mortars that were shelling the fort. We would wait until the mortars passed over us and then quickly pop up on the track so we could see over the dirt berm at the front entrance of the fort. I was standing on top of my track while the mortars were falling behind us, trying to zero in artillery on the white puffs of smoke when mortars left the tube, hoping that the NVA didn't drop a mortar round on us while we were exposed on the track.

Author at French Fort calling in artillery strikes to counter enemy mortar fire

About this time the NVA wised up and began dropping mortars on top of us. Obviously if we could see their mortar tubes firing from the jungle, they could see us standing on top of the tracks. When the first one hit too close, I jumped off the track and scrambled for the closest bunker. As I jumped inside, I knocked over a soldier who was standing in a group inside the bunker looking out of the firing aperture. Jumping or banging into someone when jumping into a bunker was a common occurrence in the infantry. This time it was a bit different! To my surprise I had bumped into a white haired Major General (two stars) and his aid, a very scared captain. The general looked very old to me and was carrying a cane! Not what one would expect in a combat base near the Cambodian border. When I stood up and recognized that he was a general, I said I was sorry for jumping into him. He said, "That's quite all right, son. I would have done the same thing!" I don't know why he was visiting French Fort, but I believe he was in the artillery. All I remember is that he stayed in our bunker until the mortars stopped, and his captain aid kept saying, "We should get out of this place before they mortar us again." The general did not seem concerned, and after the shelling stopped, they proceeded up the road to the main part of the fort. It was the first and last time I ever saw a general anyplace in Vietnam.

Ambush of Friday the 13th

Friday 13, 1968

Friday the Thirteenth: Bad Luck Day

Friday the thirteenth is considered unlucky, and it certainly was for me as it was yet another time I was faced with immediate death or worse, capture by the NVA. Friday the thirteenth was considered unlucky since Friday, October 13, 1307, when the Templars of the Crusades fame were arrested and thrown in jail by King Philip, the King of France, who trumped up charges so he could void his debts to them and because he wanted their treasure. It is usually always about "money," hence the term "follow the money." In this case the King never found the Templars' treasure, which to this day remains one of the greatest mysteries in history. However, many historians doubt just how much treasure the Templars actually had in France at the time. Still, it makes for interesting reading.

A few days after the incident with the general, September 13, we were surprised to learn that we were to "clear the road" to Tay Ninh so that a convoy could resupply the fort with artillery shells and other supplies. Supplies were running low as the fort had been cut off for some time. We were not only surprised, but very much afraid to leave the fort. We were surrounded by thousands of NVA whose headquarters, main units, and supply bases were closer to them than our supplies and the rest of our battalion soldiers were to us. Sending out an under strength platoon with four APCs down a highway, which surely was mined and which had been under NVA control for weeks, made no sense to us. We knew that we would be sitting ducks for an ambush in our "rolling coffins" as they were so easily blown up by RPGs and mines. In either case, we knew we were in for it. As usual the "higher-ups" were using us as "cannon fodder" to see if the road could be forced open for the re-supply convoys. A common role of how the army used the "draftee" infantry: dispensable, used to "draw in the enemy so we could annihilate him with superior airpower and artillery." That sounded great unless you were the "bait" who more often than not got killed or slaughtered in the process of "drawing out the enemy"!

To prepare for the fight we were positive was coming, I put on my flak vest, helmet and loaded up with ammunition. In Vietnam we were not outfitted as the modern soldier is today. Basically we wore boots, socks, pants (no underwear as it rotted away), a flak jacket when we knew we were going to have a firefight as it was too hot to wear on a foot patrol, web belt with two canteens, and lots of ammo and hand grenades. As we were going to be "running the gauntlet" down the road I figured that we should have all the firepower we could muster. Thus I grabbed an M-60 machine gun and mounted the track on the right side (front view) facing outward with my legs crossed. We always rode on top of the tracks so that we would be "blown off' in the event of a mine or RPG rather than be cooked inside of an exploding track. There were only five of us on our track including the driver, .50-caliber machine gunner, an engineer, another soldier and myself with the M-60. I believe that three of the four other men riding on my track that day were; PFC Rubin Valdez, PFC Robert Lowery, and the attached engineer Brigham. I do not recall the fifth soldier.

I loaded a 100 round linked belt of ammo for the M-60 machine gun and then linked another 300 rounds in boxes so I would not have to waste time reloading in a fight. I also placed several other boxes of 100 linked rounds each near my machines gun. Then I wrapped another 800 rounds of linked ammo around my body, seven belts around the neck and another belt around my waist. A standard combat load for an M-60 machine gunner was between 800 and 1,000 rounds in belts around his body. This was a precaution in case we had to jump or were blown off the track. A high probability as we were convinced we were going to "get hit" either by a mine or ambush or more likely both. Our platoon of four tracks and 18 soldiers was accompanied by an element of four Engineers from the 65th Engineer Battalion. They were there to clear the roads of mines with one riding on each track.

We started off early in the morning of Friday the thirteenth of September 1968. Ours was the third track of the platoon as we headed slowly down the roadway leading from French Fort to the main road, Route 4 going towards Tay Ninh. We hit the main road turning right and proceeded down the road at perhaps fifteen miles an hour. No one was anxious to hit a mine or to go too quickly into what we perceived was a suicide mission.

In traveling down a road with APCs, we traveled in a herringbone configuration with every other track facing its .50 caliber machine gun in the opposite direction from the track in front. The lead track had its machine gun facing forward. This enabled us to cover the front and both sides of the road as we proceeded ahead.

We drove down the road slowly with the track drivers following the tracks of the APC ahead to avoid triggering a mine. As we approached the first village which had just a handful of shacks on either side of the road, we noticed that there were no villagers about. This was an ominous sign which often presaged an ambush or landmines. Either way it meant trouble and we had all senses on alert. We proceeded to enter the village with all hands on triggers and safety levers off ready to fire at anything suspicious or smelling of NVA who we knew were in the area in force. After proceeding into the village perhaps twenty-five yards the first track was hit by an RPG. At the time I remember thinking it had hit a mine. Of course all we could see was smoke and heard a loud explosion. As it turned out this first rocket hit the platoon sergeant, decapitating him and wounding several others riding in the first track. This was the opening bell for the NVA to trigger an ambush and all hell broke loose! RPGs, machine guns and small arms fire immediately broke out all along the road at all four tracks simultaneously.

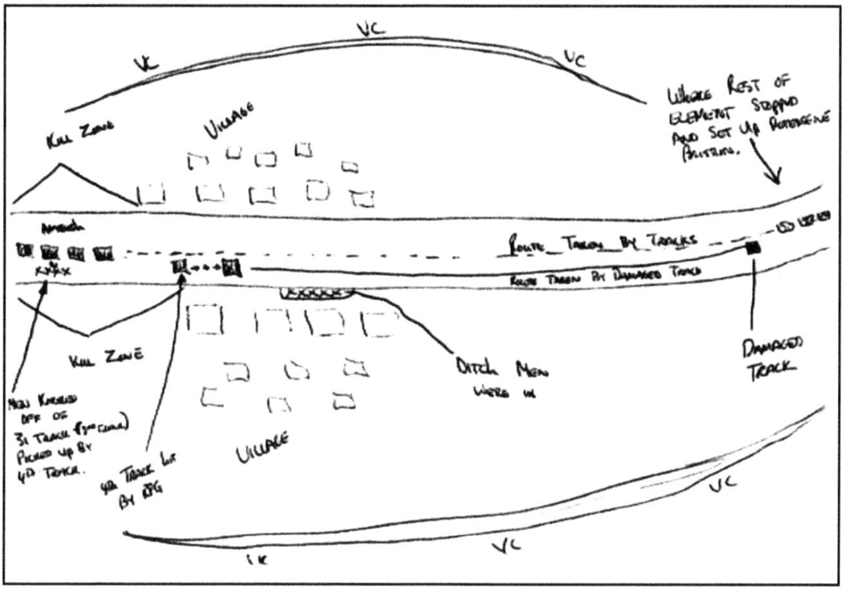

Original debriefing map of the ambush on September 13, 1968

Several RPGs and perhaps mines were going off around our tracks, with several RPGs shot over and by the sides of each of the tracks. Immediately several of the soldiers riding on top of the tracks were hit by automatic weapons fire and RPG explosions. In fact both of the first two tracks had been hit by RPGs in the opening salvo of the ambush. In addition to our platoon sergeant being decapitated, the platoon lieutenant was likewise killed, as were several others. As the drivers had been trained, they immediately floored the engines and drove on through the ambush site to get out of the killing zone. To stay in the killing zone of an ambush means certain death. Being experienced we immediately understood the danger as we were in the middle of a well-prepared ambush by a far superior force of NVA.

Immediately upon hearing and feeling the impact of the explosions, I instinctively began firing my M-60 to the right side of the track I was riding. At that instant I saw a rocket coming directly toward our track. You can see a rocket coming toward you for an instant, which looks like a fireball coming at you at warp speed! It comes so quickly you really don't have time to react, but you know it is coming and you likely have had it! We were proceeding slowly to avoid mines, and our driver had just begun to react to the explosion by speeding up. All of this took only fraction of seconds, hardly time to react. I felt the hot blast as the rocket passed over our heads. A split second later we were not so lucky. We were hit by another rocket which blew up our track, killing and wounding everyone in our squad. All of this happened so fast I likely only got off a handful of rounds from my machine gun before being blown into oblivion. In the opening seconds of the ambush, six or seven men were killed instantly and almost everyone else was wounded, some severely.

The next thing I recall, I woke up dizzy, not quite sure what was going on. I apparently ended-up on my knees in the middle of a field with the barrel of the M-60 machine gun pushed into the earth. I was blown off the track perhaps forty or so feet. When I looked up in front of me, I saw five or six NVA casually walking toward me with their AK-47 assault rifles held crossways across their bodies. I recall all of them had on clean khaki uniforms with their standard pith helmets and ammo pouches in the front. Obviously they must have thought I was dead since they were taking their time walking toward me, as if they were on a parade ground. When I came to my senses, I immediately jumped up (my adrenalin was working since I was obviously hurt but felt nothing but a cloudy head) and pulled the trigger of my M-60. Unfortunately all that happened was that the bolt rammed forward with a heavy clunk. All of the ammo belts had been blown out of the gun and also off of my body in the explosion. In fact everything I was carrying, including my canteens, ammo, knife and hand grenades were blown off my body in the explosion. Only my boots, pants and flack vest was still on me at the time. I had no clue where my helmet landed.

As soon as I jumped up, the NVA reacted and opened fire on me. I immediately took off running for my life, dodging side-to-side as I felt and heard (you can not only hear but feel the bullets wiz by you when they are close) bullets whizzing by me and kicking up dust around me. In fact, later I found a bullet hole through the inside of my pant leg, too close to the crotch for comfort. It must have been my lucky day as none of them hit me, even though I likely ran forty feet across an open field with five or six NVA chasing me with AK-47s. All of this probably took just less than a minute or two from when we were blown off the track. Our track was still in the middle of the road smoking, but it had not blow-up completely. I ran for the track still holding my useless M-60 machine gun. I knew the only place I was going to get ammo was from our damaged track, even though it was still smoking from the explosion. Without ammo I was going to get killed very quickly, so I really had no choice but to run for the track. I also was not going to get captured or surrender to the NVA.

Once I hit the road I could see a dead American soldier lying in the road. A couple others were taking cover in the ditch on the side of the road. I jumped for the safety of the ditch just down the road from where the others were trying to take shelter. I saw an M-16 lying in the ditch in front of the disabled APC and I grabbed the rifle. Luckily it had a 20 round clip in the chamber and I quickly took aim and fired at the pursuing NVA. My adrenaline was pumping and I was scared to death, thinking I would be hit any second, as we were receiving tremendous amounts of automatic fire. Bullets were bouncing off the ground and whizzing all around me. It was a miracle that I was not hit by something! I hit one enemy in the leg and knocked him down. Other enemy soldiers immediately hit the dirt and crawled for cover. I kept firing at them until I ran out of ammo! At the same time, the other survivors opened fire on other NVA trying to overrun our position from the other side of the road.

We were in the middle of the ambush "killing zone" and receiving a tremendous amount of fire coming from all sides. Just then the last and fourth track, driven by SP4 Noonan, came down the road and was yelling for everyone to get on. I jumped from the safety of the ditch, grabbed both weapons, threw them on top of the track and jumped on board. At this time I had no ammo for my M-60 or my M-16. PFC Valdez and PFC Lowery, who was shot in the arm, jumped on board at the same time as I and Noonan, the driver, took off. Several others were riding on top of Noonan's track, including Thomas Patterson. Noonan then sped up to get out of the village and ambush zone. I groped around looking for ammo for my M-60 or M-16 rifle but did not find any on top of the track, so I laid down flat as I could on the top of the APC. Things were moving very quickly at this juncture and everyone was firing everything they had. Ahead in the distance we could see that the first two tracks had made it out of the killing zone and were on the far side of the village setting up a defensive perimeter. We found out later that they too had many dead and wounded traversing the killing zone.

Proceeding through the village Noonan slowed down to pick up a troop, I believe it was SP4 Stone, who had lost the lower half of his leg and was jumping toward the road on one leg to make it to the track. He was severely wounded and carried no rifle in the middle of the ambush killing zone. With the track slowing I reached down and grabbed him by his shirt collar with my left hand and literally threw him up on top of the moving track. He screamed in pain as he hit the top of the track. I recall that he felt as light as a .50-caliber ammo can. My adrenaline was definitely pumping in high gear! SP4 Stone laid down flat like everyone else. As we didn't have a medic he just laid there suffering. For some reason he was not bleeding too much as he surely would have died from the loss of blood. If anyone rose up on the top of the track, they would have been quickly shot off. Everyone who had ammo was firing. As we were the only track still moving in the ambush zone, the NVA focused all their weapons and rockets on us. Sooner or later the odds were against us and we were going to get hit by a rocket. Seconds after we picked up SP4 Stone, one of the many RPGs fired at us finally connected, hitting the track in the transmission. We had not gone fifty yards from where Noonan had initially picked us up! I recall the track lifted off the ground and hit me rather hard on the chin since I was lying flat on the surface of the track. I felt like I had been hit in the chin by a baseball bat. It rattled my teeth, and between the hit and the explosion, I believe I lost consciousness for a few seconds. When I came to my senses and recognized where I was, the track had come to a stop. As bullets were flying all around and hitting the track, I immediately jumped off the track to the left side. Apparently we had been hit on the right side where I was lying, and the explosion shifted me to the left side of the track. Apparently everyone else on top of the track, including the driver and track commander, had been either blown off the track or had jumped off by the time I hit the dirt. Having experienced tracks hit by mines and RPGs before, we all expected the APC to explode any minute. Thus the first action for everyone was to get away from the track before it blew up! After the RPG hit the track, it was smoldering with smoke and dust all around.

We were in the middle of a road in an ambush killing zone grossly outnumbered with NVA all around and closing in on us! We all figured the game was up. Yet no one was going to give up the fight. We had to quickly begin to return fire or we were going to be overrun in minutes. I began yelling for everyone to spread out and get on either side of the road to set up some sort of defensive position. Everyone on the track had been wounded, or at least had incurred a concussion from being blown off of our track or from the recent explosion on Noonan's track. Being blown up by an RPG once is bad enough, but twice in a matter of minutes makes for a bad day! Perhaps because the RPG had hit on the right side of the track, everyone had landed on the left side, including myself. Apparently no one wanted to go near the track to risk crawling to the other side of the road. I kept yelling for everyone to begin firing and to spread out and alternately cover both sides of the road. The NVA had us surrounded, not only on both sides, but now in front and to our rear as they closed in for the kill. Basically there was too much fire and too few us to organize any meaningful defense on both sides of the road. At that point there were only five of us in the ditch with everyone hurt and SP4 Stone severely wounded with the loss of his leg. Fortunately, we still had two machine guns with us, but mine had no ammo, so I had the least wounded of us man the machine guns at either end of the ditch facing outward. Fortunately everyone in the platoon carried 200 rounds or two belts of M-60 ammo and some still had the belts on them, so we finally got my M-60 in operation. They were firing at the enemy, who was closing in on our position from all sides. We were quickly running out of time and ammo. There were far too many of them surrounding us with too much firepower for us to fight them off for long.

It was obvious to us that if we did not get help soon, we were going to be overrun. While I was trying to arrange the men into a fighting position with the M-60 at either end of the ditch, I yelled for someone to go get some M-60 ammo. We needed ammo for the machine guns if we were going to keep the enemy at bay. We only had a limited amount of rounds at that point in time. SP4 Noonan volunteered to run back to the burning track and retrieve ammo for the machine guns. We were burning M-60 ammo fast trying to keep the enemy from overrunning our position. Once I set up the position, I exchanged my M-60 for an M-16 from the soldier at the front of the ditch. I then ran back to the track to retrieve more M-60 and M-16 ammo as I was almost out of ammo myself. I jumped into the smoking track, hoping it would not blow, and grabbed some M-60 and M-16 ammo, feeling my way around in the smoke for the correct size of ammo cans. An M-16 and M-60 can is half the size of a .50-caliber box. I pitched the ammo into the ditch and ran back to get more, along with SP4 Noonan. We wanted to get as much ammo as we could before the track blew up. We continued firing from the ditch, trying to keep the NVA from overrunning our position. With the two M-60s firing at either side of the ditch, we were keeping the NVA busy, but they were still advancing on our position. The NVA were obviously experienced battle veterans who kept advancing on us from all sides. They knew we would shortly be overrun if they kept pushing towards us.

Remember everyone had been wounded or hurt from being blown up when the RPG hit the fourth track. Some of us had been blown up twice with those on our track hurt much worse since it had been a direct hit and blew everyone off several yards, killing and wounding everyone. One of the engineers who were riding on our track, SP4 Brigham, was blown off along with everyone else and was then captured by the NVA. No one saw him after the explosion, which is not surprising, considering everyone was wounded and just trying to get away from the advancing enemy.

I decided that in order to survive we needed to get to the radio in the track and call for help. We also needed the firepower of the .50 caliber machine gun if we were to fight off the overwhelming odds against us. So I told everyone to keep firing to keep the NVA at bay while I ran for the still smoking track. I jumped up on top of the track and into the .50-caliber copula standing on ammo cans inside the APC. As I manned the .50-caliber machine gun, I saw a squad of NVA coming down the middle and sides of the road. They were in formation firing AK-47s as they closed in on our position. I immediately opened up on the enemy squad with the heavy machine gun. I hit several NVA, PFC

Lowery said I killed three of them, and they scattered to either side of the road taking cover. No one wants to face a .50 caliber machine gun, not even doped up NVA soldiers.

I then noticed a helicopter flying around and quickly decided that calling them for help was our only chance. Bullets were spraying all around me hitting the sides and armor of the .50-caliber copula. I began yelling into the mike that we were still alive with many wounded. To my surprise a calm voice came on the net (radio) and said something to the effect "You need to move out of there immediately!" I think I replied something like "No shit, but how do you propose we do that since we are surrounded and half the guys are too hurt to move!" He calmly said again, "You need to move out of the ambush zone or you will all be killed!" With that, I exploded, calling him every name in the book, yelling, "We can't move, the fire is too intense, and the track has been hit" frequently calling him a stupid SOB or words to that effect. In fact, I found out later that the calm voice on the net was our brigade operations officer or S-3 Major Cain Bridgman, who was flying around in a helicopter above us.

At about that instant another Huey helicopter appeared on the scene and began firing directly at my men in the ditch! I could see the helicopter gunner leaning out of the helicopter which had turned on its side in order for the door gunner to have a direct line of fire below him. Incredibly the gunner shot directly into the ditch with all of our troopers and shot around everyone just like in the movies! Only one of my guys, PFC Lowery, who had been previously wounded and blown off the track, was shot again in the same arm by the helicopter M-60. He was the only casualty. PFC Lowery continued to fire his weapon even while being hit the second time. He was one brave soldier. On seeing this I thought for sure the Huey gunner had killed everyone in the ditch! I jumped up out of the copula onto the top of the APC standing up and started waving my arms at the helicopter trying to wave him off. If he made another run he might kill everyone. From the air it must have looked like there was a squad of NVA crawling up to the track to finish off the Americans. Of course this was the survivors of our platoon holding the ditch as a last stand against the NVA. All the time this was going on we were under intense enemy fire. After I waved them off, the Huey helicopter got the message directing their fire at the enemy rather than at us. I got back behind the .50 caliber and opened fire again at anything that moved and in all directions to keep the NVA from overrunning our position. Then I got back on the net and again began cursing my head off to Major Bridgman that they were killing us with our own helicopter.

The Major kept telling me I needed to get my men out of the ambush zone or we were going to die. I kept telling him we needed help in order to move, we had too many wounded to move on our own. Finally he said to get in the track and see if it would move. That did it for me. I told him that it was about to blow up, couldn't he see that it was smoking and about to blow! In between I continued to fire my machine gun at the enemy. Major Bridgman said that it had not blown up yet and to try it as it was our only chance to move the wounded out of the ambush zone. He said something like "If you don't get on that track and get out of the ambush zone, you are going to be overrun. It is your only chance, now MOVE, that is an order!" With a few more choice words I thought I would follow his orders and yelled and motioned for SP4 Noonan to come over to the still smoking track and see if it would move. He jumped out of the safety of the ditch and ran through the gunfire and jumped up on the track with me. When I told him to start up the track and see if it could mover he looked at me like I was nuts! But he quickly jumped into the driver's seat. The track engine was still running but the track itself was still smoldering and smoking. Both of us thought it would blow up at any moment!

To both of our surprise the track moved when Noonan put it into gear. However, it would only move at around 4–5 MPH since it was hit by the RPG in the transmission. Once the track started moving the enemy fire intensified as they focused in on the track. But luckily the machine gunfire from the two Huey helicopters was keeping them busy and they were taking cover rather than advancing toward us. I yelled and waved for the guys in the ditch, "Come on, get on the track!" They jumped out of the ditch and ran for the track. I jumped down to help PFC Lowery, who had been shot twice in the same arm; and hoist SP4 Stone on the track. The others helping each other climbed aboard. I slid back into the copula and grabbed the .50-caliber machine gun firing at everything that moved and some that didn't. We were moving agonizingly slow toward the end of the village where the first two tracks in our platoon had stopped. They were approximately one thousand yards from where we were at the beginning of the village.

Almost immediately as we began to move a lone NVA drove up to our track on a motorcycle with his AK-47 slung across the handlebars. When he saw that we were moving and I was behind the .50-caliber machine gun he tried to steer off the road on the right hand side. I let him have it with a burst of the .50 caliber bullets. He literally blew apart as he was only twenty yards away. I also recall firing to the left side on the top of a dike trying to keep the NVA heads down and prevent them from firing at us. As I was traversing the top of the berm an NVA popped up to shoot and caught a .50-caliber round in the head. It blew his head apart flinging his helmet twenty feet in the air. Interesting how you remember such things in the middle of a fight for your life. I believe I hit several other NVA with the .50 caliber. We kept firing all the way through the village. Between our machine guns firing and the helicopters we kept the NVA on the defensive and sustained only one other soldier slightly wounded on our slow crawl through the ambush site on the track. We also prevented any enemy from firing more RPG rockets at us.

We proceeded crawling at five miles an hour through the village with the helicopters firing all around us and the NVA trying their best to stop us from escaping from the ambush. As we neared the end of the village we were still being fired upon by the NVA. Just before we linked up with the first two tracks our artillery began to land on either side of the village where most of the NVA were firing upon us. The artillery was devastating to the NVA and the fire slacked off. We continued to fire our weapons on both sides of the track as we crawled up to the rest of the survivors of our platoon. They had many killed and wounded on the tracks but both appeared to be operational. A quick assessment of our platoon showed that the platoon lieutenant, Lieutenant Elbert and two of the track sergeants were killed along with others. Our new platoon sergeant, Staff Sergeant Vincent, was severely wounded. We could see other dead on top of the tracks and one in the .50-caliber copula who had been decapitated by an RPG. We were all still firing our weapons to keep the NVA in the village ambush zone away from us. The artillery barrage continued and the incoming fire had dropped off dramatically. By this time we were receiving only sporadic incoming fire.

About the time we caught up to the first two tracks at the other side of the village, a helicopter landed. Out jumped the battalion commander, LTC Clifford Neilson. I did not know who he was as I had never met nor even seen him previously. The colonel's helicopter took off and another Medevac helicopter landed to take off the most severely wounded. I hoped off our track and with one of the other soldiers helped bring SP4 Stone to the helicopter and loaded him on. Then we helped load other severely wounded including our platoon Staff Sergeant Vincent.

As the helicopter took off I joined a couple of other soldiers who were speaking with the Colonel. As I arrived and the noise of the helicopter faded, he yelled at us that we had to take the tracks back to French Fort. Even with my concussion and broken eardrums I still understood what he was saying. I thought that he had lost his mind! I yelled at him that our track was disabled and could not make it back through the ambush zone. It could only go five miles an hour and we would get slaughtered! I also yelled something like "Jesus fucking Christ, have you seen what happened to us going through that village?" He just ignored me and yelled for everyone to load up as we had to go back. There was no help coming. We were on our own! I was shocked as I thought for sure with a colonel on the ground reinforcements surely must be on the way!

Having just come out of this hellhole with the platoon devastated I thought he had lost his mind going back through an ambush. Frankly I was speechless and at that juncture too drained and pissed off at the stupidity of our leadership. They had gotten us all but wiped out sending us on this stupid mission in the first place. Now they wanted to get the rest of us killed going back through the same ambush site! My only hope at that point was that the stupid Colonel would be the first one to get killed! I stormed away to tell what was left of my squad.

I went over to my men who had taken up positions around the remaining two tracks and told them that the "crazy son of a bitch wants us to go back through the ambush to French Fort." They just looked at me in disbelief and fear in their eyes! At that juncture we all thought that we were saved and were going to be reinforced and the remaining wounded dusted off. No one imagined that with so few of us left that anyone in their right mind would send us back through the ambush killing zone! Having just gone through hell and lived none of us wanted to go through that again.

As we were deciding what to do two jets came flying over us and dropped napalm on either side of the ambush zone. Then they circled around and began firing their 20 mm cannons on both sides of the road. With the helicopters, artillery, napalm and the jets firing their 20 mm cannons the firing from the NVA had almost stopped. I assume that the NVA Company began to withdraw at this point although we were not aware of it at this time. The Colonel was yelling for us to strip our track of its radio and ammo and load it on the surviving two tracks. We took what we could quickly load on the tracks and then we hopped on the remaining two tracks. I jumped unto the first track which was one of the two tracks who made it through the initial ambush. The track commander, a sergeant, had been hit in the head by an RPG and was decapitated. I had to move his body into the belly of the track and push him aside in order for me to stand in the copula manning the .50-caliber machine gun. When I looked down at the driver he had a piece of shrapnel six inches long embedded in the neck collar of his flak vest. It had penetrated all of the Kevlar layers except the last vinyl cloth covering. The driver had a huge welt on his neck when it had been hit. Had it not been for the Kevlar vest he too would have been decapitated! I said nothing to him and he never even noticed as he was so hopped up on adrenaline.

We abandoned Noonan's track at the end of the village as it could not move more than 5 mph and no one knew if it would even make it back. Besides no one was anxious to return through an ambush site at 5 mph with a smoking APC, which could still blow-up at any moment.

Once everyone was positioned on the two tracks we moved out down the road at maximum speed firing every gun we had. The jets were flying so low you could see the details on the bottom of the planes belly and feel the heat from the exhaust. They must have been moving at hundreds of miles an hour as they flew past firing on both sides of us tearing up the sides of the road with 20 mm cannons. The fire from these two jets was unbelievable. It was like hundreds of M-79 grenades going off every ten feet on both sides of us as we raced through the village. It was scary as hell and we hoped they did not miss and hit us! Their precision flying so fast was unbelievable as the road was only perhaps twenty feet across.

Fortunately for us the jets' 20 mm cannons firing either killed or drove off the remaining NVA or certainly it kept their heads down. We managed to race back through the ambush site with no casualties and little fire from the enemy. There was so much firing and noise, and we were moving at top speed so I didn't notice any incoming fire, although there very well might have been. In either case, we made it back to French Fort. When we rolled into French Fort with our two remaining APCs we looked like we had been through hell. As we pulled up to the fort entrance road the NVA began to mortar us. Apparently they were not finished with us yet! Several of the surviving troopers were wounded again by flying shrapnel from the mortars. As soon as we entered the gate we all scrambled for the safety of the bunkers.

After the mortars stopped, "dust off" helicopters landed in French Fort, and we loaded on the worst wounded. I boarded the second dust off helicopter along with several other walking wounded. I don't remember much about the ride to the Hospital in Tay Ninh except that this would likely be my last day in the field as it was my third Purple Heart. In the 25th Infantry Division, if you were wounded three times and spent forty-eight hours in the hospital, you could ask to be assigned to a house cat, or rear job assignment.

I vaguely remember the brief dust off helicopter ride to the 12th Evacuation Hospital at Tay Ninh. It probably was no more than ten to fifteen minutes by air. As we landed I shuffled into the emergency hospital on my own but I had a hard time moving my legs. I felt like I had been run over by a truck, my head was pounding, I could barely hear and my ears were bleeding. All of a sudden my knee caps and back were killing me, and I felt like I was holding the weight of the world on my shoulders. When the adrenaline wears off, you feel like you cannot move you are so exhausted.

I don't recall much else except that I slept for a couple of days and awoke in a bed with clean sheets. The first time I had slept in a bed since the last time I was wounded three months previously. I remember being awakened by a group of officers awarding Purple Hearts to the men in the ward. I vaguely remember the officer presenting me the medal asking where or how I was wounded. I just ignored him and dozed off to sleep as I wasn't interested in anything other than getting some more rest.

Aftermath of the Ambush

The NVA force who attacked us was a company of the NVA 88th Regiment. Typically an NVA company was comprised of some 120–150 soldiers. The NVA 88th Regiment was one of three regiments ordered to capture and hold Tay Ninh. It was later estimated that approximately half of the attacking NVA force was either killed or wounded during this firefight. As we only killed a handful of enemy soldiers the majority were killed by the artillery, helicopters, napalm, and fighter jets that came to our support after the initial ambush. They had basically wiped out our platoon in the first few seconds of the ambush.

SP4 Brigham POW

The captured soldier's name was SP4 James W. Brigham. He was an engineer with the 65th Engineering Battalion attached to our platoon to sweep for mines. This was the first time we ever saw Brigham. He was riding on our track when it was hit and blown up by an RPG. After everyone was blown off the top of the track, no one in our squad saw Brigham again. Everyone assumed he was killed in the ambush along with seven others. As his body was not found at the ambush site, we were questioned by an officer from the 65th Engineering Battalion some weeks after the ambush. I told him all I knew which was that I never saw him again after the track blew up.

As it turns out Brigham was not killed in the ambush. He was captured by the NVA. On Wednesday January 1, 1969, he was one of three POWs who were released by the NVA. He was released in a field near the Vam Co Dong River in Tay Ninh Province. The two others released with Brigham were SP4 Thomas N. Jones and PFC Donald G. Smith. Smith is of interest since he was captured on Nu Ba Den Mountain and published a propaganda letter telling us to surrender to the NVA. I have a copy of the pamphlet that Donald Smith was purported to author.

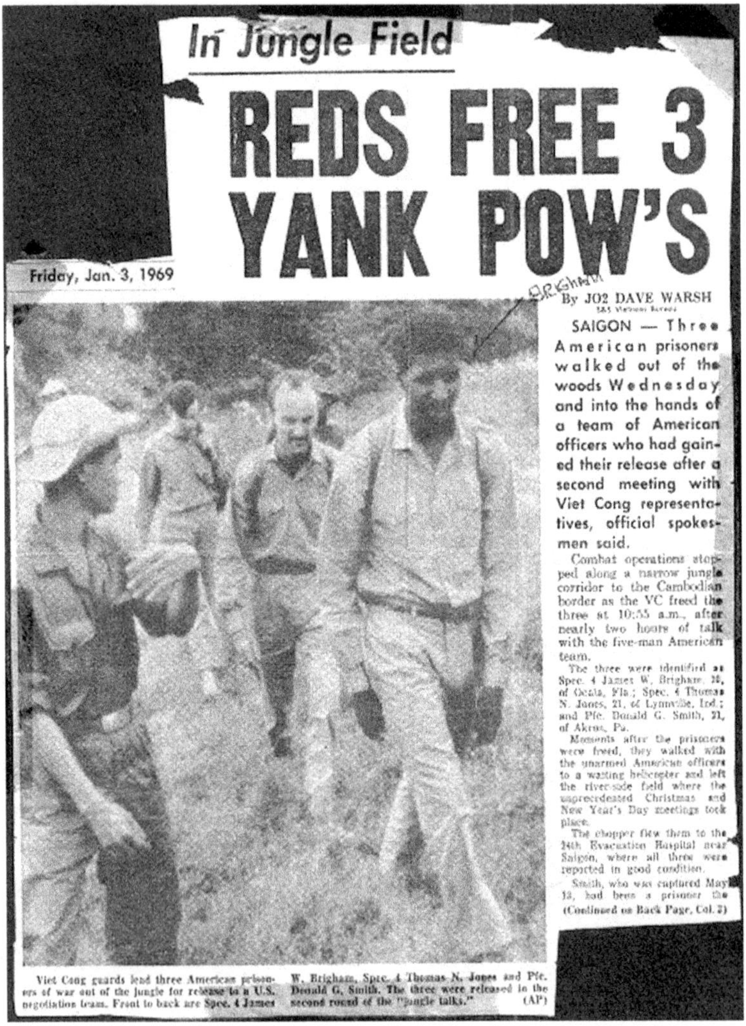

In Jungle Field

REDS FREE 3 YANK POW'S

Friday, Jan. 3, 1969

By JO2 DAVE WARSH

SAIGON — Three American prisoners walked out of the woods Wednesday and into the hands of a team of American officers who had gained their release after a second meeting with Viet Cong representatives, official spokesmen said.

Combat operations stopped along a narrow jungle corridor to the Cambodian border as the VC freed the three at 10:55 a.m., after nearly two hours of talk with the five-man American team.

The three were identified as Spec. 4 James W. Brigham, [illegible], of Ocala, Fla.; Spec. 4 Thomas N. Jones, 21, of Lynnville, Ind.; and Pfc. Donald G. Smith, 21, of Akron, Pa.

Moments after the prisoners were freed, they walked with the unarmed American officers to a waiting helicopter and left the river-side field where the unprecedented Christmas and New Year's Day meetings took place.

The chopper flew them to the 24th Evacuation Hospital near Saigon, where all three were reported in good condition.

Smith, who was captured May 13, had been a prisoner the

(Continued on Back Page, Col. 2)

Viet Cong guards lead three American prisoners of war out of the jungle for release to a U.S. negotiation team. Front to back are Spec. 4 James W. Brigham, Spec. 4 Thomas N. Jones and Pfc. Donald G. Smith. The three were released in the second round of the "jungle talks." (AP)

POW Brigham, first soldier released by the NVA

Apparently Brigham and the other two soldiers walked out of captivity on their own. Upon their release, Brigham announced, "I would like to say the National Liberation Front does treat its prisoners humanely." He later said his remarks were made "under pressure." The three POWs were flown to the 24th Evacuation Hospital and all three were reported to be "in good condition." They were to be flow back to the USA the next day! What is strange about this situation is that Brigham apparently died on January 17, 1969, in Tay Ninh Province Vietnam according to his listing as KIA on the Vietnam Memorial Wall. According to George J. Veith, author of the book *Code-Name Bright Light* (page 223–224), "Brigham had a severe head wound which a communist surgeon had operated on but which had become infected. As soon as he returned to the States, American surgeons attempted to repair the damage, but he lapsed into a coma and died a week later." More than likely he received the severe head wound when he was blown off my track by the RPG along with the rest of our squad. Again according to Vieth, "The communists accused the American of 'murdering' Brigham because he had agreed to work for the 'cause of peace' in the United States." My question today is why, if he died in the USA, does the wall list him as dying in Tay Ninh Vietnam?

Killed and Wounded In the Ambush

The discrepancy between the "Official 4/23rd Record" casualties and the actual casualties is explained by there being two different units of soldiers involved. My award states there were US casualties of "5 killed and 11 wounded in the initial attack." At the end of the day the eye witness notes state there were actually 7 killed, 11 wounded and one captured out of a total of 22 men who were sent to clear the road. Only three men escaped without being killed or wounded. I believe that the discrepancy can be explained by the fact that the "award recommendation" was generated in the 4th Battalion 23rd Infantry. Thus only 18 of the men involved were from the third platoon of A Company of the 4/23rd. The other four were assigned to clear the roads of mines from the 65th Engineering Battalion. I believe that it is likely that two of these men were killed in the initial ambush and one, Brigham, was captured. We know for sure that Brigham was captured and later released. As there were dead soldiers left at the scene of the ambush where they fell, it is very likely that this could have added to the confusion as their bodies were recovered later. With 90% casualties we were certainly no longer an effective fighting force. There was so much confusion no one kept track of anyone else as everyone was just fighting for survival. Furthermore many of the men were new to the Platoon and did not know each other. The platoon lieutenant was killed along with two new replacement sergeants and the Platoon Sergeant was severely wounded. Add to this the fact that four men were attached from the Engineers whom we had never met and you can see how confused the "facts" about wounded, killed and captured were muddled. Additionally some of the wounded were evacuated at the end of the village while others were medevac'd later after returning to French Fort. At the time no one had any idea that one of the men was captured.

Major Cain A. Bridgman

I later met Major Bridgman when I transferred to the Headquarters Company of the 1st Brigade of the 25th Infantry Division. He was the Brigade S-3 in charge of Brigade operations and I was assigned as the Brigade Casualty Clerk working for Major Norman E. Orr, the Adjutant. On my first meeting with Major Bridgman we were talking in HQ and somehow it came out that I had been in the ambush near French Fort. We both soon realized that Major Bridgman was the person in the helicopter who I was cursing and yelling at on the radio during the ambush. He dressed me down for cursing and yelling at him, but I had the feeling that he did it "tongue in cheek" as he seemed most pleased to meet me. From my perspective I didn't mind him dressing me down a bit as he was the reason that I was standing there! If it was not for him ordering and pushing me to try to get the track moving we would have never escaped from the ambush site. Furthermore he called in the helicopter, artillery, and air support that ultimately drove the NVA away from us giving us time to escape and return to French

Fort. Later Major Bridgman recommended me for the DSC which I was ultimately awarded. I saw Major Bridgman often at Headquarters, and we always had nice conversations afterward. He was one of the best officers in the Brigade along with Major Orr. Both of whom had my respect, along with the other men at the Headquarters Company. They made my headquarters' assignment interesting under difficult circumstances, and we had some stimulating conversations about the army.

After forty-four years I had the pleasure of once again connecting with Major Cain Bridgman. By this time Cain had retired from the Military as a Lieutenant Colonel and was living in Tennessee. On April 15, 2013, we met for lunch and once again I had the pleasure of thanking him for getting us out of a very tight spot in 1968.

Discrepancies

In LTC Clifford C. Neilson's Diary published in 2012, and edited with his comments at that time, he writes that the three remaining tracks which made it through the ambush returned to French Fort. He also states that "*we moved up the road at top speed*"! In fact Noonan's track could not move faster than 5 miles an hour as it was hit by an RPG in the transmission. Thus it could not have returned back through the ambush with the other two tracks. He also states, "*We got to the inoperable APC. We stopped; everyone hit the ground, stripped it of radios, weapons, and ammunition and looked for the wounded trooper. We could not find him and presumed the NVA had captured him.*" My recollection is quite different. We certainly did not stop in the middle of the ambush zone where our platoon had been wiped out! In fact we raced through the village with guns blazing and the fighter jets shooting 20 mm cannon on either side. At the time, no one was even aware that there was a wounded trooper in the ambush zone. When we left the ambush zone on Noonan's disabled APC, we thought that we had taken everyone who was still alive with us! Several dead were left at the scene of the ambush. But no one thought anyone else was left alive. Later Lieutenant Colonel Neilson states, "*The wounded man had been rescued by some villagers in the field but he died, we recovered his body the next day from them at the same time we fixed the disabled APC.*" Certainly Brigham was not dead nor was his body recovered. In fact, Lieutenant Colonel Neilson never even mentions Brigham, who was not missing or dead but was captured by the NVA. It is highly likely that after forty-four years, Lieutenant Colonel Neilson is confusing the situation with the many dead left at the scene and the story of Brigham's capture.

Lieutenant Colonel Neilson also writes that one APC was lost. He is referring to our track which was blown up at the site of the ambush. It was destroyed and thus could not have been repaired, certainly not on site. Here again I believe Lieutenant Colonel Neilson is mixing up two different tracks – our track, which was destroyed at the ambush site, and Noonan's track, which was damaged but not destroyed. It was stripped and left at the end of the village as it was incapable of "running the gauntlet" back through the ambush site. It is more likely that Lieutenant Colonel Neilson is confusing which track we "*stripped . . . of radios, weapons, ammunition.*" As our track was destroyed in the ambush zone, there is no way anything, much less ammo (which had blown up), could have been recovered! He is obviously referring to Noonan's track, which we did indeed strip of some of the ammo, weapons, and the radio. However, this did not happen in the ambush zone but rather at the end of the village before we ran back through the ambush zone.

The Lieutenant Colonel also notes that there were 2 KIA and 9 wounded. Yet he lists 5 KIA by name. Eyewitness and the official records of the 4/23 report 5 KIA and 11 WIA in the initial ambush. As previously explained, the difference between the 4/23 records and the total of 7 KIA, 11 WIA and one captured (Brigham) related to the difference between 4/23 casualties and those which include the casualties and capture of the 65th Engineering battalion troopers.

CHAPTER V

House Cat

Assigned to Brigade S-2 Intelligence

September 20, 1968

After I was released from the hospital, I flagged down a jeep which was headed toward the Alpha Company compound. Upon arrival I checked with the company clerk. He greeted me and said, "According to division policy, with three Purple Hearts and forty-eight hours in the hospital, you can 'elect' to be assigned to a job in the rear or return to the field, your choice!" Then he looked at me with a knowing smile waiting for the answer he already knew. I laughed and with a big smile on my face replied, "Well, I elect to be reassigned to a job in base camp. I have had it with getting shot up!" The company clerk laughed and said sarcastically, "Gee, I'm surprised!" Then we both laughed, and he said, "Congratulations, looks like you are one of the lucky ones who will make it home with all your parts!" I was thrilled and simply replied, "Yep, I guess so." Then he asked, "Do you feel OK and ready to return to duty, or do you want to hang around here for a while?" I told him, "I feel fine; except the doctor told me to keep from getting my bandages wet and get them changed a couple of times a week, so nothing in the field for me." The company clerk replied, "Well, we will have to get you a job back in base camp where you don't have to go to the field anymore. In the meanwhile, you are on light duty around here." He obviously was doing me a favor since I really didn't need light duty. But it was common for line units to respect the men who had been wounded multiple times and give them a break. True to his word, he called me back to his office a couple of days later. He asked, "How would you like to go work for brigade S-2?" I asked, "What is S-2?" He responded, "It's intelligence, and the top sergeant needs a driver." I jumped at the chance of being a driver where I didn't have to walk. So I replied, "Great!" So the company clerk asked, "Are you ready to go now?" I said, "Sure, just let me get my gear!" The company clerk told me I would have to return my weapons, and that I would be issued a new rifle from brigade HQ. After that, I was to report to the brigade headquarters and ask for Master Sergeant Roberts (fictitious name).

I reported to brigade HQ administration, which was a metal Quonset hut fortified with sandbags. In the back of the brigade HQ building was the communications center, which was much more heavily sandbagged and was guarded by several MPs who were at the only entrance. I asked the clerks in the HQ where I could find Master Sergeant Roberts and they told me to go to another side of the building where the sergeant had a small desk. I waited for him to return for a while and took notice of how the men worked in the HQ building. I had never seen how the administrative side of the army operated. It was very busy with phones going off and men running around. There were several senior officers coming and going but no one seemed very formal or to salute officers. Of course we never saluted officers in the field as the enemy would recognize them as officers and try to shoot them first. So only if you did not like an officer did you salute him when operating in the field. The thing I noticed most was how clean everyone was in the HQ. While they did not have shined boots nor pressed clothes they all had on clean uniforms and were clean shaven and looked healthy. They looked very different from the sad looking infantry in the field.

After an hour or so Sergeant Roberts pulled up outside the HQ in a jeep. He was muddy and his uniform was not clean like the rest of the men at HQ. It was obvious that he was out running around in the jeep. He was a big sergeant and much older than any of us in the field.

He was likely in his late thirties or early forties, but to a nineteen-year-old he seemed old to me. But I did notice he was wearing a CIB on his uniform, but no other rank or insignia.

He walked into the HQ building and did not notice me sitting by his desk. He walked by me and went into another office where the sign read S-2 Major Orr. He spent five or ten minutes with the Major then as he walked out to the clerk outside the major's office, he handed him some paperwork. Then the clerk pointed to me sitting at his desk. He got a big grin on his face and immediately came over to me shaking my hand and said, "Specialist Esher, we were expecting you. Glad to have you on board. I need an experienced troop who knows how to handle himself when the shit gets heavy." I smiled and said that I was happy to be joining the HQ. He laughed and said, "Yep, anything beats humping the boonies, right?" I replied, "That's for sure!" Then he took me over to one of the HQ clerks and told him, "Get Esher here squared away in one of the empty bunks in one of the HQ hooches." Then he turned to me and asked, "You ready to ride shotgun on a jeep?" I answered, "Whenever you're ready, Sergeant." He laughed and said, "Drop your gear off and be back here in half an hour, and I will start showing you the ropes!" I simply said, "Yes, Sergeant," and left with the HQ clerk, who walked me over to the hooches which housed the brigade enlisted men. They looked exactly like all of the other hooches in the base camp. We walked toward the back of a row of hooches and walked into one. The building looked like two or three men lived inside. It had two three-sided rooms on either side of the building at the end, which I assumed were for NCOs. He pointed to one of the bunks in the room and said, "That's my room, and you can have the one across the way." I was surprised he had his own room as he was only a SP4 like me. But I threw my gear on the bunk and began to get on my ammo and other gear. He watched me for a moment and then said, "Good luck, Sergeant Roberts is crazy, and he is always going outside the wire. Be careful when you are with him outside of the camp." With that, he walked back to the HQ building. I wondered what he meant by the warning, but figured nothing could be worse than where I had come from, so I wasn't worried. In fact things were looking up from my perspective. Not only did I have a roof over my head, but my own room with three sides at least, but of course no doors. How bad could being a house cat be anyway?

After getting on my web gear and loading my rifle, I grabbed my canteens and headed over to the mess hall to fill them up. You never wanted to run out of water or ammo. I figured if I was riding shotgun I would be prepared.

As it turned out Sergeant Roberts had eight (that's right, eight Purple Hearts), and he was on his third tour of Vietnam. He was one of the earliest soldiers in the war and kept coming back. He also owned a whorehouse in Tay Ninh and hung out at a local bar where he picked up enemy intelligence. Apparently the army looked the other way about the bar and whorehouse since he was most effective in obtaining enemy intelligence. He was able to come and go as he pleased anytime of the day or night since he was in intelligence. I drove with him, usually riding shotgun as he preferred to drive. He drove like a wild man, zipping in and out of traffic and not stopping for anything. We would go out and hang around town most of the day and then return to Tay Ninh base camp around dusk. Occasionally he and I would go out after dark, mostly to visit his whorehouse and the bar which was attached downstairs. Sergeant Roberts could speak fluent Vietnamese, so he was always speaking with informants and his hookers around Tay Ninh and the surrounding countryside.

One night we were returning from a visit to the bar around 10 p.m. and Sergeant Roberts was driving. Going through Tay Ninh we saw some soldiers placing a roadblock across the road. Sergeant Roberts as usual was racing through town. He would not stop for anything and said the faster he went the safer it was. This incident proved his theory, because we came flying out of nowhere and headed straight toward the men putting up the roadblock. They scattered and we saw they wore the distinctive NVA pitch helmets. The sergeant raced around the blockade at the last moment, running off the road and going around the barrier without even slowing down. I was hanging on for dear life as the jeep bucked around over the rough and uneven ground. I never had a chance to even fire my weapon because, if I let go of the jeep, I would have been tossed out! Jeeps did not have seat belts in those days nor did they have door or tops. The NVA soldiers were so surprised at our jeep racing toward them that they just wanted to get out of the way. They did not fire a single shot until we were far down the road. None of the bullets fired by the NVA came close to hitting us.

I went through some wild times with Sergeant Roberts for several weeks. The two of us went driving all over in his jeep, going to the cathouse, bar and generally speaking to the people around Tay Ninh to gather information on the enemy. We never had another experience like the roadblock incident in Tay Ninh, although someone would occasionally take a pot shot at us when racing down the roads. But as always Sergeant Roberts was driving so fast that we never had a close encounter, nor did any bullets strike our jeep.

One early morning when we were in base camp, the Base Commander announced that the army was changing the MPC or Military Pay Certificates, and that no one was allowed in or out of camp. All of the local Vietnamese civilians, some of whom were NVA spies, were turned away at the entrance gates.

Military Pay Certificates

MPC or military pay certificates were called "funny money' by the troops. They came in multiple denominations including both dollars and cents and typically had a military image of some type such as a submarine, on the face rather than Presidents as with US dollars. They were printed in different colors to distinguish them from US greenback dollars and they would change color when they were superseded by a new issue. All denominations were printed on paper, and there were no coins. Denominations of five, twenty five and fifty cents were used for coins. Denominations of one, five, ten and twenty dollars were used to match US greenbacks, and they held the same value as US dollars. They were used by the USA military for all military transactions since we were not allowed to have any US dollars or greenbacks. This was because a greenback dollar was worth many times the established exchange rate for Vietnamese Currency or Piasters. Anytime we wanted to exchange our MPC, we had to do so at the time we were paid at the exchange rate that was set by the military. Civilians were not allowed to have MPC, but many of them did obtain them illegally anyway, such as through prostitution. This way the Vietnamese could pay a GI to buy goods at a discount from the Military PX for a commission or for other "favors." The MPC was a printed secured currency which like a greenback was difficult to forge. But as a precaution MPC was changed without warning so that one day it was worth a US dollar and the next day it was worthless!

When the sergeant found out about the exchange he told me to load up as we were headed out to Tay Ninh. I was surprised as I thought no one was allowed to exit or enter the base camp until the MPC exchange had taken place. Anyway I did as ordered and jumped in the Jeep riding shotgun. We headed out of the gate and the sergeant showed his intelligence pass and was allowed to leave camp. We immediately went to his whorehouse. Once there he told me to wait outside in the jeep which was unusual as he always brought me along with him. I hung around outside but saw through the open door that he had gathered several of his whores and others from the bar together. From what little Vietnamese I understood, it appeared that he was getting the word out that he was buying old MPC in exchange for the new MPC. It was fortunate that I was not involved because of what happened later. Soon there was a steady stream of Vietnamese civilians headed into the bar over the next hour or so. Apparently it was common knowledge to the Vietnamese that a change in MPC was happening most likely because they were not allowed into the base camp. After an hour and a half, Sergeant Roberts came out holding a backpack and threw it into the back of the jeep and jumped into the driver's seat. He said we were going back to base camp. So we raced off to Tay

Ninh base camp which was a short distance away. At the gate the MPs recognized Sergeant Roberts and waived us through. Sergeant Roberts then parked the jeep next to our administrative building and told me to take it easy for the rest of the morning. He would catch up with me that afternoon. So I went back to my hooch and collected what little MPC I had and went down to the brigade HQ office to wait in line to exchange them. I probably only had $20 or $30 worth of MPC since I only made $190.90 plus $65 in combat pay a month and I was saving $100 a month.

That afternoon I never heard from Sergeant Roberts, so after going to the mess hall, I wandered over to the brigade HQ and figured I would wait for him by his desk. As I was always out riding around with Sergeant Roberts, I had spent almost no time at all at Brigade HQ. In fact the only people I hung around with at brigade HQ were two of the clerks who worked in Brigade. One was a clerk like me who lived and worked in the hooch next to mine and was in charge of correspondence educational programs for the brigade along with testing. The other was one of the brigade enlisted soldiers who did some administrative function for Brigade HQ. We did not have much time to ourselves, so at the time I did not get to know them very well. As I approached the desk one, of the sergeants in the HQ came over and said that Captain Murayama wanted to see me. So I left my rifle and ammo at Sergeant Roberts's desk and went over to the captain's door. I saw that Captain Murayama was speaking with another captain whom I had never seen before, so I waited outside his door. One of the clerks indicated with his finger that I should go in, so I stood at the door and asked, "Excuse me, sir, but you wanted to see me, sir?" Captain Murayama, whom I had only met once before when I joined the S-2 intelligence, looked up and replied, "Yes, come in!" With that, the other captain turned around and looked at me. The insignia on his collar indicated he was with the inspector general's office. Captain Murayama said to the captain, "This is Specialist Esher, Sergeant Roberts's driver." Then he motioned for me to sit down and said, "Have a seat. Captain So-and-So (I do not recall his name) wants to ask you some questions." I suspected it had something to do with the morning's activities with Sergeant Roberts so I was careful not to say too much. The first question the captain asked was, "Where did you drive Sergeant Roberts this morning?" I told him, "I didn't drive anyplace, as Sergeant Roberts always drove the jeep and I rode shotgun." He seemed to get annoyed by this answer and said in a demanding tone, "Well then, where did Sergeant Roberts drive you?" I answered, "We went downtown to one of the local bars where we typically stop." Then he asked, "What did you do while you were in the bar?" I replied, "I wasn't in the bar, as Sergeant Roberts told me to wait outside, which I did." Then he asked me more questions about what had happened. I told him that I had no idea, since I was outside guarding the jeep the whole time. After that, I was dismissed and told to wait outside.

After a while, another one of the clerks came by and said the captain wants to see you again. So I went back to the captain's office. This time only he was in the office and he motioned for me to come inside. Once inside he told me that Sergeant Roberts would not be coming back to the brigade and that I was going to be reassigned to work for Major Orr, the head of intelligence or G-2. I asked, "Sir, what happened to Sergeant Roberts?" He looked at me for a moment and said, "He is in big trouble for currency exchange! You are lucky you had nothing to do with it! The IG captain checked, and you only exchanged $25 this morning! So you are better off just forgetting about Sergeant Roberts and go report to Major Orr!" After that, we never saw or heard from Sergeant Roberts again. The rumor around HQ was that he had tried to exchange almost $10,000 in MPC, which triggered an immediate investigation, since there was no way a sergeant could have accumulated that much money. It was easy to find out that he and I had left the post that morning, so they simply put two and two together. The inspector general's office did not buy his story that he won the money gambling, and so they arrested him. We never did hear what ultimately happened to the sergeant. But I suspect they let him resign because of his extensive combat record and eight Purple Hearts and a host of other medals for bravery earned in combat. That was too bad, as I really did like Sergeant Roberts.

Brigade Casualty Clerk

October 1968

I had only worked for Sergeant Roberts for a month or so when he was removed from Brigade HQ. So when I reported to Major Orr, the head of G-2, he asked me a few questions and asked if I would like to replace the current casualty clerk who was rotating back to the states. Any job outside the infantry was a good job to me, and being a clerk sounded like a great job. The job of the causality clerk was to call around to all of the units in the brigade and obtain the casualties each day. These casualty figures would then be posted on a white asphalt chart listing the daily USA KIA (Killed in Action) in orange grease pencil, MIA (Missing in Action) in black grease pencil, and WIA (Wounded in Action) in blue grease pencil. Backup reports listed each casualty by unit with a cumulative total for each unit and classification of KIA, MIA and WIA. This was not as straight forward as one might expect, as it was very difficult to obtain the casualties every day from the field units. When they were engaged they went radio silent, and then gave estimates later, to be corrected when an actual count could be made. Thus there were constant updates and corrections. The fog of war certainly surrounded our casualties. That said it was a whole lot easier to report on casualties than to be one yourself. Compared to being an infantryman, it was like being on holiday every day.

We worked twelve hours a day and weekly had to pull all night guard duty for the HQ. About once a week we had to man the perimeter defense at night. Then you would go to work the next day as usual. We had little time off and no recreation at all except going to the enlisted man's club on off time which was minimal. All in all being a house cat was easy compared to being in the field.

The best part of the job was working with Major Orr who was about fifteen years older than me and a really good guy. As long as we did our job he left us alone and always came over and spoke with us before and after briefings with the Brigade Colonel. The Brigade Colonel was another matter. He rarely spoke to anyone and always seemed to be in a bad mood chewing out someone or another. Happily the colonel ignored the enlisted men, which was fine with us.

Moving Underground

October 1968

Living in an empty hooch with my own three sided wall room was quite a luxury. The only problem was that we were getting hit by mortars about every other day mostly at night. So we were constantly running for the bunkers built in-between our hooches. So to protect myself from the first mortars before I made it to the bunkers, I built a sandbag wall outside my hooch. It was high enough to cover me when I was sleeping which was about five feet high and ten feet long. This seemed like sufficient protection to me until the NVA started shooting the 122 mm rockets and 240 mm mortars into our base camp. It began one evening in the early hours of the morning when a diversionary attack was made on the perimeter. Several of the hooches directly around my area had been blown up and several men were killed or wounded. It was the largest attack on the base camp up to that point.

After that I decided it was better for me to move underground, the traditional safe haven of the infantry. So I started by using a bunker which had been partially dug out by someone else but abandoned because it was too small to house the men in the barrack hooches. However, it was fine for me and I figured a small bunker would be stronger and a smaller target. So I completed the bunker by working on it every night I had off and by scrounging around the camp for roofing and other building materials. Sandbags were not a problem as we often had extra duty in off hours of filling sandbags to reinforce various buildings and facilities around the HQ. I had a load of metal artillery shell housings dropped off at the site by some friendly artillery guys and used these to line the sides of the bunkers and make steps down into the bunker. Then I obtained a bunch of Marston mats or corrugated steel mats to use for the roof. Over these I lined the roof with tar paper to keep out the rain and then placed sandbags on top. Every night the bunker got larger as I piled on more and more sandbags until I had about five to six feet of layers of sandbags on top of the bunker. Then I went to work on placing sandbags in front of the entrance and covered that also for extra protection. I worked on improving my bunker every night I had available strengthening it against a direct hit by a mortar. Only a direct hit by a 122 mm rocket could have penetrated my bunker by the time I left Vietnam. The finished bunker was exactly large enough to house my bunk and have a few feet left over; it was about six feet long by five feet wide. I could not stand up in the bunker as the ceiling was only about five feet high, but the smaller the bunker the more it will stand up to a direct hit. The floor was lined by a couple of pieces of scrap plywood which I scrounged from someplace. Eventually I rigged up a light bulb in the bunker by running an extension cord from one of the hooches to my bunker. So this was my dog and my home for the balance of my tour as a house cat.

Black Dog

October/November 1968

While I was working on my bunker one evening, a small brown-and-black puppy wandered into my area. He seemed hungry, so I took him down to the chow hall and bummed some food scraps from the cooks. The dog ate like he had never been fed before! After that, he hung around and was waiting for me every night when I got off from my day job. When I pulled all-night duty at HQ or even when I manned the defensive line in the bunkers, Black Dog would accompany me. After a time I brought extra food home to feed Black Dog after my shift. I got Black Dog a poncho liner to sleep on, and he waited for me and slept in my bunker. Dogs were not allowed on the base camp, so I had to keep him out of sight. But since most soldiers liked dogs, everyone kind of looked the other way, except for the commanding brigade colonel.

Author with Black Dog at Tay Ninh Base Camp bunker

Truck Full of Soldiers Hit by Mortar

October/November 1968

One evening we were being attacked by mortars and rockets. This happened about every other day in Tay Ninh base camp. We were always ready to head to the bunkers whenever we were above ground. You made sure you always knew where the nearest bunker was so you could quickly get underground. Once underground you were relatively safe unless a rocket made a direct hit on your bunker which was a rare occurrence. So the odds were good if you were not caught out in the open that you would survive a mortar and rocket attack. Sometimes the rocket and mortar attack would be used by the enemy to infiltrate sappers into our base camp who would try to blow up aircraft and command bunkers. Usually the enemy sappers were killed trying to get through the barbed wire around the perimeter of the base camp but sometimes they succeeded. When they did, they often caused significant destruction and killed some of our men.

Sometimes if there was an assault or significant enemy penetration into our defensive perimeter a rapid response unit was called up to go to the aid of the sector of the perimeter which was under attack. When an infantry, mechanized infantry or armor fighting unit was in base camp for refitting, they would typically be called out for support. Sometimes the rapid response unit was drawn from ex-infantry who had been assigned to rear echelon jobs such as me. Other times, as a last resort it would be comprised of house cats that had no infantry experience and learned how to shoot a weapon in basic training.

This evening some enemy had penetrated the perimeter wire and the rapid response force was called out to respond. There was a deuce and a half truck full of soldiers who were loaded into the back of the truck to be rushed to the perimeter location where the enemy had infiltrated. As they were loading on the truck, a large 240 mm mortar round made a direct hit on the truck, killing and maiming everyone in and around it. The 240 mm mortar was the largest mortar the enemy possessed. It was a massive mortar, and it blew up the truck. There were over thirty men killed and a handful more wounded who were too near the truck as it was loading. This was the largest loss of life at Tay Ninh base camp while I was stationed there.

Snake in my Bunker

October/November 1968

One night in my bunker while I was asleep, I felt something cold and slimy crawling over me. It was hot and humid in the bunker so I slept with only my pants. I awoke immediately, jumping up and throwing whatever was crawling over me onto the floor. Black Dog, who was also sleeping in the bunker, started barking. I kept a .45 pistol next to my bunk along with my M-16 and some grenades (just in case). So I grabbed my .45 and turned on the light. As the light came on I saw a big black tail of a snake crawling in between the plywood floor and the metal artillery casings which lined the walls. So I fired a couple of shots at the snake which almost broke my eardrums and scared Black Dog out of the bunker. Then I got the heck out of the bunker in case the snake returned. That night I slept in the hooch on one of the empty bunks with Black Dog joining me.

The next day after eating dinner I went back to the bunker, this time armed with my M-16. The idea was for one of the other guys to pull up the flooring with a poker we found while I would try to shoot the snake. When we pulled up one of the plywood boards, there were snake trails everywhere but no snake! Apparently he had been living underneath my bunker for some time. We never did find out where the snake went, but he never came back again. So I must have scared him off with the shooting or he found a quieter place to live.

Attacked by a Crazy GI

November/December 1968

One of our jobs as brigade clerks was to pull night duty at our HQ and man the radios and phone lines. This entailed one of us staying up all night sitting in the HQ building answering the phones and generally keeping guard over the HQ. In the back of our building was the colonel's fortified command bunker complex which was guarded by two MPs at all times. The command bunker complex was a large series of fortified bunkers partially above ground where the colonel slept while a battery of support officers and men controlled the maneuvers of the brigade soldiers in the field.

I was sitting at my desk gathering information to update the colonel's casualty chart for the debriefing the next morning. I was alone in the HQ building. A black soldier came walking into the HQ building apparently drunk and carrying a jungle ax at his side. A jungle ax is a frightening tool looking like a cross between a machete and a meat cleaver. It is used by infantry for cutting down jungle. At first I thought he was just another drunk GI. I asked him, "What do you want?" He started saying something like "Rear echelon mother fuckers don't know nothing! You got no idea what it's like in the bush!" He was getting more and more worked up and moving closer to my desk as he was ranting. I cut off his tirade and told him, "Get out of here and go sober up!" He continued to rant about being in Indian Country and then all of a sudden he lunged at me raising the jungle ax over his head. I reacted quickly pushing back from my desk and grabbing my .45 pistol off the top of my desk and chambering a round in an instant. When the round of my .45 chambered the soldier froze! He saw I had the .45 aimed directly at his midsection. Apparently he understood what a .45 round could do to him at three feet away. He had gotten as far as my desk, and had just put a foot up on my desk and was about to jump up on top of it swinging his jungle ax when he saw my .45 leveled at his midsection. When he first came at me I was startled, but reacted quickly. I was afraid he would cleave my head in two with the jungle ax, but when I chambered the round in my .45, I got very calm knowing he was a dead man. A .45 at that close a range would have blown a hole in his midsection and knocked him back away from me. I looked at him and could see the fear in his eyes; he either sobered up real fast or was not as crazy as he was acting. I said in a threatening voice, "Drop that ax, or I'll blow a fucking hole in your gut!" The crazy GI immediately dropped the jungle ax on the floor and stepped back. Then he took off running out of the building. He didn't say a word as he was running away into the night. Then I ran out of the HQ building toward the MPs who were guarding the HQ Communications bunker. For some reason I did not have my M-16 with me that night and only had my .45 pistol which was a big mistake which I never repeated again. I was afraid the crazy GI might come back with a rifle or hand grenades. He was clearly crazy and was bent on killing me for what reason I had no clue.

Running out of my building toward the MPs, I started yelling, "Call for backup! Some crazy son of a bitch just attacked me with a jungle ax!" They immediately called for backup and chambered rounds in their M-16 rifles. I ran into the bunker with the MPs, and they asked, "What happened?" I replied, out of breath, "Some crazy son of a bitch started calling me a rear echelon mother fucker, talking about being in the field, and then came after me with a jungle ax!" They asked, "What did you do?" I told them, "I grabbed my .45 and damn near shot the son of a bitch!" One of them said, "You should have shot the stupid SOB." At that moment we saw the crazy GI running in a crouched position with an M-16 toward the back of the HQ building. He was about one hundred yards away at that time, but we could see him in the shadows. Both MPs took aim and they were about to open up on him, when at that moment an MP jeep with a mounted M-60 came racing around the HQ building toward the crazy GI. The MP manning the machine gun fired a burst from the M-60 at the crazy GI! He immediately dropped his weapon and stood up with his hands in the air. There were three MPs in the jeep. The MP in the shotgun position jumped out with his M-16 aimed at the crazy GI and ordered, "Get on the ground NOW!" The MP manning the machine gun was zeroed in on the crazy GI in the event he moved. The crazy GI got on the ground on his belly while being covered by the machine gunner and the other MP covering him with his M-16. The driver jumped out and handcuffed the crazy soldier then yanked him to his feet. All of this took about half a minute. When we saw the crazy soldier handcuffed one of the guarding MPs and I walked out of the guard bunker toward the crazy soldier. At the time we walked up to the soldier the MPs were taking a bandolier of M-16 ammo off his chest and unloading his weapon. Fortunately he had no grenades or other weapons on him. After the gunfire several soldiers and officers came out of the command bunker wanting to know what was going on.

The MPs from the jeep holding the crazy soldier asked me, "Is this the fucker who attacked you?" I looked at the crazy soldier, saying, "Yep, that's him, crazy son of a bitch!" Then I asked the crazy soldier, "What the fuck is up with you, you son of a bitch. What did I ever do to you?" He just looked down at his feet and said nothing. The MPs then took away the crazy soldier in the jeep.

When I walked back to the command bunker, a group of HQ soldiers and officers were standing outside. The Colonel was there in a t-shirt, pants and sandals. He asked me, "What happened, soldier?" I replied, "Sir, I don't really know, except that I was at my desk and this crazy soldier came into the HQ office, started calling me a REMF and telling me I didn't know how it was in the field. Then he attacked me with his jungle ax!" The Colonel asked, "Then what did you do?" I answered, "Sir, I grabbed my .45, chambered a round, and leveled it at his chest, telling him to drop the ax." The Colonel then asked, "What did he do then?" I said, "Well, sir, he dropped the jungle ax and took off." Then the Colonel said, with no change of expression on his face, "Well, you should have shot the son of a bitch and saved us all the trouble!" Several of the soldiers and officers chuckled at the comment. Then the Colonel told everyone, "Get back to your duties, I'm going back to my bunker." As he was leaving, he turned to me and said, "You were in the field, weren't you?" I replied, "Yes, sir, Alpha Company 4th of the 23rd." The Colonel shook his head and said, "Good job, soldier, we'll take care of him. We will see how brave he is in the field."

The next day Major Orr wanted to know all of the details about what happened the night before. He had heard about the incident from the colonel and wanted to hear what happened directly from me. He laughed when I told him that the Colonel said I should have shot him. Major Orr was always in a good mood even when he was disciplining you. Major Orr told me that the colonel was going to see how brave the crazy soldier was by taking him up to Nu Ba Den and dropping him off at the top and leaving him there. This is exactly what happened.

That morning after the daily briefing the Colonel took the crazy soldier on his chopper and dropped him off at the top of Nui Ba Den Mountain. Apparently the soldier told the colonel on the trip to Nu Ba Den Mountain that if he dropped him off he would walk down the mountain. The colonel was a tough soldier and apparently told the soldier, "Go ahead, I would like to see that!" If the crazy soldier did try to walk down the mountain, he would surely wind up dead or captive. The NVA controlled the mountain below the radar installation at the top and the rock pile at the bottom. When the colonel dropped him off, he told the officer in charge at the top of Nui Ba Den to walk the crazy soldier to the defensive perimeter, give him a rifle and some ammo, and wish him well going down the mountain.

Apparently the crazy guy was not as crazy as he appeared, because he would not walk down the mountain. He stayed inside the perimeter for three days and would not go near the defensive perimeter. I am sure he was immediately disarmed and closely watched by the GIs on top of the mountain. If he pulled any nonsense out in the field, the soldiers would have taken care of him very quickly and he knew it. Thus he was the perfect guest and did not threaten anyone nor walk down the mountain, much to the disappointment of all concerned, especially the colonel. After three days the crazy soldier was flown back off the mountain and taken under guard to LBJ (Long Ben Jail) jail. That was the last any of us heard of him.

Christmas in Vietnam

December 25, 1968

On Christmas Eve 1968 I was in Tay Ninh base camp. There was a truce declared for Christmas by the NVA, but I don't think anyone on either side paid much attention to the truce. Based on the sneak attack of the Tet celebration in February 1968 there was not much faith that the NVA would honor any truce. So rightly no one paid much attention to the NVA's declared truce. That said the day before Christmas our artillery guns in Tay Ninh went silent. It was an eerie feeling since we were used to constant artillery firing day and night around the clock. Some infantry unit was always in engaged with the enemy and needed artillery support someplace near Tay Ninh. We had grown accustomed to hearing the boom and flashes of artillery, and helicopter and gunships firing rockets, cannons, mini-guns which were Gatling guns that could shoot up to 6,000 rounds a minute and machine guns around our perimeter at both day and night. At night you could see the red tracers, one out of every five rounds fired, would shoot down from helicopters and the NVA would return fire with green tracers firing up at the helicopters. Sometimes we would sit on our bunkers drinking beer and watch the show. I for one was thankful that I no longer was the subject of all the weapons firing at one another.

On Christmas Eve I pulled guard duty at our operations HQ. So I settled down for what I thought would be an uneventful and lonely night. Sometime during the early evening a battery of artillery broke the silence. They fired an artillery mission for perhaps twenty to thirty minutes then went silent. The next day we found out that a leg infantry unit had spotted a large regiment-sized NVA unit of around five hundred to one thousand troops crossing an open field and had called in the artillery on top of them. The NVA took heavy casualties as they were caught out in the open by our artillery—so much for the Christmas truce. We got back somewhat for the enemy breaking the truce earlier that year.

Company Overrun One Night

Winter 1968/Spring 1969

Being the casualty clerk, I handled all of the casualty statistics for each unit. In fact when I came home from Vietnam I did not believe that only 58,000 or so men had been killed over the entire war. I thought the government was suppressing the facts on casualties since our one brigade, comprising some three thousand to four thousand men at full strength in the half a year I was reporting on casualties, had so many killed and wounded. I could not believe that we could have so few casualties over a decade in total. What I later found out was that during the time I served in the infantry and while I was reporting on casualties that this was one of the worst times in Vietnam for casualties. In fact 1968 was the worst year for casualties, and May of that year was the worst month when I was wounded the first time and Tom Foster for the second time. My unit, the 25th Division, had the most casualties of any army division. In 1968 90% of the casualties were infantrymen. So I was in the worst position as a light weapons infantryman, in the worst place at the worst time in the worst Army unit. This is why I experienced and reported on so many casualties.

One night, when we were listening to the radio at HQ, a company of infantrymen was being overrun by a vastly superior NVA Regiment. They called in artillery on their position since the NVA had penetrated the perimeter wire and were running over the company position. I do not recall which leg infantry unit it was, but it could have been the Wolfhounds, who were always in the thick of the fighting. Anyway this evening we listened to the artillery FO and captain desperately calling for help and support. Unfortunately, there was no unit who was close enough to come to their support in time, and the air and artillery support they received was too little too late. As a result, almost the entire company was a casualty, and it was no longer an effective fighting unit. I recall that they had almost half the men killed and almost everyone else wounded. This was a company of slightly over one hundred men, or a typical under-strength grunt company. While these casualties were somewhat high for a single night battle for a company-sized unit, they were not unusual for multiple-day battles, which happened quite often in 1968.

25th Infantry Division Casualties

The 25th Infantry Division comprised of some 15,000–17,000 soldiers at full strength and suffered some 34,484 killed or wounded casualties during the Vietnam War. This is almost twice the casualties it experienced in WWII (5,432) and the Korean War (13,685) combined. This compares to the total hostile action casualties during the entire decade of war for the army of 232,404 (30,868 KIA and 201,536 WIA) or almost 15% of the total casualties for all of the army which had two thirds of all casualties of all branches of the military who served in Vietnam.

Ammo Dump Hit by Rocket and Plane Crash

Winter 1968/Spring 1969

One night when we were attacked by rockets and mortars, they hit our ammunition dump inside our base camp. I was in our HQ when the rocket and mortar attack began, and I ran for the bunker. We were in our HQ bunker for only a few minutes when we heard a huge explosion larger than anything we had heard before. At first we thought it was some type of new rocket which had hit near our bunker as it rattled the ceiling and shook the ground. We stayed in the bunker for a while until someone came running into our bunker and yelled that the ammo dump had been hit and it was on fire. We ran out to see for ourselves and there was a huge flame in the distance along with ammunition cooking off and exploding in the air. It was quite a show and burned all night with explosions.

The next day a C-130 propeller driven aircraft was hit by a rocket or mortar as it tried to land or take off from the runway. We heard the incident over the radio, and I grabbed my camera and jumped into a jeep with some other officers. We raced to the runway arriving to see the plane burning and explode in flames. I don't recall how many men were killed in the attack but the plane was a total loss and made quite a mess of the runway.

This was the only time I recall that the enemy hit a plane landing or taking off from our runway. Most of the time planes were hit while on the ground parked behind their protective barriers. Whenever we loaded or unloaded from aircraft on the runway, we moved very quickly as the plane hardly came to a stop and kept its propellers running all the time. Often mortars would hit as soon as the plane touched down, and when it was taxing down the runway for take-off. When we were unloading, the crew would push out the supplies on pallets while the plane was moving, and we had to exit by running besides the pallets and trying not to get run over by them as the plane continued down the runway. When everything was unloaded the plane kept going and took off. We would run for the ditches to avoid being killed by the mortars following the aircraft as it took off down the runway. I never liked getting on or off planes in Tay Ninh and avoided the airfield as much as possible. It was target number one for the enemy who had it zeroed in thanks to the Vietnamese spies on base.

Another incident I recall with aircraft was when a single engine prop aircraft of WWII vintage was hit by ground fire flying over our base camp. We heard a plane in trouble with the engine going in and out flying very low over our building. The plane crashed and burned just outside our perimeter while attempting to land on the runway. I do not recall if the pilot made it out alive or not. I have pictures of both of these plane incidents, along with many other pictures of mortars and rockets hitting the runways and revetments holding parked aircraft in Tay Ninh.

Invasion of the Ants

January 1969

Another night I was sleeping in my bunker and Black Dog started barking and jumped up on my bunk. I thought the damn snake had returned. I did not like snakes, and after being in the jungle with them I disliked them even more. I grabbed my .45 pistol and turned on the light (by screwing it into the socket). To my surprise the floor and walls were alive with millions of small black ants. The ants were the same type like you see at home, except there were millions of them swarming all over my bunker. Once again I retreated and spent the night in the hooch with Black Dog. Next day I got bug spray from the Combat Engineers who were always giving us things we needed and sprayed down my bunker. After they were killed I swept them up in buckets there were so many bodies. Then it took a couple of more days for Black Dog and me to return to the bunker as it had to air out because there was so much bug killer inside. Of course the enemy did not accommodate us and we had to make a quick dash to another bunker when the mortars began dropping in near us. We received mortars and/or rockets in Tay Ninh base Camp about every other day. The mortars were not too worrisome unless you were caught out in the open or in one of the hooches. However, the rockets were big enough that a direct hit could penetrate a bunker and kill everyone inside. We worried more about the rockets as a result.

HQ Guard Duty and Attacked by a Drunken Soldier

February 1969

I was pulling guard duty at our HQ administrative building along with the acting Officer of the Day or OD. The OD was not an officer, but one of the sergeants assigned to HQ. I was required to be in full combat gear with flak vest, helmet, ammo, grenades, and my M-16 rifle. It was late in the evening when a drunken soldier came crashing through our front screen door flinging it open with a bang. At the time I was standing next to the desk with my rifle slung over my shoulder talking to the sergeant. Neither the sergeant or I was sure what he wanted but it was clear that he was angry, drunk and looking for trouble. The soldier was a large Latino soldier several inches taller than I was and quite a bit heavier. At the time I stood around five feet eleven inches and probably weighed in around 170 pounds. I had gained back some of the weight I had lost in the field but was still 15 pounds lighter than when I entered the army. After crashing through the door the drunken soldier started cursing and yelling something in Spanish. He kept coming toward the desk where we were standing. The sergeant yelled at him, "Get the hell out of here!" He didn't hesitate and quickly took another couple of steps closer to us. As I was the closest to him he took a round house swing at my head. I was not expecting a punch, but I managed to duck a couple of inches and his fist hit the top of my helmet and sent it flying along with my rifle which was still slung over my shoulder. Fortunately I did not have my helmet strap on so the punch did not hurt me nor yank my head back. I was in a crouch position directly under the drunken soldier who had taken another wild swing with his other arm after hitting my helmet with his right-hand fist. So I used my legs and drove a punch with my right fist as hard as I could into his nose. The punch using my full body weight drove into this face and knocked him backward over the desk, just like in the movies. By this time the sergeant had moved away from the back of the desk and was coming around to the front to assist me. The punch had broken the drunken soldier's nose and had split it open down the center. When he recovered and got up he had his hands on the desk and was spurting blood everywhere. He stood there for a moment leading with his hands on the top of the desk just spurting blood, cursing and yelling something in Spanish. Then he began to climb over the desk coming toward us again. The sergeant had come around the desk and was standing next to me, but he had left his rifle behind him at the desk. The drunken soldier glared at us as he climbed over the desk, and we thought he was going to attack us again. However, the fight had gone out of him, and he realized that he was hurt badly since he was having difficulty breathing and was spitting blood all over the orderly room. By this time I had retrieved my rifle, and I quickly chambered a round. The sergeant told him to "stay put," then to me said, "Shoot him if he moves." The drunken soldier just stood there for a moment, and then he made a dash for the door. Both of us stood there with me keeping my rifle pointed at him while he took off. I didn't want to shoot the drunken soldier unless he came at us again. I was just glad he took off.

As soon as the drunken soldier took off running out the door the sergeant called the MPs explaining that a raging soldier had attacked us but appeared to be unarmed. Both of us then took off from the building and ran outside to get under cover, in case the drunken soldier returned with a weapon or hand grenade. In Vietnam one never knew what a soldier would do in a rage, especially since it was such a violent environment with everyone armed. Fortunately the drunken soldier was picked up by the MPs as he headed to the hospital to get his nose sewed up.

Apparently what had happened was that the soldier had been drinking all day, celebrating going home the next day. After consuming too much alcohol and taking some drugs, he flipped out and began to get in fights and attack people. After leaving the Enlisted Man's Club he saw the light on in our HQ building and decided to come attack us. This was strange since neither the sergeant nor I had ever seen the man before.

When we went back to the orderly room, there was blood everywhere. The drunken soldier had spurted blood on all of the wall charts, desks, wall, and floor. It looked like someone had been killed in the room there was so much blood spattered everywhere.

The next morning day I reported to my desk as usual. Major Orr was not in his office, but pulled up in a jeep about an hour later. As he walked by my desk he gave me a strange look as if he was surprised and said, "Esher, come into my office!" I worked directly for Major Orr, so it was not unusual for him to call me into his office. However, he was usually in a good mood and always a real gentleman to all of the enlisted soldiers. He was a good guy and I especially liked him. When I walked into his office, he did not look happy. He looked me up and down and then said with a stern face, "So, Esher, I heard you were fighting in the orderly room last night and put a soldier in the hospital. What have you got to say for yourself?" I was surprised that he was angry with me as I had done nothing wrong and was on guard duty when I was attacked. I said, "Sir, I wasn't fighting, I was on duty when this lunatic attacked me!" Then Major Orr said, still in a stern voice, "Well, have you seen what a mess you made of the orderly room? It looks like someone was killed, there is blood everywhere!" Then not giving me time to answer, he said, "That poor soldier was headed home today, and now he is in the hospital with a broken nose and his face bashed in and black and blue. He is in no shape to go home like that! So what have you got to say for yourself?" I did not get that he was joking, so I replied, "Major Orr, sir, I only hit him once after he took a swing at me and knocked off my helmet. He attacked me, I didn't fight with him!" Then still with the same expression he said, "Well, you can't go around beating up on soldiers, especially ones so much larger than you. You should be ashamed!" Then he got a big smile on his face and said, "I was just kidding. You did a good job last night. I thought I would come in today and see you all banged up after seeing that soldier this morning. He looks like he got hit by a truck. What did you do to him anyway?" I explained what happened, and he wanted to know all of the details. He apparently had heard all about what happened from the MPs and the sergeant on duty. He also had stopped by the orderly room and had seen all of the blood splattered everywhere. Thus he assumed some of the blood was mine and that I would be in a sling or something, given that the drunken soldier was so much larger than I. He chucked as I told him the story, and he said again, "I was expecting to see you all banged up, but you didn't have a scratch on you!"

Later we heard that, after a few days of recovery, the soldier was let out of jail and returned to his company. He missed his flight home, which frankly was punishment enough for anyone. I guess his CO felt sorry for him as he was really a mess and didn't hurt anyone but himself. He was given an Article 15 (similar to a reprimand) by his CO, who fined him a few dollars and then allowed to go home.

AWOL In Saigon

March 12–16, 1969

I had been in the 1st Brigade headquarters as a house cat since October of 1968. I was getting "short," meaning I was getting ready to go home from Vietnam. I was sent down to Tan Son Nhut Air Base in Saigon for some reason which I cannot recall. As I had some time before I could catch a ride back to Tay Ninh, I decided to go visit Saigon. In those days you could simply walk off the base and go into Saigon without a pass or any paperwork. I carried my sidearm .45 with me but had no other weapon. I had been to Saigon before when we were running convoys and before and after going on R&R.

As I wandered down the street, I saw an attractive looking Vietnamese girl and started up a conversation. Her name was Lynn, and we hit it off. So I decided to stay in Saigon for a while. Later we went out to dinner and one thing led to another, and we went back to her home and spent the night together. Then we hung out in Saigon for the next few days. Her home was near the Truman Key Marketplace. I remember this because once some MPs began to approach Lynn and me when we were walking down the street near her home. I was AWOL so I didn't want to be questioned by the MPs. Thus we quickly walked into the Vietnamese market near her home. The MPs saw us and began to follow us into the market. As soon as we made it past a few stalls, we began to run. Lynn was familiar with the market, and we quickly ducked into a side ally. The MPs were slowed by the vendors, and they went past the alleyway where we had hidden. As soon as they had passed, we went through a maze of tight alleyways and eventually emerged across the street from Lynn's home. So we looked around before crossing the street and when there were no MPs we crossed the street and entered her home. Thus, we lost the MPs.

Author AWOL in Saigon with Lynn.

After three to four days of spending time together I thought I had better get back to Tay Ninh as I knew that I was going to be in trouble for going AWOL. I also knew that I would be going home soon so I didn't want to push things too far. So I simply walked back to the air base boarded a C-47 transport plane and flew back to Tay Ninh. Once I arrived back, I went directly to the HQ. I don't recall exactly what happened next, but I was dressed down by Major Orr who was very angry with me for not coming back from Saigon on time. He then dismissed me and sent me to the HQ captain who was in charge of administrative actions. I was given an Article 15 discipline for not completing the colonel's casualty book on time. Although he never admitted it, I am certain Major Orr intervened and covered for me because I only received punishment for not completing the colonel's casualty report for apparently one day. So obviously Major Orr covered for me the other three or four days I was AWOL. Thus the Article 15 I received was basically a "slap on the wrist" administered by Captain Murayama. According the Article 15, I was given a written reprimand as follows: "*Did, without proper authority, fail to go at the tine prescribed to your appointed place of duty, to wit; brigade S-1 Section for completion of Colonel's information book, by 0700 hours on 16 March 1969."* An interesting note on the Article 15 document, it details my pay as: $177.90 base pay and $13 over sea or foreign duty pay for a total of $190.90. I received no other punishment and the incident was forgotten. Like I have mentioned several times, Major Orr was a really great guy who obviously intervened to keep me out of trouble. Unfortunately I have been unable to make contact with him, although I have tried many times during the years to thank him.

Black Dog is Poisoned

March 1969

I had Black Dog with me for almost five months since I had been assigned to the brigade HQ. He was still a puppy at that time. We had many Vietnamese working on our base and most of us believed a good many were spies for the NVA/Vietcong. Periodically we would find a few of them pacing off the distance to various installations to zero in mortars and rockets. I for one didn't trust them at all and never had them do any work for me other than laundry. I didn't like them hanging around my bunker and chased them away if I saw any of them around.

One evening I came back to my bunker expecting to be greeted by Black Dog who as always was anxious to eat. When he didn't come running out of the bunker, I called for him but he didn't come. I immediately got a bad feeling because he never missed meals and did not wander very far from our bunker or hooch. So I began looking around for him, calling his name. The soldier who lived in the hooch next to mine came out and started helping me look for Black Dog. He liked Black Dog and also brought him scraps from the mess hall. It was getting dark, and we looked all over but could not find my dog. I began to wonder if the MPs had found him and taken him away or shot him, which is what they did to dogs they found on base camp.

Next morning I got up early to look around some more. Then I saw Black Dog curled up in a drainage ditch under some branches. He was dead, with his tongue swollen and bulging out of his mouth.

He looked to me like he had been poisoned! My soldier friend came out when he saw I had picked up Black Dog and said what I had been thinking, "I'll bet the damn gooks poisoned him!" I felt like I had lost my best friend and cursed the Vietnamese and the whole of Vietnam. I hated being in this god-forsaken country where everything seemed to get killed or screwed up. I buried Black Dog next to my bunker and went to my assigned place at HQ as I was already late.

The guys in the office had covered for me, and I quickly completed the morning casualty report for Major Orr to present to the colonel. As most of the information had been complied the day before, all I had to do was to update the grease charts. Later after lunch I ran back to my bunker and grabbed my jungle ax. Then I rounded up all of the Vietnamese I could find who were milling around my bunker area. I lined them up next to my hooch and started yelling at them in broken Vietnamese and English asking who poisoned my dog? I threatened them with my jungle ax yelling, "I cat dauyou," meaning "I will cut your head off" (actual translation "cut head"). Swinging a jungle axe at your head is a scary proposition especially if someone is serious about harming you. The Vietnamese were terrified that if they lost any part of their body that is how they would spend eternity in heaven or wherever they went after death. So the threat terrified them. However, none of them would tell me anything, and I was not sure that any of them was responsible. It was possible, with all of the rat poison around to keep away the giant rats, that Black Dog may have eaten some rat poison and killed himself. Since none of them could tell me anything, and they were all terrified by my being raging mad at the fact that I had lost my dog, I let them go. They all took off running to get away from me. My soldier friend who lived and worked next door to my bunker witnessed the episode and came over to me after the Vietnamese had taken off and said, "I thought for sure you were going to chop one of their heads off. You scared me too!" That broke my spell, and I chuckled and went back to Brigade HQ.

That night and every night there after I missed Black Dog coming to greet me when I got home and spending the night with me in the bunker. It made me feel more alone than ever. I always loved dogs and grew up with them and have three today.

CHAPTER VI

Back to the World

Orders Back to the World

March 27, 1969

On March 27, 1969, I received my orders to return to the "world" (USA). I was to report to Cu Chi and from there to Long Ben and the 90th Replacement Depot or the "REPO Depo." Then out-process and fly back to the USA from Ton San Nut Air Base. I was to report two days before my DEROS or Date of Estimated Return to States. Once I received my orders, I worried that I would be killed by a rocket or mortar attack just before I was to leave. This was a fear of everyone before he left for the USA. No one wanted to die in Vietnam after spending a year in hell, especially for grunts in the field. My orders stated that once back in the USA I was to have a thirty-day leave and then to report to Fort Hood, Texas, which I knew was an Armor base. I didn't want to go to another army base where I would have to continue as an infantry soldier, but at least I was going home.

I became very careful to always be near a bunker or a ditch just in case. This was normal as we were rocketed and mortared about three times every week in Tay Ninh base camp. I was extra careful these last few days, and almost didn't want to come out of my bunker after I got off from my normal duties.

On the afternoon of April 7, Major Orr told me I could leave for Cu Chi anytime. He shook my hand and said I was free to go home. Nicer words could not have been said. So I picked up my personnel file, said goodbye to everyone I worked with at HQ, and then ran to my bunker to pack up the few things I had. It took me about twenty minutes to get to my bunker and pack. Then I took off for the airstrip to see if I could catch a ride to Cu Chi. When I arrived at the airstrip I checked in to the transport sergeant, and he said there was a chopper leaving for Cu Chi in ten minutes if I wanted to catch a ride. I ran to the airstrip to make sure I didn't miss my opportunity to get out of Tay Ninh. After a few nervous minutes (you always thought something was going to go wrong and you would not get to leave), I saw a helicopter loading up and I ran over. I asked if they were going to Cu Chi, and the door gunner said, "Yes, hop on!" It was almost 4:00 p.m. by the time I made it to the chopper. I threw my duffel bag on the chopper and hopped on. I had my weapon, ammo, and of course, my hand grenades with me. Some other soldiers boarded and we took off. It was a strange feeling leaving Tay Ninh, almost like a bad dream. You could see the base camp and smoke from the fires burning the shit as we climbed higher and higher away from my life in Vietnam. Fortunately the NVA did not attack the airfield, nor did they shoot at us as we were leaving. I was still afraid that something would happen as we left—a rocket, or anti-aircraft round, or engine trouble—and we would not make out of Tay Ninh. But as we climbed higher, I grew happier and more confident that we would make it after all.

The flight from Tay Ninh to Cu Chi was uneventful as the sky began to turn to dusk. We landed at the Cu Chi airstrip and I hopped off the chopper waving goodbye to the crew. I went to the transportation hut and asked if I could hop a ride to Long Ben. I was told that there was a flight out on a Caribou aircraft early next morning. The sergeant in charge looked at my orders and said I could spend the night at the replacement depot where I could get something to eat. He told me to be back by 6:00 a.m. tomorrow to catch a ride to Long Ben.

I hopped on a jeep and went to the replacement depot. There I walked into the operations building and was told I could take a bunk in such and such a building and get something to eat. The sergeant in charge told me I could catch a ride back to the airfield in the morning. First thing I did was to select a bunk nearest the door so I could get to the bunker first. The hooch was empty except for two others who were returning home the next day. I was hungry so I strolled over to the mess hall hooch. The food was lousy, but better than C-rations, and I could have all I wanted to eat, which was a big deal. Later I was told to report to the armory along with all of the others going home. At the armory we had to hand in our; rifles, pistols, bayonets, knives, grenades, ammo, packs and web gear. I felt very uncomfortable being without my rifle and grenades for the first time in Vietnam. We were only allowed to keep our duffel bags. We were warned that trying to smuggle any; NVA military items, drugs, arms, ammo, grenades, body parts, knives, pornographic material or other contraband would result in us being sent back to our units for punishment and not going home. Several 55 gallon drums were provided in the hooches for "no questions asked" contraband. It was amazing what contraband and weapons of all types' soldiers tried to take home which wound up in the 55 gallon drums. I am sure the house cats and officers had some nice war memorabilia to take home with them and make up stories about how they got them.

I spent a restless night thinking about going home and hoping that we would not get attacked. I missed my rifle and grenades, just in case! I was ready to run for the bunker the minute I even thought I heard incoming enemy mortars, artillery or rockets. Fortunately it was a quiet night. The closer you were to Saigon, the less likely you were to be attacked. Next morning I went to get a quick breakfast of "shit on a shingle" (chipped beef on toast with some sort of white gravy which was always disgusting). Then I hopped a deuce and a half truck ride to the airstrip. I was early so as not to miss the ride to go home. The Caribou aircraft landed and turned around back to us, where it unloaded its cargo and personnel very quickly. As the pallets of supplies were on rollers in the aircraft, the unloading went very fast. As soon as the pallets were out of the way, those of us waiting for a ride ran onto the aircraft and sat in the red nylon seats running alongside of the plane. Everyone including the pilots was anxious to get away from Cu Chi, so loading didn't take very long. The aircraft didn't even turn off its engines; it simply closed up the back ramp as soon as everyone was on board and started to take off down the runway. This was a most dangerous time as the enemy was known to shoot mortars and rockets at the airstrip when planes were taking off and landing. The pilots knew this and tried to take off as rapidly and steeply as possible so as to make the smallest target for the smallest amount of time.

We had an uneventful flight to Long Ben Airstrip. Things seemed much more relaxed at Long Ben than at Tay Ninh or Cu Chi. When we unloaded, we were directed into the transportation hut where we were provided transportation to the 90th Repo Depot. You could tell the infantry from everyone else because they didn't say much and had a gaunt far-away look in their eyes. No one said much to anyone else on the ride to the Repo Depot. Everyone kept his thoughts to himself and just wanted to go home and get out of Vietnam. We arrived at the Repo Depot and were greeted by a house cat sergeant who assigned us to hooches. Then we were told that we had to meet for a "short arm inspection" (medics and doctors checked your genital area for VD) at 10:00 a.m. at the processing center. We were also told that we had to meet three times a day to receive our place in line for aircraft leaving for the US. In the meanwhile we were to keep out of trouble or we could be held in Vietnam. Frankly no one was much in the mood to do anything except get home. Getting in trouble was the last thing anyone wanted as it would mean a delay in getting home.

I proceeded to my hooch and grabbed a bunk near the door and looked around for a bunker. The bunkers looked like they had never been used. I guessed that this was a good sign and remembered when I arrived a year earlier that there were never any rocket or mortar attacks while I was in the Repo Depot.

At 10:00 a.m. I reported to the processing center and lined up with everyone else for a short arm inspection. We had been warned by the rumor mill which is typically how we learned things, that if you had any type of VD you would stay in Vietnam until it was cured regardless of how long it took. No one wanted to be held back from going home. A couple of the troops were called out for further inspection and taken away to the medical facility. I don't know if they ever returned as I did not know any of them. In fact I knew no one in the Repo Depot. I was on my own as I had been for most of my time in the military. We were dismissed and told to report to our barracks (hooches) for an inspection of our possessions and gear.

At our barracks the sergeant told us that there would be an inspection of our personal gear in fifteen minutes, and that if any contraband was found, we would be turned over to the MPs and sent back to our units for punishment. He said he would return with MPs, and that anything placed in the 55 gallon drums in the center of the room would be placed there with no questions asked. He said we were to lay out everything we had on our bunks for inspection. He then left and people started pulling all sorts of contraband and weapons out of their duffel bags. I had no contraband, so I simply laid out what little I had on my bunk for inspection. About twenty minutes later the sergeant returned with several MPs who inspected every one's gear and removed the fifty-five-gallon drums, which were full of contraband and weapons.

I hung around the depot, going to eat and not doing much of anything else, as I waited for them to call my name to board the plane. Hurry up and wait was the army's Standard Operating Procedure. While I was going to eat, I bumped into one of the men who attended AIT with me in Tigerland, Fort Polk. Both of us were surprised that we did not see any others from our AIT class returning home since we all had the same DEROS date. Later we bumped into one other soldier whom we recognized from AIT. We swapped stories about the soldiers we knew who had been killed or wounded from our AIT class. Of course, as we were all sent to different units, few of us knew what happened to most of our classmates. As I recall, both of the soldiers had been wounded, but they both served the full time in the field infantry. Neither one was in the mechanized infantry. One story I recall was about one of the toughest guys in our class, a steel worker who worked on the steel infrastructure of high rise buildings in NYC. Apparently he had stepped on a Bouncing Betty mine and lost both his legs. But he survived. A Bouncing Betty mine was a nasty weapon because when you stepped on it, it sprang up to groin height and exploded. It was made to sever the lower half of the body to strike fear into the survivors. It certainly achieved its goal! I hung out with the two soldiers going to formation to see if any of us was called to depart for the world.

At the 4 p.m. formation my name was called to ship out at 5:30 a.m. the next morning. I was elated and couldn't wait for the night to end. Neither of the other two soldiers was called to go home in the morning. They would have to wait for the next formation. They congratulated me on going home, and we spent the rest of the night at the enlisted man's club drinking beers, swapping war stories, and talking about what we were going to do when we got home. I recall telling them I was going to "kiss the ground" when I got off the airplane. I was up early; in fact, I never really went to sleep. I went to the chow hall and was at the assembly line by 5:00 a.m.

It turned out that I wasn't the only one waiting early as it seemed everyone had the same idea. Our names were called and we boarded buses which were the same ones that took us off the planes a year earlier, for the ride to the airstrip. At the airstrip we waited in formation lined up according to our names. You could tell the men who spent time in the field versus the house cats. The men in the field were all skinny and had a faraway look in their eyes, and their uniforms were all faded and boots beat to hell. The housecats had newer clothing and shined boots. Only the house cats said much of anything.

The charter airplane which was going to take us home came in very steeply and landed abruptly. It never turned its engines off but simply opened the doors and began to discharge new replacements from the USA as soon as the ramp was wheeled up to the door. The soldiers were off loaded very quickly and most looked scared as they walked by us. Some of the "house cat" soldiers made fun of the new replacements telling them they were going into hell and such. The infantry who had seen real combat said nothing at all. The new troops seemed to sense this and stared at the guys who were in the infantry. You could also recognize infantry men as the only insignia most wore was the CIB's or Combat Infantry Man Badge, on their fatigues'. Infantry did not wear rank or any other insignia on their uniforms for good reason. The enemy would single out officers and non-commissioned officers to shoot first. Thus no one wanted to be identified as either in combat.

As soon as the last man departed from the airplane the line started moving to board. Everyone's name was called and checked off as we entered the plane. Most carried only a less than full duffel bag on the plane. Both officers and enlisted men boarded the plane at the same time and sat in any seat available. At the head of the door was a good-looking stewardess greeting us as we entered the plane. They quickly guided everyone into seats loading back to front as there were no assigned seats as you just filled the next vacant one. The boarding was the fastest you have ever seen as the men were all anxious to leave. The Stewardesses and sergeants kept pushing everyone to move faster like they anticipated incoming mortars at any minute! One of the men in front of me fainted as he was approaching the sergeant who was calling out names to board. No one stopped to pick him up as they were afraid they might lose their seat in the plane. I don't remember if he made it or not as I also stepped over him and boarded the plane. The plane had six seats across and when it was my turn to sit down, the next seat that was open was a window seat. Thus I would have a final view of Vietnam as we pulled away.

As soon as everyone was on board the sergeant left and said good luck going home and then shut the door. The ramp was pulled away and the plane started out down the runway without ever turning off its engines. In no time we were off the ground in a steep accent. As soon as the wheels left the ground the plane roared with cheers from everyone inside the plane. Then it was dead silence as everyone was lost in their thoughts watching Vietnam fade away as we climbed. All I keep thinking was that I hope no one shoots a rocket at us as I watched the land fall behind. Vietnam looks green and pretty from the air, a real difference than the reality on the ground. I had been in Vietnam eleven months and twenty-seven days.

Our plane departed Vietnam and traveled to Alaska to refuel. Everyone cheered as we landed for the first time in a year in the USA. We were not allowed off the plane in Alaska, and watched the snow from inside the plane as it refueled. After the plane refueled, we were off again to the Air Force Base and Army Replacement Depot in Oakland, California.

Arrival Back in the World

April 11 or 12, 1969

I watched out the window as the plane approached the Air Force base in Oakland, California. The stewardess came on the speaker and announced that we would be landing in Oakland, and that produced another cheer, even though we had been on the plane 18 or so hours. As they plane touched down, everyone went crazy yelling and cheering!

When the plane came to a stop and they rolled the boarding ladder up to the aircraft, everyone was anxious to get off the plane and place their feet on the ground of the USA. When I exited the plane and stepped on the ground, I made good on my comment and kissed the ground! For too long in Vietnam I never thought I would make it back, and yet here I was back in the good old USA.

After leaving the plane we were brought to a very large building where we were told to strip and to throw all of our clothes into a huge two story circular bin which was perhaps twenty feet in diameter. Everyone threw their clothes into this bin along with their duffel bags and all of its contents. Then we were led into mass showers where we scrubbed down with soap and delousing shampoo. Then we were marched into a medical section where we were once again examined by medics and doctors. Our "shot records" were examined, and we were given any missing inoculations. A shot record was a record of all of your inoculations. If you lost it, you would be required to take all of your injections over again as this was the only record of your inoculations. Thus you never wanted to lose your shot record. I carried mine though out Vietnam and still have it in my possession today. After that we were routed to a supply section where we were given new dress uniforms, underclothing, boots, shoes, socks, fatigues, hats, and a new duffel bag to hold everything. Once we were clothed we were told we could go to the chow hall and get a steak dinner. Unbelievably for army cooks it was one of the best steak dinners I had in the army along with real French fries. They even let us go back for more as many times as we wanted. We could also make phone calls home or to anyone on the army's dime. I called my parents and told them I was back from Vietnam and would stop by to see them. I also called Barbara, who was a girl friend of mine when I was drafted, and asked her if she could meet me at the airport.

I filled my belly with seconds and then reported to the administrative center to get my orders and administrative file for my new assignment. I was given orders to report to Fort Hood Texas for my next assignment. In those days a soldier had to carry orders with them so that, if stopped by MPs, they could check the orders to see if the soldier was AWOL. You also carried your administrative file with you to your new assignment, which allowed you to be paid at your new station. In Vietnam many of these files were incomplete or missing altogether as was the case with my file. The file was incomplete as it lacked some of my medical records from when I was wounded. Then we were given our pay some of which was withheld during our stay in Vietnam. As an incentive to save money in Vietnam the government increased any monies you saved by 10% so I saved up as much as I could and had accumulated over $1,100 which was a lot of money when you only made a few hundred dollars a month.

After receiving our orders, personnel file and pay, we were free to go home on leave. I had accumulated thirty days of leave, so I wanted to get home as fast as I could. We were driven in army buses to San Francisco airport to board planes. In those days you could get on a plane with your orders to go on leave or to your new assignment on the government's dime. It was about the only concession the army provided to us. I hopped on the first plane going out to the east coast to Newark Airport. My destination was Morristown, New Jersey, where my parents lived. But first I wanted to spend some time with my old girlfriend.

In spite of the stories about people spitting on soldiers returning from Vietnam, no one paid much attention to me at all. If someone had spit on me, they likely would have lost a few teeth in the process. Basically as soldiers we were ignored. No one said anything much to us at all. They just stayed away and sat at the other end of the waiting room. No parades, no recognition, no anything. But at the time, I didn't care. I was just glad to be alive and be on my way home. I met my girlfriend, whom I had not seen in a year, in Newark and spent a couple of days with her. Then I went home to see my parents in Morristown, New Jersey.

Welcome Home Party

April 13–15

I stayed at my parents' house for one night and got in an argument with my dad, whom I never really got along with even before the army. So the next day I said goodbye and went to stay with my friend, Frank Dolan. Frank had been a friend since high school and had a one-bedroom apartment in Parsippany, New Jersey. Frank had recently been discharged from the army and was working at the Grand Union where we both worked before we were drafted. Frank had served in Korea before his discharge. Frank let me live with him while I was on leave. I slept on the couch in the living room.

A bunch of my friends had a welcome home party for me a couple of days after I returned. During the party I was sitting on the couch with friends. In front of us was a coffee table full of drinks and snacks. I was busy talking to the people around me when a gunshot went off. I hit the deck, diving to the ground and knocking over the drinks on coffee table. Everyone stopped and looked at me like I was crazy. The "shot" I heard was a champagne cork popping. To me it sounded like a rifle shot, and my immediate reaction was to hit the ground. I was embarrassed and full of spilled drinks. But in Vietnam that quick reaction could save your life. We went on with the party, but incidents like this are where some of the rumors about crazy returning Vets likely originated.

From the Stone Age to Landing on the Moon

April 15–18

While we were in the army, and especially in Vietnam, we received no news from the "outside world" other than a letter now and then and whatever the army wanted to tell us. In spite of the movies about

"Good morning, Vietnam," we did not have radios, and in fact I never even heard about an army broadcast until I saw the movie years later. The only news we received was the *Tropic Lighting News*, which was the newspaper of the 25th Infantry Division. In fact today you can see copies online by going to the 25th Infantry Association web site. Remember, in the 1960's there was no Internet, no cell phones, and no phone connections back to the USA from Vietnam. During my time there, the rural areas of Vietnam were more like the Stone Age than the jet age. People lived in mud huts with dirt floors and straw thatched roofs. They did not have running water, bathrooms, or electricity in their huts. Thus they had no appliances or light bulbs or any modern conveniences at all. They drew water from a common well and went to the bathroom in the fields of rice to use as fertilizer. You can imagine what we smelled like when we walked and crawled through the rice paddies for days on end with no showers or way to clean ourselves. The rural Vietnamese lived like people did centuries before and had no concept of the outside world. Most of these people never went more than a few miles from their home, and had never even been to a major city like Saigon. Saigon was likewise primitive by our standards, being more like the turn of the century (1900s) than 1960s USA living standards. Even in our base camps, while we had electricity provided by generators, we had no running water or electrical conveniences. We still defecated in steel drums and "burned shit" in the camps. I lived in a bunker the entire time I was a house cat or REMF, due to the constant bombardment of enemy mortars and rockets hitting our base camp.

So when I came back to the United States, I was shocked to learn that we were planning to land a man on the moon! I have never even heard we were attempting such a project! I felt like I had come full circle, from the Stone Age to science fiction of landing on the moon. But on July 16, 1969, Apollo 11 with three astronauts took off for the moon. On July 20 two of the astronauts landed on the moon, and on the twenty-first, Neil Armstrong walked out of his lunar landing capsule and became the first man ever to walk on another planet!

Trip To The Pentagon

April 18–20, 1969

After being home a couple of days, I decided to attempt to get my orders changed so I could spend the last few months in the service closer to my home. I didn't really know much about how the army operated, but I knew that a general was like a god and could do about anything. So I thought I would go see a general. I had only seen one general in my entire time in the army, and that was for a brief moment in French Fort while under a mortar attack. He seemed like a decent guy after I ran into him so I thought it was worth a try. The only place I knew that had generals was in the Pentagon in Washington, DC. So I decided to go there to see a general. To the make the trip more enjoyable I took Barbara, my girlfriend at the time, along for the ride. Thus we hopped in a car and drove to Washington, DC. When I arrived at the Pentagon I was in my full dress uniform with all of my medals on my breast. We simply walked up to the Pentagon and the guards let both Barbara and I enter. I didn't have a clue as to where I should go or who I should see. I was just looking for an army general. So we walked around these huge corridors looking at the names and ranks of the people on the doors. After walking for a while and not seeing any generals on the door plaques, I finally saw a three-star Lieutenant General Black. We went into his office. Sitting behind the desk was a Lifer Master Sergeant. As we entered he looked up from his desk and asked, "What is your business?" I responded, "I would like to see the general!" He looked confused and said, "For what purpose?" This was likely the first and last time the sergeant had a lowly SP4 enlisted man asking to see the general. I responded, "I just got home from Vietnam and I am being sent to another lousy assignment. I want to get my orders changed, and I know a general can change my orders, so that's why I want to speak with him." With that the sergeant came out of his chair and started dressing me down saying that I had nerve coming to see a general, that he was too busy and that I should follow my orders and not bother officers with my problems, etc. Frankly I didn't really care what he said since he could not change my orders, so I didn't even respond to him. The door to the general's office was open and thus he heard the commotion outside his office and came to see what the fuss was all about. The general was a three–star or lieutenant general, and he was a large rather imposing figure standing in the doorway. He asked, "What's going on here?" Luck was with me in that the general was in the 25th Infantry Division in WWII and had fought in combat. As the sergeant stood at attention I responded, "General, sir (as I didn't know how to properly address a general), I am a draftee. I just got back from Vietnam where I was shot up and before that I was in Tigerland in Fort Polk and Fort Dix in the winter, and now they are sending me to another rotten outpost, and I would like to spend my last few months in the army near my home and family! I was hoping that you could possibly help me." The sergeant went to say something, but the general put up his hand and said, "Who is the young lady?" I said, "General, sir, she is my girlfriend." He then asked what unit I was with in Vietnam. I told him, "The 25th Infantry Division, 4/23 Mechanized Infantry, Company A, sir!" He then asked, "What did you do in the 4/23, son?" I told him I was a grunt and squad leader. He laughed and said, "An 11Bravo, huh, and a squad leader as a specialist 4th class?" I said, "Yes, sir, we were kind of short of sergeants, sir." Then looking at my medals, he said, "Looks like you were in the thick of things based on your medals." I responded, "Yes, sir, more than I care to remember, General, sir." Then he said, "Come into my office, Specialist Esher (we wore name tags on our uniforms). I would like to speak with you!" Then he turned to the sergeant and said, "Please make the young lady comfortable, will you, Sergeant." The sergeant, who had a look of I don't believe this on his face, simply stuttered, "Yes, General."

After I entered the general's office, he told me to sit down and he took a chair across from me in front of his desk. It was obvious to me that he had been in combat, not only because he had a CIB, but in the detailed and knowledgeable questions he asked.

The general asked questions about the leadership, operations, the NVA, supply, food, weapons, artillery, air support and many other detailed questions. I recall telling him that the leadership was a bunch of idiots in that they sent us out to find the enemy, who always outnumbered us and was just waiting to wipe us out. The theory was we would find the enemy, hold him in place and then destroy him with superior air and artillery. Unfortunately it didn't work like that, and all they accomplished was to get us killed for nothing! I also told him that the NCOs all got jobs in the rear, and that we had little or no leadership in the field. Since we were doing the fighting, we should have received promotions rather than the house cats in the rear. All in all I communicated that the war was not being well run from my perspective, and that if the ARVN or South Vietnamese Army took over, the NVA would overrun them in no time. They ran instead of fighting!

We spoke for about an hour, and then the general said he had to go to a meeting. He thanked me for my candor and said that this discussion was most helpful to him, as he rarely spoke to enlisted men who returned from the front lines in Vietnam. He said he always got filtered information from the returning officers. Then he asked me what he could do for me. I said for the last few months of my service, I would like to be posted near my home. He said, "That should not be a problem," and then got up and shook my hand. He walked outside and told the master sergeant outside his office to send me down to the enlisted personnel office and "let this soldier go to whatever base he wishes." The master sergeant said, "Yes, General," and then gave me a dirty look! With that, the general left the office and said goodbye again. My girlfriend and I were left alone with the master sergeant. He started to ball me out, talking about how I had gone over many NCOs' and officers' heads and that I was in big trouble. I ignored him, as the general already told him what to do, so I said, "Look, Sergeant, I don't give a damn what you think, as I will be getting out of your army very soon. Besides, the general told you what to do, so I suggest you get on with it and let me go to the personnel office!" The sergeant was fuming at this juncture, but what more could he say? He handed me a note and said to take this to room such and such in the basement and see Master Sergeant So-and-So.

I left the general's office on a high, knowing I was going to get my wish, thanks to General Black. We walked around the Pentagon, which is a huge building where you could drive trucks down the hallways and get lost, looking for the room where we were to report. Finally after asking several people where the office was located we arrived at a group of offices in the basement floor level (or at least one of them). There I met another lifer master sergeant who obviously had been briefed by the general's master sergeant, and told me that I must be something special to have a lieutenant general send me down to his office. Then he took us to a room with a large wall map with US Army bases listed by name. He asked, "Where is your home?" I told him Morristown, New Jersey. Then he said, "Well, as an 11 Bravo, you can go to Fort Dix, which is in New Jersey." I told him I had been to Fort Dix and didn't want to go back. He said, "Well, how about Fort Wadsworth in New York City?" I asked, "Do they have infantry there?" He said, "Yes." So I replied, "I'm not interested." Getting a bit frustrated, the sergeant said, "Well, those are the closest forts to where you live, so you need to pick one." Then I saw another fort on the map called Fort Monmouth in southern New Jersey. I asked, "What about Fort Monmouth?" The sergeant replied, "It's a signal post, and they don't have any infantry there!" That was music to my ears, so I said, "I will go there!" The sergeant started to argue telling me how there would be no job for me at that post, as it was a signal corps post. I said, "I don't care, I will do whatever until I get out of the army!" The sergeant shook his head and then filled out some paperwork and asked where I would be staying so he could send me my new orders. I gave him my parents' address, and he told me to go back on leave and wait for my new orders to be cut. Then I would be reporting to Fort Monmouth to serve out my remaining service commitment. He then said, "That's all, you may go now," and dismissed us from his office with a strange, confused look on his face. I thanked him, and then we left his office and the Pentagon to go celebrate. Sure enough, about two weeks later, orders came for me to report to Fort Monmouth, New Jersey, at the end of my leave.

CHAPTER VII

Fort Monmouth New Jersey

May 1969

After my leave I reported to Fort Monmouth in New Jersey. During my leave I retrieved my car which was a '63 Chevy Impala 327 with a 3 shift stick on the floor, from my parent's house where I had left it before I departed for Vietnam. I reported into the Post Processing Center and handed in my orders directing me to report to the post. The SP4 behind the desk looked at my infantry MOS and said, "What are you doing here?" I said, "This is where I was ordered to report, so here I am, but if you want, I can go back home!" He laughed and said, "Well, can you type?" I said, "Yes!" He then explained, "Look, I am going to be leaving next week, and I don't have a replacement. Would you be interested in replacing me?" I said, "Sure." Anything behind a desk beats being a grunt. That is how I became the company clerk for the Fort Mammoth Enlisted Processing Center. As it turned out, this assignment was a completely different life than being an infantryman—and not too bad at that.

Learning How the Army Worked

May 1969

I met with the Executive Officer called the "XO" who approved of my assignment as the company clerk of the Fort Monmouth Enlisted Man's Processing Company. Our job was to process in all enlisted soldiers assigned to Fort Monmouth. Typically they were assigned to us for a week or two before they received their final posting within the fort. In addition to having these newly assigned soldiers go through the paperwork to join the post, we were supposed to employ them in a variety of jobs around our company and the fort in general. Their assignments were; Kitchen Patrol, manhandling supplies, moving equipment, and doing a variety of manual jobs around the post.

For two weeks or so I learned as much as I could about being a company clerk. I really knew little to nothing about how the army worked and certainly nothing about being a company clerk. What I learned quickly was that, as the company clerk, I could give out assignments, and more importantly I could give the enlisted men processing into the fort a pass. This turned out to me my ace in the hole. As many lifer sergeants were assigned to the fort and had to pass through our processing center, I would ask the new soldiers being processed if any knew how to do company paperwork. Since many had been in the service for years, and a few had even been company clerks, I would assign these soldiers to work with me in the office. This way I learned more about the army, and we ran the office rather smoothly. I told all of the sergeants who worked with me that if they helped me and did a good job, I would give passes to them. They all jumped at the chance and without exception they did a great job of getting our company administration in order. As a result they received lots of passes, and whenever any of them needed to go do something, they were free to go. Thus I made friends of many senior NCOs at the base. This helped me out later whenever I needed a favor.

Since we only had a cadre of some 18 or so enlisted men to operate our processing company, we relied on the men being processed to do much of the work. We had several barracks and, since I was permanent company, I took over one of the two NCO rooms in the barracks. However, almost every weekend I was able to leave the fort, and I made myself as scarce as possible whenever I could get a way. I was dating several girls in the Morristown area so I spent most of my time there. I often stayed with my friend, Frank, and we would have some really drunken good times. Later when I got out of the army and went to college, I lived with Frank in the dining room of his single bedroom apartment. We had a blast, but that is another story.

Shake and Bake Ordered to Nam

July 1969

One of the men assigned to our unit was a good guy we called Shake and Bake, as we often used nicknames for soldiers. This name was given to him because he had been selected to attend the "instant NCO" course where a new soldier who showed leadership was sent to take a course called NCO Candidate Course, or NCOCC for short. When they completed the course they would be made buck sergeants (E-5). This program was created during the Vietnam War because of the severe shortage of combat NCOs due to casualties, retirements, and the limitation on redeployment of twenty-five months between tours. Also, from what I saw, the lifer sergeants were experts at finding ways to avoid being assigned to the infantry. So there was always a shortage of NCO leadership in the infantry. This certainly was the situation in our company for the entire time I was in the field.

Shake and Bake was one of the lucky men who took this course. For some reason he was not sent to Vietnam, even thought that is why the army sent men to this course. More unusual was the fact that he was sent to Fort Monmouth. He was a draftee and had something like nine months left to serve. He was scared to death about going to Vietnam. But he felt that with so few months remaining he had "dodged the bullet" and would not be sent to Vietnam. He and I shared billets together where we both had separate NCO rooms. We would go out drinking together, and I would tell him stories about my experience in the infantry. He was always asking me what it was like to be in combat. As I mentioned previously, he was terrified about being sent to Vietnam.

He and I were always kidding around with each other. He had played a trick on me a few weeks before, so it was my turn to get even. I thought I would play a trick on Shake and Bake by making up fake orders sending him to my old unit in Vietnam. So I got a friend who worked in HQ to make up phony orders and forged the signature of the Major who issued such orders. Then I had the phony orders sent down in an official manila envelope in triplicate. They looked exactly like real orders with other names of soldiers on the same orders. Of course, being the company clerk, I had access to all of his personal information including his service number, which I included in the proper sequence.

When I had the fake orders, I sealed them and went to deliver them to Shake and Bake with a worried look on my face. I handed him the orders in the sealed envelope and said I hope it is good news. He opened the orders and his face got gray, and he just sat down on his bunk. I asked him what they said. He didn't say anything just handed me the orders. I pretended to read them and said, "Oh my god. You have been assigned to my old unit!" With that he grabbed the orders and read where he had indeed been assigned to my old unit the 4th of the 23rd Mech. He just shook his head and said, "Jesus Christ! I thought I was too short to go!" Then he mumbled, "Holy shit, holy shit, what can I do now?" He was in shock. I started feeling bad as he really was scared stiff. But I thought I would play one more trick on him. I said, "You know, I know a guy who works in HQ and may be able to do something about changing these orders. However, it may cost you." Shake and Bake looked up with a ray of hope in his eyes and said, "Anything, anything you can do, please help me." So I took his orders and said let me see what I can do. The reason I took his orders is that I would be in a world of trouble if anyone had found those phony orders. So I didn't want them out of my hands.

I let him stew for a while, and then I went back and told him that for $10,000, a fortune in those days, I could get his orders changed. He jumped up and said, "OK, I will get it!" His demeanor changed to one of hope. I figured I had gone far enough with this scam as I didn't want him running off trying to gather the $10,000. So I took out the orders and ripped them up in front of him. He looked shocked and said, "What are you doing?" I told him, "It was a joke!" He still didn't believe it, as he saw the orders himself and said, "I don't believe it. Are you fucking with me, or what?" I replied, "No, I am serious. They are fake orders. I had them made up." He looked at me and still was not convinced. He asked, "Really, let me see the orders." I said, "No way, I need to destroy these before I get in trouble." After that he finally understood that he had been had. He started a string of cursing at me and then hugged me. He said, "Shit, I thought I was going to die, you bastard! You even assigned me to your old unit. That really did it for me; I thought I had bought the farm!" We both laughed, and he swore he would get even with me for almost giving him a heart attack. He never did go to Vietnam and is likely one of the luckiest draftees ever.

IG or Inspector General Inspection

August 1969

One of the issues I faced when I took over the company from the prior company clerk was that we had an inspector general inspection scheduled for August. Thus I had to hustle to make sure the company passed the IG inspection. As I knew little about what to expect, I enlisted the help of the more experienced sergeants processing through our company. Fortunately I got a lot of help from some really competent lifer sergeants. The bad news was that they only stayed with our processing company a week or two before they were given permanent assignments. So I had a rotating group of sergeants working in the office. As their tours overlapped, it turned out to be less of an issue than I thought. Besides they would work very hard to complete whatever task they were working on before they left. They were really a good bunch of guys. Of course, the freewheeling atmosphere and passes every night and weekends helped to keep them motivated.

Anyway when the IG inspection day came, it turned out to be a rather perfunctory inspection which took only a few hours. We passed with flying colors. The XO was happy and pretty much left me alone to do my thing. This was a completely different side of the army than I had experienced up to that date.

As I only had five months of my two-year commitment remaining when I was assigned to the post, I was a short-timer in the service. I wanted to go back to college and complete my degree so I could someday be the boss and give orders rather than take them. So I asked one of the sergeants helping out in the office to help me submit an "early out" application to go back to college. In those days a draftee could get out of the service early to go to college. So I took advantage of this option since it would both get me out of the army and back in school earning a degree. I applied to and was accepted into the College of Business of Fairleigh Dickinson University, the same school where my brother Bob had been attending for his doctorate degree. My application for an "early out" was approved and my date of separation was the Sunday before I began classes on Monday morning. Life was looking up for me.

"Section 8" Dishonorable discharge for "Klinger"

August 1969

One of the more interesting characters I came across at the processing center was a soldier who had been drafted, but claimed he was "queer" and was being held in our unit pending discharge from the service. In 1969, "queers," as we called them, or "gays," as they are called today, were not allowed to serve in the military. They were dishonorably discharged with a "Section 8 dishonorable discharge." At this time many of the men running the country had served in WWII and Korea and did not look kindly on anyone with a dishonorable discharge. So it was difficult to get a job if you were dishonorably discharged, especially for homosexuality.

This soldier seemed to me to be a decent guy who just wanted to get out of the military. Nothing wrong with that since that was my goal also. I hated the army and couldn't wait to get out. Anyway, this soldier (I will call him Klinger after the character in the TV show *MASH)* didn't seem very gay to me. The only time I saw him act queer was around the officers. For the most part he kept to himself and did as he was told. He lived in a separate barracks as no one would stay with him. Several of the guys in our company teased and taunted him, but he just ignored them. Frankly he never did anything to me so I never bothered him. What he did was his own business, not mine, and if he wanted out of the army, so what. Anytime an assignment came up, I assigned him like anyone else. Some of the sergeants in the company, but not Shake and Bake, who thought like me, gave him shitty assignments, while others simply treated him like everyone else at his rank. He was a buck private, so he was at the bottom of the ladder.

Finally after a couple of months Klinger got what he wanted and his Section 8 dishonorable discharge papers came through. When I received his discharge papers I had one of the soldiers go tell him to come to the company office. He showed up expecting some type of assignment as usual. I handed him his discharge papers and said, "You're finally out!" His face turned from the dour expression he carried into the happiest face I had ever seen on him. He shook my hand and said, "Thank you, do I need to do anything else?" I said that he needed to be out-processed and turn in his gear and he was free to go. He almost floated out of my office; he was so happy. Later that day, he brought me all of his out-processing paperwork confirming he had turned in all of his gear and other administrative paperwork. I checked it over and brought in the paperwork for the XO to sign. He signed it right away and did not even want to interview or talk to Klinger, which was unusual. He just said, "Get him out of here as soon as possible." I saluted and said, "Yes, sir." So I gave Klinger the final paperwork and told him he was free to go! He shook my hand again and started out the door. I got up from my desk and said to him, "Hey, Klinger, tell me the truth, are you really a queer, or did you just want to get out of the army?" He looked at me and smiled with the kind of smile like he had just pulled over something on someone. All he said was, "What do you think?" I shrugged my shoulders, and he left with a huge smile on his face. I never did find out if he was queer or not. However, both Shake and Bake and I believed it was all an act to get out of the service!

Early Out

August 24, 1969

My "early out" date was scheduled for August 24, 1969. A couple of days before I was ready to leave, I had all of my paperwork completed and gear turned in. I had duly met with the recruiting officer who laughed when I saw him to get his sign-off, saying, "Esher, do you think I could talk you into reenlisting and going back to Vietnam?" I just laughed and said kiddingly, "Let me think about it for a moment. NO!" I had served one year, nine months, and twenty-nine days in the army. When I was discharged, I owed the army seventeen days' pay for taking more leave than what I earned due to the early out cutting my service short. I was very happy to return the $6.25 a day I was earning as an E-4. My discharge orders stated, *"AR635-200 SPN, to attend school,"* with an honorable discharge date of August 24, 1969.

On the Sunday before I was to begin college at Fairleigh Dickinson University in Morristown, New Jersey, I was released from the army. It was on Sunday, August 24, 1969, when I got to leave Fort Mammoth and return back to the civilian world. The week before I was discharged from the army, one of the enlisted men who was discharged from the army took off his uniform and threw it on the ground as he was exiting the post. He was arrested by the MPs and detained for punishment back in the army again. All of us went into reserve duty after our active service. We served two years of active service and four years of inactive reserves for a total of six years after being drafted. Thus I was careful just to leave the base and not look back. I didn't want any trouble with the army or any excuses for them to keep me in even for another day.

I drove off base elated to finally be done with the army. The next day I went to class. It was very strange being a student with all of the draft dodgers and anti-war students and liberal professors.

CHAPTER VIII

After the Army

GI Bill and Fairleigh Dickinson University

August 25, 1969

On Monday morning it was my first day out of the army after almost twenty-two months. I was on top of the world. No more military "chicken shit" to deal with and I was free to do what I wanted when I wanted. Plus I had gotten into college and was prepared to change my life. Never again would I be the low man on the totem pole taking directions from idiots just because they had been in the service longer or they had bars on their collars. I was committed to being a successful businessman and one day to be the leader, giving orders rather than taking them. I would, however, always remember what it was like being on the bottom so I would be a different type of leader who cared about his people. To say I was driven to succeed would be an understatement. I always recalled that day lying in a field behind the berm not being able to move and thinking about LBJ having a steak dinner in a tuxedo surrounded by good-looking women without a worry in the world. I had vowed to myself that if I ever made it out of this crap alive I would change my life and earn enough money so that I could be independent and rely on no one but myself. This is how I conducted myself from that day forward! It has paid dividends for me ever since and certainly changed my life.

Award of the Distinguished Service Cross (DSC)

June 16, 1972

In December 1971 I had graduated from Fairleigh Dickinson University with a Bachelor of Science degree in Business Management Magna Cum laude and a minor in mathematics. I had graduated in two-and-a-half years, which is why I graduated at year-end instead of in the spring with the rest of the class. In school I did not socialize with any particular class as I took a heavy course load of 24 or so credits each semester and I went year round. I also took any courses during the holidays which would count toward my 128 credit hours to earn my BS degree. As I had to pay for everything with the miserly GI bill plus my $2.50 an hour full time job at Morristown Airport, I made sure I did not take a single extra course. I couldn't afford it as I was constantly watching pennies.

As soon as I graduated I had a job waiting for me. As always I had planned ahead and sent out many résumés and went on interviews so I would have a job upon graduation. In January 1972 I started work as an assistant to the engineering administrator at a company called Litton Advanced Retail Systems or Litton ARS for short. I was to be a management trainee rotating between different jobs in the company, which I did about every three to four months.

In May of 1972 I received a letter from the US Army in Fort Monmouth, New Jersey, my last duty station. As I was still in the inactive reserves for several more years, my heart sank! At that time, draftees served two years on active duty and four more years in the reserves. Fortunately, because I was wounded I was assigned to the "Inactive Army Reserves," which meant I did not have to attend drills each month and go away for two weeks each summer for training. I wanted nothing at all ever to do again with the army or Government. I was afraid to open the letter as I was afraid they were going to call me back again for service. Since I had left the army, I periodically have a reoccurring dream that I have been recalled. In my dream, I am going through base camp all over again, destined to go back to Vietnam.

Some forty-five-plus years later, it is the only nightmare I have from Vietnam which occurs about once every few years. Then I usually wake up and am sure glad it was a bad, really bad, dream!

Anyway, I opened the letter, and it was from a Captain Thomas Finnegan, writing to me on behalf of Major General Hugh F. Foster Jr. (no relation to Tom Foster, my friend). The letter stated that I had been awarded the Distinguished Service Cross (DSC) in October of 1969, and that the general wanted me to come to Fort Monmouth for an awards ceremony and parade. I wasn't quite sure what it all meant, as I didn't even know I had been awarded the DSC. Enclosed with the letter was a copy of the general orders for the medal. After reading it, I realized that the Silver Star medal I had been awarded on October 7, 1969, had been upgraded to a DSC sometime later. Apparently it needed the approval of higher-ups which took some time. I had no clue as to why they waited for over 2 ½ years to send me the notice of this award. Perhaps they had no address for me, as I never heard from the army once I was discharged. Frankly, I didn't really care as I was just very happy that I was not being recalled for duty! That was worth more to me than any medal the army could award. A week or so after receiving the letter, Captain Finnegan called me at work. How he found out where I was working, I do not know. The captain told me, "The general wants to give you a parade and awards ceremony at Fort Monmouth to honor your award." I replied, "Well, I am working and am quite busy, so can you thank the general and just send me the award?" The captain replied, "You don't understand. This award is the second-highest award for bravery, just below the Medal of Honor, and the general wants to give it to you personally." I said, "Thank you, but I don't think I would be able to come." The captain replied, "Well, like I said, the general wants you to come to an awards ceremony. He has never had someone in his command awarded such a high medal and he wants to make a big deal about the award and have a ceremony to honor you." At this point I was getting frustrated as he was not taking no for an answer, so I said, "Well, I am just too busy at work right now to come." With that the captain said, "Well, that should not be a problem. I will call your CEO and get him to give you permission to attend the ceremony." That made me a bit nervous as I knew our CEO was a graduate of the naval academy and had served as a naval officer. So I said, "Well, let me see what I can do." With that the captain said, "Son, you don't understand. The general, a major general in fact, wants to pin this medal on you personally. This is a great honor to be awarded this medal. I hesitate to remind you that you are still in the military, and if need be, you could be activated so that you could be ordered to come receive this medal. Now I wouldn't want to have to take things that far, but like I said, the general wants you to come to a ceremony so he can personally award you this medal!" That made things crystal clear to me. I was going "voluntarily" because the last thing in the world I wanted was to be reactivated. So I quickly replied, "When would the general like me to attend?" With that the captain understood he had made his point and gave me a couple of dates. We settled on June 16, 1972, as the date. Then I mentioned to him that I no longer had a military uniform. The captain said, "That's not a problem. You can come in civilian clothes." I was relieved as I did not want to get in my uniform ever again. Being slightly embarrassed about the whole situation, I asked, "Could you ask the general for one favor?" He asked, "What's that?" "Could you ask if we can forgo the parade and ceremony and just have a small presentation?" He replied, "I will ask the general, but either way, we are confirmed for June, correct?" I said, "Yes, sir, I will be there." He thanked me and said he would get back with me on the details and my request. You have to keep in mind that at that time the Vietnam War was very unpopular. Almost no one supported the war, and the veterans were treated like lepers and "baby killers." Many returning veterans did not even list their service on résumés for fear no one would hire them. Many companies at that time would not hire Vietnam veterans, as the "elite media and Hollywood" portrayed them as outcasts and murderers. Much of this was a myth created by the millions of draft-age men who either were draft dodgers, went to Canada, refused to serve (such as President Clinton), or joined the National Guard to avoid going to Vietnam, or used some other method to avoid being drafted to go fight. Today many of these men are old, and now question what they did and their motives, and are trying to twist the facts and go overboard praising those who serve today.

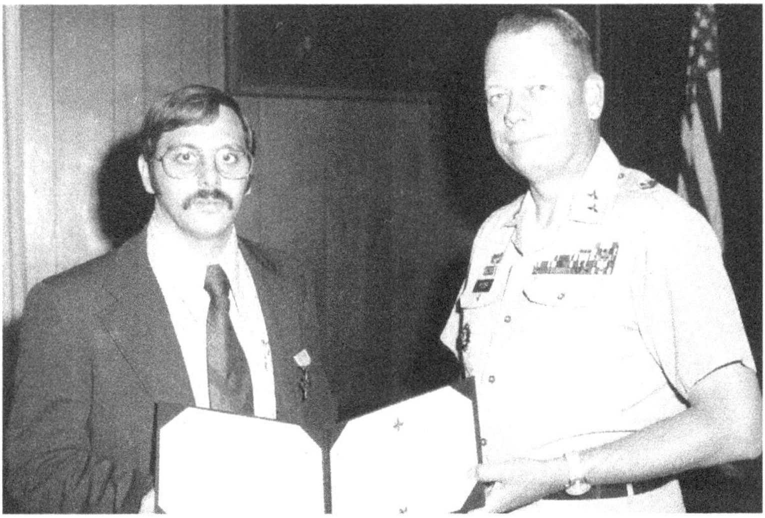

Author receiving Distinguished Service Cross from Major General Foster

The CEO of our company, Harry Martel, got wind of my award and asked me to come to his office. I had never had a one-on-one session with the CEO. As I suspected, being a naval officer, he was very gracious and congratulated me on receiving such a high honor. He asked to see the award and spent over an hour asking me questions about what had actually happened and how things were in Vietnam. Years later after he left the company, he and I would become close and we started a computer company together along with another executive.

On June 16, 1972, I drove down from where I was living in Northern New Jersey, to Fort Monmouth. At the gate I was greeted by the MPs who manned the front gate. When I gave them my name, they both saluted me and said Captain Finnegan was waiting for me. As I had left the army as an enlisted man, it was not normal for other soldiers to salute you. Besides I was in a suit and tie and not a uniform. The MPs escorted me to Captain Finnegan who was waiting to take me to the general's headquarters. I followed him in my car to the HQ building. I had never been in that building when I served at the post.

I entered the general's office and was warmly greeted by the Major General Hugh F. Foster, Jr. He was much taller than me, perhaps six feet three or four inches, and he was in dress uniform. In those days you wore a dress uniform if you were in an administrative job. He introduced me to several of the officers on his staff and then sat down and talked about what had happened that day in 1968. After our discussion he presented me with the DSC medal with my name engraved on the back. Then a photographer took several pictures of the award ceremony. Later the general kindly sent me several photos of the ceremony, along with an army green award presentation book with a picture of him pinning the DSC on my chest. I did not look happy in the picture, mostly because I was embarrassed about the whole affair. I had received several medals during my service, including the Silver Star and Bronze Star and three Purple Hearts, and never once did anyone pin a medal on my chest or even have a formal presentation. I just got the awards handed to me at a later date, usually by the company clerk. Then I just mailed the awards home because they would be lost of destroyed if we kept them in Vietnam.

After the ceremony I thanked the general and the others, shook hands and drove to my work office. I put the DSC award in a shoe box along with my other medals. Sometime after that the director of the advertising department of our company asked if I would bring in my medals for him to see. So I brought them in one day and showed him the medals. He took them away to "show some of his guys," and at the end of the day presented me with a beautiful case with all of my medals displayed. He and the CEO had conspired together and he put all of my medals in a glass case, which I still have hanging in my office. It was a very thoughtful action by these gentlemen.

Distinguished Service Cross

The DSC is the nation's second-highest medal for valor after the Medal of Honor. During the ten years of the Vietnam War the army awarded only 1,051 DSC's, 500 of which were awarded posthumously.

Author's award of the DSC
The Distinguished Service Cross

DEPARTMENT OF THE ARMY
Headquarters, United States Army Vietnam
APO San Francisco 96375

GENERAL ORDERS
NUMBER 3794

7 October 1969

AWARD OF THE DISTINGUISHED SERVICE CROSS

1. TC 320. The following AWARD is announced.

ESHER, BRIAN R 107-38-9777 SPECIALIST FOUR United States Army, Company A, 4th Battalion, 23d Infantry, 25th Infantry Division, APO 96225

Awarded: Distinguished Service Cross
Date of action: 13 September 1968
Theater: Republic of Vietnam
Reason: For extraordinary heroism in connection with military operations involving conflict with an armed hostile force in the Republic of Vietnam: Specialist Four Esher distinguished himself by exceptionally valorous actions on 13 September 1968 during a mine sweep operation south of Fire Support Base Santa Barbara in Tay Ninh Province. As his unit proceeded along Route 4, a North Vietnamese unit sprang an ambush employing rocket-propelled grenades. In the initial barrage, the first three armored personnel carriers were struck and disabled. Specialist Esher along with four other men who survived the salvo scrambled aboard the following vehicle as the platoon attempted to move out of the ambush site. When their armored vehicle was stalled by an exploding rocket grenade, they quickly dismounted and established a defensive perimeter around the personnel carrier. Setting up a machine gun position, Specialist Esher unleashed a suppressive barrage on the hostile force who sought to close in on the element now cut off from the rest of the platoon. Twice he returned to the smoking vehicle to obtain ammunition and once more to call in and direct gunship fire on hostile positions. Receiving orders to rejoin the platoon, Specialist Esher positioned his men advantageously on the vehicle and set off in the badly damaged vehicle at a painfully slow speed. After finally reaching the location of his unit, he helped supervise the evacuation of the more seriously wounded. Only after he and his comrades had retraced their path through the ambush site and returned to the fire base did Specialist Esher accept medical care for his wounds received in the initial attack. Specialist Four Esher's extraordinary heroism and devotion to duty were in keeping with the highest traditions of the military service and reflect great credit upon himself, his unit, and the United States Army.

Author's medals

Offered an Officer Commission

1985–86

Years later, I was working as the vice president and general manager of the largest and most profitable business unit of a company called ITEK Graphics. I was part of a four-man team who had just completed a successful leveraged buyout of this company from Litton Industries. One of the directors who worked for me ran our Operations Maintenance and Facilities Groups. He was a lieutenant colonel in the Army Reserve. In this position he was the Commanding Officer of a Battalion of Engineers. He was aware of my service, but we never really spoke about it. One day he approached me and said, "You know, the army these days is having a lot of difficulty keeping soldiers of all ranks in the military." I replied, "I'm not surprised." Then he said, "Well, we could use someone like you in our unit, and I could offer you a direct commission as my adjutant with a rank of major if you're interested." I was shocked, but I had less than no interest in ever being in the army or working for the government again. My big fear in life at that time is that the army would try to call me back again, even though I had served my time and was not eligible to be called up again. So I said,

"Well, thanks for the offer, but I would never want to go back in the army even if they made me a general!" He laughed and said, "Well, if you ever change your mind, let me know!" I said, "Not likely in this lifetime!" He was a good man, and I appreciate his offer, but even the thought of going back in the army gave me shivers down my spine!

EPILOGUE

I have read many books on military history. It is interesting how, even though the many wars throughout history have been different, there are many experiences of the front line infantry that are similar. For the most part, men were scared, exhausted, and miserable living and fighting in the difficult conditions of the infantry in all theaters of war. Vietnam was most closely associated with the Americans fighting the Japanese in the island battles of WWII. Above all else, Vietnam was a small-unit infantryman's war with soldiers fighting yards apart. During the war, I saw the best and worst of men. I also learned how unfair life was and how easily men could be killed and maimed. Most eye-opening was how luck played such a significant part in surviving a battle. Too many times I attacked the enemy with men on my right and left, only to see both killed or wounded while I survived and lived on. The contrast between an infantry soldier fighting day in and day out with a determined and skilled enemy and American soldiers in the rear areas was dramatic and bore little resemblance to their experiences.

As a nineteen-year-old soldier, I quickly learned many things about life, leadership, people, and myself during the war. It is true that one never knows how he will react in combat. The strongest and seeming most brave during training and civilian life may turn out to be the most timid and even cowardly during battle. Rank and position also meant little as leadership qualities in combat are different than in peacetime. Too many leaders in Vietnam did not measure up, and too many draftees and low-level enlisted men carried the ball when the career soldiers found ways to get out of combat and secure rear echelon positions. What we lacked the most in the infantry was experienced leadership. It has been said that we did not fight a decades-old war in Vietnam but ten one-year wars! In my experience we rarely had any experienced officers and NCOs, who are the backbone of the infantry. The failure of Johnson and his military advisors to call up the reserves of experienced leaders was another catastrophic failure on the part of our war leaders. The officers we had rarely lasted more than a few months, and some should not have been there at all. None of the front line officers I served under had any previous combat experience, and they learned by getting too many of their men killed, then trying something else. Worst of all were the officer warmongers who rarely, if ever, risked their own skin, but were most aggressive in sending others to their death in search of their own recognition and promotions. Most of the enlisted men I served with in the infantry were draftees. This was because if you enlisted for three years you could get assigned to a rear echelon job, which did not involve fighting. Many men chose this path when they were confronted with fighting as infantry. Thus the bulk of the fighting in our company fell to the draftees. Even the NCOs we had were mostly inexperienced draftees who had been sent to the instant NCO school and awarded their stripes, not by earning them in combat or with experience, but through stateside training. We had little, if any, real-life-combat-experienced leaders to teach us how to fight and survive. The failing of the military to place experienced officers and NCOs in the field with the infantry resulted in many more casualties than was necessary. It is also a condemnation on the leadership of the military that they allowed so many experienced combat NCOs from WWII and Korea to avoid combat and serve in rear echelon positions while placing the burden of fighting on young draftees and volunteers with no military or combat experience. The result was that most soldiers in my unit did not survive more than three months, and many were killed or wounded the first few days of combat.

The other major failing in Vietnam was that we were sent into combat units as individuals. We had zero unit cohesion as we did not know anyone in the units we were joining. There is not a scarier feeling than to go into battle not knowing anyone or anything about combat and having no one to even care enough to learn your name. In fact the "veteran combat soldiers" avoided even getting to know your name as you were likely to be killed or wounded in your first few days of combat. Thus they did not want to get to know you or have anything to do with you since your mistake could get them killed. Thus there was no buddy system or unit cohesion. This was certainly my experience throughout my time in the field. In my company if you survived three months, you were considered an experienced combat veteran. The majority did not make it that long and most veterans had been wounded at least once.

It is also true that the most effective combat troops are those who survived and fought for the first 90 days or so of combat. After that your effectiveness steadily declines. After 140 to 180 days of combat the majority of front line infantry soldiers steadily become more and more ineffective. Combat is the most stressful and taxing of any life experience, both physically and mentally, which was certainly the case in my situation. It is also said that a veteran soldier is a scared soldier. In my situation, before I ever got to fire my rifle, I experienced the extreme violence, death, and terror of the battlefield by being blown off a track and almost killed by our own artillery. Then I was thrown into combat the next morning, still in shock with a concussion and no sympathy or understanding from my leaders or fellow soldiers. We were treated like cannon fodder and, from the military point of view, worth less than an APC because the military only paid our surviving relatives $10,000 for our deaths. This is why we were ordered to walk out in front of our APCs to protect them at supreme risk to ourselves.

What also made little sense to us was how the army used up our lives. We were sent out to seek the enemy in his home territory and almost always outnumbered and expected. The NVA enemy who were tough, determined, and experienced soldiers, prepared positions with artillery proof bunkers, ambushes, and booby traps and waited for us to walk into their ambushes. When they were not prepared, they retreated or melted away in small groups back to their safe havens in Cambodia where we were not allowed to follow or bomb. They were often better fed, better rested, and from an infantryman's point of view, as well equipped as we were to fight small unit battles. What they lacked in airpower and artillery, they made up for with surprise, planning and overwhelming manpower. Typically we would only find the enemy when we stumbled into his prepared base camps or ambushes. Rarely did we surprise the enemy or start the battle at a time and place of our choosing. Rather we found them on their ground, when and where they wanted to fight. When they had inflicted sufficient casualties or determined the odds were not in their favor, they retreated.

We also could not understand why our "leaders," both civilian and military, would not bomb the enemy directly. They bombed South Vietnam rather than Cambodia, Laos, and North Vietnam where the enemy sheltered and stored their arms and supplies. Instead the army sent us out in far too-small units to find temporary enemy base camps and soldiers operating in South Vietnam. Then after we bumped up against mostly larger enemy formations or they attacked us when they wished, our strategy was to bring in overwhelming firepower in terms of artillery and airstrikes to kill as many enemies as possible, at our expense of course. McNamara's "body count" metric was likewise a mistake, as the enemy was willing to take casualties far in excess of what we would stand. At one point Ho Chi Minh said "*You will kill 10 of our soldiers for every one of yours we kill, but in the end you will give up!*" His prophecy turned out to be true, even though we killed something more like twenty soldiers to one of ours. Keep in mind that the enemy, not our side, controlled when and where to fight. Thus, he controlled how many of his soldiers became casualties. On the other hand, as defenders, USA casualties were determined by the actions of the enemy. What is most discouraging is that in 1972 when the NVA invaded South Vietnam, Nixon ordered the mining of Haiphong Harbor and the bombing of Hanoi with B-52 bombers. In eleven days of bombing, the North Vietnamese had had enough and returned to the peace negotiations in Paris. One can only speculate the outcome of the war and the many soldiers' lives which would have been saved if the USA had bombed Hanoi earlier in the war. By fighting a limited defensive war, the USA signaled to the enemy that we would not invade his homeland or his safe havens in Cambodia and Laos. This was a huge strategic error by our leadership and, as always, the leaders themselves did not suffer, but rather it was the fighting troops who bore this burden. I have always believed, and still do today, that a primary object of a war should be to kill the leadership of the enemy. If more leaders had to stand with the fighting men in battle, there would be a lot less wars. It is always the old men who send the young men into battle to die!

Another interesting comparison of what we endured as civilian soldiers in Vietnam versus the professional soldiers of today is the Osama Bin Laden raid by specially-trained forces. Most everyone in our country acknowledges that the men who made this raid are national heroes, and this is true. But what is not as well recognized is that in many ways we front line soldiers in Vietnam were thrown into equally, if not more difficult situations on a daily basis. Let me explain by using this extreme example. The special operations soldiers who made the Bin Laden raid had been trained for years to execute just such a mission. They were all experienced professional soldiers who spent many years in the military and everyone volunteered for this mission. For the most part they were senior NCOs. They routinely practiced with their weapons and knew their specialized gear by heart. They had night vision equipment to gain an edge over the enemy and were trained to fight at night as a team. They also had top-of-the-line weapons and equipment which were tailored to exactly what they needed to do for this specific mission. They also trained and worked together as a team, not only with their team members, but their support infrastructure and leaders as well. Before the raid they were well fed, well rested and in prime physical condition. They had support from the commander-in-chief down the line and access to whatever resources they needed. They were recognized as valuable soldiers who should not be risked unless it was a very important mission. Before the raid, they were given excellent intelligence (including live observation) and had a very good idea of the layout and defense of the compound. They practiced on life-sized mock-ups of the site until they knew how they would approach the assault by heart. They also knew the exact strength of the enemy, that they were only armed with small arms, and that they were, for the most part, amateur soldiers living with their family. Most importantly they were in control of the battlefield and had the element of surprise. They picked when and where they were going to attack and how they would go about making the assault. They also understood the importance of their mission and that the man they were going after had been responsible for an attack on our homeland that killed thousands of our unarmed citizens. They also understood Bin Laden was waging war against our country and had to be destroyed.

Now compare this to how we went into battle in Vietnam as civilian soldiers. First of all, most of us had only been trained for a few months in basic military skills. For example, I took three months of basic military training and three months of advanced infantry training, much of it spent doing drills and other such non-combat training. Our training for combat was rudimentary at best. In fact we were never even trained on some of the weapons we used and on how to operate with armor or helicopters. We were in large part draftees who were still civilians at heart and did not want to be in Vietnam in the first place. Many of us joined units as replacements who were operating in the field. Thus, we joined units where we knew no one, much less trained with any of them. Yet we were dependent on these people for our lives! In the field we were mostly dead tired, dirty, underfed, under the constant strain of battle, and living a primitive existence with no rest or relaxation. Our equipment was minimal to the point where we were supplied used clothing, and many times went weeks when our tracks were destroyed before receiving replacement clothing and gear. Once I was given boots off of a soldier who had been killed because the heel of my boot had been blown off by a mortar. When your track was destroyed, you lost everything except the clothes, ammo, and rifle you were holding at the time. I went through five tracks during my five months in the infantry, not counting the ones I hopped on in a battle which were also destroyed! Most of us understood that Vietnam was not a threat to our country, and that we were wasting our time and lives in Vietnam for no reason. We could not at the time, and still do not today, understand why we were there, what we were fighting for, and what the overall strategy, if any, there was—not so good for morale or teamwork.

We went into battle, not as a well-planned, well-organized team, but rather feeling our way along unfamiliar jungle trails and territory with little or no understanding of the enemy strength, disposition or where they were located. Most veterans who survived a couple of months in our unit understood we were being used as bait to draw the enemy into battle so they could be destroyed (or so the theory went) by our air and artillery power. We knew from experience that the enemy would only fight when he chose to fight, and that was when he had the advantage of surprise and superior numbers and firepower. Every day we knew someone would be killed or wounded when we walked into an enemy trap or base camp because they were expecting us and were prepared to fight. Once were engaged, we immediately took casualties and, more often than not, we were pinned down until artillery or airstrikes drove back the enemy. Too often we could not get support because of other priorities, and then we were on our own.

Then we paid in blood for our supporting team's mistakes. Our own artillery short rounds dropped on us and helicopters shooting at us all made being in the infantry very dangerous. While I was in the infantry I estimate we lost around one in four or five of our men to friendly fire or accidents. Then remember that this was not a one-time raid like the bin Laden raid where you went back to a warm bed, good food, and congratulations. We did this every day, and if you survived, you went back to digging a fox hole or bunker and sleeping on the ground eating C-Rats if you were not going out on an ambush or pulling listening post duty outside the wire. Rarely did we receive any recognition, promotions, or medals other than Purple Hearts for our efforts.

Given the two situations which one would you rather participate in if given the choice?

Another unfair reality of the army was that, as draftees, we were almost never given promotions, even when we acted in NCO positions. For example, track commanders and squad leaders were NCO positions. The majority of the time we had SP4 grade enlisted men functioning in these positions. Yet they rarely if ever received promotions to NCO because they were draftees, and the military wanted to promote regular army soldiers instead of "wasting the promotion slot" on draftees. So the soldier handing out boots and socks in the rear who had enlisted in the army got the promotion, while the men doing the fighting did not. In the infantry we were paid the same as a clerk sitting behind a desk in Saigon who collected combat pay yet was likely safer than being on the streets of Detroit at night.

What I took away from my army and combat experiences was worth a lifetime of understanding human nature. Before the army, I was more independent than most, relying primarily on myself. After Vietnam, I was more independent than ever and obsessed with becoming financially independent so I would not have to rely on anyone ever again. I had learned the hard way that relying on my own judgment, rather than blindly following orders, was much more fruitful and beneficial to my own well-being. I also came away with a deep distrust of our government and leaders, knowing full well that they lied to us during Vietnam and many other times, and placed their own interest above that of our country or its citizens. With the poor and unqualified leadership we have today in Washington, this is more than ever true. I also learned about leadership, team work, and motivating people, mostly by understanding what not to do versus what to do correctly. I applied these techniques to my career as a business leader most successfully. I made sure throughout my career to see things for myself, and asked the people who were doing the work how the designs, systems, and processes actually work. Many times I knew more than the designers about what worked and didn't work because I saw it for myself, not from some office computer or chart. I adopted the philosophy of "management by walking around" far before it was made popular in management books.

The other positive contribution I took away from my Vietnam experiences was how very fortunate I was to be alive. Every day above ground was a good day for me, and I approached my life in a positive manor. Even a bad day for me was a good day compared to a normal day in the life of a combat infantryman. I would think to myself, how bad can it be? No one is trying to kill me, I have all I want to eat, I can sleep in a bed, no bugs are biting me, and for the most part I am free to do as I please. That put things into perspective for me, and I approached problems with a positive attitude which is one of the keys to success. Even minor business failures were not catastrophic, since no one was killed or maimed by a wrong decision, and most problems, if recognized early, can be easily rectified. Overall this experience made me a better man and leader. Best of all, I have no regrets about how I conducted myself during the war and have a clear conscience with no nightmares about what I experienced. The only nightmare I have, if one could call it that, is that I was once again drafted into the army. Then I began to go through basic training, thinking to myself how unreal and easy basic training is compared to combat. Then I wake up!

All in all, I can sum up my experiences in a statement attributed to an infantry soldier in WWII: "I would not go through that again for a million dollars, but I would also not trade my experiences for a million dollars either!"

I am proud of my service and that, as a teenager, I faced my greatest fears and did not shrink in the face of adversity. I was a simple soldier who did his duty when called upon by his country.

APPENDIX

Vietnam War Statistics

Vietnam War:

- USA casualties through 1975-entire war:
    - KIA, 58,202–58,260
        - Battle deaths, 47,378
        - 10,824 non-hostile deaths (18.6%)
        - Total, 58,202
        - 11 B (light weapons infantryman) had 18,465 or 31.76% of the KIAs.
    - WIA, 304,704–390,00 (figures are different from different sources-approximately a 7:1 ratio)
        - 153,329 required hospitalization (50.3%)
        - 75,000 severely disabled
        - permanently disabled, 21,000–23,214 (100% disabled)
        - 5,283 lost limbs
        - 1,081 multiple amputations
    - MIA, 2,338
    - CIA, 766
        - Died in Captivity 114
    - USA KIA in 1968, 14,589, most for one year and almost 31% of total battle deaths during the entire Vietnam War. 1969 had 9,414 the second highest year of battle deaths. Together they comprised 51% of all battle deaths during the Viet Nam War.

- USA ARMY from January 1968 thru September 1968 (9 months)
    - KIA, 6,607
    - WIA, 49,202
    - Enemy KIA, 152,387
- USA KIA in May 1968, 2169 (most ever for a month)
    - For the week ending May 11, 1968, some 562 were KIA
    - For the month some 7,602 were WIA.
    - Of these 3,954 were hospitalized
- Of the KIA:
    - 61% were younger than 21
    - 11,465 younger than 20 years old
    - Average age of men KIA 23.1 years
    - Army had approximately 2/3 of the battle deaths in Vietnam.
    - Of these 73% were 11B (light weapons infantry)
- SURRENDER:
    - No American unit, not even the smallest unit, a squad of 11 men or less, surrendered during the entire war!
    - As the war was primarily a small unit war of company size and below this is extraordinary as in the height of the war it was a common for small units to be cut off and surrounded by superior enemy forces. These brave soldiers fought to the death rather than surrender!
    - Contrast this to WWII where tens of thousands of American surrendered.
    - After the war one of the NVA generals asked one of our retired generals who were visiting Vietnam, "Why, when your soldiers were surrounded and about to be overrun, did they not surrender?" The US retired general said, "Think of how you treated our prisoners, and that's why!"

- ARVN-ARMY OF THE REPUBLIC OF VIETNAM:
    - KIA, 223,748
    - WIA, 1,169,763
    - MIA/CIA, N/A
    - Vietnamese civilians KIA, 2,000,000 (both North and South)
- NVA/VC:
    - KIA/Missing, 1,100,000 to 1,400,000 range as multiple sources claim different numbers (this does not include non-battle deaths)
    - WIA, 1,169,763
    - MIA, N/A
    - CIA/surrendered, 26,000
    - Hoi Chanh defectors, 101,511
    - According to McNamara in his book in 2003 he claims that the NVA lost some 3,400,000 men in the war from all causes.
        - ** The NVA VC battle deaths do not include non-battle deaths. It is estimated that deaths from noncombat causes; falling, snakes, drowning, infections, etc. are estimated at several times the battle deaths!
        - Given that the North of Vietnam had a population of 38,000,000 during 1954–1975 casualties represents 12%–13% of the population.
- VC/NVA casualties in Tet '68....100,000–160,000 est., essentially wiped out the VC which is why we fought hard core NVA after March '68
    - Estimated some 45K-60K KIA.
    - 100,000 WIA
    - 7,000 CIA

- Some 55,000 Soviet Union "advisors" supported the NVA in North Vietnam
- Some 327,000 Chinese troops served in North Vietnam (we killed one of these in S.VN)
- SOME OTHER STATISTICS ABOUT THE WAR AND FAKE WANNABES:
- There were some 26,800,000 young American males in the USA who were eligible for military service during the war according to the 1948 Selective Service Legislation.
  - If women were counted (equal rights and equal responsibility) you could double this figure.
  - 8,720,000 men volunteered for service, and 2,215,000 were drafted.
  - Only 23% of college graduates were drafted.
  - Only 45% of high school graduates were drafted.
  - This left 15,980,000 men who never served.
  - Of these 570,000 or 3.5% were technically draft dodgers.
  - Thus 15,410,000 men were disqualified or obtained deferments or exemptions from military service.
- These are many of the men today who are the most critical about Vietnam, and many are in the Obama administration!
- From August 5, 1964, to May 7, 1975, some 9,087,000 military personnel served on active duty during the official Vietnam era.
  - This represents some 9.7% of their generation or less than 1:10 who served.
  - Some 2 million were drafted.
- Of these some 2,709,918 served in Vietnam (all services)....29.8%
  - Of these 2.7MM who served in Vietnam only 2,594,000 served inside the country.

- Only 25% of those who served in Vietnam were draftees.
- Average education for those serving in Vietnam one year of college (thirteen years)
- .79% had high school diplomas.
- Blacks accounted for 10.5% of combat deaths in Vietnam. They accounted for 13.5% of the American population of 220,000,000.

- As of August 1995 only 1,713,823 Vietnam vets were still alive (census figures), 63.2%
- During the 1995 census some 9,492,958 Americans falsely claimed to have served in the country in Vietnam, 5.5:1 ratio, thus only 18% of those who claimed to serve actually served in Vietnam!
- During the 2000 census there were only 1,002,511 Vietnam vets still alive; that is a loss of 390 per day from the prior census!
    - This means that in 2000 only 37% were still alive (approximately 1 in 3).
    - If we extrapolate into 2013 using a rate of deaths of 10% per year (likely higher as vets age). Then in 2013 there would only be about 300,000 or so Vietnam vets left alive!
- During this same census 13, 853,027 American falsely claimed to be Vietnam vets, or a ration of almost 14:1; thus 93% of those claiming to be Vietnam vets are false!
- In December 1969 a lottery system for the draft was instituted by Nixon.
- In 1966 McNamara created "Project 100,000." This was an attempt to use the armed forces as a dumping ground for those of low intelligence.
    - This is what I experienced with some of the draftees who could not even dissemble and reassemble a rifle!

Combat related:

- On the best day ever for combat troops at the peak of the war only 43,500 of the 545,000 (the peak of troops was in January of 1969 with 549,500 troops) troops in the country were out in the field!
    - That means on the BEST DAY EVER less than 8% or one in twelve and a half were actually in the field.
    - Considering that we were mostly at half strength in the field most of the time that means that for each of us in the field there were more than 12 support troops!
    - According to some estimates only 300,000 troops served in the field (infantry, armor, artillery, support, etc.) out of a total during the war of 2.7MM men.
- During WWII the USA executed 300 of its own troops. In Vietnam none were executed.
- Battle Fatigue evacuations in Vietnam were 5 per 1,000 troops.
    - In Korea it was about 50 per 1,000 troops, over ten times the rate.
    - In WWII some units experienced over 100 per 1,000 troops.
- 25th Infantry division had the highest number of casualties of all army divisions during the Vietnam War even though it did not serve the longest in the country (January 1966–April 1971).
    - KIA and WIA during Vietnam, 34,484.
    - WWII, KIA and WIA, 5,432
    - Korea, KIA and WIA, 13,685
- In Vietnam the average infantry soldier spend 240 days in combat. The average infantry soldier in WWII spent some 40 days.
    - A ratio of 6 times as long in combat (if you lasted that long)

- Of course in our units at the time we served we spent much less time as we kept getting wounded.

- The USA military never lost a Major battle in Vietnam.
- For "ARMY Maneuver Battalions" the annual KIA rate using 100 as an average strength during select periods in 1968 was as follows:
  - January–March, 147.3
  - April–June, 123.8
  - July–September, 79.7
  - You can see why we didn't fare so well while we were in the field in Vietnam. Remember this is only the KIA rates and does not count the WIA or CIA!
- If you use the ratio of 7:1 (WIA to KIA) these figures would look more like what we experienced:
- January–March WIA and KIA, 1,178 or almost 100% each month!
- April–June WIA and KIA, 990
- July–September WIA and KIA, 638.
- Battle deaths in various wars:
  - WWI, 53,513
  - WWII, 292,131
  - Korea, 33,629
  - Vietnam, 47,378
- Causes of Casualties in Vietnam 1/65–6/70:

USA KIA/WIA

- Small arms, 51%/16%.
- Fragments, 36%/65%
- Booby traps/mines, 11%/15%
- Other, 2%/4%

GLOSSARY OF TERMS AND ABBREVIATIONS

AIT: Advanced Individual Training.

AK-47: Assault rifle developed by the Russians, 7.62 mm the most popular rifle in history.

AO: Area of operations.

AP: Ambush patrol.

APC: Armored Personnel Carrier or M-113. Also called a viper, track, or rolling coffin.

Article 15: Non-judicial punishment for less serious offenses.

ARVN: Army of the Republic of Vietnam.

AWOL: Absent without leave.

Azimuth: Compass heading for navigating.

Beehive round: Ammunition packed with thousands of 2 ¼ steel darts, nicknamed for the sound made when fired. Deadly against ground troops.

Boonies: Out in the field, Indian country, or enemy territory.

Boonie hat: A type of military issued soft head cover used in Vietnam to keep the sun and rain off your head.

Bug juice: An insect repellent used to ward off bugs and to get leeches off your skin. It came in a camouflaged plastic container often carried in the helmet camouflage band.

C-4: A powerful military explosive which was white in color and had the properties of molding clay.

C-47: Fixed-wing propeller-driven transport aircraft.

Canister round: Main gun ammunition packed with metal cylinders for antipersonnel fire.

Chinook: CH47 two blade helicopter for heavy lifting of cargo and troops.

Chopper: Generically a helicopter but most often referring to a Huey helicopter or UH1.

CIA: Captured in Action.

Claymore mine: Antipersonnel mine placed above ground facing the enemy, filled with C-4 explosive and 700 steel balls. Has the same effect of multiple shotguns shooting all at once.

Click: Kilometer or approximately 6/10 of a mile.

CO: Commanding officer.

C-Rats or C-rations: Cardboard box containing a canned meal carried by field maneuver units in Vietnam.

Concertina wire: Reusable barbed wire which comes in three-foot-diameter coils used to quickly set up a defensive perimeter for field fortifications. Often used with three coils with one on top and two coils on the bottom in a triangle formation.

DEROS: Date eligible for return from overseas.

Doc: Combat medic who accompanied infantry in the field.

Dust off: Slang for medical evacuation flights from the field, typically on Huey helicopters.

E-1: Enlisted pay grade for recruit private, the lowest enlisted rank.

E-2: Enlisted pay grade for private.

E-3: Enlisted pay grade for private first class.

E-4: Enlisted pay grade for corporal or specialist fourth class.

E-5: Enlisted pay grade for sergeant or specialist fifth class.

E-6: Enlisted pay grade for staff sergeant or specialist sixth class.

E-7: Enlisted pay grade for sergeant first class.

E-8: Enlisted pay grade for first sergeant or master sergeant.

E-9: Enlisted pay grade for sergeant major or command sergeant major the highest enlisted rank.

Eagle flight: A formation of Huey helicopters used to ferry troops into an area for operations. Typically, it included twelve helicopters with two parallel formations of five slicks carrying troops and two gunship helicopters providing covering fire.

Electric strawberry: disrespectful nickname of the 25th Infantry Division based on its insignia of a yellow lightning bolt on a read taro leaf.

FAC: Forward air controller.

FF: French Fort or Fort Santa Barbara.

FSB: Fire support base. A temporary field position which contained artillery and defending soldiers who supported field maneuver units (infantry and armor) with covering artillery. Typically FSBs were established in open fields in a circular form with bunkers and barbed wire around the perimeter for protection.

Grunt: Slang for an infantryman. Based on the sound one makes when an infantryman is loading a heavy pack or rucksack on his back.

Gook: In Vietnam, a derogatory term to describe oriental people, especially Vietnamese. It originated as a Korean word which meant "foreigner."

Gunships: Typically a HU1 or Huey helicopter armed with machine guns and rockets which provided fire support to the ground troops.

HE Round: High explosive ammunition for artillery or recoilless rifles.

Herringbone: Formation used by armor and mechanized infantry units when a column of armored vehicles is halted with every other vehicle facing left or right to cover all sides of the column.

Hooch: Nickname for USA base camp living quarters with a tin roof, wood and screen sides, and a wooden floor sometimes surrounded on the sides with sandbags.

House cat: A soldier who is assigned to a position in the rear or not in the field. A noncombatant position. Also referred to as a REMF (rear echelon mother f——er) by infantry troops.

KIA: Killed in action.

Laager: Slang name for a temporary circular night defensive position.

Laterals: Straps or metal extensions used on an Armored Personnel Carrier to enable the driver to drive the vehicle by sitting on top of the APC to help protect against mines and RPG explosions.

LP: Listening post.

LZ: Landing zone. Area designated for helicopter to land.

M-14 rifle: USA standard 7.62 mm automatic rifle. In our unit it was only used as a sniper rifle mounted with an infrared scope for night use.

M-16 rifle: USA standard 5.56 mm automatic rifle. Basic rifle used by the infantry in Vietnam.

M-60 machine gun: USA standard 7.62 mm machine gun, also called the pig.

M-79 grenade launcher: USA standard grenade launcher, single-shot breach loading weapon which fired 40 mm grenades.

M-113 APC: Armored Personnel Carrier.

Marston mats: Also called PSP, or pierced steel planks, used for construction of runways, bunkers, and hung over the sides of APCs to protect against RPGs.

Mad minute: All weapons fired at once around a defensive perimeter designed to disrupt possible enemy formations preparing for an attack.

MIA: Missing in action.

MOONSOON: in South Vietnam, the rainy season or monsoon season begins in mid-May and ends in mid-November. The heaviest rainfall is during the months of June–September where the monthly average rainfall is about 300 mm.

MOS: Military occupational specialty.

MOS 11B: Light weapons infantryman.

MP: Military police.

MSB: Main supply base.

NCO: Noncommissioned officer (pay grades E-4 to E-9).

NPD: Night laager position.

NVA: North Vietnamese Army.

OD: Olive drab, the color of army fatigue uniforms and equipment.

PIASTER: South Vietnamese currency with an official rate of exchange 100 to 1 US dollar.

Point: First man walking in front of a row of soldiers.

POW: Prisoner of war.

PX: Post Exchange.

REMF: Rear echelon mother f——ker. Infantry slang for rear echelon troops also called house-cats.

RIF: Reconnaissance in force.

RPD: Main enemy machine gun using a 200-round drum with a high rate of fire.

RPG: Rocket-propelled grenade. A shaped charge antitank weapon used to destroy enemy armor and bunkers. In Vietnam, two primary types were used by the NVA: an RPG 2 and an RPG 7, the RPG 7 being a larger and more powerful version of the RPG 2.

R&R: Rest and recreation, or rest and recuperation. A seven-day leave outside of Vietnam granted to soldiers during their one-year service in Vietnam.

RTO: Radio-telephone operator.

SGT: Sergeant.

SPOOKY: Nickname for a C-47 propeller-driven aircraft fitted with Gatling guns to support infantry field night laagers and fire support bases.

Staff: Support staff for military organizations:

- S-1: Personnel
- S-2: intelligence
- S-3: Operations
- S-4: Logistics

Saddle up: An order given to infantry to pick up their packs, weapons, and gear and prepare to move out on maneuvers.

Sapper: Enemy soldier trained in demolition and infiltrating through defensives.

Shake and Bake: An instant NCO. An army soldier who was sent to the NCO training school and made a noncommissioned officer, typically a buck sergeant (E-5) or sometimes a staff sergeant (E-6).

SKS rifle: Enemy semiautomatic rifle with built-in bayonet.

Short-timer: Term used to describe when US soldiers in Vietnam were getting close to returning home.

Slick: A Huey or UH1 helicopter used to carry troops, typically eight to ten soldiers per helicopter.

Starlight Scope: A USA handheld night scope used to intensify light from stars and moon so that the user could see in the dark. The scope illuminated the night with a green coloring.

Straight leg: Nickname for infantrymen.

TC: Track or tank commander.
TNBC: Tay Ninh Base Camp.
TOC: Tactical Operations Center.
TOE: Table of Organization and Equipment
Top: Nickname for first sergeant.
Track: APC 113 or viper.
Triple-canopy jungle: very thick jungle which has trees and vegetation which cover the ground, shutting out much of the sunlight.
Tropic Lightning: Nickname for the 25 Infantry Division based on its divisional patch with a yellow streak of lightning on a red-leaf background. The name originated from WWII due to its rapid advances in the Guadalcanal campaign.
VC: Vietcong.
VTR: Vehicle track recovery. A tank recovery vehicle with a large boom for lifting tanks and tank parts built on an M-48 tank chassis.
White Mice: South Vietnamese Police, called White Mice because of their small stature and white uniforms.
WIA: Wounded in action.
Willie Peter or WP: A white phosphorous hand grenade.
Wolfhounds: 27th Infantry Regiment of the 1st Brigade.
World: As in "back to the world" US soldiers' slang for the USA.
Xenon spotlight: A 75-million-candlelight searchlight mounted on the barrel of an M-48 tank.
XO: Executive officer or second in command of a unit typically overseeing administrative matters.

SELECTED BIBLIOGRAPHY

I have read many books, articles, and studied historical information on Vietnam to better understand where, how, and in what overall context we fought while I was in Vietnam. I have also read well over a thousand books on war and history. I also have my personal material from my days in service and books full of pictures to help me put events in context. Likewise, I have spent many hours with two veteran soldiers, Tom Foster and Cain Bridgman, both of whom served with the 4/23rd Mechanized Infantry. I have collected notes and information for many decades in the hope that someday I would have the time to write my experiences as an infantry soldier and place my actions in some semblance of historical context. This book is the culmination of these efforts. The bibliography below does not list all of the books, articles, and historical information I have researched over the years, but it includes the most important.

25th Infantry Division WEB Site; 25ththida.org/tln.Tropic Lightning News, 1968/69.

4/23 Infantry battalion WEB site; www.tomahawks.us/fsb's.

Ambrose, Stephen. *Citizen Soldiers.* USA: Simon & Schuster Inc., 1997.

Anderson, Christopher. *Grunts US Infantry in Vietnam.* London: Greenhill Books, 1998.

Appleyard, Anthony. *Wikipedia.* English Wikipedia project/flame thrower.

Arnold, James. *The Illustrated History of Armor. The Viet Nam War.* Toronto: Bantam Books, 1987.

Arnold, James. Tet Offensive 1968. London. Osprey Publishing Ltd. 1990.

Bendell, Don. *Valley of Tears*. New York: Dell Publishing, 1993.

Bergerud, Eric. *Red Thunder, Tropic Lighting*. USA: Penguin Group, 1993.

Bergerud, Eric. *Touched with Fire: The Land War in the South Pacific*. New York: Penguin Group, 1996.

Birdwell, Dwight. *A Hundred Miles of Bad Road. An Armored Cavalryman in Vietnam 1967–68*. California: Presidio Press, 1997.

Bonds, Ray. *The Vietnam War: The Illustrated History of the Conflict in Southeast Asia*. New York: Crown Publishers Inc., 1979.

Brennan, Mathew. *Hunter Killer Squadron Vietnam 1965–1972*. New York: Pocket Books, 1990.

Brown, John. *Rice Paddy Grunt*. Lake Bluff: Regnery Books, 1986.

Browne, Malcom. *The New Face of War*. Toronto: Bantam Books, 1965.

Burke, Tracy. *The Tet Offensive, January–April 1968*. NYC: Combined Books, 1998.

Butterfield, Fox. *The Vietnam War Almanac*. USA: World Publications, 1985.

Callaway, Joseph, Jr. *Mekong First Light*. New York: Random House Publishing Group, 2004.

Canfield, Roger. *Comrades in Arms*. January 2010.

Caputo, Philip. *A Rumor of War*. Toronto: Holt, Rinehart and Winston, 1977.

Carhart, Tom. *The Offering*. New York: Warner Books, 1987.

Chambers, Larry. *Recondo: LRRPs in the 101st Airborne*. New York: Ballantine Books, 1992.

Don, Tran Van. *Our Endless War*. San Rafael, California: Presidio Press, 1978.

Donahue, James. *Blackjack-34*. New York: Ballantine Publishing Company, 1998.

Donovan, David. *Once a Warrior King. Memories of an Officer in Vietnam*. USA: McGraw-Hill, 1985.

Distinguished Service Cross.www.homeof heros.com/DSC.

Didley, Wade. "What We Learned from the Tet Offensive." *Military History Magazine*, January 2011 issue.

Essame, H. *Patton: A Study in Command.* New York: Charles Scribner's Sons, 1974.

Esper, George. *The Eyewitness History of the Vietnam War 1961–1975.* USA: Associated Press Inc., 1983.

Evans, Daniel, Jr. *Doc: Platoon Medic.* New York: Pocket Books, 1998.

Foster, Thomas. "Yes, Our Cause in Viet Nam Was Noble." Peoria. *Peoria Journal Star* newspaper, September 6, 1980.

Fowler, Will. *The Vietnam Story.* London: Winchmore Publishing Services Limited, 1983.

Gadd, Charles. *Line Doggie: Foot Soldier in Vietnam.* Pocket Books, 1987.

George, Robert. *The Vietnam Experience.* 12 volume series. Boston: Boston Publishing Company Inc., 1982.

Guilmartin, John. *America in Vietnam.* Godalming: Colour Library Books Ltd., 1991.

Hartline, David. *Vietnam What a Soldier Gives.* Summerville: Espy Publishing Company, 1984.

Hardwick, William. *Down South One tour in Vietnam.* New York: Random House Publishing Group, 2004.

Hayes, Roger. *On Point: A Rifleman's Year in the Boonies, 1967–1968.* Novato: Presidio Press Inc., 2000.

Hobbes, Nicholas. *Essential Militaria.* New York: Atlantic Books, 2003.

Kamps, Charles, Jr. *The History of the Vietnam War.* London: Aerospace Publishing Ltd., 1988.

Karno, Stanley. *Vietnam: A history, The First Complete Account of Vietnam at War.* New York: Viking Press, 1983.

Laurie, Bill. Whitewash/blackwash; myths of the Viet Nam war. 2005.

Leninger, Jack. *Time Heals No Wounds.* New York: Ballantine Books, 1993.

Leppelman, John. *Blood on the Risers: An Airborne Soldier's Thirty-Five Months in Vietnam.* New York: Ballantine Books, 1991.

Mangold, Tom. *The Tunnels of Cu Chi.* New York: Random House, 1985.

Maclear, Michael. *Vietnam: A Complete Chronicle of the War.* New York: Black Dog & Leventhal Publishers Inc., 1981.

Maclear, Michael. *Vietnam: A Complete Photographic History.* New York: Black Dog & Leventhal Publishers Inc., 2003.

Mangold, Tom. *The Tunnels of Cu Chi.* Berkley Book, 1985.

Martinez, Reynel. *Six Silent Men.* New York: Ballantine Books, 1997.

Mersky, Peter. *The Navel Air War in Vietnam.* Annapolis: The Nautical and Aviation Publishing Company of America, 1981.

Mertel, Kenneth. *Year of the Horse-Vietnam.* New York: Bantam Books, 1968

Middleton, Drew. *Air War-Vietnam.* New York: Arno Press Inc., 1978.

Mills, Hugh, Jr. *Low Level Hell.* New York: Dell Publishing, 1992.

Moriarty, J. M. *Ground Attack Vietnam: The Marines Who Controlled the Skies.* New York: Ballantine Books, 1993.

Morris, Jim. *War Story.* New York: Paladin Enterprises Inc., Dell Publishing, 1979.

Murphy, Edward. *Vietnam Medal of Honor Heroes.* New York: Ballantine Books, 1987.

Murry, Stuart. Eyewitness Vietnam War. London. DK Publishing. 2005.

Nelson, Clifford. Daily diary transcript of LTC Clifford C. Nelson (col. Ret.). Commanding Officer 4/23 mechanized Infantry regiment, 25th Infantry division 12 May–13 November 1968. 2003–4. www.tomahawks.us/commander's_page.htm.

Nolan, Kieth. *Ripcord: Screaming Eagles Under Siege Vietnam 1970.* New York: Random House Publishing, 2000.

Olson, James. *Where the Domino Fell: American and Vietnam, 1945–1990.* New York: St. Martin's Press Inc., 1919.

Palmer, Bruce. *The 25-Year War.* Lexington: The University Press of Kentucky, 1984.

Palmer, Dave. *Summons of the Trumpet.* New York: Ballantine Books, 1978.

Pimlott, John. *Nam: The Vietnam Experience 1965–75.* London: Orbis Publishing Ltd., 1988.

Pimlott, John. *Vietnam the Decisive Battles.* Edison: Chartwell Books, 2003.

Pisor, Robert. *The End of the Line: The siege of KheSanh.* New York: Ballantine Books, 1982.

Prados, John. *Valley of Decision. The Siege of KheSanh.* New York: Doubleday Dell Publishing Group Inc., 1919.

Robinson, Anthony. *Weapons of the Vietnam War.* New York: Bison Books, 1983.

Rogers, Bernard. *Vietnam Studies: Cedar Falls-Junction City.* Washington, DC: US Gov't Printing Office, 1974.

Rottman, Gordon. *US Army Infantryman in Vietnam 1965–73.* UK: Osprey Publishing, 2005.

Russell, Norman. *Suicide Charlie.* New York: Pocket Books, 1993.

Sears, K. G. Vietnam; looking back at the facts. Mrken@saigonnet.vn.

Shaplen, Robert. *The Road from War.* New York: Harper & Row, 1970.

Shook, John. *One Soldier.* New York: Bantam Books, 1986.

Sloan, Bill. *The Ultimate Battle; Okinawa 1945-The Last Epic Struggle of World War II.* New York: Simon & Schuster Paperbacks, 2007.

Soiset, Roger. *The Two-Dollar Bill: One Man's Year in Vietnam.* Columbia: Palmetto Bookworks, 1993.

Sorley, Lewis. *A Better War: The Unexamined Victories and Final Tragedy of America's Last Years in Vietnam.* Orlando: Harcourt Brace & Company, 1999.

Spector, Ronald. *After Tet: The Bloodiest Year in Vietnam.* New York: Vintage Books, 1993.

Stanton, Shelby. *Anatomy of A division: The 1st Cav. in Vietnam.* New York: Warner Books Inc., 1987.

Stanton, Shelby. *Rangers at War: LRRPs in Vietnam.* New York: Ballantine Books, 1992.

Starry, Donn. *Armored Combat in Vietnam.* New York: Arno Press Inc., 1980.

Summers, Harry, Jr. "Deliberate Distortions Still Obscure Understanding of the Viet Nam War." *Vietnam Magazine*, August 1989.

Summers, Harry, Jr. *Historical Atlas of the Vietnam War* Boston: Houghton Mifflin Company, 1995.

Summers, Harry, Jr. *Vietnam War Almanac.* NYC: Facts on File Publications, 1985.

United States Army. The United States Army Training Center Infantry, Fort Dix, New Jersey, Combat Training.

Veith, George. *Code-Name Bright Light*. New York: Bantam Doubleday Dell Publishing Group, 1998.

Vietnam Veterans. www.Vietnam-veterans.us.

Warr, Nicholas. *Phase Line Green: The Battle for Hue, 1968*. New York: Ballantine Publishing Group, 1997.

Webb, James. Heroes of the Vietnam Generation. January 3, 2011. www.vidol-america.us/.

West, Francis Jr. *Small Unit Action in Vietnam: Summer 1966*. New York. Arno Press Inc., 1967.

Wikipedia; numerous references.

WWW.inetres.com/gp/military.

WWW.grunt.space.swri.edu/visit/maps.

www.mrfa.org/vnstats.htm.

www.nexus.net/nq119fx/vietnam.

ABOUT THE AUTHOR

Brian Richard Esher was born in New York City. He was drafted into the army in October of 1967 and was sent to Vietnam as a combat infantryman in April of 1968, the worst year in terms of causalities. He served with the 25th Infantry Division, 4th Battalion of the 23rd Infantry Mechanized. After being wounded three times and receiving several medals, including the Distinguished Service Cross (our nation's second-highest medal for valor), he was assigned to the 1st Brigade Headquarters in Tay Ninh, Vietnam. After serving his tour in Vietnam, he was assigned to Fort Monmouth, New Jersey. Upon receiving an honorable discharge, he went back to college, finishing his Bachelor of Science degree in business management, magna cum laude, and later a master's degree in business administration with highest honors.

Mr. Esher is currently the founder and CEO and Chairman of STORM Consulting LLC, a consulting business focusing on tackling difficult situations and turning them into superior returns for investors. The unusual aspect of Mr. Esher's career, spanning more than forty years, is that he has operated as the CEO of several companies under different situations, with large and smaller companies both public and private, and in a wide variety of industries. This has included both hi-tech and traditional businesses engaged in manufacturing, distribution, and services. He has been the CEO/COO of more than ten companies, two of which were public. He has also operated as the Chief Restructuring Officer of several other companies emerging from bankruptcy and has served on numerous company boards of directors.

Mr. Esher lives in Johns Creek, Georgia, with his loving wife, Cristina, and has two sons, Justin and Christopher.

CPSIA information can be obtained
at www.ICGtesting.com
Printed in the USA
FFHW021245010319
50802591-56214FF

9 781634 171106